Entertainment industry economics

A guide for financial analysis

SECOND EDITION

Entertainment industry economics

A guide for financial analysis

SECOND EDITION

HAROLD L. VOGEL

First Vice-President, Merrill Lynch Capital Markets

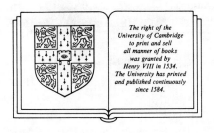

The right of the
University of Cambridge
to print and sell
all manner of books
was granted by
Henry VIII in 1534.
The University has printed
and published continuously
since 1584.

CAMBRIDGE UNIVERSITY PRESS

Cambridge

New York   Port Chester   Melbourne   Sydney

TO MY DEAR FATHER
– WHO WOULD HAVE BEEN SO PROUD

Published by the Press Syndicate of the University of Cambridge
The Pitt Building, Trumpington Street, Cambridge CB2 1RP
40 West 20th Street, New York, NY 10011, USA
10 Stamford Road, Oakleigh, Melbourne 3166, Australia

© Cambridge University Press 1990

First edition 1986
Second edition 1990

Printed in Canada

British Library Cataloguing in Publication Data

Vogel, Harold L., 1946–
    Entertainment industry economics : a guide for financial analysis.–2nd ed.
    1. United States. Entertainment industries
    I. Title
    338.4'7791'0973

ISBN 0-521-38500-8 hard covers

Contents

Preface

en·ter·tain·ment – the act of diverting, amusing, or causing someone's time to pass agreeably; something that diverts, amuses, or occupies the attention agreeably.

in·dus·try – a department or branch of a craft, art, business, or manufacture: a division of productive or profit-making labor; esp. one that employs a large personnel and capital; a group of productive or profit-making enterprises or organizations that have a similar technological structure of production and that produce or supply technically substitutable goods, services, or sources of income.

ec·o·nom·ics – a social science that studies the production, distribution, and consumption of commodities; considerations of cost and return.

Webster's Third New Unabridged International Dictionary, G. & C. Merriam Company, Springfield, Massachusetts, 1967.

Each year Americans cumulatively spend at least 60 billion hours and over $60 billion on legal forms of entertainment. So we might begin by asking: What is entertainment, why is there so much interest in it, and what do its many forms have in common?

At the most fundamental level, anything that stimulates, encourages, or otherwise generates a condition of pleasurable diversion could be called entertainment. The French word, *divertissement,* perhaps best captures this essence.

Although life is full of constraints and disciplines, responsibilities and chores, and a host of things disagreeable, entertainment, in contrast, encompasses activities that people enjoy and look forward to doing. This is the basis of the demand for or the consumption of entertainment products and services; this is the primary attribute shared by the many diverse topics – from cinema to sports, from theme parks to theater – that are discussed in the pages that follow.

Entertainment – the cause – is thus obversely defined through its effect: a satisfied and happy psychological state. And it matters not whether the effect is achieved through active or passive means. Playing the piano can be just as pleasurable as playing the stereo. Indeed, entertainment may include everything from visiting museums and going shopping to having sex.

Entertainment, in fact, means so many different things to so many different people that manageable analysis requires that a sharper boundary be drawn. Such a boundary is here established by classifying entertainment activities into industry segments – that is, productive or profit-making enterprises or organizations of significant size that have similar technological structures of production and that produce or supply goods, services, or sources of income that are substitutable.

Classification along those lines facilitates contiguous discussion of entertainment *software,* as we might more generically label films, records, and video games, and *hardware,* the physical appurtenances and equipment on which or in which software, the instruction sets, are executed. Such classification also allows us to more easily trace the effects of technological developments in this field.

So accustomed are we now to continuous improvements in the performance of entertainment hardware and software that we have difficulty remembering that early in the twentieth century moving pictures and music recordings were novelties, radio was regarded as a modern-day miracle, and television was a laboratory curiosity. Simple transistors and lasers had yet to be invented; lightning-fast electronic computers and man-made orbiting satellites were still in the realm of science fiction.

These fruits of applied technology have nevertheless spawned new art forms and vistas of human expression, and have brought to millions of people around the world, at virtually the flick of a switch, a much more varied and higher-quality mix of entertainment than has ever before been imagined feasible.

Little or none of this, however, has happened because of *ars gratia artis* (art for art's sake) – in itself a noble but ineffectual stimulus for technological development. It is *economic forces* – profit motives, if you will – that are always behind the scenes regulating the flows and rates of implementation. Those are the forces that shape the relative popularity and growth patterns of competing, usually interdependent, entertainment activities and products. And those are the forces that ultimately make available to the masses what was previously affordable only by upper-income classes.

It is therefore somewhat surprising to find that most serious examinations of the economics of entertainment are desultorily scattered among various pamphlets, trade publications and journals, stockbrokers' reports, and incidental chapters in books on other topics. The widely available popular magazines and newspapers, biographies, histories, and technical manuals do not generally provide in-depth treatments of the subject.

This book is a direct outgrowth of my search for a single comprehensive source. It attempts to present information in a style accessible and interesting to general readers; yet it can be used as a text for graduate or advanced undergraduate students in applied economics and management/administration courses in film, music, communications, professional sports, performing arts, and hotel-casino operations. But it should also prove a handy reference for executives, financial analysts and investors, agents and legal advisors, accountants, economists, and journalists. To that end, extensive supplementary data are presented in a Supplementary Data appendix following the Notes.

The material included has been selected on the basis of industry size measured in terms of consumer spending and employment, length of time in existence as a distinct subset, and availability of reliable data. In a larger sense, however, topics were chosen with the aim of providing no more and no less than would be required by a "compleat" entertainment industry investor. Inevitably, then, the perspectives are those of an investment analyst, portfolio manager, and economist.

Whereas this decision-oriented background leads naturally to an approach that is more practical and factual than highly theoretical, it nevertheless assumes some familiarity with the language of economics and finance, and readers without fluency in those areas may encounter occasional difficulties. For their assistance, a Glossary has been appended.

This second edition has been revised and broadened to include more detailed discussion of areas that are of growing interest to readers. Of special significance is the greatly enlarged section on television production and barter-syndication, and the addition of a major section on the toy industry. In recent years, an important relationship between toy manufacturers and television and film companies has emerged.

Also, of course, wherever relevant new statistical information has become available since release of the first edition, it has been included in this revised version. An example of this can be found in Chapter 4's discussion of film accounting, in which the different accounting policies of various film companies can now be more effectively compared against the industry-wide averages that are shown.

I am especially grateful to Elizabeth Maguire, editor at Cambridge University Press, for her early interest and confidence in this project. Thanks, too, to Cambridge's Rhona Johnson and production editor Michael Gnat, who worked on the first edition, and to Matthew N. Hendryx, economics editor who worked on the second.

I am further indebted to those writers who earlier cut a path through the statistical forests and made the task of exposition easier than it would otherwise have been. Particularly noteworthy are the books of John Owen on demand for leisure, David Leedy on movie industry accounting, David Baskerville on the music business, John Scarne and Bill Friedman in the gaming field, and William Baumol/William Bowen on the performing arts. Extensive film industry commentaries and data collections by A. D. Murphy of *Variety* (and the University of Southern California) were important additional sources.

My thanks also to the following present and former senior industry executives who generously took time from their busy schedules to review and to advise on sections of the first edition draft. They and their company affiliations as of that time were, in alphabetical order, Michael L. Bagnall (The Walt Disney Company), Jeffrey Barbakow (Merrill Lynch), J. Garrett Blowers (CBS Inc.), Erroll M. Cook (Arthur Young & Co.), Michael E. Garstin (Orion Pictures Corp.), Kenneth F. Gorman (Viacom), Harold M. Haas (MCA Inc.), Howard J. Klein (Caesars New Jersey), Donald B. Romans (Bally Mfg.), and James R. Wolford (The Walt Disney Company). Greatly appreciated too was the comprehensive critique provided by my sister, Gloria. Acknowledgments for the second edition are also owing to Arnold W. Messer (Columbia Pictures Entertainment) and to Angela B. Gerken (Viacom).

Although every possible precaution against error has been taken, for any mistakes that may inadvertently remain, the responsibility is of course mine alone.

I've been most gratified by the success of the first edition, and as before, my hope and expectation remains that this work will provide valuable insights and a thoroughly enjoyable adventure.

Now, on with the show.

                                                                                    Harold L. Vogel

New York City

Note to the reader

Investors should be aware that the opinions and interpretations expressed herein are those of the author and do not necessarily reflect the current opinions or attitudes of Merrill Lynch & Co. in regard to the investment merits of the industries or securities of the companies mentioned.

Part I
Introduction

1
Economic perspectives

To everything there is a season, and a time to every purpose under the
heaven. – Ecclesiastes

Extending this famous verse, we can also say that there is a time for work
and a time for play. There is a time for leisure.

An important distinction, however, is to be made between the precise
concept of a time for leisure and the semantically different and much fuzz-
ier notion of *leisure time,* our initial topic. In the course of exploring this
subject, the fundamental economic forces that affect spending on all forms
of entertainment will be revealed, and our understanding of what moti-
vates expenditures for such goods and services will be enhanced. Moreover,
the perspectives provided by this approach will enable us to see how entertainment is defined, and how it fits into the larger economic picture.

1.1 Time concepts

Leisure and work

Philosophers and sociologists have long wrestled with the problem of defining *leisure* – the English word derived from the Latin *licere,* which means
"to be permitted" or "to be free." In fact, as Kraus (1978, p. 38) and Neu-

3

linger (1981, pp. 17–33) have noted, leisure has usually been described in terms of its sociological and psychological (state-of-mind) characteristics.

The classical attitude was epitomized in the work of Aristotle, for whom the term *leisure* implied both availability of time and absence of the necessity of being occupied (DeGrazia 1962, p. 19). According to Aristotle, that very absence is what leads to a life of contemplation and true happiness (for an elite few, who would not have to provide for their daily needs). Veblen (1899) similarly saw leisure as a symbol of social class. To him, however, it was associated not with a life of contemplation but with the "idle rich," who identified themselves through its possession and its use.

Leisure has more recently been conceptualized either as a form of activity engaged in by people in their free time or, preferably, as time free from any sense of obligation or compulsion.[1] As such, the term *leisure* is now broadly used to characterize time not spent at work (where there is an obligation to perform). Naturally, in so defining leisure by what it is not, metaphysical issues remain largely unresolved. There is, for instance, the question how to categorize work-related time such as that consumed in preparation for and in transit to and from the workplace. And it may happen that one person's vocation is another's avocation: Consider a carpenter and an executive whose hobby is cabinetmaking. Fortunately, for our purposes, these problems of definition have little bearing on the analysis that follows.

Recreation and entertainment

In stark contrast to the impressions of an Aristotle or Veblen, today we rarely, if ever, think of leisure as contemplation, or as something to be enjoyed only by the privileged. Instead, "free" time is used for doing things and going places, and the emphasis on activity more closely corresponds to the notion of recreation – refreshment of strength or spirit after toil – than to the views of the classicists.

The availability of time is, of course, a precondition for recreation, which can be taken literally as meaning re-creation of body and soul. But because such active re-creation can be achieved in many different ways – by playing tennis, or by going fishing, for example – it encompasses aspects of both physical and mental well-being. As such, recreation may or may not contain significant elements of amusement and diversion, or occupy the attention agreeably. Amateurs training to run a marathon would, for instance, normally be experiencing recreation without much entertainment content.

On the other hand, as noted in the Preface, entertainment is defined as that which produces a pleasurable and satisfying experience. The concept of entertainment is thus subordinate to that of recreation: It is more specifically defined through its direct and primarily psychological and emotional effects.

Time

Most people have some hours left over – "free time," so to speak – after subtracting the hours and minutes needed for subsistence (mainly eating and sleeping), for work, and for related activities. But this remaining time has a cost in terms of alternative opportunities forgone.

Because time is needed to use or to consume goods and services as well as produce them, economists have attempted to develop theories that treat it as a commodity with varying qualitative and quantitative cost features. However, as Sharp (1981) notes in his comprehensive coverage of this subject, economists have been only partially successful in this attempt:

> Although time is commonly described as a scarce resource in economic literature, it is still often treated rather differently from the more familiar inputs of labor and materials and outputs of goods and services. The problems of its allocation have not yet been fully or consistently integrated into economic analysis. (Sharp 1981, p. 210)

Nevertheless, investigations into the economics of time, including those of Becker (1965) and DeSerpa (1971), have suggested that the demand for leisure is affected in a complicated way by the cost of time to both produce and consume. For instance, according to Becker (see also Ghez and Becker 1975),

> The two determinants of the importance of forgone earnings are the amount of time used per dollar of goods and the cost per unit of time. Reading a book, taking a haircut or commuting use more time per dollar of goods than eating dinner, frequenting a night-club or sending children to private summer camps. Other things the same, forgone earnings would be more important for the former set of commodities than the latter.
> The importance of forgone earnings would be determined solely by time intensity only if the cost of time was the same for all commodities. Presumably, however, it varies considerably among commodities and at different periods. For example, the cost of time is often less on week-ends and in the evenings. (Becker, 1965, p. 503)

From this it can be seen that the cost of time and the consumption-time intensity of goods and services are significant factors when selecting from among entertainment alternatives.

Expansion of leisure time

Most of us do not normally experience sharp changes in our availability of leisure time (except on retirement or loss of job). But there is nevertheless a fairly widespread impression that since the Industrial Revolution more than a century ago, leisure time has been steadily increasing. Still, the evidence on this is mixed. In examining the length of an average workweek for agricultural and nonagricultural industries, we can see that significant

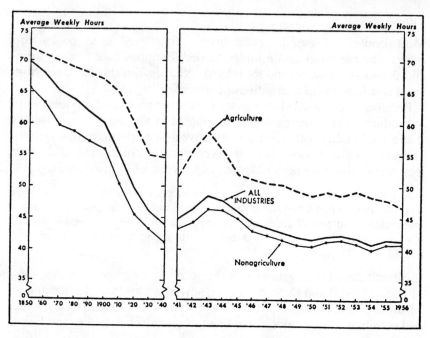

Figure 1.1. Estimated average weekly hours for all persons employed in agricultural and nonagricultural industries, 1850–1940 (10-year intervals) and 1941–56 (annual averages for all employed persons, including the self-employed and unpaid family workers.) *Source:* Zeisel (1958).

increases in leisure time (workweek reductions) were achieved prior to 1940 (Figure 1.1); more recently, however, the lengths of average workweeks, as adjusted for increases in holidays and vacations, have scarcely changed (Figure 1.2 and Table 1.1).

Although this indeed suggests that there has been little, if any, expansion of leisure time in most years, Hedges and Taylor (1980), with a more detailed breakdown of labor-force statistics, were able to show that between 1968 and 1979, work time for wage and salary employees tended to decline (their data appear in Supplementary Data Table S1.2 in Appendix C). This decline was attributed to changes in industry and occupation structures, in federal laws, and in collective-bargaining agreements. In fact, weekly hours worked in private industry as a whole have declined modestly since 1965, although remaining fairly constant in the manufacturing segments; the sharpest drop appears in services (Table 1.2).

Data from so-called Area Wage Surveys conducted by the Bureau of Labor Statistics in fact suggest that the average workweek has not shrunk at all in recent years. What has apparently happened instead is that the work schedules now available provide greater diversity: "A larger percentage of people worked under 35 hours or over 49 hours a week in 1985 than

Weekly hours

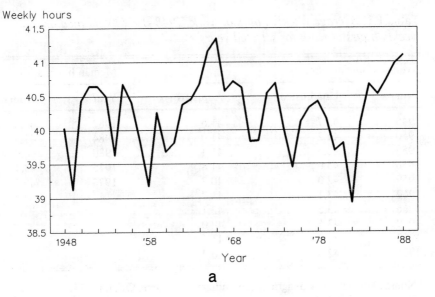

a

Weekly hours

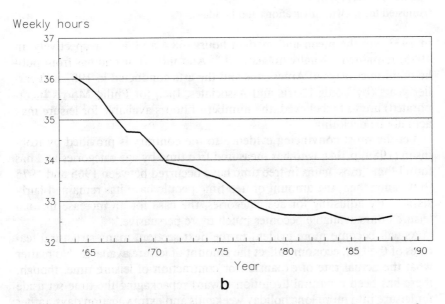

b

Figure 1.2. Average weekly hours worked by production workers in: (a) manufacturing, 1948–88; and (b) service industries, 1964–88. *Source:* U.S. Department of Commerce.

Table 1.1. *Average weekly hours at work, 1948–1975,[a] and median weekly hours at work for selected years[b]*

Average hours at work			Median hours at work	
Year	Unadjusted	Adjusted[c]	Year	Hours
1948	42.7	41.6	1987	46.8
1950	42.2	41.0	1984	47.3
1953	42.5	41.4	1980	46.9
1956	43.0	41.8	1975	43.1
1959	42.0	40.7	1973	40.3
1962	43.1	41.7		
1966	43.5	42.1		
1969	43.5	42.0		
1972	42.9	41.4		
1975	42.5	40.9		

[a]Nonstudent men in nonagricultural industries. *Source:* Owen (1976).
[b]*Source:* Harris (1988).
[c]Adjusted for growth in vacations and holidays.

in 1973, yet the mean and median hours (38.4 and 40.4, respectively, in 1985) remained virtually unchanged."[2] And indeed, if findings from public-opinion surveys of Americans and the arts conducted in 1987 and earlier years (by Louis Harris and Associates, Inc., for Philip Morris Incorporated) are to be believed, the number of hours available for leisure may actually be declining.[3]

Yet the most convincing evidence to the contrary is provided by Robinson (1989, p. 34), who has measured free time by age categories and has found that "most gains in free time have occurred between 1965 and 1975 [but] since then, the amount of free time people have has remained fairly stable." By adjusting for age categories, the case for an increase in total leisure hours available becomes much more persuasive.[4]

As will become more evident in the next section, many structural features of the U.S. economy affect the amount of leisure available. No matter what the actual rate of expansion or contraction of leisure time, though, there has been a natural evolution toward repackaging the time set aside for leisure into more long holiday weekends and extra vacation days, rather than in reducing the minutes worked each and every week. Particularly for those in the higher-income categories – conspicuous consumers, as Veblen would say – the result is that personal-consumption expenditures (PCEs) for leisure activities are likely to be intense, frenzied, and compressed instead of evenly metered throughout the year. Estimated apportionments of leisure hours among various activities and the differences in such apportionments between 1970 and 1988 are indicated in Table 1.3.

Table 1.2. *Average hours and earnings for production or nonsupervisory workers, selected industry categories, 1965–88*

Year	Total private[a]			Manufacturing			Services		
	Weekly hours	Hourly earnings	Weekly earnings	Weekly hours	Hourly earnings	Weekly earnings	Weekly hours	Hourly earnings	Weekly earnings
1965	38.8	$2.46	$ 95.45	41.2	$ 2.61	$107.53	35.9	$ 2.05	$ 73.60
1966	38.6	2.56	98.82	41.4	2.71	112.19	35.5	2.17	77.04
1967	38.0	2.68	101.84	40.6	2.82	114.49	35.1	2.29	80.38
1968	37.8	2.85	107.73	40.7	3.01	122.51	34.7	2.42	83.97
1969	37.7	3.04	114.61	40.6	3.19	129.51	34.7	2.61	90.57
1970	37.1	3.23	119.83	39.8	3.35	133.33	34.4	2.81	96.66
1971	36.9	3.45	127.31	39.9	3.57	142.44	33.9	3.04	103.06
1972	37.0	3.70	136.90	40.5	3.82	154.71	33.9	3.27	110.85
1973	36.9	3.94	145.39	40.7	4.09	166.46	33.8	3.47	117.29
1974	36.5	4.24	154.76	40.0	4.42	176.80	33.6	3.75	126.00
1975	36.1	4.53	163.53	39.5	4.83	190.79	33.5	4.02	134.67
1976	36.1	4.86	175.45	40.1	5.22	209.32	33.3	4.31	143.52
1977	36.0	5.25	189.00	40.3	5.68	228.90	33.0	4.65	153.45
1978	35.8	5.69	203.70	40.4	6.17	249.27	32.8	4.99	163.67
1979	35.7	6.16	219.91	40.2	6.70	269.34	32.7	5.36	175.27
1980	35.3	6.66	235.10	39.7	7.27	288.62	32.6	5.85	190.71
1981	35.2	7.25	255.20	39.8	7.99	318.00	32.6	6.41	208.97
1982	34.8	7.68	267.26	38.9	8.49	330.26	32.6	6.92	225.59
1983	35.0	8.02	280.70	40.1	8.83	354.08	32.7	7.31	239.04
1984	35.2	8.32	292.86	40.7	9.19	374.03	32.6	7.59	247.43
1985	34.9	8.57	299.09	40.5	9.54	386.37	32.5	7.90	256.75
1986	34.8	8.76	304.85	40.7	9.73	396.01	32.5	8.18	265.85
1987	34.8	8.98	312.50	41.0	9.91	406.31	32.5	8.49	275.93
1988	34.7	9.29	322.36	41.1	10.18	418.40	32.6	8.91	290.47

[a]Data relate to production workers in mining and manufacturing, construction workers in construction, and nonsupervisory workers in transportation and public utilities, wholesale and retail trade, finance, insurance, real estate, and services.
Source: Employment and Earnings, U.S. Department of Labor, Bureau of Labor Statistics.

Table 1.3. *Time spent by adults on selected leisure activities, 1970 and 1988*

Leisure activity	Hours per person per year[a]		% of total time accounted for by each activity	
	1970	1988	1970	1988
Television	1,226	1,550	46.5	45.3
Network affiliates		900		26.3
Independent stations		365		10.7
Basic cable programs		190		5.5
Pay cable programs		95		2.8
Radio	872	1,160	33.1	33.9
Home		560		16.4
Out of home		600		17.5
Newspapers	218	180	8.3	5.3
Records & tapes	68	220	2.6	6.4
Magazines	170	110	6.5	3.2
Leisure books	65	95	2.5	2.8
Video games (home)		15		0.4
Movies	10	12	0.4	0.4
Spectator sports	3	14	0.1	0.4
Videocassette recorder		60		1.8
Video games (arcade)		4		0.1
Cultural events	3	5	0.1	0.1
Total	2,635	3,425	100.0[b]	100.0[b]
Hours per adult per week	50.7	65.9		
Hours per adult per day	7.2	9.4		

[a]Averaged over participants and nonparticipants.
[b]Totals not exact due to rounding.
Source: CBS office of Economic Analysis, Wilkofsky Gruen Associates, Inc.

1.2 Supply and demand factors

Productivity

What ultimately makes more leisure time available through reductions in the length of the average workweek is not government decree, nor strikes by labor unions, nor altruism from factory owners. It is the continuation of the rising trend in output per person-hour – in brief, rising productivity of the economy. Quite simply, technological advances embodied in new capital equipment and in the training of a more skilled labor pool enable more goods and services to be produced in less time or by fewer workers.

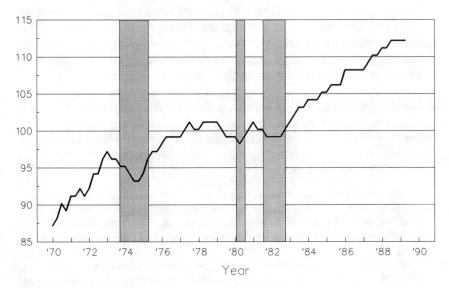

Figure 1.3. Nonfarm business productivity in the U.S., 1970–89, shown by output per hour. Index 1977 = 100. Bars indicate periods of recession. *Source:* U.S. Department of Labor.

Thus, it happens that long-term growth in the leisure-time-related industries depends on the rate of technological development throughout the economy.

The U.S. Commerce Department's National Income Accounting (NIA) figures – official compilations of data concerning economic activities – provide us with imperfect but still useful information concerning trends in productivity. For instance, according to those figures, productivity during the 1970s rose at an average annual rate of only about 1.5%, as compared with rates averaging 2.9% during the 20 years immediately following World War II.[5] The apparently reduced rate of improvement in this period may have been caused by unexpected sharp cost increases for energy and capital (interest rates), or perhaps by the burgeoning "underground" (off-the-books) economy not directly captured in (and therefore distorting) the NIA numbers. Annual productivity gains have averaged 1.8% or so during the 1980s. Whatever the rate, however, the potential for leisure-time expansion has always been and always will be linked to changes in productivity (Figure 1.3).

Demand for leisure

All of us can choose to either fully utilize our free time for recreational purposes (defined here and in NIA data as being inclusive of entertainment activities) or use some of this time to generate additional income. How we allocate free time between the conflicting desires for more leisure and for additional income then becomes a subject that economists investigate with standard analytical tools.[6] In effect, economists treat demand for leisure as if it were, say, demand for gold, or for wheat, or for housing.

Without going into great detail, it is sufficient to note here that consumers tend to substitute less expensive goods for more expensive ones, and the total amounts they can spend – their budgets – are limited or constrained by income. The effects of such substitutions and changes in income as related to demand for leisure have been extensively studied by Owen (1970), who observed:

> An increase in property income will, if we assume leisure is a superior good, reduce hours of work. A higher wage rate also brings higher income which, in itself, may incline the individual to increase his leisure. But at the same time the higher wage rate makes leisure time more expensive in terms of forgone goods and services, so that the individual may decide instead to purchase less leisure. The net effect will depend then on the relative strengths of the income and price elasticities ... It would seem that for the average worker the income effect of a rise in the wage rate is in fact stronger than the substitution effect. (Owen 1970, p. 18)

In other words, as wage rates continue rising, up to point A in Figure 1.4, people will choose to work more hours to increase their income (income effect). But they eventually begin to favor more leisure over more income (substitution effect, between points A and B), with the result of a backward-bending labor-supply curve.[7] Although renowned economists, including Adam Smith, Alfred Marshall, Frank Knight, A. C. Pigou, and Lionel Robbins have substantially differed in their assessments of the net effect of wage-rate changes on the demand for leisure, it is clear that "leisure does have a price, and changes in its price will affect the demand for it" (Owen 1970, p. 19). Indeed, results from a Bureau of Labor Statistics survey of some 60,000 households in 1986 suggest that about two-thirds of

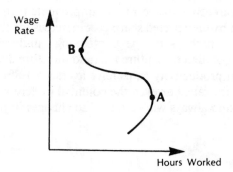

Figure 1.4. Backward-bending labor-supply curve.

those surveyed do not want to work fewer hours if it means earning less money.[8]

As Owen (1970) has demonstrated, estimation of the demand for leisure requires consideration of many complex issues including the nature of "working conditions," the effects of increasing worker fatigue on production rates as work hours lengthen, the greater availability of educational opportunities that affect the desirability of certain kinds of work, government taxation and spending policies, market unemployment rates, and several other variables.[9]

Expected-utility comparisons

Individuals differ in terms of the sense of psychic gratification experienced from consumption of different goods and services. And so it is difficult to measure and compare the degrees of satisfaction derived from, say, eating dinner as opposed to buying a new car. To facilitate comparability, economists have adapted an old philosophical concept known as utility.[10] As Barrett (1974, p. 79) has noted, utility "is not a measure of usefulness or need but a measure of the desirability of a commodity from the psychological viewpoint of the consumer."

Of course, rational individuals try to maximize utility – in other words, make decisions that provide them with the most satisfaction. But they are hampered in this regard because decisions are normally made under conditions of uncertainty, with incomplete information, and therefore with risk of an undesired outcome. Human beings thus tend to implicitly include a probabilistic component in their decision-making processes – and they end up maximizing *expected utility* rather than utility itself.

The notion of expected utility is especially well applied in thinking about demand for entertainment goods and services. It helps, for example, to explain why people may be attracted to gambling, or why they are sometimes willing to pay scalpers enormous premiums for theater tickets. Its application also sheds light on how various entertainment activities compete for the limited time and dollars of consumers.

To illustrate, assume for a moment that the cost of an activity per unit of time is somewhat representative of its expected utility. If the admission price to a two-hour movie is $6, and if the purchase of video-game software for $25 provides six hours of play before onset of boredom, then the cost per minute for the movie is 5.0 cents, and that for the game is 6.9 cents. Now, obviously, no one decides to see a movie or buy a game based on explicit comparisons of cost per minute. Indeed, for an individual, many qualitative (nonmonetary) factors may affect the perception of an item's expected utility. But in the aggregate, and over time, such implicit comparisons do have a significant cumulative influence on relative demand for entertainment (and other) products and services.

Demographics and debts

Over the longer term, the demand for leisure goods and services can also be significantly affected by changes in the relative growth of different age cohorts. For instance, teenagers tend to be important purchasers of recorded music; people under the age of 30 are the most avid moviegoers. Accordingly, a large increase in births following World War II created a market highly receptive to movie and music products in the 1960s and 1970s. As this postwar generation matures into its years of family formation and peak earnings power, it is easy to visualize increasing interest in amusement/theme parks, and video cameras and casinos, whereas demand for, say, rock 'n' roll recorded music albums will likely become relatively weaker.

The broad demographic shifts most important to entertainment industry prospects include (1) a projected shrinkage of 19% in the numbers of 15- to 19-year-olds during the 1980s (6 million fewer teens in 1990 than in 1980), (2) a projected rapid growth in the large group age 30 to 44 (up from 47 million in 1982 to 64 million in 1995), and (3) a significant expansion of the population over age 65 (Table 1.4).

Of particular importance going into early next century is that for the first time since the 1960s, the number of people in the 45 to 60 age group will be gaining rapidly in proportion to the number of people in the 20 to 34 age group. The significance is that those in the younger category are generally spenders as they enter the labor force and form households. Those in the older category, however, are already established and are thus more likely to be in a savings mode in order to finance college educations for their children and/or to prepare for retirement, when earnings are lower. This ratio of people in the younger group to those in the older group, in effect, the spenders versus the savers, is illustrated in Figure 1.5a and suggests that relatively small-ticket expenditures for software might be favored at the expense of big-ticket hardware expenditures until well past the turn of the century.

Depending on the specific industry component to be analyzed, proper interpretation of long-term changes in population characteristics may also require that consideration be given to several additional factors including dependency ratios,[11] fertility rates, numbers of first births, numbers of families with two earners, and trends in labor-force participation rates for women.

Two paychecks have indeed become an absolute necessity for many families as they have attempted to service relatively high (to income) installment and mortgage debt obligations that have been incurred in the household-formative years. As such, this element of consumer debt, weighted by the aforementioned demographic factors, probably explains why, according to the aforementioned Louis Harris surveys, leisure hours per week

Table 1.4. *U.S. population by age bracket, components of change and trends by life stage, 1970–95*

Components of population change

| | Percentage distribution | | | | | Change (millions) | | |
Age	1970	1980	1985	1990[a]	1995[a]	1970–80	1980–90[a]	1990–95[a]
Under 5	8.4	7.2	7.7	7.7	7.2	− 0.7	2.7	− 0.6
5–19	29.3	24.6	21.7	21.0	21.2	− 4.1	− 3.6	2.7
20–29	15.1	18.2	18.1	16.0	13.8	10.4	− 1.3	− 4.1
30–59	33.2	34.3	35.9	38.3	40.9	10.0	17.6	10.4
60 and over	14.0	15.7	16.6	17.0	16.9	7.1	6.6	1.5
Total	100.0	100.0	100.0	100.0	100.0	22.7	22.0	9.9

Population trends by life stage (millions)

Life stage	1970	1980	1990[a]	1995[a]
0–14 Children	57.9	51.3	54.6	56.7
15–24 Young adults	36.5	42.7	35.5	34.1
25–34 Peak family formation	25.3	37.6	43.5	40.5
35–44 Family maturation	23.1	25.9	37.8	42.0
45–54 Peak earning power	23.3	22.7	25.4	31.4
55–64 Childless parents	18.7	21.8	21.1	21.0
65 and retirement	20.1	25.7	31.8	34.0
Total	205.1	227.7	249.7	259.6

[a]Forecast.
Source: U.S. Department of Commerce.

seem to have declined noticeably since the early 1970s. These very same elements, however, may combine in the 1990s to at least slow if not abate recent pressures on time availability.

1.3 Personal-consumption expenditure relationships

Recreational goods and services are those used or consumed during leisure time. As a result, there is a close relationship between demand for leisure and demand for recreational products and services. As can be seen from Table 1.5, NIA data classify spending on recreation as a subset of total personal-consumption expenditures (PCEs). This table is particularly important because it allows comparison of the amount of leisure-related spending to the amount of spending for shelter, transportation, food, cloth-

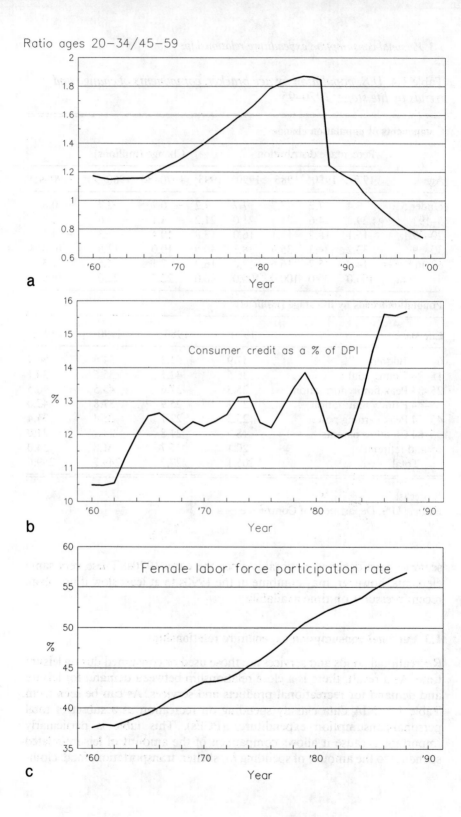

Ratio ages 20–34/45–59

a

Consumer credit as a % of DPI

b

Female labor force participation rate

c

Table 1.5. *PCEs for recreation, 1970–88[a]*

Type of product or service	1970	1975	1980	1985	1988
Total recreation expenditures	42,718	70,233	114,972	185,689	246,845
Percentage of total personal consumption	6.7	6.9	6.6	7.1	7.6
Books and maps	2,922	3,570	5,595	8,109	9,842
Magazines, newspapers, sheet music	4,097	6,356	10,438	13,150	15,960
Nondurable toys and sport supplies	5,498	8,954	14,633	21,127	28,118
Wheel goods, durable toys, sports equipment[b]	5,191	10,514	17,185	26,727	36,504
Radio and TV receivers, records, musical instruments	8,540	13,489	19,888	36,968	48,780
Radio and television repair	1,383	2,229	2,555	3,236	3,850
Flowers, seeds and potted plants	1,798	2,659	4,047	5,518	6,803
Admissions to specified spectator amusements	3,296	4,317	6,490	9,453	11,885
Motion picture theaters	1,629	2,197	2,671	3,571	4,225
Legitimate theaters and opera, and entertainments of nonprofit institutions[c]	531	787	1,786	2,973	4,424
Spectator sports	1,136	1,333	2,033	2,909	3,236
Clubs and fraternal organizations[d]	1,465	1,921	3,020	4,805	5,902
Commercial participant amusements[e]	2,367	4,858	9,666	15,124	18,936
Pari-mutuel net receipts	1,096	1,662	2,095	2,569	2,800
Other[f]	5,065	9,704	19,360	38,903	57,465

[a]In millions of dollars, except percentages. Represents market value of purchases of goods and services by individuals and nonprofit institutions. See *Historical Statistics, Colonial Times to 1970,* series H 878–893, for figures issued prior to 1981 revisions.
[b]Includes boats and pleasures aircraft.
[c]Except athletic.
[d]Consists of dues and fees excluding insurance premiums.
[e]Consists of billiard parlors; bowling alleys, dancing, riding, shooting, skating, and swimming places; amusement devices and parks; golf courses; sightseeing buses and guides; private flying operations and other commercial participant amusements.
[f]Consists of net receipts of lotteries and expenditures for purchase of pets and pet care services, cable TV, film processing, photographic studios, sporting and recreation camps, and recreational services, not elsewhere classified.
Source: U.S. Bureau of Economic Analysis. *The National Income and Product Accounts of the United States, 1929–1976;* and *Survery of Current Business,* July issues.

←

Figure 1.5. (a) Ratio of spenders to savers, 1960–99. (b) Consumer credit as a percentage of personal income, 1960–88. (c) Labor force participation rate for women, 1960–88.

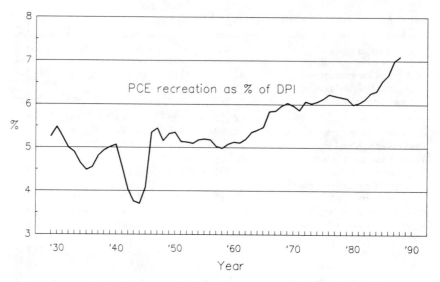

Figure 1.6. PCE for recreation as percentage of disposable income, 1929–88.

ing, national defense, and other items.[12] For example, in 1988, spending
for food amounted to 17.3% of all PCEs, for clothing 5.8%, and for transportation 12.6%.

That spending on total recreational goods and services responds to prev-
alent economic forces with a fair degree of predictability can be seen in
Figure 1.6 and in Supplementary Table S1.1.[13] Figure 1.6 illustrates that
PCEs for recreation as a percent of total disposable personal incomes (DPI)
have held in a band of roughly 4.0% to 6.5% for the fifty-five years beginning in 1929. It is only since the late 1980s that new heights have been
achieved as a result of a relatively lengthy business cycle expansion,
increased consumer borrowing ratios, demographic and household formation influences, and the proliferation of leisure-related goods and services utilizing new technologies.

Measuring real (adjusted for inflation) per capita spending on total recreation, and on recreation services – the entertainment services subsegment that excludes durable products such as television sets but includes
movies, cable TV, sports, theater, commercial participant amusements,
lotteries, and pari-mutuel betting – provides yet another long-term view of
how Americans have allocated their leisure-related dollars. A steady
increase in real per capita PCEs on total recreation and on recreation services beginning around 1965 is suggested by Figures 1.7 and 1.8.

It might be noted from Figure 1.8, however, that the entertainment services series as a percentage of total recreation spending has demonstrated
considerable volatility. This series hit a peak of nearly 50% in the early
1940s, when there were relatively few consumer durables available. Then,

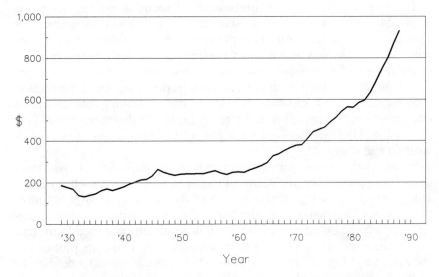

Figure 1.7. Real annual per capita spending on recreation and on recreation services, 1929–88.

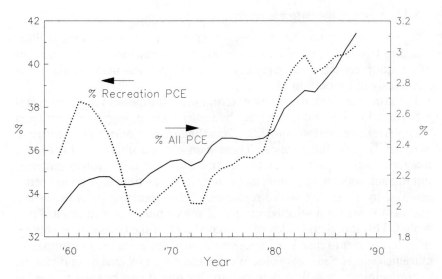

Figure 1.8. PCE for recreation *services* as percentage of all PCE and total PCE on
recreation, 1959–88.

for a dozen or so years ending in the late 1970s, the percentage had been
confined to a fairly narrow band of 32.0% to 36.0%. But more recently,
with the growth of cable television and lotteries in particular, the percentage has rapidly climbed above 40%.

Thus we can see that the composition of spending on recreation has noticeably shifted away from durables and toward service segments. This shift is a reflection of relative market saturation for durables, relative price patterns, and changes in consumer preferences that are a function of the development of new goods and services that compete with more established outlets for such spending. In these series, even small percentage changes nevertheless represent billions of dollars flowing into or out of entertainment businesses. And for many firms, the direction of that flow makes the difference between an experience of prosperous growth or of struggle and decay.

Because various entertainment sectors have markedly different responses to changing conditions, the degree of recession resistance or cyclicity of the entertainment industry relative to that of the economy at large is unfortunately not well depicted by the NIA series. For example, broadcasting-revenue trends are known to closely follow advertising-expenditure patterns, which in turn are known to be dependent on corporate profits. But the movie and theater segments often exhibit contracyclical tendencies. In order to effectively study these business-cycle relationships, data at a less aggregated level must be used.

1.4 Overview of industry segments

The relative economic importance of various industry segments is illustrated in Figure 1.9, from which it is possible to conclude that the amount of attention certain areas regularly receive in popular news media is not necessarily in proportion to size.

Performance comparisons for entertainment businesses versus the aggregate for all service industries may be futher seen in Supplementary Data Table S1.4, derived from U.S. Department of Commerce *Census of Selected Services* information. These data provide important long-range macroeconomic perspectives of entertainment-industry growth patterns, but financial operating performances over a shorter time horizon are better revealed by Table 1.6, where revenues, pretax operating incomes, assets, and cash flows for a selected sample of major public companies are presented. This sample includes an estimated 80% of the transactions volume in entertainment-related industries and provides a means of comparing efficiencies in various segments. We can learn a lot by analyzing it closely.

For example, cash flow is important because it can be used to service debt, or to acquire assets, or to pay dividends. Representing the difference between cash receipts from the sale of goods or services and cash outlays required in production of goods and services, operating cash-flow figures are defined as pretax income before interest and depreciation. Cash flow, so defined, is the basis for valuing all kinds of media and entertainment properties because the distortionary effects of differing tax and financial

Table 1.6. *Entertainment-industry composite, 1988 (in $ millions)*

Compound annual growth rates: 1984–8

Industry segment	No. of companies in sample	Revenues	Operating income	Assets	Operating cash flow
Broadcasting	64	7.0	6.4	21.6	7.9
Cable	44	22.9	30.3	41.1	27.9
Filmed entertainment	53	16.5	14.0	21.3	17.5
Gaming (casinos)	19	8.1	9.6	8.8	9.6
Recorded music	3	22.3	32.6	22.9	32.0
Theatrical exhibition	6	17.0	−7.9	47.4	7.9
Theme parks	4	13.9	25.9	10.6	21.4
Toys	12	6.3	−10.5	9.6	−5.7
Total	205				

Total composite

Year	Pretax return on Revenues	Assets	Revenues	Operating income	Assets	Operating cash flow
1988	14.2%	9.1%	58,188.0	8,242.0	90,693.9	12,076.9
1987	13.8	11.6	50,729.6	7,020.8	60,607.8	30,512.4
1986	14.0	9.4	44,603.9	6,265.7	66,792.7	8,719.6
1985	14.3	12.2	39,506.1	5,649.2	46,236.1	7,741.5
1984	14.1	12.9	36,335.1	5,112.4	39,505.8	6,954.1
CAGR[a]			12.5	12.7	23.1	14.8

[a]Compound annual growth rate, 1984–8(%).
Source: Company 10-K reports, and *Communications Industry Report,* November 1989. New York: Veronis, Suhler & Associates, Inc.

structure considerations are stripped away: the business property can be evaluated from the standpoint of what it would be worth to a private buyer who can deploy the cash in whatever way he chooses (or must).

This concept of operating cash flow, which will appear throughout the book, however, may also be specifically employed here in studying the entertainment industry aggregates shown in Table 1.6. In the table, we see that entertainment industries generated revenues (on the wholesale level) of nearly $60 billion in 1988, and that annual growth between 1984 and 1988 has averaged approximately 12.5%. Over the same span, operating income has risen at a rate of 12.7%, whereas assets have increased at a rate of 23.1%. Clearly then, we can see that operating cash flows, rising at a rate

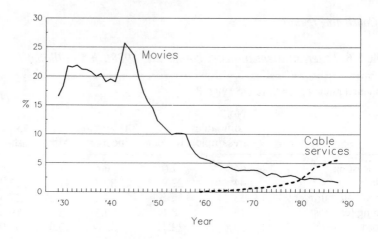

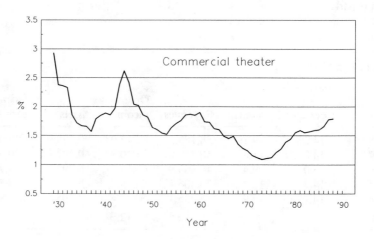

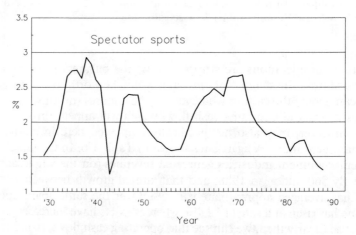

Figure 1.9. PCEs by entertainment category as percentages of total PCE on recreation, 1929–88.

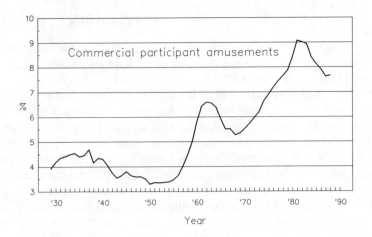

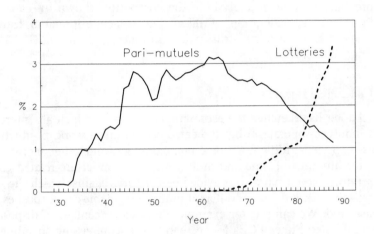

Figure 1.9. (*cont.*)

of 14.8%, have not kept up with the growth of assets, and that therefore, assets have been to a large extent financed by borrowings, and/or by sales of equity (i.e., shares of stock).

Another interesting aspect revealed in the data from Table 1.6 is that rapid expansion of the cable industry – highest in measures of revenue and earnings growth – did not translate into substantial pretax income growth acceleration for filmed entertainment programmers and distributors. Between 1984 and 1988 pretax income for the cable segment rose at a compound rate of 30.3%, whereas pretax income for a 53-company composite in filmed entertainment rose only 14.0% over the same period.

More worrisome, still, is that returns on composite industry assets decreased from 12.9% in 1984 to 9.1% in 1988. A smaller sample of similar companies generated returns on assets averaging 19.1% in 1979. Of course, a more than superficial analysis of the composites shown in Table 1.6 would require consideration of many business-environmental features including interest rates, anti-trust policy attitudes, and the trend of dollar exchange rates since 1979.

1.5 Concluding remarks

This chapter has sketched the economic landscape in which all entertainment industries operate. It has indicated how hours at work, productivity trends, expected utility functions, demographics, and other factors can affect the amounts of time and money we spend on leisure-related goods and services. And it has also provided benchmarks against which the relative growth rates and sizes of different industry segments or composites can be measured. We can see, for example, that as a percentage of disposable income, United States PCEs for recreation – encompassing spending on entertainment as well as other leisure-time pursuits – rose to a record high of well over 6% in the 1980s. And we can see that entertainment is big business: at the wholesale level it generated over $60 billion in 1988. Moreover, as measured in dollar value terms, entertainment has also consistently been one of the largest export categories for the United States.[14]

Past, though, is not necessarily prologue – especially in a field where creative people are constantly finding new ways to turn a profit. The broad economic perspectives discussed in this chapter, however, provide a common background for all that follows.

Selected additional reading

Bowers, D. A., and Baird, R. N. (1971). *Elementary Mathematical Macroeconomics.* Englewood Cliffs, N.J.: Prentice-Hall.

Frank, A. D. (1987). "The Fault Is Not in Our Stars," *Forbes,* 140(6)(September 21):120.

Hedges, J. N. (1973). "New Patterns for Working Time," *Monthly Labor Review* 96(2)(February):3.

(1980). "The Workweek in 1979: Fewer but Longer Workdays," *Monthly Labor Review* 103(8)(August):31.

Meyersohn, R., and Larrabee, E. (1958). "A Comprehensive Bibliography on Leisure, 1900–1958," in *Mass Leisure*. Glencoe, Ill.: The Free Press; also in *American Journal of Sociology* 62(6)(May 1957):602–15.

Moore, G. H., and Hedges, J. N. (1971). "Trends in Labor and Leisure," *Monthly Labor Review* 94(2)(February):3.

Owen, J. D. (1971). "The Demand for Leisure," *Journal of Political Economy* 79(1)(January/February):56–75.

Staines, G. L., and O'Connor, P. (1980). "Conflicts Among Work, Leisure, and Family Roles," *Monthly Labor Review,* 103(8)(August):35.

"The Productivity Paradox," *Business Week* No. 3055 (June 6, 1988):100.

"The Revival of Productivity," *Business Week* No. 2828 (February 13, 1984):92.

"The 21st Century Family," *Newsweek,* special edition, 1989.

Part II
Media-dependent entertainment

2
Movie macroeconomics

You oughta be in pictures!

A more appealing pitch to investors would be hard to find. Yet, ego gratification, rather than money, is often the only return for investment in movies. Many people imagine that nothing could be more fun, and potentially more lucrative, than making them. After all, in its first four years, *Star Wars* returned profits of over $150 million on an initial investment of $11 million for the negative (i.e., the negative film stock from which prints are made). But, as in other endeavors, what you see is not always what you get. In fact, of any 10 major theatrical films produced, on the average 6 or 7 are unprofitable, and 1 will break even. As we shall soon discover, however, there are many reasons why the success ratio for studio/distributors is considerably better than for individuals.

Be that as it may, moviemaking is still truly entrepreneurial: It is often a triumph of hope over reality, where defeat can easily be snatched from the jaws of victory. But its magical, mystical elements notwithstanding, it is also a business, affected as any other by basic economic principles.

This chapter is concerned with macroeconomic trends and movie asset valuations; the next two chapters deal with operational structure, accounting, and television-related microeconomics.

2.1 Flickering images

Snuggled comfortably in the seat of your local theater or, as is increasingly likely, in front of the screen attached to your videocassette machine, the lights are dimmed and you are transported far away by your imagination as you watch – a movie. Of course, not all movies have the substance and style to accomplish this incredible feat of transportation, but a surprising number of them do. In any case, what is seen on the screen is there because of a remarkable history of tumultuous development that is still largely in process.

Putting pictures on a strip of film that moved was not a unique or new idea among photographers of the late nineteenth century. But the man who synthesized it all into a workable invention was Thomas Edison. By the early 1890s, Edison and his assistant, William Dickson, had succeeded in perfecting a camera ("Kinetograph") that was capable of photographing objects in motion. Soon thereafter, the first motion picture studio was formed to manufacture "Kinetoscopes" at Edison's laboratory in West Orange, New Jersey. These first primitive movies – filmstrips viewed through a peephole machine – were then shown at a "Kinetoscope Parlor" on lower Broadway in New York, where crowds formed to see this sensational novelty.

The technological development of cameras and films and projection devices accelerated considerably at this stage, and astute businessmen were quick to understand the money-making potential in showing films to the public. The early years, though, were marked by a series of patent infringement suits and attempts at monopolization that were to characterize the industry's internal relations for a long time. As Stanley (1978, p. 10) notes:

movies were being shown in thousands of theaters around the country, . . . After years of patent disputes, the major movie companies realized it was to their mutual advantage to cooperate . . . A complex natural monopoly over almost all phases of the nascent motion picture industry was organized in December 1908. It was called the Motion Picture Patents Company.

This company held pooled patents for films, cameras, and projectors, and apportioned royalties on the patents. It also attempted to control the industry by buying up most of the major film exchanges (distributors) then in existence and organizing them into a massive rental exchange, the General Film Company.

The Patents Company and its distribution subsidiary (together known as the "Trust") often engaged in crude and oppressive business practices that fostered great resentment and discontent. Eventually the Trust was overwhelmed by the growing numbers and market power of the independents that sprang up in all areas of production, distribution, and exhibition (i.e., theaters). The Trust's control of the industry, for example, was undermined by the many "independent" producers who would use the Patent

Company's machines, without authorization, on film stock that was imported. But more significantly, it was from within the ranks of these very independents that there emerged the founders of companies that later were to become Hollywood's giants: Carl Laemmle, credited with starting the star system and founder of Universal; William Fox, founder of the Fox Film Company, which was combined in 1935 with Twentieth Century Pictures; Adolph Zukor, who came to dominate Paramount Pictures; and Marcus Loew, who in the early 1920s assembled two failing companies (Metro Pictures and Goldwyn Pictures) to form the core of MGM.

At around the same time, there began a distinct movement of production activity to the west coast. Low-cost nonunion labor available in Los Angeles provided an economic incentive that was reinforced by Southern California's advantageous climate and geography for filming. Thus, by the mid-1920s, most production had shifted to the west, although New York retained its importance as the industry's financial seat.

However, not long thereafter, the industry was shaken by the introduction of motion pictures with sound, and by the onset of the Great Depression. In that time of economic collapse, the large amounts of capital required to convert to sound equipment could only be provided by the eastern banking firms – who refinanced and reorganized the major companies. Ultimately, it was those companies with the most vertical integration – controlling production, distribution, and exhibition – that survived this period intact. Those companies were Warner Brothers, RKO, Twentieth Century–Fox, Paramount, and MGM. On a lesser scale were Universal and Columbia, who were only producer-distributors, and United Artists, essentially a distributor. The Depression, moreover, also led to the formation of powerful unions of skilled craftsmen, talent guilds, and other institutions that, of course, now play an important role in the economics of filmmaking.

Except for their sometimes strained relations with the unions, the eight major companies came out of this period of restructuring with a degree of control over the business that the early Patents Company founders could envy, and the complaints of those harmed in such an environment began to be heard by the Justice Department. After five years of intensive investigation, the government filed suit in 1938 against the eight companies, charging them with illegally conspiring to restrain trade by, among other things, causing an exhibitor who wanted any of a distributor's pictures to take all of them (i.e., block booking them). Yet, by agreeing to a few relatively minor restrictions in a consent decree signed in 1940, the majors were able to settle the case without having to sever the link between distribution and exhibition. Because of this, five majors retained dominance in about 70% of the first-run theaters in the country.

Not surprisingly, complaints persisted, and the Justice Department found it necessary to reactivate its suit against Paramount in 1944. After several years more of legal wrangling, the defendants finally agreed in 1948

Table 2.1. *Chronology of antitrust actions in the motion-picture industry*

1908	Motion Picture Patents Co. established; horizontal combination of 10 major companies that held most of the patents in the industry; cross-licensing arrangement
1910	General Films Co. purchased 68 film exchanges (local distribution companies) (vertical integration)
1914	Five film exchanges combined as Paramount to distribute films (vertical integration)
1916	Famous Players merged with Lasky to form major studio (horizontal integration)
1917	Famous Players–Lasky acquired 12 small producers and Paramount (vertical and horizontal integration)
1917	Motion Picture Patents Co. and General Films Co. dissolved as a result of judicial decisions and innovations by independents
1917	3,500 exhibitors became part of First National Exhibitors Circuit; financed independents, built studios (vertical and horizontal integration)
1918	Exhibitor combination formed in 1912 partially enjoined
1925	Series of federal suits brought against large chains of exhibitors for coercing distributors
1927	Paramount ordered to cease and desist anticompetitive practices
1929	Standard exhibition contract struck down as restraint of trade
1929	Exhibitor suit resulted in injunction against restrictive practices of sound manufacturers (talkies)
1930	Full vertical integration established as norm (production/ distribution/exhibition); major exhibitor circuits given special treatment such as formula deals, advantageous clearances; studios owned supply of natural resources (stars)
1932	Uniform zoning and protection plan for the Omaha distributing territory enjoined
1938	Start of a series of Justice Department antitrust actions against the industry (Paramount case I)
1940	Major studios entered into a series of consent decrees
1944	Justice Department brought Paramount case II, asked for divestiture of exhibition segment of major studios; District Court stopped short of divestiture, but ordered other practices to cease; both parties appealed
1948–49	Supreme Court (in effect) ordered divestiture Under jurisdiction of District Court, major studios divested themselves of their theaters and entered into consent decrees in other areas
1950–87	Series of antitrust actions (private and federal) against various segments of the industry for past practices, violations of the consent decree, price fixing, block booking, product splitting, and other anticompetitive activities

to sign a decree that separated production and distribution from exhibition. It was this decree – combined with the contemporaneous emergence of television – that ushered the movie business into the modern era (Table 2.1).

2.2 May the forces be with you

Evolutionary elements

The major forces shaping the structure of the movie industry have included (1) technological advances in the filmmaking process itself and in the development of television, cable, satellites, video recorders, and laser discs, (2) the need for ever-larger pools of capital in order to launch motion-picture projects, (3) the 1948 consent decree separating distribution from exhibition, (4) the emergence of large multiplex theater chains in new suburban locations, and (5) the constant evolution and growth of independent production and service organizations. Each of these items will be discussed in the context of a gradually unfolding larger story.

Technology Unquestionably the most potent impetus for change over the long term has been, and probably will continue to be, the development of technology. As Fielding has observed:

> If the artistic and historical development of film and television are to be understood, then so must the peculiar marriage of art and technology which prevails in their operation. It is the involvement of twentieth-century technology which renders these media so unlike the other, older arts. (Fielding 1967, p. iv)

In the filmmaking process itself, for instance, the impact of technological improvements has been phenomenal. To see how far we have come, we need only remember that "talkies" were the special-effects movies of the late 1920s; indeed, it was not until the 1970s that special effects began to be created with the help of advanced computer-aided designs and electronic editing and composition devices. The *Star Wars* series and *Top Gun* are examples of films that would not and could not have been made without the new machines and methods.

Television, cable, and other modern home video devices have also been important in changing the movie industry's economic and physical structure; film presentations on these devices are competitive as well as supplementary to theatrical exhibitions – historically the core business. Advancements in program distribution and storage capabilities have made it possible to see a wide variety of films in the comfort of our homes, and at our discretion, and a broad selection from network or local-station broadcasts, pay-cable channel offerings, and purchased or rented videocassettes and videodiscs is now widely available. Such unprecedented access to filmed entertainment – enabling viewers to control the time and place of viewing – has redirected the economic power of studios/distributors and opened the way for new enterprises to flourish.

This, however, is merely an introduction, and we shall later have much more to say about how the new distribution and storage media fit into the whole picture.

Capital After technology, the second most important long-term force for change has been the packaging and application of relatively large amounts of capital to the total process of production, distribution, and marketing. In this regard, financing innovations (as discussed in the next chapter) have played a leading role. Without the development of sophisticated financing methods and access to a broad and deep free capital market, it is doubtful that the movie industry could have arrived at the position it occupies today.

From an economist's standpoint, it is also interesting to further observe that the feature-film and television businesses do not easily fit the usual molds. Industries requiring sizable capital investments can normally be expected to evolve into purely oligopolistic forms: steel and automobile manufacturing, for example. But because movies – each uniquely designed and packaged – are not stamped out on cookie-cutter assembly lines, the economic structure is somewhat different. Here, instead, we find a combination of large oligopolistic production/distribution/financing organizations regularly interfacing with, and highly dependent on, a very fragmented assortment of small specialized service and production firms.

At least in Hollywood, energetic little fish often can swim with great agility and success among the giant whales, assorted sharks, and piranha.

Pecking orders

Exhibition Back in the 1920s, a 65-cent movie ticket would buy a comfortable seat in the grandeur of a marbled and gilded theater palace in which complimentary coffee was graciously served while a string quartet played softly in the background. But that was to be no more.

The aforementioned 1948 antitrust consent decree had considerable impact on movie industry structure because it disallowed control of the retail exhibition side of the business (local movie theaters) by the major production/distribution entities of that time. Disgruntled independent theater owners had initiated the action leading to issuance of the decree because they had felt that studios were discriminating against them: Studios would book pictures into their captive outlets without public bidding. However, the divestiture – ordered in the name of preserving competition – turned out to be a hollow victory for those independents. Soon after the distribution–exhibition split had been effectuated, studios realized that it was no longer necessary to supply a new picture every week, and they proceeded to substantially reduce production schedules. Competition for the best pictures out of a diminished supply then raised prices beyond what many owners of small theaters could afford. And by that time, television had begun to wean audiences away from big-screen entertainment; the number of movie admissions had begun a steep downward slide. The 1948 decree (now largely an irrelevant artifact) thus triggered and hastened the arrival of a major structural change that would anyway have eventually happened.[1]

In the United States, exhibition is dominated by several major theater chains including those operated by General Cinema, UA Communications (formerly UA Theater Circuit), Cineplex Odeon (Plitt, Walter Reade, and RKO), AMC Entertainment (American Multi-Cinema), Carmike Cinemas, Redstone (National Amusements, Inc.), Commonwealth, Columbia Pictures (Loews), and Marcus Corp. In aggregate, these companies operate approximately 7,500 of the best-located and most modern urban and suburban (primarily in shopping malls) movie screens, with most of the other 15,000 or so older single-screen theaters still owned by individuals and small private companies. As such, the chains control 35% of the screens, but probably account for at least 80% of the total exhibition revenues generated.

In Canada, however, two chains, Cineplex Odeon and Famous Players Ltd. (owned by Paramount Communications, formerly Gulf & Western), are estimated to control about 65% of annual theatrical revenues that are roughly 10% of those in the United States.

In both the United States and Canada, construction of conveniently located multiple-screen (i.e., multiplexed) theaters in suburban areas by these large chains has more than offset the decline of older drive-in and inner-city locations, and has accordingly helped to stave off competition from other forms of entertainment, including home video. The chains, moreover, have brought economies of scale to a business that used to be notoriously inefficient in its operating practices and procedures. As a result, control of exhibition is gradually being consolidated into fewer and financially stronger hands.[2] Indeed, the six companies aggregated in Table 2.2 together account for over 40% of total industry dollar volume.

Production and distribution Theatrical film production and distribution have evolved into a multi-faceted business, with many different sizes and types of organizations participating in some or all parts of the project development and marketing processes. Historically, however, companies with important and long-standing presences in both production and distribution, with substantial library assets, and with some studio production facilities (although nowadays this is not a necessity) have been collectively known as the "Majors." As of the end of 1989, subsequent to several mergers and restructurings, there were seven major theatrical-film distributors (studios): Buena Vista (The Walt Disney Company), Columbia Pictures Entertainment[3] (wholly owned by Sony), MGM/UA Communications

Table 2.2. *Exhibition company revenues and earnings[a]: composite of six companies,[b] 1984–8*

Year	Revenues	Operating income	Operating margin (%)	Assets	Operating cash flow
1988	2,009.1	96.7	4.8	2,832.8	233.5
1987	1,759.9	151.8	8.6	2,261.6	252.8
1986	1,369.5	123.4	9.0	1,621.9	187.7
1985	1,091.3	127.0	11.6	735.8	169.0
1984	1,071.2	134.3	12.5	600.7	172.1
CAGR[c]	17.0	−7.9		47.4	7.9

[a]In millions of dollars except for operating margin (%).
[b]The number of screens for each of these companies, as of the end of the 1988 fiscal year, was as follows: AMC, 1,695; Carmike, 701; Cineplex, 1,825; General Cinema, 1,359; UA Communications, 2,677; Marcus Corporation, 151.
[c]Compound annual growth rate, 1984–8 (%).

(restructured several times in the 1980s), Paramount (Paramount Communications, formerly Gulf & Western), Twentieth Century Fox (owned by Rupert Murdoch's News Corp.), Warner Bros. (Time Warner Inc.), and Universal (MCA Inc.). These companies produce, finance, and distribute their own films, but also finance and distribute pictures initiated by so-called independent filmmakers who either work directly for them or have projects "picked up" after progress toward completion has already been made.

Of somewhat lesser size and scope in production and distribution activities is a so-called "mini-Major" like Orion Pictures (Formerly Filmways), and many smaller production companies which sometimes have distribution capabilites in certain market segments. Generally, these companies do not present a theatrical product line as broad and as deep as the majors, nor do they have the considerable access to capital that a major would have. Nevertheless, these smaller companies occasionally produce and nationally distribute pictures that outperform those of the majors.[4]

Several smaller so-called independent producers also either feed their production into the established distribution pipelines or have smaller distribution organizations of their own. In addition, there are a slew of executive production and project development firms that themselves do no physical production, but that option existing literary properties and/or develop new ones for others to produce.

To handle distributions in local and regional markets not well covered by the majors or submajors, there are furthermore small independent firms, sometimes known as states-righters.[5] They have counterparts in overseas markets, where distributors of various sizes operate.

Although at first it may be a bit startling to learn of the existence of so many different production and service organizations, their enduring presence underscores the entrepreneurial qualities of this business. The many "independents" have been a structural fact of life since the industry began; they add considerable variety and spice to the filmmaking process, and they help prevent the onset of stagnation.

2.3 Ups and downs

Admission cycles

There has long been a notion, derived from the depression-resistant performance of motion-picture ticket sales, that the movie business has somewhat contracyclical characteristics. Indeed, it may be theorized that as the economy enters a recessionary phase, the leisure-time spending preferences of consumers shift toward lower-cost, closer-to-home entertainment activities than when the economy is robust and expansionary (Figure 2.1). If so, this would explain why ticket sales often remain steady during the early to middle stages of a recession, faltering only near the recession's end. By that stage, many people's budgets are apt to be severely stretched, and long-postponed purchases of essential goods (e.g., new cars) and services (e.g., fixing leaky ceilings) will naturally take priority over spending on entertainment. The performance of movie-ticket sales via-à-vis the economy during recessionary episodes since 1929 is illustrated in Figure 2.2.

The most detailed attempt to assess the contracyclicity of ticket demand was made by Albert Kapusinski (see Nardone 1982), who matched 42 economic measures of the motion-picture industry for the 1928–75 span against similar variables used to assess the performance of the whole economy. The variables were then subjected to five tests of cyclical movement which indicated that the motion-picture industry acts contracyclically to the economy 87.5% of the time in peaks and 69.3% of the time in troughs.

Preliminary experiments using spectral-analysis techniques[6] also hint at the possibility of a 4-year cycle and a 10-year cycle in movie admissions, but the statistical evidence in this regard is inconclusive at this time. A more heuristic approach based on unit ticket sales and general operating conditions also seems to suggest the existence of a 25-year cycle. Ticket sales peaked in 1946, and troughed in 1971 – a time when the economic survival of several major distributors was seriously in question.

Seasonal demand patterns are, fortunately, much easier to discern and to interpret than are the long-wave cycles. Families find it most convenient to see films during vacation periods such as Thanksgiving, Christmas, and Easter, and children out of school during the summer months have time to frequent the box office. Contrariwise, in the fall, school begins again, new television programs are introduced, and elections are held; people are busy with activities other than moviegoing. And in the period just prior to

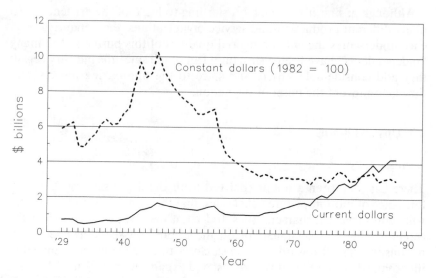

Figure 2.1. PCEs on movies, 1929–88.

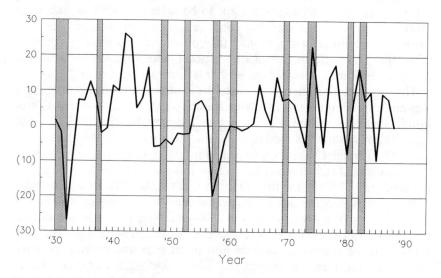

Figure 2.2. Motion-picture receipts: percentage change over previous year's
receipts, 1929–88. Bars indicate periods of recession.

Christmas, shopping takes precedence. Thus the industry tends to concentrate most of its important film releases within just a few weeks of the year.
This makes the competition for moviegoers' attention and time more
expensive than it would be if audience attendance patterns were not as sea-

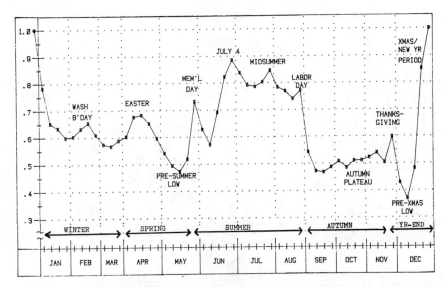

Figure 2.3. Normalized weekly fluctuations in U.S. film attendance, 1969–84.
Source: Variety, copyright 1984 by A. D. Murphy.

sonally skewed (see section 3.4 on marketing costs). Normalized seasonal
patterns are illustrated in Figure 2.3.

Prices and elasticities

Ticket sales for new film releases normally are not very responsive to
changes in box-office prices per se, but there may be sensitivity to the total
cost of moviegoing, which can include fees for babysitters, restaurant
meals, and parking. Although demand for major-event movies backed by
strong word-of-mouth advertising and reviewer support is essentially price-
inelastic, exhibitors often are able to stimulate admissions by showing
somewhat older features at very low prices during off-peak times (e.g.,
Tuesday noon screenings when schools are in session). Many retired and
unemployed people, and probably bored housewives and truants, like to
take advantage of such bargains. There is, moreover, a widespread impression that ticket prices have risen inordinately. Yet, as Figure 2.4 indicates,
movie-ticket prices, as deflated by the consumer price index for the same
period, remain below the peak of the early 1970s.

Production starts and capital

In at least one respect, the movie industry is no different from the housing-
construction industry. The crucial initial ingredient is capital. Without

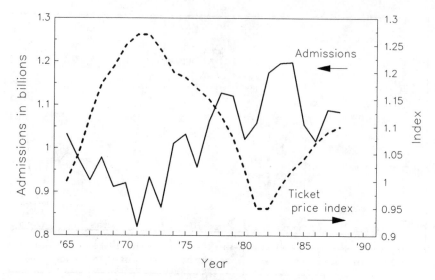

Figure 2.4. Motion-picture ticket sales (solid) and average real ticket-price index, 1966–88.

access to it, no project can get off the ground. It should thus come as no surprise to find that the number of movies started in any year may be sensitive to changes in interest rates and in the availability of credit. To illustrate this relationship, a statistical experiment was conducted using the *Daily Variety* end-of-quarter production-start figures from 1969 to 1980, the quarterly average bank prime interest rate adjusted by the implicit gross-national-product (GNP) deflator for the same period, and the banking system's borrowed reserves (also deflated) as a proxy for the availability of capital. The results were as follows:

1. There may be a moderate, statistically significant inverse correlation, with at least a one-quarter lag, betweeen real interest rates and the number of production starts.
2. There probably exists, with a six-quarter lag, an inverse relationship between production starts and borrowed reserves (credit availability) (Figure 2.5).

That production starts should lag behind changes in the availability of capital by as much as six quarters should not be unexpected in view of the long time usually required to assemble the many diverse components required for motion-picture productions. Beginning with a rudimentary outline or treatment of a story idea, it can often take over a year to arrange financing, final scripts, cast, and crew. And, in total, it normally requires at least 18 months to bring a movie project from conception to the answer-

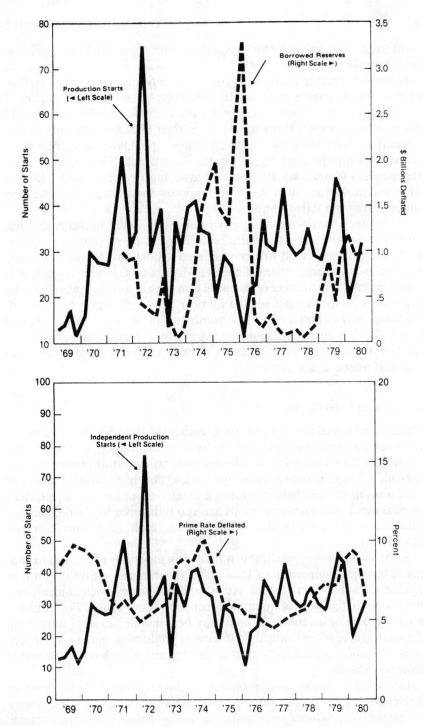

Figure 2.5. Production starts, interest rates, and borrowed reserves lagged six quarters, 1969–80.

print stage – the point at which all editing, mixing, and dubbing work has been completed.

Moreover, because the industry ordinarily depends on a continuous flow of cash, when credit is restricted by the Federal Reserve Bank, sources of funding for movie projects rapidly dry up: Everyone in the long chain of revenue disbursement slows payments on their bills, and it becomes more difficult to effectively attract relatively scarce capital flows away from alternative uses that promise higher returns for less risk. Thus, especially for independent filmmakers, the cost and availability of credit with which to finance a project are often the most important variables affecting the time that elapses from start to finish.

No matter what the monetary environment, however, in theory (but not always in practice) only the worthiest of projects are supported – with the best concepts presumably first being offered to (and sometimes erroneously rejected by) the large studios/financiers/distributors. In this respect, it is significant that the number of potential film projects on Hollywood's drawing boards always far exceeds the number that can actually be financed. Parkinson's law applies here: The number of projects will always expand to fully absorb the capital available, regardless of quality, and almost certainly without regard to the quantity of other films scheduled for completion and release at about the same time.

Releases and inventories

Variations in production starts are eventually reflected in the number of films released (supplied) to theaters. In turn, the number of releases and the rate of theater admissions influence industry operating profits. But it is difficult to estimate (using regression models) how large this effect may be; variations in the numbers of releases and admissions are not independent of each other, and aggregate profits are also influenced by the demand for filmed entertainment products in television, cable, and other markets[7] (Table 2.3).

Sometimes, a more practicable way to view the effects of changes in supply is through comparison of total dollar investments in film inventories against sales (i.e., film rentals). As in other industries, such comparisons often lead to discovery of important economic relationships. For instance, a falling ratio of inventory to sales may be a manifestation of improving demand and/or of declining investments in production; either way, inventories become less financially burdensome to carry as cash is being recycled relatively rapidly.

Estimated inventory-to-sales figures for the major studios are shown in Table 2.4, where proper interpretation requires recognition that *many independently produced projects are carried off-balance-sheet* until release impends. The visible ratios – generally in the range of 0.4 to 0.6 since the early 1970s – are consequently somewhat akin to the tip of an iceberg, the size of which is often more easily gauged from the number of films rated each year by the Motion Picture Association of America (MPAA).[8]

Market-share factors

Many consumer-product industries rely on market-share information to evaluate the relative positions of major participants. However, because consumers have little, if any, brand identification with movie distributors (or most producers), and because market share tends to fluctuate considerably from year to year for any one distributor, such data generally have limited applicability and relevance. In the picture business, the approach is of necessity far different than in market-share research for soaps, cigarettes, or beverages.

This kind of information therefore seems suited for contrasting the major distributor organizations on the basis of relative long-term effectiveness, or for comparing a film's short-term rental performance in one region against that for another film in the same region. In long-term analysis, for example, averaging of Disney's share and those of other distributors over the dozen years beginning in 1970 would quantify that company's significant erosion of market presence (Supplementary Data Tables S2.4 and S2.5 in Appendix C).

Exchange-rate effects

Between 30% and 45% of gross rentals earned by the majors usually are generated outside of the so-called domestic market, which includes both the United States and Canada (about 10% of the U.S. total). Swings in foreign-currency exchange rates may therefore substantially affect the profitability of U.S. studio/distribution organizations.

For instance, during most of the 1970s and after 1985, with the U.S. dollar relatively weak against major export-market currencies (Japanese yen, British pound sterling, West German deutsche mark, French franc, and Swiss franc), studio profitability was significantly enhanced as movie tickets purchased in those currencies translated into more dollars. Contrariwise, in the late 1970s and early 1980s, a strengthening dollar probably reduced the industry's operating profits by some 10%–20% ($50 million to $100 million) under what would otherwise have been generated. Estimates of the importance of foreign-currency translation rates on industry profits are shown in Figure 2.6, and aggregate theatrical admissions in seven developed countries are shown in Figure 2.7.

Although there is some countervailing effect from the higher costs of shooting pictures in strong-currency countries and from maintaining foreign-territory distribution and sales facilities in such locations, a weakening dollar exchange rate can noticeably improve movie industry profitability.

Table 2.3. *Motion-picture-theater industry statistics, 1965–8[a]*

Year	Total U.S. box office revenues ($ million)	MPAA U.S. rentals[b] ($ million)	MPAA Canadian rentals ($ million)	MPAA U.S. rentals as % of B.O.[c] (%)	U.S. + Canadian rentals % of B.O. (%)	Worldwide (U.S. + foreign) rentals ($ million)	Foreign rentals ($ million)	Foreign as a % of total (%)
1988	4,458	1,413.6	125.2	31.7	34.5	2,433.9	1,020.3	41.9
1987	4,253	1,244.5	96.7	29.3	31.5	2,179.6	935.1	42.9
1986	3,778	1,165.1	86.8	30.8	33.1	1,963.4	798.3	40.7
1985	3,749	1,109.1	76.8	29.6	31.6	1,729.0	619.9	35.9
1984	4,031	1,313.2	111.0	32.6	35.3	1,967.2	654.0	33.2
1983	3,766	1,297.4	94.2	34.5	37.0	2,136.2	838.8	39.3
1982	3,453	1,342.7	99.8	38.9	41.8	2,061.3	718.6	34.9
1981	2,966	1,163.6	88.7	39.2	42.2	2,015.0	851.4	42.3
1980	2,749	1,182.6	91.5	43.0	46.4	2,093.7	911.2	43.5
1979	2,821	1,067.7	75.0	37.8	40.5	1,966.6	911.4	46.3
1978	2,643	1,119.9	77.6	42.4	45.3	1,949.4	829.5	42.6
1977	2,372	868.0	66.8	36.6	39.4	1,466.8	597.6	40.7
1976	2,036	576.6	60.8	28.3	31.3	1,147.5	570.9	49.8
1975	2,115	628.0	63.2	29.7	32.7	1,232.2	604.2	49.0
1974	1,909	545.9	54.4	28.6	31.4	1,040.7	494.8	47.5
1973	1,524	390.5	39.9	25.6	28.2	819.3	428.8	52.3
1972	1,583	426.4	38.7	26.9	29.4	827.7	401.3	48.5
1971	1,350	336.7	29.4	24.9	27.1	684.7	348.0	50.8
1970	1,429	381.3	27.4	26.7	28.6	741.7	360.4	48.6
1969	1,294	317.4	27.7	24.5	26.7	665.8	348.4	52.3
1968	1,282	372.3	30.0	29.0	31.4	711.3	339.0	47.7
1967	1,110	355.9	28.1	32.1	34.6	713.7	357.8	50.1
1966	1,067	319.5	26.4	29.9	32.4	680.9	361.4	53.1
1965	1,042	287.2	23.2	27.6	29.8	630.7	343.5	54.5
CAGR[d]	6.5%	7.2%	7.6%			6.0%	4.8%	
Avg.				31.7%	34.3%			

[a]Totals may be affected by rounding.
[b]Motion Picture Association of American (MPAA) rentals are assumed to be about 95% of total U.S. rentals. Remainder is from non-MPAA-member companies.   [c]Rentals percentage for U.S. is understated by 1%–2% because state admissions taxes are not deducted from box office figures.
[d]Compound annual growth rate, 1965–88 (%).

44

Year	U.S. no. of admissions (billion)	Avg. ticket price	Total no. of MPAA releases	Number of domestic screens			Average per screen		Screens per release
				Total	Indoor	Drive-in	Dom. box office ($)	Admissions	
1988	1.085	$4.11	157	23,234	21,689	1,545	191,891	46,690	148.0
1987	1.089	3.91	128	23,555	21,048	2,507	180,552	46,211	184.0
1986	1.017	3.71	133	22,765	19,947	2,818	165,957	44,683	171.2
1985	1.056	3.55	149	21,147	18,327	2,820	177,302	49,941	141.9
1984	1.199	3.36	166	20,200	17,368	2,832	199,535	59,361	121.7
1983	1.197	3.15	190	18,884	16,032	2,852	199,428	63,382	99.4
1982	1.175	2.94	173	18,020	14,977	3,043	191,604	65,228	104.2
1981	1.060	2.78	173	18,040	14,732	3,308	164,390	58,758	104.3
1980	1.022	2.69	161	17,590	14,029	3,561	156,254	58,073	109.3
1979	1.121	2.52	138	16,901	13,331	3,570	166,913	66,327	122.5
1978	1.128	2.34	114	16,251	12,671	3,580	162,636	69,411	142.6
1977	1.063	2.23	110	16,041	12,434	3,607	147,871	66,268	145.8
1976	0.957	2.13	133	15,832	12,197	3,635	128,600	60,447	119.0
1975	1.033	2.05	138	15,030	11,402	3,628	140,719	68,729	108.9
1974	1.011	1.89	155	14,417	10,839	3,578	132,413	70,126	93.0
1973	0.865	1.76	163	14,420	10,765	3,655	105,687	59,986	88.5
1972	0.934	1.70	193	14,428	10,694	3,734	109,717	64,735	74.8
1971	0.820	1.65	183	14,055	10,335	3,720	96,051	58,342	76.8
1970	0.921	1.55	185	13,750	10,000	3,750	103,927	66,982	74.3
1969	0.912	1.42	183	13,480	9,750	3,730	95,994	67,656	73.7
1968	0.979	1.31	196	13,190	9,500	3,690	97,195	74,223	67.3
1967	0.927	1.20	199	13,000	9,330	3,670	85,385	71,308	65.3
1966	0.975	1.09	181	12,930	9,290	3,640	82,521	75,406	71.4
1965	1.032	1.01	210	12,825	9,240	3,585	81,248	80,468	61.1
CAGR:									
1983–88	−1.9%	5.5%		4.2	6.2	−11.5	−0.8	−5.9	
1978–88	−0.4	5.8		3.6	5.5	−8.1	1.7	−3.9	
1973–88	1.5	5.8		3.2	4.8	−5.6	4.1	−1.7	
1965–88	0.2	6.3		2.6	3.8	−3.6	3.8	−2.3	

Note: In traditional industry parlance, the term *domestic* includes U.S. and Canadian rentals. In this table, *foreign* includes Canada.

Source: Variety and *Daily Variety* as based on MPAA–MPEAA data.

45

Table 2.4. *Filmed entertainment industry operating performance, major theatrical distributors, 1973–88[a]*

Year	Revenues ($ million)	Operating income ($ million)	Margin (%)	Film inventory ($ million)	Inventory/ revenue
1988	9,112.3	1,147.6	12.6	5,088.9	0.56
1987[b]	8,242.6	931.8	11.3	4,709.7	0.57
1986[c]	6,847.0	807.5	11.8	4,457.5	0.65
1985	6,359.5	464.8	7.3	4,215.9	0.66
1984[d]	5,838.8	515.5	8.8	3,370.4	0.58
1983[e]	5,323.8	589.6	11.1	2,980.1	0.56
1982[f]	4,548.4	565.0	12.4	2,729.3	0.60
1981[g]	3,748.8	301.3	8.0	2,267.0	0.60
1980[h]	3,997.4	489.4	12.2	1,422.6	0.36
1979	4,009.0	661.4	16.5	1,537.8	0.38
1978	3,498.4	606.3	17.3	1,212.1	0.35
1977	2,739.0	405.9	14.8	973.3	0.36
1976	2,335.6	336.3	14.4	936.2	0.40
1975	2,077.9	352.8	17.0	822.3	0.40
1974	1,802.7	259.5	14.4	862.4	0.48
1973	1,485.3	108.9	7.3	839.7	0.57

5-, 10-, and 15-year compound annual growth rates (%)

1988/83	11.3	14.2		11.3	
1988/78	10.0	6.6		15.4	
1988/73	12.9	17.0		12.8	

[a]Includes fiscal year data for Columbia Pictures, Disney, MCA, MGM/UA and predecessor companies, Twentieth Century Fox, Warner Communications, and for Paramount after 1978, Tri-Star beginning in 1984, and Orion Pictures beginning in fiscal year ended February 1982 and included in prior calendar year figures.

[b]Tri-Star changed from calendar year to fiscal year ended February in 1987. Fiscal year end results are thus included in prior calendar year, except 1987, where nine months' period ends in November. Figures for Columbia in 1987 end December 17 and reflect new February fiscal year. Data from November 1987 to February 1988 are essentially lost for Tri-Star.

[c]Fiscal year on Twentieth Century–Fox was changed from August to June in 1986. MGM/UA figures beginning in 1986 are for reconstituted company, MGM/UA Communications. Gulf & Western changed from a July to an October fiscal year in 1986.

[d]Fiscal 1984 operating income does not reflect Disney pretax film writedowns totaling $112 million.

[e]MGM operating income for 1983 and prior years includes a small amount of music publishing income.

[f]Fiscal 1982 figures omit results of about $150 million in revenues and about $30 million in operating income not reported during transfer of Columbia Pictures to Coca-Cola.

[g]Consistency of data series are also affected by transfer of and change in fiscal years at Twentieth Century–Fox in 1981. Gulf & Western data prior to 1981 also contain theater chain results.

[h]United Artists revenues in 1980 and prior years double-count some MGM revenues.
Source: Corporate reports and 10-K statements.

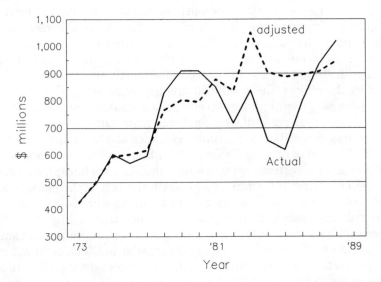

Figure 2.6. Film industry foreign theatrical rentals as adjusted for dollar exchange rate effects, 1973–88.

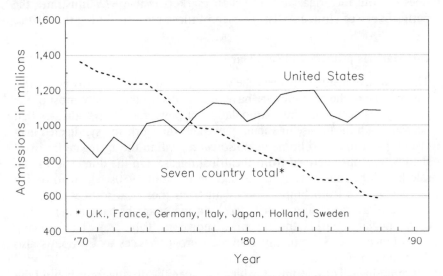

Figure 2.7. Theatrical admissions in the United States and in seven major developed countries, 1970–88. *Source:* Country statistical abstracts and MPAA data.

Financial aggregates

As we have already seen, for all its purported sophistication and glamor, the movie industry remains highly fragmented in both physical organizational structure and mental disposition. It is very much still a cottage industry, and there are good economic reasons to believe that it will remain so, if only because many small, privately owned service firms and production units are frequently much more efficient than the behemoth studios.

The majors, though, generate most of the industry's income, and when they have problems, so does everyone else in the business. Because an estimated 85%–90% of gross domestic film rentals are consistently generated by the majors, the combined financial statements of those companies provide a useful (though overly generalized) representation of the industry's financial performance. Such aggregate data for revenues, and for operating profits before corporate expenses and taxes, are presented in Table 2.4 (where data for Orion and Tri-Star have been included).

Of course, what we really want to know, and what will be explained later, is where entertainment companies generate the best profit margins and growth rates. That cannot be seen in this data set because corporations report only aggregate operating profits for filmed entertainment; they do not separately indicate profits derived from theatrical, television, and ancillary market sales because it is well-nigh impossible to match overhead and other production costs unarbitrarily against revenues from specific sources. However, the former United Artists subsidiary of Transamerica, which did not engage in series production activities, reported operating income on sales to both theatrical and television markets. Table S2.7 illustrates the performance of United Artists in each of those markets during the 1970s.

2.4 Markets primary and secondary

Theaters have historically been the primary retail outlet for movies; that is, where most of the revenues are have been collected and where most of the viewing has occurred. But extrapolation of powerful trends indicates that licensing of films for use in ancillary markets (network and syndicated television, pay cable, and home video software) will in the aggregate far overshadow revenues derived from theatrical release. On the domestic wholesale level, the major distributors had by the mid 1980s begun to derive more revenues from home video than from theatrical sources. And, by 1990, an "average" film distributed by a major might have generated in each ancillary market the revenues shown in Table 2.5. The growing importance of U.S. company television program sales to Europe is also illustrated in Figure 2.8.

Technological development, which has been the driving force behind the transition to dominance by formerly ancillary markets, has led to sharp decreases in the costs of distributing and storing the bits of information that are contained in software. But whether such unit-cost decreases are in themselves sufficient to sustain the industry's profitability cannot just yet be readily ascertained from the information thus far presented.

An individual seeing a newly released feature film in a theater would, for example, ordinarily generate revenue (rental or gross) to the distributor of anywhere between $1.50 and $3.00. However, viewing on pay

Table 2.5. *Estimated ancillary revenues for an "average" MPAA-member film[a] and worldwide average theatrical rentals, 1990 ($ million)*

Typical license fees or revenues	
per film[b]	
Pay cable	6.0
Home video (cassettes and discs)	8.0
Network TV licenses	1.5
Syndication	1.0
Foreign TV	0.5
Total	17.0
Average theatrical rentals	
Domestic	10.5
Foreign	5.5
Total	16.0

[a]Per-film figures for ancillary markets represent the approximate going rate for representative pictures. However, they are not derived by dividing total ancillary-market revenues by an exact number of releases. Averages would, of course, be much lower if non-MPAA member films were to be included.

[b]Also see section 3.5, where it is explained why averages such as those used here require careful interpretation. Examples of wide positive and negative deviations from these approximate averages are shown in Table 4.8.

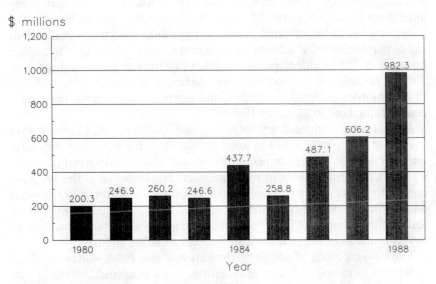

Figure 2.8. U.S. company television program sales to Europe. *Source:* Motion Picture Association of America.

television, or from a rented prerecorded videocassette, sometimes results in revenue per person-view of as little as ten to twenty cents. That happens when several people in a household watch a film at the same time, or when an individual watches several times without incurring additional charges.

It may, of course, be argued that for most of the 1980s, declining average unit costs at home have had no discernible effect on theater admissions and that, indeed, markets for filmed entertainment products have been broadened by attracting, at the margin, viewers who would anyhow not pay the price of a ticket. In addition, it seems that no matter how low the price at home, people still enjoy going out to the movies.

But as sensible as this line of reasoning appears (it is platitudinous within the industry), there are several problems in accepting it without challenge. One of the most noticeable tendencies, for instance, has been the virtual dichotomization of the theatrical market into a relative handful of "hits" and a mass of also-rans. This can be seen from several recent peak-season box-office experiences, in which four out of perhaps a dozen major releases have generated as much as 80% of total revenues.

Although "must-see" media event films are as much in demand as ever, such dichotomization suggests that admissions to pictures requiring less immediate responsiveness probably are being replaced by home screenings that on average generate much less revenue per view. The new home video options obviously allow people to become more discriminating as to when and where they spend an evening out.

Those video options, moreover, were just beginning to penetrate a significant percentage of households in the early 1980s. For example, in many large cities it was not until 1983 and 1984 that cable systems began to be constructed or to be activated. And it was not until 1985 that video recording or playback-only machines were present in over 20% of U.S. television households. When videocassette recorders (VCRs) reached into more than 20% of households in Germany and Australia, theatrical admissions in those countries declined noticeably, and pretty much the same thing happened in the United States in 1986.

All this is a roundabout way of saying that what is gained in one market may be at least partially lost in another; that is, in the aggregate, ancillary-market cash flow is often largely substitutional and thus does not necessarily lead to net increments in total revenues. For evidence of this we have merely to notice that extensive exposures on pay-cable prior to showings on network television have sharply reduced network ratings garnered by feature film broadcasts. The networks have accordingly been unwilling to pay as much as in the past for feature-film exhibition rights.

The development of ancillary markets has also been widely heralded as a boon to movie industry profitability. Yet a case could be made that the contributions from new ancillary revenue sources, especially those

Table 2.6. *Filmed entertainment company revenues and earnings[a]: composite of 53 companies, 1984–8*

Year	Revenues	Operating income	Operating margin (%)	Assets	Operating cash flow
1988	12,392.0	1,098.8	8.9	17,606.2	1,387.3
1987	11,003.1	1,073.1	9.8	17,016.2	1,306.1
1986	8,911.7	903.3	10.1	14,650.9	1.078.4
1985	7,506.3	741.0	9.9	10,148.2	817.7
1984	6,731.3	615.5	9.7	8,142.1	726.9
CAGR[b]	16.5	14.0		21.3	17.5

[a] In millions of dollars except for operating margin (%).
[b] Compound annual growth rate, 1984–8 (%).
Source: Communications Industry Report, 1989. New York: Veronis, Shuler & Associates, Inc.

from pay cable and home video, have merely offset the sharply diminished profitability of theatrical production and release.

The data in Table 2.6, for example, indicate that despite the effective doubling of industry revenues over five years beginning in 1984 – with much of the gain derived from the growth of new media sources – aggregate industry *profits* have increased at a compound rate of only 14.0%, and industry operating margins have remained well below the peaks of the late 1970s (see also Table 2.4). Production and releasing costs for the industry majors have risen far faster than revenues generated in the still-important but relatively stagnant (as measured by admissions and real unit prices) theatrical markets.

Just as significantly, however, the existence of ancillary markets has enabled many independent producers to finance their films through so-called *presales* of rights. Presales often support projects that perhaps could not and should not otherwise have been made, and as such, presales do not enhance industry profitability because the cash flow so generated is not necessarily in excess of that required to cover production *and* marketing costs. Moreover, projects financed in this manner swell the supply of films and at the same time heighten the demand for and thus the cost of various input factors (screenplays, actors, sound stages, etc.).

Companies generally relying on presale strategies manage to cushion but not eliminate their downside risks while giving away much of the substantial upside profit and cash flow potential from hits. Such companies will also inevitably have a relatively high cost of capital compared to a major studio, and will encounter a significant time lag between the start of production and establishment of library asset values. Thus, over the longer run, the relatively few hits such firms produce (if lucky) are often insufficient in number or in degree of success to cover their many losing or break-even projects. In the mid-1980s, the poorer but wiser shareholders of Cannon Group and DeLaurentiis Entertainment were able to attest to this.

As we can see from the data, ancillary market development has not as yet been (and may never be) fully translated into the industry profitability enhancements that many forecasters had anticipated at the dawn of the new-media age circa 1980. There are many reasons for this, but essentially it all boils down to weak cost constraints and increased competition. Between 1980 and 1989, the cost of the average picture made by a major studio rose from $9.4 million to over $20.0 million, and marketing costs more than doubled (Table 3.3).[9]

It is somewhat simplistic and unpopular, but nonetheless accurate, to then portray new-media revenues as thus far having been more important as a prop than as a source of improved aggregate industry profitability. Yet there is no denying that the new media have forever changed the income structure of the film business at large. As Table 2.7 illustrates, as recently as 1980, theatrical sources accounted for over half of all industry revenues. Ten years later, theatrical sources account for only about a fourth of all such revenues (Figure 2.9).

Industry profit trends clearly depend on the amount of time and money consumers are willing and able to spend on entertainment that is purchased directly in the form of movie tickets, pay-cable services, and videocassettes (sales and rentals) rather than obtained for "free" in the form of advertiser-supported programming that is shown by television networks,

Table 2.7. *Film industry sources of revenue estimated, 1980 and 1990*[a]

	1980		1990	
	$ millions	%	$ millions	%
Theatrical:				
Domestic	1,183	29.6	2,100	15.9
Foreign	911	22.8	1,200	9.1
Home video	280	7.0	5,100	38.6
Pay cable	240	6.0	1,100	8.3
Network TV	430	10.8	100	0.8
Syndication	150	3.8	600	4.6
Foreign TV	100	2.5	1,000	7.6
Made for TV films	700	17.5	2,000	15.2
Total	3,994	100.0[b]	13,200	100.0[b]

[a]Major filmed entertainment companies in the United States.
[b]Total not exact due to rounding.

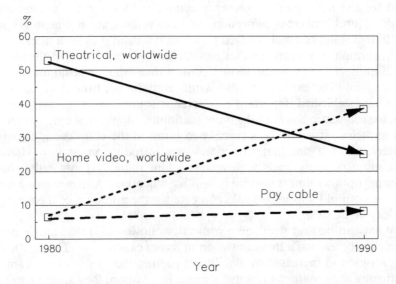

Figure 2.9. Estimated percentage of film industry revenue derived from feature film exploitation in theatrical, home video, and pay cable markets, 1980 and 1990.

stations, and some cable channels. As of 1988, consumers spent almost $26 billion on direct purchases ($4.5 billion in tickets, $13.7 billion on cable, and $7.5 billion for home video), whereas advertisers spent about $23 billion to sponsor programming.

Although the entertainment industry derives revenues from both sources, a distinct shift of preference toward the direct-purchase category would imply a significant improvement in profitability. To see this, note that consumers' out-of-pocket costs per hour of entertainment generally range from approximately fifty cents to two dollars, with pay-per-view events occasionally at three dollars or more. On average, a typical household may buy about 100 hours of such entertainment in a year.

Still, that same average household spends about 2,500 hours per year (almost seven hours per day) in front of free advertiser-supported television. Sponsors reach this audience at a cost of around ten cents per hour per household ($23 billion divided by 2,500 hours divided by 92 million households). If it were possible to sell another 100 hours or so per household per year at fifty cents rather than at ten cents, all other things being equal (and they never are), entertainment industry revenues would be enhanced by about $3.7 billion. That, however, is easier said than done if we take into account the time and income constraints discussed in the previous chapter.

Some large corporations have, of course, already made important strategic decisions under the assumption that such a positive shift will occur.

But for the most part, inherent uncertainties have created a constantly shifting jumble of cross-ownership and joint-venture arrangements (Figure 2.10) that more resemble hedged bets than bold and insightful maneuvers.

In summary, we can see that new technology has provided the viewer with unprecedented access to and control over when entertainment may be enjoyed. Technology has also significantly lowered the price per view and has established important new revenue sources, thus generally diffusing the economic power of the more traditional suppliers of entertainment. Nevertheless, it would be a mistake to jump to the conclusion, as many observers often do, that the continuous introduction of new viewing options necessarily leads to heightened film industry profitability. New viewing options almost invariably displace older ones. And marketing costs rise as both old and new media compete for the attention of increasingly finicky audiences.

What can be said with some conviction, however, is that movie companies have learned a thing or two from recent experiences. They are looking forward to increased availability of pay-per-view cable as a means of enriching their marginal revenue stream. In addition, they appear eager to prevent loss of control in nascent foreign (primarily European) cable and satellite-distributed television markets, where major program-wholesaling organizations are being established through joint ventures.[10]

2.5 Assets

Film libraries

In studies of the financial economics of moviemaking, perhaps no area suffers more from guesswork and vagueness of understanding than evaluation of film-library assets. Yet this topic is of prime concern to investors, who over the years have staked hundreds of millions of dollars on actual and rumored studio takeovers. Twentieth Century Fox, United Artists, and Columbia Pictures have been among the many major acquisitions in an industry long rife with buy-out attempts, a few successful, many others not. Factors that might not at first glance be considered significant – technological advances, interest rates, legislative developments, previous and anticipated near-term utilization (depletion) rates, and prevailing social temper – all affect a library's perceived value.

Technology Of all these factors, technological advances have been by far the most important and have generated the most controversy. On the one hand, the flourishing new electronic media have increased the demand for programming, effectually providing opportunities to sell a lot of old wine (software) in a wide variety of new bottles. But on the other hand, new entertainment delivery and storage technology has made it possible for virtually anyone to conveniently and inexpensively replicate expensive-to-

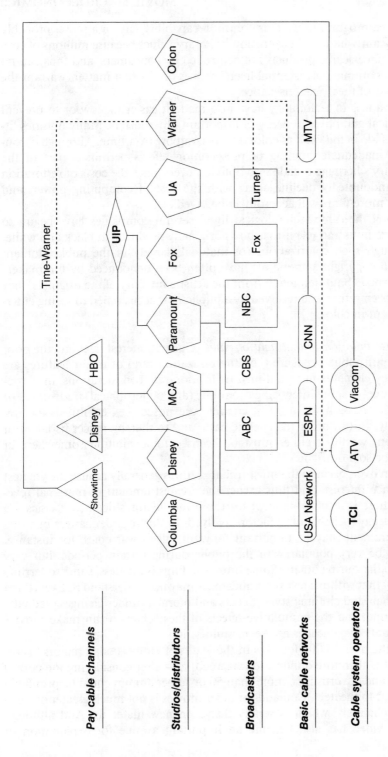

Figure 2.10. Significant entertainment company interrelationships, 1990. Dashed lines indicate indirect relationships.

produce programming. This common capability has, in a sense, probably significantly hastened the erosion of library values because millions of copies of once-scarce products are controlled by consumers, and thus can no longer command substantial licensing fees or, for that matter, warrant the expense of theatrical reissuance.

Advances in technology have also made it easier to slow or to prevent chemical and physical decay of important film masters. Many libraries literally fade in the vault as color dyes decompose over time. Although chronically inadequate funding of preservation efforts permits a part of the industry's heritage to fade into oblivion every year, the costs of restoration will undoubtedly decline along with the cost of computing power, and many more films will accordingly be saved.

Along the same technological lines, several companies have begun to colorize films and television shows originally produced in black and white. Although such colorizations (of materials largely in the public domain from a copyright standpoint) have often been denounced by filmmakers concerned about detracting from the artistic integrity of the originals, they have been rather well received by a public now accustomed to seeing entertainment in color.[11]

Interest, inflation, and utilization rates Current interest rates and the prior degree of public exposure (i.e., the utilization rate) of major features are also key elements in valuations. Utilization-rate considerations, in particular, involve some interesting economic (and philosophical) trade-offs: For a library to be worth a lot, it cannot be exposed (i.e., exhibited) too frequently. But in order to generate cash, and to thereby reflect its latent or inherent worth, it either must be licensed for exhibition somewhere or must be sold outright.

Moreover, because the most recent pictures generally arouse the greatest audience interest, and thus garner the greatest amount of marginal revenue, there is usually – except for those rare features deemed classics – a time-decay (perishability) factor involved. In this regard, changes in social temperament may be important. A vault full of war epics, for instance, might be very popular with the public during certain periods, but very unpopular during others. Some humor in films is timeless, some so terribly topical that within a few years audiences may not understand it. Everything from hair and clothing styles to cars and moral attitudes changes gradually over time, and the cumulative effects of these changes can make movies from only two decades ago seem stultifying.

Of the over 15,000 features in the vaults of Hollywoods's majors (Table 2.8), it is therefore difficult to imagine that – after considering the cost of prints and advertising – more than 50 or so per annum could be profitably reissued to theaters. Demand for older movies is not much greater on pay-cable channels, which generally thrive on new materials. And although home video has also become an important avenue for exploitation of

Table 2.8. *Approximate number of majors' feature titles as of 1988[a]*

Studio	Approximate no. of titles
Columbia	2,700
Disney	300
MGM (Turner)	3,600
Orion	800
Paramount	800
Twentieth Century Fox	1,400
United Artists	1,000
Universal	3,100
Warner Bros.	1,800
Total	15,500

[a]Universal owns pre-1948 Paramount features, and UA owns pre-1950 Warner Bros. films. UA also owns free-TV rights to 700 pre-1950 RKO pictures. Also see chapter note 12.

libraries, the major studios find it difficult to promote effectively an average of more than one package per week – which means that each year the industry might deliver some 500 distinct titles, with the bulk being of fairly recent vintage. Syndicated television – long the main market for older features – also relies heavily on the relative handful of titles that have proved strong enough to consistently attract audiences. In all, then, the structural constraints are such that the industry probably cannot regularly deploy in the domestic markets more than about 800 or so items (5.0%) a year from its full catalog of features. Perhaps another 5% can be deployed in foreign venues.

The effect of interest rates can be understood by visualizing a portfolio of licensing contracts (lasting for, say, the typical three to five years) as entitling the holder to an income stream similar to that derived from an intermediate-maturity bond or annuity. As in the bond market, rising interest rates diminish a portfolio's value, and vice versa. In other words, the net present value (NPV) of a library is the sum of all discounted cash flows, risk-adjusted for uncertainties, that are estimated to be derived from the future licensing of rights or from outright sales of films in the group. A discounted cash-flow concept of this kind may be mathematically presented in its most elementary form as

$$\text{NPV}_a = \sum_{t=0}^{n} A_t/(1 + r)^t$$

where r is the risk-adjusted required rate of return (which is linked to interest rates), A_t is the estimated cash to be received in period t for film a, and

n is the number of future periods over which the cash stream is to be received. Because it is often procedurally difficult to make precise estimates of revenues and net residuals and other participant costs more than a few years into the future, normally relatively large adjustments for risk must be assumed either directly in the formula (by raising the assumed r) or by further trimming of the calculated NPVs.

Inflation is, of course, one of many possible reasons for license fees to rise over time. But to the extent that license fees reflect general inflationary pressures, there is merely an illusion of enhanced worth. Another inflation illusion appears when people speak of "priceless" assets that are often priceless in an artistic sense. Many animated Disney classics, for example, could not be made today at less than astronomical cost, and these pictures are widely considered to be "priceless." However, that does not necessarily mean that these films can consistently generate high license fees or box-office grosses every year. Most of them, in fact, cannot.

Collections and contracts Other factors entering into an evaluation process include questions of rights ownership and completeness. As in philately or numismatics, a complete collection of a series (e.g., all *Rocky* or James Bond or Marx Brothers films) is obviously more valuable than an incomplete set. Control over a complete series of related films makes full marketing exploitation much more efficient.

In addition, rights-ownership splits can present especially nettlesome problems. To fully assess a library, many hundreds of detailed contracts signed over many years must be reviewed to determine the sizes of participations and residual payments. But because such contract stipulations are never well documented (or, for that matter, made available to outsiders), most evaluations must be made at a distance from extrapolations of what is known about available rights to a few key properties. The total number of films in a library may thus provide only a rough measure of its potential value.

Library transfers From the outside, the most obvious method of determining what a library might be worth is to study previous asset-transfer prices for comparable film portfolios. After all, what people actually pay is more significant than what they say. This approach, however, may be difficult to implement because library sales are fairly infrequent, and because the conditions under which such trades take place may differ significantly. The motives for transfer and the prevailing market sentiment for entertainment products at the time of transfer often carry great weight in establishing a transfer price. Consequently, even for two libraries of substantively the same size and quality, the prices may be greatly dissimilar.[12]

From the information in Table 2.9, we can pretty well determine that in the late 1980s, major features have, on the average, been sold for under

Table 2.9. Selected film library transfers, 1957–89[a]

Year	Assets transferred	Sold by	Bought by	Approximate price
1957	700 Warner Bros. features, shorts, cartoons	Associated Artists	United Artists	$30 million
1958	750 pre-1948 features	Paramount	MCA	$50 million
1979	500 features	American International Pictures	Filmways	$25 million
1981	2,200 features, shorts, studio, and distribution system	Transamerica	MGM	$380 million
1981	1,400 features, Aspen Skiing, Coke Bottling, Deluxe Film Labs, 5 TV stations, Intl Theater Chain, studio real estate	Twentieth Century Fox	Marvin Davis, private investor	$722 million
1982	1,800 features, studio property, TV stations, arcade games manufacturing	Columbia Pictures	Coca-Cola	$750 million
1982	500 features	Filmways	Orion Pictures	$26 million
1985	4,600 features, 800 cartoons, shorts, Metrocolor Lab, studio property	MGM/UA Entertainment (K. Kerkorian)	Turner Broadcasting (T. Turner)	$1.5 billion
1985	950 features, distribution system, and other rights to MGM library	Turner Broadcasting	United Artists (K. Kerkorian)	$480 million
1989	2,700 features and 20,000 TV episodes plus distribution system, 800 screens, and other rights	Columbia Pictures Entertainment and Coca-Cola	Sony Corp	$4.8 billion[b]

[a]Several other transactions or proposed transactions reflect library values. In 1985, a half interest in Twentieth Century–Fox was obtained by magnate Rupert Murdoch for $162 million in cash and an $88 million loan, equivalent to about $180,000 a title if real estate, studio assets, and distribution are assumed to comprise half of the asset valuation.

In 1982, the pre-1948 Warner Bros. library including 745 features, 327 cartoons, all the outstanding syndication rights, and the MGM/UA music publishing business was almost sold to Warner Communications for around $100 million. Adjusting for the non-film assets in the proposed sale would indicate a per title average of somewhat under $100,000 a title.

[b]Includes assumption of debt of $1.4 billion. In addition, subsequent buyout of Guber-Peters Entertainment assets required several hundred million dollars more.

$500,000 per title. We can also say that the film-asset evaluation process is neither simple nor precise. As with assessments of beauty, value is often only a function of the beholder's imagination.

Real estate

For a long time, the Hollywood majors neglected and underutilized their real estate assets. But that is no longer the case.[13] By the early 1980s, studio real-estate assets were in the middle of a steep up trend as proximity to major urban growth areas, inflation, and the numbers of made-for-television movies, theatrical features, and cable productions rose to new heights.[14]

Compared with the neglect and downsizing of a generation ago, it is clear that movie-company real-estate assets are now being actively managed and are becoming more impressive all the time. The scope of those assets and development plans is revealed in Table 2.10.

As always, real-estate values in Hollywood or elsewhere will be sensitive to changes in interest rates and to the growth rates of the economy as a whole. But anticipated rising demand for new entertainment software-production facilities and completion of ambitious property-development plans suggest that these assets have become much more significant for financial analysis of film companies and their corporate parents.

Table 2.10. *Major studio real estate assets, 1990*

Studio	Assets
Columbia Pictures (Sony Corp.)	44 acres in Culver City, near Los Angeles (formerly MGM)
Walt Disney Company	27,500 acres, Disney World, Florida 160 acres, Disneyland, California 44 acres, Burbank, California headquarters 691-acre ranch outside Los Angeles
Fox (News Corp.)	63 acres, studio and headquarters, Los Angeles
MCA Inc.	420 acres, Los Angeles headquarters and studio-tour 444 acres, Orlando, Florida, studio-tour
Paramount	50 acres, studio, Los Angeles
Warner Bros.	140 acres, Burbank studios

2.6 Concluding remarks

This chapter has taken a macroeconomic view of the movie industry. As we have seen, many of the things that affect other industries – economic cycles, foreign exchange rates, antitrust actions, technological advances, and interest rates – also affect profits and valuations here. From this angle, moviemaking is a business like any other. How the film business differs from other businesses will more easily be seen from the microeconomic and accounting perspective that is presented in the next two chapters.

Selected additional reading

Cieply, M. (1984). "Movie Classics Transformed to Color Films," *Wall Street Journal,* September 11.

Egan, J. (1983). "HBO Takes on Hollywood," *New York* 17(24)(June 13):40.

Izod, J. (1988). *Hollywood and the Box Office, 1895–1986.* New York: Columbia University Press.

Landro, L. (1984). "Parent and Partners Help Columbia Have Fun at the Movies," *Wall Street Journal,* December 6.

Sherman, S. P. (1984). "Coming Soon: Hollywood's Epic Shakeout," *Fortune* 109(9)(April 30):204–16.

  (1986). "Movie Theaters Head Back to the Future," *Fortune,* 113(2)(January 20).

  (1986). "Ted Turner: Back from the Brink," *Fortune,* 114(1)(July 7).

Smith, P. A. (1987). "Film Colorists Forecast Royalty Payoff," *Wall Street Journal,* May 15.

Steinberg, C. (1980). *Reel Facts.* New York: Vintage Books (Random House).

Thompson, K. (1986). *Exporting Entertainment: America in the World Film Market, 1907–1934.* London: British Film Institute.

3
Making and marketing movies

Dough makes bread and dough makes deals.

Some people would argue that deals, not movies, are Hollywood's major product.

Although we frequently think of studios as monolithic enterprises, in actuality they are simultaneously engaged in four distinct business functions: financing, producing, distributing, and advertising movies. Each function requires application of highly specialized skills that include raising and investing money, assessing and insuring production costs and risks, and planning and executing marketing and advertising campaigns. This chapter describes the framework in which these functions are performed.

3.1 Properties physical and mental

A movie screenplay begins with a story concept based on a literary property already in existence, a new idea, or a true event. It then normally proceeds in stages from outline to treatment, to draft, and finally to polished form. Root (1979) and Nash and Oakey (1974), for example, explain the screenplay development process.

Prior to the outline, however, enter the literary agent, familiar with the latest novels and writers and always primed to make a deal on the client's behalf. Normally, unsolicited manuscripts make little or no progress when submitted directly to studio editorial departments. But with introduction from an experienced agent – who must have a refined sense of the possibility of success for the client's work and of the changing moods of potential producers – a property can be submitted for review by independent and/or studio-affiliated producers. Expenditures to this stage usually involve only telephone calls and some travel, reading, and writing time.

Should the property attract the interest of a potential producer (or perhaps someone capable of influencing a potential producer), an option agreement will ordinarily be signed. Just as in the stock market or real-estate market, such options provide, for a small fraction of the total underlying value, the right to purchase the property in full. Options have fixed expiration dates and negotiated prices, and, depending on the fine print, they can sometimes be resold. Literary agents usually begin to collect at least 10% of the proceeds at this point.

Assuming, against considerable odds, that a film producer decides to adapt one of the many properties offered, the real (and reel) fund-raising effort begins. If the producer is affiliated with a major studio, the financing problem is considerably reduced because a distribution contract can be used to secure bank loans. The studio may also invest its own capital. But in what is now the more common case, "independent" producers have to obtain the initial financing from other sources, which means, of course, that they are thus not completely independent. However, in the pursuit of start-up capital, many innovative, if not truly ingenious, financing structures have in recent years been devised.

Even so, funding decisions are normally highly subjective, and mistakes are often made: promising projects are rejected or aborted, and whimsical ones accepted (i.e., "green-lighted" in industry jargon). The highly successful features *Star Wars* and *Raiders of the Lost Ark,* for instance, were shopped around to several studios before Twentieth Century Fox and Paramount, respectively, agreed to finance and distribute them. *Jaws* was nearly canceled midway in production because of heavy cost overruns. And the script for *Back to the Future* was initially rejected by every studio.

Of course, in order for funding to be obtained, a project must already be outlined in terms of story line, director, producer, location, cast, and estimated budget. To reach this point, enter the talent agents or, pejoratively, the "flesh peddlers." Agents play an important role in obtaining work for their clients, sometimes by assembling into "packages" the diverse but hopefully compatible human elements that go into the making of good feature films or television programs.[1]

The largest multidivision talent agencies are the privately owned William Morris Agency and International Creative Management (ICM), a subsidiary of the formerly publicly owned Josephson International.[2] The Creative Artists Agency (CAA) became a Hollywood powerhouse in the 1980s.

And there are also many smaller and highly specialized firms, among which are the recently emerging "discount" agencies that place top talent for fees of less than the standard 10% of income.

In aggregate, agents perform a vital function by generally lowering the cost of searching for key components of a film project, and by providing and replenishing that constant and necessary industry data base known as gossip. As such, gossip is a natural offshoot of an agent's primary purpose, which is to advance the careers of clients at whatever price the talent market will bear. The use of agents also permits talent employers to confine their work relations to artistic matters, and to delegate business topics to expert handling by the artists' representatives.

3.2 Financial foundations

Some of the most creative work in the entire movie industry is reflected not on the screen but in the financial offering prospectuses that are circulated in attempts to fund film projects. As we shall see, financing for films can be arranged in many different ways, including the formation of limited partnerships and the direct sale of common stock to the public.

Common-stock offerings

Common-stock offerings are structurally the simplest of all to understand. A producer hopes to raise large amounts of capital by selling a relatively small percentage of equity interest in potential profits.

However, as historical experience has shown, common-stock-based offerings do not, on the average, stand out as a particularly easy method of raising production money for movies. Unless speculative fervor in the stock market is running high, movie-company start-ups usually encounter a long, tortuous, and expensive obstacle course.

The main difficulty is that a return on investment from pictures produced with seed money may take years to materialize, if it ever does, and underlying assets intitially have little or no worth. Hope that substantial values will be created in the not too distant future is usually the principal ingredient in these offerings. In contrast to boring but safe investments in Treasury bills and money-market funds, new movie-company issues promise excitement, glamor, and risk. The following examples of common-stock offerings in the 1980s are illustrative.

In the case of a Kings Road Productions offering in the early summer of 1981, rapidly deteriorating market conditions caused withdrawal of the proposed sale of 1.8 million shares at prices between $10 and $12 per share through a large managing underwriter. Experienced producer Stephen Friedman contributed as a core of assets his previously released theatrical features *Slapshot, Blood Brothers, Fast Break, Hero at Large,* and *Little*

Darlings – several of which had already been profitable. United Artists, moreover, was at that time about to distribute Friedman's *Eye of the Needle*, a $15-million picture based on the best-selling novel of the same title.[3] Options on several promising literary properties were also among the Kings Road assets.

It was not until 1985, however, that Kings Road Entertainment finally raised capital from the public in an offering of 1.5 million shares at $10 a share led by two smaller underwriters. The assets included profit participations in the aformentioned pictures and in five others, the most prominent of which was *All of Me*. At the time of the offering, MCA Universal had been granted domestic theatrical and most other distribution rights (except for home video) in most of the company's upcoming productions. MCA, in turn, had agreed to provide material cash advances for the production of those films.

In the 1980s, many other new companies raised or attempted to raise public capital through common stock offerings at low prices. Although most of these small companies began with an intention to eventually produce films on their own, some of them were organized solely for the purpose of developing and arranging financing, production, and distribution for others; that is, they functioned as executive production outfits. Laurel Entertainment, one such example, in 1980 sold 1 million shares of stock at $3.25 each through a small New York investment firm.

Straight common-stock offerings of unknown new companies are difficult to launch except in all but the frothiest of speculative market environments, and, strictly from the stock market investors' viewpoint, experience has shown that most of the small initial common stock movie offerings have in recent years provided at least as many investment nightmares as tangible returns.

Combination deals

Common stock is often sold in combination with other securities so as to appeal to a wider investor spectrum or to more closely fit the financing requirements of the issuing company. This is illustrated by the Telepictures equity offering of the early 1980s. At that time, Telepictures was primarily a syndicator of television series and feature films and a packager and marketer of made-for-television movies and news.

As of its initial 1980 offering by a small New York firm, Telepictures had distribution rights to over 30 feature films and to about 200 hours of television programming in Latin American territories. The underwriting was in the form of 7,000 units each composed of 350,000 common shares, warrants to purchase 350,000 common shares, and $7 million in 20-year 13% convertible subordinated debentures. In total, Telepictures raised $6.4 million.

Another illustration of a combination offering was that of DeLaurentiis Entertainment Group Inc., which separately but simultaneously sold 1.85 million shares of common stock and $65 million in 12.5% senior subordinated 15-year notes through PaineWebber Inc. in 1986. In this instance, the well-known producer Mr. Dino DeLaurentiis contributed his previously acquired rights in the 245-title Embassy Films library and in an operational film studio in North Carolina to provide an asset base for the new public entity. Among the several major films in the library were *The Graduate, Carnal Knowledge,* and *Romeo and Juliet.*

The underlying concept for this company, as well as for many other similar issues brought public at around the same time, was that pre-sales of rights to pay cable, home video, and foreign theatrical distributors could be used to cover, or perhaps more than cover, direct production expenses on low-budget pictures. The subsequent difficulties experienced by this company and several others applying the same approach, however, showed that the concept most often works better in theory than in practice. The reason is that companies in the production start-up phases of development normally encounter severe cash-flow pressures unless they are fortunate enough to have a big box-office hit early on.[4]

Limited partnerships and tax-shelters

Limited partnerships have in the past generally provided the opportunity to invest in movies with the government sharing some of the risk. In fact, before extensive tax-law adjustments in 1976, movie investments were among the most interesting tax-shelter vehicles ever devised. Prior to that revision, limited partners holding nonrecourse loans could write down losses against income several times the original amount invested; they could experience the fun and ego gratification of sponsoring movies and receive a tax benefit to boot.

Such agreements were in the form of either purchases or service partnerships. In a purchase, the investor would buy the picture (usually at an inflated price) with, say, a $1 down payment and promise to pay another $3 with a nonrecourse loan secured by anticipated receipts from the movie. Although the risk was only $1, there was a $4 base to depreciate, and on which to charge investment tax credits.

In the service arrangement, an investor would become a partner in owning the physical production entity rather than the movie itself. Using a promissory note, deductions in the year of expenditure would again be a multiple of the actual amount invested – an attractive situation to individuals in federal tax brackets of over 50%.

Tax-code changes applicable between 1976 and 1986 permitted only the amount at risk to be written off against income by film "owners" (within a strict definition). The code also specified that investment tax credits

Table 3.1. *SLM Entertainment Ltd.*

Distribution	Limited partners (%)	General partners (%)
Until limited partners have received total cash distributions equal to their initial capital contributions:		
Income, gains, credits, distributions	99	1
Losses and deductions	90	10
After limited partners have received total cash distributions equal to the following percentages of their initial capital contributions:		
100% all items	80	20
200% all items	70	30
300% all items	60	40

(equivalent to 6⅔% of the total investment in the negative, assuming that more than 80% of the picture had been produced in the United States) were to be accrued from the date of initial release.[5] Revised tax treatment also required investments to be capitalized – a stipulation that disallowed the service-partnership form.

Beginning with the Tax Reform Act of 1986, however, the investment tax credit that many entertainment companies had found so beneficial because it had helped them to conserve cash was repealed. And as significantly, so-called "passive losses" from tax shelters could no longer be used to offset income from wages, salaries, interest, and dividends. Such passive losses became deductible only against other passive activity income. Accordingly, since 1986, there have been notably fewer and differently structured movie partnerships offered to the public.

For illustrative purposes, though, it is nevertheless of interest to examine more closely several of the widely distributed pre-1986 limited partnerships. Good examples are to be found in the 1981 SLM Entertainment Ltd. offerings of participations in a package of MGM's films, and in the 1982, 1983, and 1984 Delphi-series packages of Columbia Pictures films that Merrill Lynch originated.

The SLM limited partnership was sold in units valued at $5,000, and with a general partners' contribution of 1% (Table 3.1). Investors shared up to 50% ownership with MGM of some 15 films (5 films were initially specified), and were entitled to 99% of capital-contribution recoupment and then a sliding percentage of profits generated by those productions.

In Delphi II (1983), similarly, the partnership retained all distribution rights, and until the limited partners received cash equal to their investment they were entitled to 99% of all cash distributions and equal allocation of all income, loss, or credits. After cash payments to limited partners equaled the proceeds of the offering (less selling commissions and marketing and sales management fees), the general partners were to receive 20% of all cash distributions. In other words, any partnership losses were compensated out of distribution fees due the studio.

Delphi III (1984), also offered in units of $5,000 (for a total of $60 million), was even more favorable to investors because all distribution fees were to be deferred until the partnership recouped 100% of its share of a film's negative (production) costs. Only after that condition had been satisfied was the distributor entitled to recoup its deferred distribution fee of 17.5% of gross receipts from the film. In addition, Delphi III partners were entitled to 25% of net proceeds earned by a film (after deducting a 17.5% distribution fee), or 8% of gross receipts, whichever was greater. This ensured some payment to the partnership even if the film was unsuccessful.

More prototypical of the current partnership structures was the first Silver Screen Partners, brought public by E.F. Hutton in 1983. Strictly speaking, it was not a tax-sheltered deal. Here, Home Box Office (HBO, the Time Inc. wholesale distributor of pay-cable programs) guaranteed – no matter what the degree of box-office success, if any – return of full production costs on each of at least 10 films included in the financing package. However, because only 50% of a film's budget was due on completion, with five years to meet the remaining obligations, HBO in effect received a sizable interest-free loan,[6] while benefiting from a steady flow of fresh product. For its 50% investment, HBO also retained exclusive pay-television and television syndication rights and 25% of network TV sales. This meant that partners were largely relying on strong theatrical results, which, if they occurred, would entitle them to "performance bonuses."[7] Subsequent Silver Screen offerings of substantially the same structure but of larger size (up to $400 million) have been used to finance Disney films (Table 3.2).[8]

In addition to the aforementioned widely distributed partnership units are quasi-public offerings that fall under the Securities and Exchange Commission's Regulation D. Independent filmmakers might sometimes consider structuring such so-called Regulation D financings for small corporations or limited partnerships as a means of establishing themselves. Perhaps the most prominent of recent Regulaton D partnerships was FilmDallas, originally established in 1984 as a private limited partnership with an initial capital contribution of $2.4 million. This company subsequently produced the well-regarded low-budget pictures *Kiss of the Spider Woman* and *The Trip to Bountiful*. Regulation D offerings allow up to 35 private investors to buy units in a corporation or a partnership without registration under the Securities Act of 1933.[9]

Limited-partnership financing appeals to studios because the attracted

Table 3.2. *Movie partnership financing: a selected sample, 1981–7*

Partnership	Total amount sought ($ million)	Minimum investment ($ thousand)	Management fee as % of funds raised	Limited partners' share of profits
Delphi III (January 1984)	60	5	1.16% for 1985–9, then 0.67% for 1990–4	99% to limited partners, 1% to general partners until 100% capital return; then general partners entitled to 20% of all further cash distribution
SLM Entertainment Ltd. (October 1981)	40	10	2.5% of capitalization in 1982, 3% in 1983–7, and 1% in 1988–94	99% until 100% returned, then 80% until 200% returned, and 70% afterward
Silver Screen Partners (April 1983)	75	15	4% of budgeted film costs + 10% per year to the extent payment is deferred	99% until limited partners have received 100% plus 10% per annum on adjusted capital contribution, then 85%
Silver Screen Partners III (October 1986)	200	5	4% of budgeted film cost + 10% per year on overhead paid to partnership	99% to investors until investors have received an amount equal to their modified capital contribution plus 8% priority return

Source: Partnership prospectus materials.

incremental capital permits greater diversification of film-production portfolios: Cash resources are stretched, and there are then more films with
which to feed ever-hungry distribution pipelines.[10] Also, a feature may not
provide any return to investors owning a percentage of the negative, yet
(depending on the partnership structure) may contribute to coverage of
studio fixed costs (overhead) via earn-out of distribution fees that are taken
as a percentage of rentals.

From the standpoint of the individual investor, most movie partnerships
cannot be expected to provide especially high returns on invested capital.
Few of them have historically returned better than 10% to 15% annually.
Yet, such partnerships occasionally generate significant profits, and they
can provide small investors with an opportunity to participate in the
financing of pictures like *Annie, Poltergeist, Rocky III, Flashdance,* and
Who Framed Roger Rabbit. All of these, for instance, had originally been
included in partnership financing packages arranged for major studios.
More often than not, however, when the pictures in such packages succeed
at the box office, most investors would probably find that they could have
done at least as well by investing directly in the common stocks of the production and/or distribution companies (if for no other reason than considerations of liquidity) as in the related limited partnerships.

3.3 Production preliminaries

The big picture

Data from the Motion Picture Association of America (Table 3.3) indicate
that between 1976 and 1988, the average cost of production, or *negative
cost,* for features distributed by the majors rose at a compound annual rate
of 12.9% – thereby far exceeding the rate of inflation over that span. Costs
in this industry always tend to rise faster than in many other sectors of the
economy because moviemaking procedures, although largely standardized,
must be uniquely applied to each project, and efficiencies of scale are not
easily attained.

But especially during the seventies, fiscal sloppiness pervaded the industry as soon as it became relatively easy to finance using other people's tax-
sheltered money. Indulgence of "auteurs," who demanded unrestricted
funding in the name of creative genius, further contributed to budget bloat-
ing. And, certainly, inept management characterized by a copycat, bigger-
is-better mentality (as is still happening today) had its effect.

At the same time, well-heeled people outside the Hollywood establishment decided to apply to the movie business their fortunes earned in shopping centers, real estate, oil and gas exploration, and other diverse endeavors. Otherwise coolheaded neophyte moguls and many smaller investors
were especially attracted by the widely heralded start of the "new-media

revolution"[11] and by undue extrapolations from the record-breaking box-office performances of *Jaws* and *Star Wars.*

In particular, it was those infusive and intrusive disturbances to the industry's normal, internally generated cash-flow and financing rhythms and processes that caused rampant production-cost inflation manifested by aggressive bidding for scarce talent resources. The environment enabled "bankable" actors and directors (popular and well-known person-alities who could be expected to draw an audience simply by virtue of their presence) to command millions of dollars for relatively little expenditure of time and effort.

With prices for the services of the movie colony's leading lights rising rapidly, it was only a short while before every one else also demanded more. Guilds of actors, writers, directors, and stagehands all participated in the largesse, which then spilled over into the southern California housing market and injected an additional speculative element.

Although production costs rose somewhat more gradually in the 1980s than in the 1970s, the rate of gain still exceeded that of inflation in the overall economy. The highly visible potential of burgeoning new media revenue sources, primarily in cable and home video, attracted (until the 1986 tax code changes) relatively large and eager capital funding commit-ments for investments in movie and television projects. And this, in turn, led to continuing upward pressures on the prices of scarce talent resources and physical production facilities.

Even under the best of circumstances, though, production budgets – in which there are thousands of expense items to be tracked – are not easy to control. The basic cost components that go into the making of a film neg-ative are, for example, illustrated in Figure 3.1.

In the category of *above-the-line-costs* – that is, the costs of a film's cre-ative elements including cast and literary-property acquisition – contracts are signed and benefits and payments administered for sometimes hun-dreds of people. Good coordination is also required when budgeting *below-the-line costs* – the costs of crews and vehicles, transportation, shelter and props.[12] For each film, wardrobes and props must be made or otherwise acquired, locations must be scouted and leases arranged, and scene pro-duction and travel schedules must be meticulously planned. And should any one of those elements fall significantly out of step – as happens when the weather on location is unexpectedly bad, or when a major actor takes ill or is injured – expenses skyrocket.[13]

Major cost pressures notwithstanding, however, there are still a few places where feature films have been produced by small studios for sums of often less than $1 million. The most notable of these smaller entities are Troma Inc., based in New York City, and EO Corporation (Earl Owensby), a North Carolina outfit. Troma has specialized in the production and the-atrical distribution of raunchy comedies that are also of interest to pay-

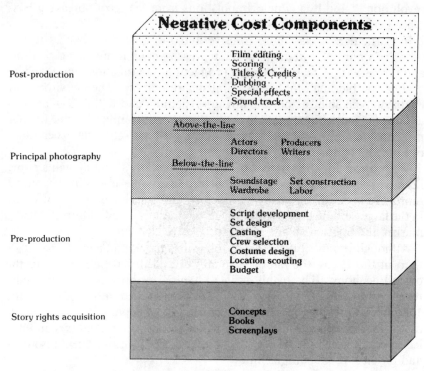

Figure 3.1. Negative cost components.

cable networks. Earl Owensby specializes in films that appeal primarily to working-class and rural audiences.[14] In addition, several other independent filmmakers now specialize in the production of low-budget features.

Labor unions

Unions have a significant influence on the economics of filmmaking, beginning with the very first phase of production. The major unions in Hollywood include the Writers Guild of America, the Directors Guild of America, the Producers Guild of America, the Screen Actors Guild (SAG), the American Federation of Television and Radio Artists (AFTRA), and the International Alliance of Theatrical and Stage Employees (IATSE). Individuals who function in more than one capacity, such as a writer-director, belong to more than one guild and are known as *hyphenates.*

Hollywood unemployment rates, as estimated from industry pension-plan contributions that depend on person-hours worked, are chronically high; they vary cyclically with changes in production starts and, to a lesser extent, secularly with growth of new entertainment media.

Negotiations between the studios' bargaining organization, the Alliance of Motion Picture and Television Producers (AMPTP), and the guilds have historically not been cordial. Relations became especially vitriolic during bargaining sessions in 1980 and 1981 when SAG and the Writers Guild demanded significant participation rights in license fees from new-media sources such as pay-cable, discs, and cassettes.[15] Then, again in 1988, the Writers and the AMPTP sustained a lengthy strike centered on the issue of television residual payments.

Incentives to create for new media are of obvious importance in view of the high unemployment rates among guild members. But because it is possible to produce a film with no noticeable qualitative differences for up to 40% less in nonunion or flexible-union territories outside of Hollywood, it may be argued that the unions' featherbedding and work-restriction rules have also contributed to unemployment. In the absence of featherbedding, the available capital resources for production could be spread over more film starts, and moviemakers would have less incentive to shift production to overseas locations where wages are lower.[16]

Labor inefficiencies further raise the cost of capital by inordinately increasing investors' risk of loss. Over the long run, high capital costs reduce opportunities for growth in entertainment industry employment.

3.4 Marketing matters

Distributors and exhibitors

Sequencing After the principal production phase has been completed, thousands of details still remain to be monitored and administered. Scoring, editing, mixing sound and color, and making prints at the film laboratory are but a few of the essential steps. Once in the postproduction stages, however, perhaps the most critical preparations are those for distribution and marketing.

Sequential distribution patterns are determined by the principle of the second-best alternative. That is, films are normally first distributed to the market that generates the highest marginal revenue over the least amount of time. They then "cascade" in order of marginal-revenue contribution down to markets that return the lowest revenues per unit time. This has historically meant theatrical release, followed by licensing to pay-cable program distributors, home video duplicators, television networks, and finally local television syndicators. But the number of households with video recorders has grown so rapidly that release to home video now regularly follows closely after theatrical release and is positioned just ahead of or at the same time as release to cable (Figure 3.2).

Sequencing is always a marketing decision that attempts to maximize income, and so it is not surprising to find occasional deviations from the usual pattern. One such exception, for example, occurred in 1980, when Twentieth Century Fox showed *Breaking Away* on network television

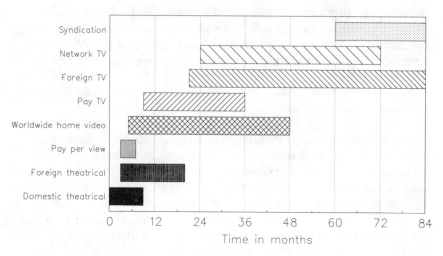

Figure 3.2. Market windows from release date, circa 1990.

before pay-cable. Fox even contemplated simultaneous release in theaters and on videocassettes. However, the market was not and still is not quite ready for that idea because for most pictures the greatest marginal revenue per unit time is still likely to be derived from theatrical issue. Moreover, most pictures require theatrical release in order to generate interest from sources further down the line. Thus, for the foreseeable future, theatrical release will come first for the great majority of films. (Also see section 2.4.)

Nevertheless, there are important adjustments ahead for all industry segments. With widespread availability of pay-per-view cable, for instance, studios will have the potential to generate millions of dollars by one-night showings of their most important films. This would, in effect, raise viewing prices per person well beyond those traditionally received from subscription-television channels (see Chapter 7).

All this, of course, threatens exhibitors, who – if they were to lose first-play rights on important films – would find it difficult, if not impossible, to survive on just leftovers. The resulting shrinkage of the theatrical-distribution pipeline obviously would also make it more difficult to nurture lightly marketed but nonetheless promising releases to the point at which such releases could attract enough attention to be profitable.

In addition, total revenues might be adversely affected by diminishing contributions from markets pushed farther downstream in the distribution sequence: For example, now that films are first widely exposed to large pay-cable audiences, television networks are no longer as interested in bidding aggressively for licenses to run theatrical features. They are most interested in first-run made-for-television productions, which are both less expensive and more effective in generating high ratings.

In sum, it seems unlikely that studios, distributors, and exhibitors will make abrupt changes in product sequencing – excitement over the new-media environment notwithstanding. After all, maximum revenues still are realized only when there is favorable word-of-mouth advertising by satisfied theatergoers.

Distributor-exhibitor contracts Distributors normally design their marketing campaigns with certain target audiences in mind, and they are always interested in efficiently reaching those audiences. Distributors will thus typically attempt to align their releases with the most demographically suitable theaters, subject to availabilities of screens and previously established relationships with the exhibition chains. They accomplish this by analyzing how similar films have previously performed in each potential location, and by then developing a releasing strategy that provides the best possible marketing mix, or platform for the picture. Sometimes the plan may involve a slow build-up through limited local or regional release, and at other times it may involve a broad national release on literally thousands of screens simultaneously.

Of course, no amount of marketing savvy can make a really bad picture play well, but an intelligent strategy can almost certainly help to make the box office (and ultimately the home video and cable) performance of a mediocre picture better. It has thus now become most common for distributors to negotiate arrangements with exhibitors for specific theater sites. Significant growth (through multiplexing) in the number of screens per release (Figure 3.5) has undoubtedly contributed to this trend in recent years.

Nevertheless, instead of negotiating, distributors may sometimes elect, several months in advance of release, to send so-called bid letters to theaters located in regions in which they expect (because of demographic or income characteristics) to find audiences most responsive to a specific film's theme and genre.[17] This would normally be the preferred method of maximizing distributor revenues at times when the relative supply of pictures is limited, as had happened in the late 1970s. Theaters that express interest in showing a picture then usually accept the *terms* (i.e., the actual cost of film rental and the playing times) suggested by the distributor's regional branch exchange (sales office).

Such contracts between distributors and exhibitors are usually of the boilerplate variety (fairly standard from picture to picture), and are arranged for large theater chains by experienced film bookers who bid for simultaneous runs in several theaters in a territory. Smaller chains or individual theaters might also use a professional agency for this purpose.

Still, there can be variations. For example, in the early 1970s the film *Billy Jack* received wide publicity for its distribution through "four-wall" contracts. Here the distributor in effect rents the theater (four walls) for a fixed weekly fee, pays all operating expenses, and then mounts an advertising blitz on local television to attract the maximum audience in a minimum of time. Yet another simple occasional arrangement is flat rental: The exhibitor (usually in a small, late-run situation) pays a fixed fee to the distributor for the right to show the film during a specified period.

Most contracts between distributors and exhibitors, however, would almost always call for a sliding percentage of the box-office gross after allowance for the exhibitor's "nut" (house expenses, which include location rents and telephone, electricity, insurance, and mortgage payments). Whether assumed or negotiated, the nut can be inflated to provide the exhibitor a somewhat disguised additional profit source.

For a major release, sliding-scale agreements may stipulate that 70% or more of the first week or two of box-office receipts after subtraction of the nut are to be remitted to the distributor, with the exhibitor retaining 30% or less. Every two weeks thereafter, the split may then be adjusted downward by 10% as 60:40, then 50:50, and so forth.

The distributor's gross (in the vernacular known as "rentals") is thus in effect received for a carefully defined conditional lease of a film over a specified period. Lease terms may include bid or negotiated "clearances," which provide time and territorial exclusivity for a theater. No exhibitor would want to meet high terms for a film that would soon (or, even worse, simultaneously) be playing in a theater down the block.

Should a picture not perform up to expectations, the distributor also usually has the right to a certain minimum or "floor" payment. These minimums are direct percentages (often more than half) of box-office receipts prior to subtraction of house expenses, but any previously advanced (or guaranteed) exhibitor monies can be used to cover floor payments owed. For a film that is a total flop, though, the distributor may reduce the exhibitor's burden through a quietly arranged settlement.[18]

Consequently, it often happens that the biggest profit source for many exhibitors is not the box office, but the candy, popcorn, and soda counter – where the operating margin may exceed 50%. Theater owners have full control of proceeds from such sales; they can either operate food and beverage stands (and, increasingly, video games) themselves or lease to outside concessionaires. The importance of these concession profits to an exhibitor can be seen in the numerical example in Table 4.7.

Given the high percentage normally taken by the distributor, it is in the distributor's interest to maintain firm ticket pricing, whereas it may be in the exhibitor's interest to set low ticket prices to attract high-margin candy-stand patronage. In most instances, ticket prices are set by exhibitors, and the potential for a conflict of interest does not present any difficulty to either party. However, there have been situations (the releases of *Superman, Annie,* and a few Disney films) in which minimum per-capita admission prices have been suggested by the distributor to protect against children's prices that are too low. What distributors fear is that low ticket prices will divert spending from ticket sales (where they get a significant cut) to the exhibitor's high-margin concessions sales.

Release strategies, bidding, and other related practices Large production budgets and high interest rates provide strong incentives for distributors to release pictures as broadly and as soon as possible. A film's topicality and anticipated breadth of audience appeal will then influence the choice of marketing strategies that might be employed to bring the largest return to the distributor over the shortest time.

Many alternatives are available to distributors. Some films are supported with national network-television campaigns arranged months in advance; others with only a few carefully selected local spots, from which it is hoped that strong word-of-mouth advertising will build. Sometimes a picture will be opened in one or two theaters in New York or Los Angeles (at a cost of perhaps half a million dollars) the last week of the year in order to qualify for that year's Academy Award nominations, and then be broken wide the following spring. Or there may be massive simultaneous release on over 2,000 screens around the country at the beginning of summer. Regional or highly specialized release is, of course, appropriate if a picture does not appear to contain elements of interest to a broad national audience.

In any case, different anti-blind-bidding laws (laws that prohibit completion of contracts before exhibitors have had an opportunity to view the movies on which they are bidding) are effective in at least 23 states. This legal mosaic tends to make the release strategies of distributors more complicated than they would otherwise be.

Anti-blind-bidding statutes were passed by state legislatures in response to exhibitor complaints that distributors were forcing them to bid on and pledge (guarantee) substantial sums for pictures they had not been given an opportunity to evaluate in a screening: in other words, buying the picture sight unseen. Distributors now generally screen their products well in advance of release, but large pledges are still required to obtain important pictures in the most desirable playing times, such as the week of Christmas through New Year's. For these seasonal high periods, the terms at many major-city theaters may require that upward of $125,000 in nonrefundable cash advance against future rentals owed (i.e., guarantees) be paid 10 days in advance of issuance.

Whereas in theory, movie releases from all studios can be expected to play in different houses depending only on the previously mentioned factors, in reality, some theaters, mostly in major cities, more often than not end up consistently showing the products of one particular distributor. Industry jargon denotes these as theater "tracks" or "circuits." Tracks can evolve from long-standing personal relationships (many going back to before the Paramount Consent Decree) that are reflected in negotiated rather than bid licenses, or they may indicate de facto *product-splitting* or *block-booking* practices.

Product splitting occurs when several theaters in a territory tacitly agree not to bid aggressively against each other for certain films – the intention being to reduce average distributor terms. Each theater in the territory then has the opportunity, on a regular rotating basis, to obtain major new films for relatively low rentals percentages.[19]

Interestingly, the practice of product splitting was brought to the attention of the Department of Justice by distributors in response to exhibitors' charges that distributors had been illegally engaged in the practice of block booking. In block booking, a distributor will accept a theater's bid on desirable films contingent on the theater's commitment that it will also run less popular pictures.

As may be readily inferred, symbiosis between the exhibitor and distributor segments of the industry has not led to mutual affection. The impending growth of pay-per-view cable, and the possibility of simultaneous releases (known as day and date in the industry) on videocassettes, may further strain their relations.

Exhibition industry characteristics: (a) Capacity and competition The long-run success of an exhibition organization is highly dependent on its skill in evaluating and arranging real-estate transactions. Competition for good locations (which raises lease payment costs), as well as too many screens in a small territory, can significantly reduce overall returns.

To achieve economies of scale, since the 1960s exhibitors have tended to consolidate into large chains operating multiple screens located near or in shopping-center malls. Meanwhile, older movie houses in decaying center-city locations have encountered financial hardships as the relatively affluent consumers born after World War II have grown to maturity in the suburbs, and as rising crime rates and scarcity of parking space have become deterrents to regular moviegoing by city residents. (Ironically, the very same social pressures contributed to the disappearance of many drive-in theaters situated on real estate too valuable to be used only for evening movies.[20])

In 1988 there were about 23,000 screens, a diminishing proportion of which were drive-ins. The total has been increasing since 1965 at an average rate of 2.6%, with box-office gross per screen rising an average 3.8% per year (see Table 2.3). During this time, operating incomes and market shares for large, publicly owned theater chains (especially regionals) have obviously gained rapidly at the expense of single-theater operators. For example, as of 1982, the top-grossing one-third of screens generated half of the box office, with the bottom third generating about one-sixth of the box office (Murphy 1983) (Figure 3.3); currently the top one-third of screens probably account for 70% of all theater grosses.

In effect, the number of screens has increased (Figure 3.4), while the number of separate theater locations has stayed about the same in recent years. And whereas a film formerly could be "platformed" because there used to be at least three tiers of theater quality ranging from first-run fancy theaters to last-run small neighborhood "dumps," now there are only key first-run multiple-screen houses, and all others.

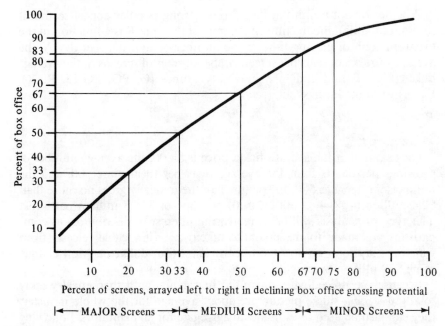

Figure 3.3. Domination of box-office performance by key U.S. movie theaters. *Source: Variety,* July 7, 1982. Copyright 1982 by A. D. Murphy.

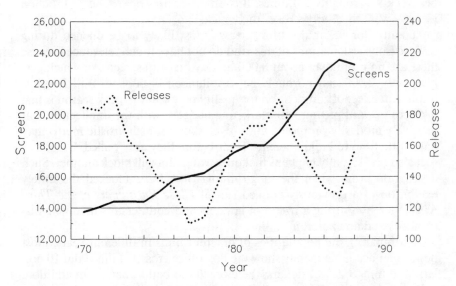

Figure 3.4. Number of screens and MPAA-member releases, 1970–88.

Whether or not a film has "legs" (i.e., strong popular appeal so that it runs a long time), the maximum theoretical revenue R is a function of the average length of playing time P, the number of showings per day N, the average number of seats per screen A, the number of screens S, the average ticket price T, and audience suitability ratings (G, PG, PG-13, R, X). Exclusive of the ratings factor,

$$R = N \times S \times T \times A$$

where $N = f(P)$.

For example, if the average ticket price is \$4.00, the average number of showings per day is four, the average seats per theater are 300, and the number of screens is 500, the picture can theoretically gross no more than \$2.4 million (4 × 4 × 300 × 500) per day, or \$16.8 million per week. This type of analysis will be of increasing interest to distributors as comparisons are made to the potential of pay-per-view cable release, from which it may soon be possible to earn, on a four-dollar per-view charge, some \$20 million overnight.[21]

Because the preceding figures used in calculating a theoretical weekly total gross for a single picture are about average for the whole industry, they can also be used to estimate an aggregate for all exhibitors. Following this line, we can determine that in 1988, the maximum theoretical annual gross, based on 23,000 screens, was about \$110.4 million per day, or about \$40.3 billion per year. The industry obviously operates well below its theoretical capacity because there are many parts of the week and many weeks of the year during which people do not have the time or inclination to fill empty theater seats. In 1989, the industry's average occupancy rate per seat per week was roughly 3.4 times. Box-office receipts of around \$5.0 billion in 1989 were thus only 11% of theoretical capacity.

Actually, for the major film releases most likely to be opened during peak seasons, calculations of this kind do not have much relevance because there are no more than about 6,000 quality first-run screens, of which perhaps only 2,000 can normally be simultaneously booked. But the most important effect of competition for quality play dates in peak season is that it places upward pressure on marketing budgets, with the implication that relatively modestly promoted films (even those of high artistic merit) may have little time to build audience favor before they are "pulled."

It also occasionally happens that one strong film will block another. Such a situation arose when the long-running *Star Wars* blocked the timely exhibition of a previously booked run of *Close Encounters of the Third Kind*, thereby starting a round of lawsuits and countersuits involving distributors and an exhibitor.[22]

In comparing the popularities of different films in different years, most newspaper accounts merely show the box-office grosses: Film A did 10 dollars, and film B did 11 dollars; therefore B did better than A. In addition, a deeper, but still often misleading, comparison is sometimes derived by

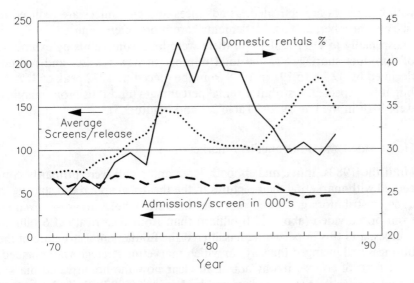

Figure 3.5. Exhibition industry trends, 1970–88.

calculating an average gross per screen. However, as can be seen from the preceding discussion, close analysis and comparison of box-office figures require that variables such as ticket-price inflation, film running time, season, weather conditions, number and quality of theaters, average seats per theater, and types of competing releases be considered.

Moreover, in theory, an even better measure of how one film has performed as compared with another can be derived by calculating the percentages of potential total weekly exhibitor capacity that the films have utilized. It would, for instance, be interesting to see how opening-week receipts from *Indiana Jones* compared against opening-week receipts from *Superman* by deriving for each picture a capacity-utilization percentage – profiled first across the whole industry's capacity, and then across the capacity of theaters that played both pictures in their initial weeks of release. Unfortunately, data of this kind are rarely available.

(b) Rentals percentages All other things being equal, when the supply of films is small compared with exhibitor capacity, the percentage of box office reverting to distributors (the rentals percentage) rises.[23] Faced with a relatively limited selection of potentially popular pictures, theater owners tend to bid more aggressively, and to accede to stiffer terms than they otherwise would. To some extent, however, the rentals percentage also depends on ticket prices and on how moviegoers respond to a year's crop of releases (Figure 3.5). A poorly received crop tends to reduce the average distributor rentals percentage as "floor" (minimum) clauses on contracts

with exhibitors are activated, as advances and guarantees are reduced in size and number, and as "settlements" are more often required.

Especially in 1977 and 1978, there were loud complaints by exhibitors of "product shortage" as the total number of new releases and reissues declined by 39.7% to 191 in 1978 from the preceding 1972 peak of 317. As might be expected, distributor rental percentages (and thus profit margins) were high in the late 1970s (Table 2.3 and Figure 3.5).

Home video and other ancillary markets

Until the 1980s, moviemakers both large and small were primarily concerned with marketing their pictures in the theatrical arena. But starting in 1986, distributors generated more in domestic wholesale gross revenues from home video (about $2.0 billion) than from theatrical ($1.6 billion) sources, and this in particular has altered the fundamental structure of the business and changed the ways in which marketing strategies are pursued.

At first, of course, it was not at all clear how the home video market would evolve. As described in detail by Lardner (1987), the videocassette recorder (VCR) was introduced by the Sony Corporation in 1975, yet it was not then at all evident that it would prevail. The machine was not perceived as something for which plentiful software in the form of movies would be available: at the time, there was no prerecorded software. And the machine, known as the Betamax, could only record on magnetic tape for one hour. Worse still, it soon faced competition from a noncompatible but similar two-hour videocassette format, the VHS system (Video Home System), that was quickly introduced by Sony's manufacturing rival, Matsushita. This battle of the formats caused great confusion and hampered the initial growth of the market for VCRs, following as it did close on the heels of earlier home-video technologies that had notoriously failed.[24]

That was not all, however. By the late 1970s, consumers were also being introduced to so-called videodisc players that did not have a recording capability, and were therefore useless for "time-shifting," i.e., recording a program off-the-air for delayed viewing. These videodisc machines were developed in two versions: a laser/optical system (closely related to the now standardized system in compact disc players) that used a laser beam to read (without touching the surface of the recording) encoded video and audio signals, and a capacitance system that used a stylus to skim a recording and measure changes in electrical capacitance. Both versions fared poorly, and were eventually withdrawn by their respective corporate sponsors.[25]

VCRs have by now, of course, become a familiar item in households around the world; total unit sales through 1988 are estimated to have been at least 175 million, with the effective installed base (i.e., net of replacements) still growing by a projected 10% annually. And in most developed countries, including the United States, Japan, Britain, France, Germany, Italy, Holland, and the Scandinavian countries, VCRs are found in over

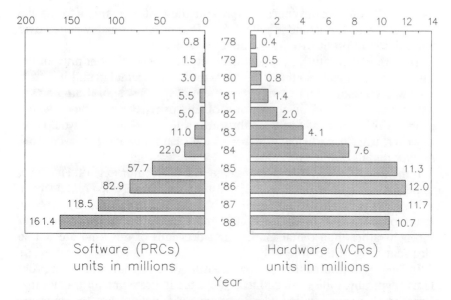

| 200 | 150 | 100 | 50 | 0 | | 0 | 2 | 4 | 6 | 8 | 10 | 12 | 14 |

	0.8	'78	0.4
	1.5	'79	0.5
	3.0	'80	0.8
	5.5	'81	1.4
	5.0	'82	2.0
	11.0	'83	4.1
	22.0	'84	7.6
	57.7	'85	11.3
	82.9	'86	12.0
	118.5	'87	11.7
	161.4	'88	10.7

Software (PRCs)   Hardware (VCRs)
units in millions   units in millions
Year

Figure 3.6. Hardware and software trends in the home video market, 1978–88.

half of the television households. This enormous installed base has already turned out to be an incredibly powerful funds flow engine for filmmakers: the machines, it seems, have evinced a voracious appetite for new entertainment products.[26] And upcoming digital disc and tape hardware formats should be just as hungry.

As a result, from virtually zero in 1980, the prerecorded home video software business (Figure 3.6) will have grown in the space of just 10 years to over $10 billion in domestic retail revenues – with the bulk of those revenues derived from sales or rentals (to the consumer) of feature films. It would appear highly probable, then, that the proportion of feature films to other home video software categories will in the foreseeable future remain fairly close to the two-to-one ratio that has prevailed in the 1980s.

The very size of the home video business thus demands that filmmakers and distributors now pay close attention to home video when they prepare marketing campaigns. One of the most important decisions for the major studios, all of which have their own home video divisions, is how to price the videocassette. Since the cost of manufacturing and shipping is about the same for all regular feature films (under $4.00 a unit), the marketing decision always comes down to whether the distributor can earn more by pricing high and thus targeting the rental market, or by pricing low in order to attract the individual buyer. On *Top Gun,* for example, Paramount decided to promote a sell-through by going with a suggested retail price of around $25 (but with the tape including a brief Pepsi-Cola advertisement). Paramount ended up selling almost three million units, thereby generating over $60 million in revenues. Given that the cost of manufacturing the physical product was (and is still) so low, Paramount probably netted over $40 million in profits from this one home video release.[27]

The other alternative, as noted, is to set the suggested retail price of the cassette much higher, so that it becomes primarily a rental item. Most such "A"-title releases, as films with the potentially widest appeal are known, would list for $79.95 or above, and of this price, the distributor would probably retain around $50 from the initial sale. The distributor would not, however, usually participate further in the cash flow that is derived from retailer rentals of the tape.[28]

If the title is indeed in strong demand, the distributor might then expect to be able to place as many as half a million units with video rental stores, and to thus generate $25 million or so in revenues. In the case of *Top Gun,* Paramount almost surely generated more profit in targeting the sell-through rather than rental market, but decisions of this kind are not so clear-cut most of the time.

Independent filmmakers, on the other hand, face a different set of problems. Typically, indies will be most interested in preselling (or fractioning) rights to their pictures in order to finance production. For this purpose, they can approach one of the majors or submajors, or go to an independent home video distributor.[29] However, in recent years it has become increasingly difficult to fractionate rights because virtually all theatrical distributors now also have video distribution arms.

Film distributors will, of course, also have to take the projected rapid growth of pay-per-view (PPV) cable into consideration. In all likelihood, PPV will noticeably dampen the growth of home video demand and alter the sequential release patterns for certain types of films. Already, there is evidence that the frequency of home video rental – which had averaged almost one tape a week for the typical VCR-owning household of the late 1980s – is declining despite the low cost of overnight rental (an average of around $2.50 in 1989).[30]

No matter which media prevails into the future, however, the importance of marketing decisions in filmmaking and distribution cannot be underestimated. Initial marketing decisions made prior to theatrical release, as we have seen, can critically affect the income-generating potential of a film in all subsequent markets.

Last, but certainly far from least, are the profit opportunities that for some films may arise in the area of product merchandising – a whole ancillary market in and of itself. Merchandising license fees and royalties from sales of toys and trinkets and all sorts of other items may amount to many millions of dollars, and contribute significantly to profits.[31]

Marketing costs

During the 1970s, expenditures on the marketing of films rose steadily at an average annual rate of over 12.5%, but more recently the rate of gain (especially as measured in constant dollars per picture) has been moderating. Nevertheless, advertising and publicity may add 50% or more to the cost of releasing a new feature, and so marketing is far from an inconsequential expense item (Table 3.3).

The more "megabudget" pictures there are in simultaneous release, the more intensive are the marketing efforts required for each. This is because capital turnover usually must be maximized at times when quality, peak-season exhibitor play dates are at a premium. Hence, there is a virtual necessity to employ expensive national and sometimes local cooperative (with exhibitors) television advertising so as to efficiently cover all the hundreds of theaters in which a widely released picture is playing.

In theory, studios have much greater cost-control potential in a film's marketing than production and financing phases, but in practice, restraint in marketing expenditures frequently is not possible. It is, moreover, inaccurate to attribute rising costs in this area primarily to acceleration in media prices.[32] As already noted, seasonal, cyclical, and other factors contribute to the bunching of important releases and therefore to the necessity of spending a lot in order to attract attention.[33]

3.5 Profitability synopsis

That a person can drown in a river of six inches average depth points to an important difficulty in analyzing data by means of averages alone. Many, if not most, films do not earn any return even after taking account of new-media revenue sources; it is the few big winners that pay for the many losers. This is especially true for outside investors, who, in terms of the funds flow sequence, are usually among the first to pay in and the last to be paid out.

Moreover, because pictures are financed largely with other people's money, there is an almost unavoidable bias for costs to rise (Parkinson's law again) in synchrony with anticipated revenues. This implies that much of the incremental income expected to be derived from growth of the new-media sources is likely to be absorbed, dissipated, and diverted as cost – an especially important consideration if, as is now common for a film released by a major studio, only about 70% ($\pm$ 10% or so) of the negative cost is recovered from theatrical revenues. Plainly, enhancement of the average film's profitability is an ever-moving target (see Figure 3.7).

Using data on the number of releases, the effects of ancillary-market revenue growth (sections 2.4 and 3.4), average negative costs, average marketing costs, and aggregate rentals (section 2.3), there emerges a profile indicating that, in a statistical sense, the average major-distributed film may at best be a breakeven proposition.[34] However, this statement should be interpreted with great care because (as shown in section 4.3) deviations from the mean can be extreme in both directions, and it so happens that despite the potential for loss on an "average" picture, major studios have been profitably engaged in this business for a long time.

Table 3.3. *Marketing and negative cost expenditures[a] for major film releases, 1970–88*

Year	MPAA releases[b] Total	Negative costs Average	Theatrical rentals U.S.	Theatrical rentals Total	Domestic advertising[c] Total	Net TV	Local TV	Newspaper	Radio	Magazine	Cable	Other[d]	Average ad spending per picture	Average print cost per picture
1988	157	18.1	1,413.6	2,433.9	1,409.4	183.9	186.0	968.2	30.7	5.5	19.5	15.6	9.0	1.4
1987	128	20.1	1,244.5	2,179.6	1,150.4	146.0	170.3	780.9	29.8	4.9	17.2	1.3	9.0	1.4
1986	133	17.5	1,165.1	1,963.4	978.8	143.1	120.1	674.5	17.4	6.7	17.0		7.4	1.2
1985	149	16.8	1,109.1	1,729.0	849.5	142.6	86.1	578.0	20.9	3.3	18.6		5.7	1.2
1984	166	14.4	1,313.2	1,967.2	877.5	167.2	72.6	609.8	23.0	4.9			5.3	1.3
1983	190	11.9	1,297.4	2,136.2	831.8	133.2	97.9	592.0	8.7				4.4	1.0
1982	173	11.8	1,342.7	2,061.3	767.1	109.6	90.4	554.4	12.7				4.4	0.9
1981	173	11.3	1,163.6	2,015.0	726.1	112.5	99.4	501.3	12.9				4.2	0.9
1980	161	9.4	1,182.6	2,093.7	703.8	103.3	102.4	486.1	12.0				4.4	0.8
1979	138	8.9	1,067.7	1,966.6	600.1	64.1	94.2	433.6	8.2				4.3	
1978	114	5.7	1,119.9	1,949.4	513.4	44.9	72.2	389.5	6.8				4.5	
1977	110	5.6	868.0	1,466.8	410.0	30.7	55.1	321.1	3.1				3.7	
1976	133	4.2	576.6	1,147.5	372.5	14.8	64.1	291.8	1.8				2.8	
1975	138	3.1	628.0	1,232.2	341.4	13.4	59.3	267.7	1.0				2.5	
1974	155	2.6	545.9	1,040.7	296.4	10.4	55.9	229.1	1.0				1.9	
1973	163	2.3	390.5	819.3	254.3	6.0	30.8	216.5	1.0				1.6	
1972	193	2.0	426.4	827.7	236.6	4.0	23.6	208.0	1.0				1.2	
1971	183	1.6	336.7	684.7	223.7	3.9	21.6	197.7	0.5				1.2	
1970	185	1.5	381.3	741.7	207.7	3.9	15.5	187.8	0.5				1.1	
CAGR[e]		14.8	7.6	6.8	11.2	23.9	14.8	9.5	25.7				12.2	

[a]In millions of dollars.

[b]The series for MPAA and total releases was revised in 1982.

[c]Advertising data differ slightly from MPAA averages, and are independently derived from Television Bureau of Advertising, Newspaper Bureau of Advertising, and Radio Advertising Bureau estimates, particularly prior to 1984.

[d]Includes syndicated TV beginning in 1988 and outdoor advertising.

[e]Compound annual growth rate, 1970–88.

Source: MPAA and TV, Radio, and Newspaper Advertising Bureaus.

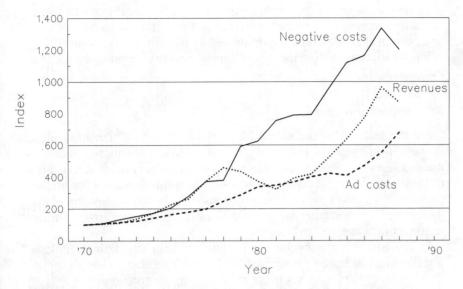

Figure 3.7. Revenue and cost trends for theatrical releases by major distributors, 1970–88 (1970 = 100).

The apparent discrepancy between large average losses per picture and the existence of profitable studio enterprises is resolved when it is realized that the heart of a studio's business is distribution and financing and that, therefore, the brunt of marketing and production cost risk is often deflected and transferred to (sometimes tax-sheltered) outside investors and producers. As the following chapter will indicate, studio profits are highly dependent on distribution and other fee income.

Nevertheless, even with the aforementioned advantages, it is not always easy for a studio to show a profit. Assuming a full production slate of 20 pictures per year made at an average cost of $15 million (which includes overhead and operating expenses), and prints and advertising at an average of $6 million per movie, there is a total of $420 million to be amortized over the releasing cycle. Further assuming that half of this cost is amortized against theatrical revenues (see Chapter 4), the minimum distributors' gross in order to reach break-even would be $210 million, which (using an approximate industry rentals percentage of 42%) is equivalent to about $500 million (in retail terms) at the box office. With total domestic box-office figures in 1989 at around $5.0 billion, this implies that a studio requires a minimum market share of over 10% in order to break even. Yet, as of the late 1980s, with the equivalent of some 10 major studios in operation, a share of that size has become much more difficult to regularly obtain. As shown in Table S2.5, there have been many years when – in a less crowded field than today – various studios have achieved much less than 10% share.

Finally, it should be noted that although it is not usually practicable to calculate precisely the return on investment (ROI) for a specific production, such a figure could be approximated by taking the total profit (if any) of all participants, adding the cost of capital, and then dividing by the total investment.[35]

3.6 Concluding remarks

Since the mid-1970s, the movie industry has been in a transition phase characterized by increasing dominance of electronic distribution and storage media and less control of distribution and product pricing through traditional organizational arrangements. Although this transition has already provided consumers with an increasing and widely varied selection of easily accessed low-cost entertainment, it creates problems for certain industry segments such as small exhibitors.

In all, however, the movie business will remain fascinatingly unique. That feeling has been summarized by *Variety's* veteran movie writer. A. D. Murphy (1982), who has made the following observations:

Even after a history of nearly 100 years, the business remains entrepreneurial and capitalistic.

Films are by nature research-and-development products; they are perishable and cannot be test marketed in the usual sense.

The film industry manufactures an art form for the masses.

There appears to be a long-term business cycle lasting approximately 25 years. Within that cycle, the industry has demonstrated recession-resistant characteristics.

Seasonal changes in theatrical attendance are radical, but domestic attendance over two decades has fluctuated within a fairly narrow range.

Despite long-standing trade restrictions, a fairly stable domestic market is reinforced by a strong export market.

From acquisitions of literary properties to final theater bookings, virtually every phase of the industry's operations is negotiated, and this, contrary to widespread opinion, implies that personal trust and high standards of professional integrity largely prevail.

As Squire (1983, p. 3) further said:

In no other business is a single example of product fully created at an investment of millions of dollars with no assurance that the public will buy it. In no other business does the public "use" the product and then take away with them [as Marx (1975) observed] merely the memory of it.

Selected additional reading

Akst, D. (1987). "Directors and Producers Face Showdown Over Residuals," *Wall Street Journal,* June 11.

Attanasio, P. (1983)."The Heady Heyday of a Hollywood Lawyer," *Esquire* 99(4)(April): 91.

Bach, S. (1985). *Final Cut: Dreams and Disaster in the Making of "Heaven's Gate."* New York: Morrow.

Baumgarten P. A., and Farber, D. C. (1973). *Producing, Financing, and Distributing Film,* New York: Drama Book Specialists.

Canby, V. (1990). "A Revolution Reshapes Movies," *New York Times,* January 7.

Cieply, M. (1986). "An Agent Dominates Film and TV Studios with Package Deals," *Wall Street Journal,* December 19.

Cooper, M. (1987). "Concession Stand: Can the Hollywood Unions Survive?" *American Film,* XIII(3)(December):33.

Cox, M. (1984). "A First Feature Film Is Made on the Cheap, Not Hollywood's Way," *Wall Street Journal,* May 14.

Daly, M. (1984). "The Making of *The Cotton Club:* A True Tale of Hollywood," *New York* 17(19)(May 7):40.

Denby, D. (1986). "Can the Movies Be Saved?" *New York,* 19(28)(July 21).

Evans, D. A. (1984). "Reel Risk: Movie Tax Shelters Aren't Box-Office Boffo," *Barron's,* January 9.

Garcia, B. (1989). "Who Ya Gonna Call If a Ghostbuster's Proton Pack Breaks?: Insurance Helps Hollywood Survive Almost Anything," *Wall Street Journal,* August 24.

Goldman, W. (1983). *Adventures in the Screentrade: A Personal View of Hollywood and Screenwriting.* New York: Warner Books.

Gregory, M. (1979). *Making Films Your Business.* New York: Schocken Books.

Gubernick, L. (1988). "Miss Jones, Get Me Film Finances," *Forbes,* 142(14)(December 26).

Harmetz, A. (1987). "Hollywood Battles Killer Budgets," *New York Times,* May 31.

Hirschhorn, C. (1979). *The Warner Bros. Story.* New York: Crown Publishers.

"How Paramount Keeps Churning Out Winners," *Business Week* No. 2846 (June 11, 1984):148.

Knowlton, C. (1988). "Lessons from Hollywood Hit Men," *Fortune,* 118(5)(August 29):78.

Landro, L. (1983). "If You Have Always Wanted to Be in Pictures, Partnerships Offer the Chance, but With Risks," *Wall Street Journal,* May 23.

    (1984). "Frank Mancuso's Marketing Savvy Paves Ways for Paramount Hits," *Wall Street Journal,* June 27.

    (1985). "Movie Partnerships Offer a Little Glitz, Some Risk – and Maybe a Decent Return," *Wall Street Journal,* May 20.

    (1989). "Sequels and Stars Help Top Movie Studios Avoid Major Risks," *Wall Street Journal,* June 6.

    (1990). "'Godfater III' Filming Begins After 15 Years And 3 Studio Regimes," *Wall Street Journal,* February 9.

Lees, D., and Berkowitz, S. (1981). *The Movie Business.* New York: Vintage Books (Random House).

Magnet, M. (1983). "Coke Tries Selling Movies Like Soda Pop," *Fortune* 108(13)(December 26):119–26 (also see counterpoint by A. D. Murphy, "In Defining 'Hit Film' Economics, 'Fortune' Looks in Wrong Eyes," *Variety,* December 14, 1983).

McClintick, D. (1982). *Indecent Exposure: A True Story of Hollywood and Wall Street,* New York: Morrow.

Mayer, M. F. (1978). *The Film Industries: Practical Business/Legal Problems in Production, Distribution, and Exhibition,* 2d ed., New York: Hastings House.

Minard, L. (1984). "Givebacks, Hollywood Style," *Forbes* 133(7)(March 26):182.

Moldea, D. (1986). *Dark Victory,* New York: Viking.

Robichek, A. A., and Myers, S. C. (1965). *Optimal Financing Decisions.* Englewood Cliffs, N.J.: Prentice-Hall.

Rudell, M. I. (1984). *Behind the Scenes: Practical Entertainment Law,* New York: Harcourt.

Salmans, S. (1984). "A Nose for Talent – and for Tradition," *New York Times,* May 20.

Sansweet, S. J. (1982). "Who Does What Film? It Depends on Who Talks to What Agent," *Wall Street Journal,* June 23.

Sansweet, S., and Landro, L. (1983). "As the Money Rolls in, Movie Makers Discover It Is a Mixed Blessing," *Wall Street Journal,* September 1.

Sherman, S. P. (1986)."A TV Titan Wagers a Wad on Movies," *Fortune,* 113(10)(May 12).

Spragins, E. (1983). "Son of Delphi," *Forbes,* 132(2)(July 18):156.

Thomas, T., and Solomon, A. (1979). *The Films of Twentieth Century-Fox: A Pictorial History.* Secaucus, N.J.: Citadel Press.

Tromberg, S. (1980). *Making Money Making Movies: The Independent Moviemaker's Handbook,* New York, New Viewpoints/Vision Books (Division of Franklin Watts).

Turner, R. (1989). "A Hot Movie Studio Gobbles Up the Cash but Produces No Hits," *Wall Street Journal,* June 14.

(1989). "A Showdown for Discount Movie Houses," *Wall Street Journal,* July 18.

Wiese, M. (1986). *Home Video: Producing for the Home Market.* Stoneham, Massachusetts: Butterworth.

Zweig, P. L. (1987). "Lights! Camera! Pinstripes!" *Institutional Investor,* XXI(9)(September).

4
Financial accounting in movies and television

Happy trails to you, until we meet again. – Dale Evans.[1]

This song is perhaps more appropriately sung by Hollywood accountants than by cowboys, but as this chapter indicates, the problems that arise in accounting for motion-picture and ancillary-market income are more often due to differing viewpoints and interpretations than to intended deceits.

4.1 Dollars and sense

Contract clout

No major actor, director, writer, or other participant in an entertainment project makes a deal without beforehand receiving some kind of high-powered help, be it from an agent, personnel manager, lawyer, accountant, or tax expert. In some cases, platoons of advisors are consulted; in others, all functions may be performed by only one person or a few individuals. Thus an image of naive, impressionable artists negotiating out of their league with large, powerful, knowledgeable, and greedy producer or distributor organizations is most often not accurate.

As in all loosely structured private-market negotiations, bargaining power (in the industry's jargon, "clout") is the only thing that matters. A new, unknown talent who happens on the scene normally will have little if any clout with anyone. Top stars, by definition, have enough clout to command the attention of just about everyone.

By hiring people whose ability to attract large audiences has already been proved, a producer can gain considerable financial leverage. It may be less risky to pay a star $1.5 million than to pay an unknown $100,000; the presence of the star may easily increase the value of the property by several times that $1.5-million salary through increased sales in theatrical and other markets, whereas the unknown may contribute nothing from the standpoint of return on investment. Clout, it seems, is best measured on a logarithmic scale.

Contracts are usually initially agreed on in outline (a deal memo), with the innumerable details being structured later by professionals representing both sides. But final contracts normally are complex documents, and those with imprecisely drawn clauses that are open to different interpretations can lead to disputes. It is the nature of this industry to attract a disproportionate amount of publicity when such disputes arise.

Orchestrating the numbers

Accounting principles provide a framework in which the financial operating performance of a business can be observed and compared with the performance of others. But it was not until 1973 that the American Institute of Certified Public Accountants (AICPA) published an accounting guide *(Accounting for Motion Picture Films)* that pragmatically resolved many (but far from all) controversial issues. Publication of that guide significantly diminished the number of interpretations used in describing film industry transactions, and thus made comparisons of one company's statements with those of another considerably easier and more meaningful than before.

The AICPA guide, however, has not prevented accountants from tailoring financial reports, starting with a set of base figures, to suit the needs and purposes of the users and providers. Just as there are different angles from which to photograph an object to illustrate different facets, there are different perspectives from which to examine the data derived from the same base. In fact, given the complexity of many contracts, it is an absolute necessity to view financial performance from the angle that suits the needs of the viewer.

For example, outside shareholders generally need to know only the aggregate financial position of the company, not the intricate details of each participant's contract. Those participants, by the same token, usually will care only about their own share statements, from which the aggregates are constructed. In the sections that follow, the two different accounting perspectives are more fully described.

4.2 Corporate overview

Because this is not strictly an accounting text, no attempt will be made to describe the full terminology used by CPAs. However, it will be useful to note instances in which movie-business definitions are different from those used in other industries.

Revenue-recognition factors

Industry practice with regard to recognition of revenues from theatrical exhibition is fairly straightforward. With either percentage or flat-rent contracts, revenues from exhibitors are accrued and recognized by distributors when receivable, which, because of cash intake at the box office, is almost immediately. Contrariwise, ancillary-market revenue recognition is potentially much more complex. Prior to issuance of the aforementioned accounting guide, four methods existed:

1. Contract method: All revenue is recognized on contract execution.
2. Billing method: Revenue is recognized as installment payments become due.
3. Delivery method: Revenue is recognized on delivery to the licensee.
4. Deferral or apportionment method: Revenue is recognized evenly over the whole license period.

To place the entire industry on a uniform basis, the AICPA guide indicated that television-license revenues for feature films should not be recognized until all the following conditions are met:

1. The license fee (sales price) for each film is known.
2. The cost of each film is known or reasonably determinable.
3. Collectibility of the full license fee is reasonably assured.
4. The film is accepted by the licensee in accordance with the conditions of the license agreement.
5. The film is available; that is, the right is deliverable by the licensor and exercisable by the licensee.

Although there are many further complicating elements – discounting for the time value of money on long-term receivables, or the possibly different methods used for tax-reporting purposes as compared with those (as described earlier) used for shareholder reports – for most analytical purposes only a few points need be noted.

Availability (item 5) is most important with regard to television or other ancillary-market licenses. Although contract-specified sequencing to downstream markets may somewhat constrain a distributor from making films available at certain times, the distributor often retains great discretion as to when product is to be made available. For example, television networks interested in obtaining a movie may be totally indifferent as to whether the picture is available on September 30 or on October 1. But to a distributor company trying to smooth its reported quarterly earnings results, the difference of one day could be substantial.

Another sensitive and potentially litigious area concerns fees allocated to films in a package of features that might be sold to a network.[2] Packages usually contain a dozen or so films, with, of course, some titles much stronger than others. Theoretically, each film is individually negotiated, but in practice the package is offered as whole. The problem is then to allocate the total-package revenues among all of the films according to a proportion formula based on relative theatrical grosses. Previously, a rule of thumb was that the strongest film in a package might be worth 2.5 times the value of the weakest, with strength being defined by box-office performance figures. Allocation procedures are further discussed in section 4.4.

Of further significance are "backlogs" – the accumulation of contracts from which future license fees will be derived. Important contracts for ancillary-market exhibition are often written far in advance, sometimes even before the film is produced or released in theaters. Such backlogs generally do not appear directly anywhere on the balance sheet as contra to inventories, except when there are amounts received prior to revenue recognition. In those cases, the amounts are carried as advance payments and are included in current liabilities.

It has with some justification thus been argued that film company financial statements only partially reflect true corporate assets. However, companies ordinarily will indicate in balance-sheet footnotes or other reports, such as annuals and 10-K filings with the Securities and Exchange Commission, the extent to which backlogs have changed during the reporting period.

Inventories

Perhaps the greatest conceptual difference between the movie industry and other industries is in the definition of inventory, which is normally taken to be a current asset (i.e., an asset that is used for production of goods or services in a single accounting period). Because the life cycles of filmed entertainment products (from beginning idea or property to final distribution) are measured in years, entertainment company inventories are, in balance sheets that are classified, categorized into current-period and non-current-period components. Included as inventories are the costs of options, screenplays, and projects in the preproduction, current-production, and postproduction phases awaiting release.

More formally, according to the accounting guide, inventories classified as current assets include the following:

1. For films in release, unamortized film costs allocated to the primary market.
2. Film costs applicable to completed films not released, net of the portion allocable to secondary markets.
3. Television films in production that are under contract of sale.

Costs allocated to secondary markets and not expected to be realized within 12 months, and all other costs related to film production, are classified as noncurrent. Typically, a film company will include the following captions:

Film productions:
   Released, less amortization
   Completed, not released
   In process
   Story rights and scenarios

Amortization of inventory

Inventories are matched in a "cost-of-goods-sold" sense against a forecasted schedule of receipt of income. Of course, forecasts of film receipts are mostly best guesses, although in aggregate it is fairly certain that, on the average, perhaps 75% of all theater-exhibition revenues will be generated in the first nine months of release, and almost all the remainder by the end of the second year.

Rather than using a cost-recovery theory in which no gross profit is recognized until all costs and expenses have been recovered, the film industry's theoretical approach is based on a system whereby costs are amortized in a pattern that parallels income flows. With this flow-of-income approach, gross profit is recognized as a standard portion of every dollar of gross revenue recorded.

Prior to implementation in 1981 of statement 53 of the Financial Accounting Standards Board (FASB), which essentially formalized the aforementioned AICPA guidelines, there were two amortization approaches generally applied. A company could use separate estimates of gross revenue for each film, or it could use average tables (as in Supplementary Data Table S4.1 in Appendix C) based on the combined experience for many films. Companies using amortization tables periodically tested their continuing validity based on actual experience, with most tables amortizing total production costs allocated to theatrical exhibition over a 104-week period by charges to income equal to about 65% of such costs in the first 26 weeks of release, and 90% in 52 weeks.

Although FASB statement 53 still allows the use of either method as long as the table leads to a result equivalent to amortization on a film-by-film basis, the use of such tables is essentially no longer practicable. MCA Inc., for example, had amortized according to tables prior to FASB statement 53, but found that such estimates were not consistent with those on an individual-picture basis. In order to restore consistency, in 1981 the company adjusted its inventories on films already released by taking a "write-down" of about $50 million against previous years' retained earnings (Table 4.1).

With costs in the industry now reported according to FASB statement 53 at the lower of unamortized cost or net realizable value on a film-by-film basis (i.e., on an individual rather than group average), accountants' procedures require that estimates be reviewed periodically (at least quarterly and at the end of each year) to be sure that the best available data are used. If there are material revisions in gross-revenue estimates, either up or down, amortization schedules must be recomputed, but previously reported interim-period results are not to be restated. For this reason, films performing very poorly in early release are quickly written down. Moreover, a write-down before release will be required in the rare situations in which the cost of a production obviously exceeds expected gross revenues.

The rules also presume that if story rights have been held for three years and not been set for production, those story costs will be charged to production overhead. Properties are to be reviewed periodically, and if it is determined that they will not be adapted for film projects, their costs are to be charged to current-period overhead.

Unamortized residuals

Before the days of television, pay-cable, and home video, theatrical exhibition was virtually the only source of income for a film.[3] But that gradually began to change as television's appetite for movies increased and as receipts grew with audience size. In order to more closely match revenue and cost, a portion of a production's cost known as an unamortized residual was therefore set aside to be written down against expected future income from television.[4] For a major feature, an unamortized residual of $750,000 or so was typical in the 1970s.

As revenues from pay-cable, home video, and syndication – so-called income "ultimates" because they are gross revenues that are ultimately receivable – have become proportionately more significant in comparison with those derived from theatrical exhibition, unamortized residuals have also been set aside, pro rata, for those markets. Such residuals have on the average accordingly become much larger than in the past, and may lead to instances in which the bulk of a picture's cost will be written down against future revenues from nontheatrical sources.

Table 4.1. *Individual-film-forecast-computation method of amortization: an example*

Assumptions:	
Film cost	$10,000,000
Actual gross revenues:	
First year	12,000,000
Second year	3,000,000
Third year	1,000,000
Anticipated total gross revenues:	
At end of first year	24,000,000
At end of second and third years	20,000,000

Amortization

Amount of amortization

First-year amortization

$$\frac{\$12,000,000}{\$24,000,000} \times \$10,000,000 = \$5,000,000$$

Second-year amortization (anticipated total gross revenues reduced from $24,000,000 to $20,000,000)[a]

$$\frac{\$3,000,000}{\$8,000,000^b} \times \$5,000,000^c = \$1,875,000$$

Third-year amortization

$$\frac{\$1,000,000}{\$8,000,000^d} \times \$5,000,000^d = \$\ 625,000$$

---

[a]If there were no change in anticipated gross revenues, the second-year amortization would be as follows:

$$\frac{\$3,000,00}{\$24,000,000} \times \$10,000,000 = \$1,250,000$$

[b]$20,000,000 minus $12,000,000 or anticipated total gross revenues from beginning of period.

[c]$10,000,000 minus $5,000,000 or cost less accumulated amortization at beginning of period.

[d]The $8,000,000 and $5,000,000 need not be reduced by the second-year gross revenue ($3,000,000) and second-year amortization ($1,875,000), respectively, because anticipated gross revenues did not change from the second to the third year. If such reduction were made, the amount of amortization would be as follows:

$$\frac{\$1,000,000}{\$5,000,000} \times \$3,125,000 = \$625,000$$

Source: Appendix to FASB statement 53. © Financial Accounting Standards Board, High Ridge Park, Stamford, CT 06905, USA. Reprinted with permission. Copies of the complete document are available from the FASB.

In the late 1970s and early 1980s, unanticipated rapid growth of revenues from the new-media sources did, in fact, upwardly bias reported industry profits. At the time, amortization was primarily against income derived from initial theatrical release, so that there was little if any cost left over to match against windfall receipts from burgeoning pay-cable and home video markets. The industry, moreover, had experienced a spate of unusual write-downs in those years, and the Securities and Exchange Commission (SEC) then reacted by expressing concern that investors did not have enough information about the timing and recoverability of film costs. In response to those concerns, the AICPA appointed a task force to study these matters and to arrive at recommended disclosures that would better explain cost-recoverability methods without unduly burdening the industry. As a result, companies now disclose information about (a) their assumed revenue cycles and the composition of their film costs, and (b) the expected timing of future amortization of the unamortized costs of released films.

Interest expense and other costs

As interest rates and average production budgets have soared, interest expense has become a proportionately more important component of feature filmmaking. Until 1980, when FASB statement 34 concerning treatment (capitalization) of interest was issued, such costs were written off as incurred. Under the new standard, interest costs are capitalized, and then charged as part of the negative cost.

Although studio period outlays, including those for rents and salaries, fall into a normal-expense category, studios also incur other costs of distribution (exploitation) that are capitalized. These may include, but are not limited to, prints and advertising and payments of subdistribution fees. For example, prints typically cost over $1,500 each (and much more in 70mm with Dolby® sound), and because simultaneous saturation booking is now common and often requires that over 1,000 copies be made, this can add up to a substantial sum. Print costs are usually amortized according to a formula similar to that used for amortization of the negative.

According to FASB statement 53, all exploitation costs (for prints, advertising, rents, salaries, and other distribution expenses) that are clearly to benefit future periods should be capitalized as film-cost inventory and amortized over a period in which the major portion of gross revenue from the picture is recorded. This method especially pertains to national advertising, in which expenses before release can be considerable. Local and cooperative advertising expenditures, however, are generally closely related to local grosses and are normally expensed as incurred because they usually do not provide any benefits in future periods.

Calculation controversies

For sure, FASB statement 53 has contributed to a much improved basis for comparison of film and television company financial data over the relatively amorphous conditions that had prevailed prior to its issuance. Yet the statement has nevertheless drawn criticism for allowing considerable discretionary variation in the treatment of marketing and inventory cost amortizations in particular. In films and television such costs are proportionately far more important in their effects on earnings than in other industries. And, furthermore, cost amortizations are not related to the projected useful life of an asset based on prior experiences with other similar assets.

Instead, according to the rules for movies and television, the rate of amortization depends on *management's* projections (market-by-market and media-by-media) of often uncertain *revenue* streams that are expected to be ultimately received sometime in the possibly distant future. Moreover, because income recognition is generally unrelated to cash collections, it is entirely possible to report earnings and be insolvent at the same time. It is thus often argued that the accounting picture rendered by application of FASB statement 53 may not accurately reflect the true earnings power, cash flow potential, or asset value of a company.

Some companies, for example, might assume that all advertising costs incurred during theatrical release create values in the ancillary markets, and as such, they will capitalize the costs regardless of the fact that local advertising in Tampa will ordinarily have no effect on video market sales in Toronto or Tanzania. And some companies will amortize prints over estimated revenues from all markets rather than against revenues generated in specific markets, for instance, domestic versus foreign.

Other companies may assume long lives for their films and television series, and thus include second- or third-cycle syndication sales even though such syndication sale events may not be known in terms of precise timing or pricing. Yet still others may differ on how long or through what means development project costs from in-house independent producers are capitalized and then written off as studio overhead; the costs of abandoned properties should be amortized as soon as it is clear that the property will not be produced, but it is not unusual for many projects to be lost in creative limbo for relatively long periods. Even receivables under FASB statement 53 present problems: Receivables, according to the rules, are shown on the balance sheet as *discounted* to present value while estimates of far more uncertain revenue ultimates are not.

Clearly, then, there is room under FASB statement 53 for substantial variations in earnings reporting practices to appear, and it is essential for the analyst comparing one company to another to understand such differences.[5] The mean values for several commonly computed financial state-

Table 4.2. *Accounting ratio benchmarks for major film studio/ distributors, 1982–8*

Year	Film cost amortization as % of			Unamortized film costs of released films as a % of inventories	Additions to film costs as a % of film cost amortization
	Revenues	Inventories	Operating cash flow		
1988	43.8	86.0	74.6	62.4	113.5
1987	44.1	89.1	79.2	64.0	109.5
1986	47.7	69.7	85.1	51.5	112.2
1985	52.6	80.9	88.8	65.4	128.3
1984	46.4	77.1	87.7	66.6	131.2
1983	44.8	78.9	92.6	52.8	122.6
1982	38.6	65.2	71.0	42.7	107.7

Source: Company 10-K reports.

ment ratios that are presented in Table 4.2 should prove useful in this regard.

Finally, it helps to remember that at the core of many accounting problems and controversies between studio corporations and individuals are differences in assumptions about the timing of receipts and subsequent disbursements to participants. For example, distributors would normally use accrual accounting methods (booking income when *billed*) for their own financial-statement reporting purposes, and they would use cash accounting methods (based on revenues when *collected* and out-of-pocket expenses when incurred) for tracking disbursements to producers and others.[6] Because of this, all levels of the industry are extremely sensitive to cash-flow considerations, and delays of payments tend to rapidly compound on the way to downstream receivers.

Merger and acquisition issues

Preceding sections have outlined the most frequently encountered aspects of corporate accounting for filmed entertainment products. But several others are also noteworthy.

In business combinations or reorganizations, for example, two different methods can be used to integrate the balance sheets of separate corporate entities. As described by Accounting Principles Board opinion 16, the "purchase" method accounts for business combinations as the acquisition of one company by another, with the acquiring corporation recording as its cost the assets less liabilities assumed. Under this method, goodwill (generally to be amortized in equal annual amounts over a period not to exceed 40 years) is a difference between the cost of an acquired company and the sum of the fair values of tangible and identifiable intangible assets less liabilities. With "pooling of interests," however, a business combination is viewed as "the uniting of the ownership interests of two or more companies by exchange of equity securities. No acquisition is recognized because the combination is accomplished without disbursing resources of the constituents. Ownership interests continue and the former bases of accounting are retained."

Although neither the purchase nor the pooling method is unique to this industry, films are by nature intangible assets, and valuations are thus often highly subjective. The quasi-reorganization of Filmways Corporation in 1982 illustrates this point well. A spate of expensive box-office failures had led Filmways into financial difficulties, and it was only through injection of fresh capital and reorganization that the company was saved from probable bankruptcy.[7]

As we have seen, accounting methods contain elements of both art and science. That will be further amplified as we next explore specific financial relationships between studios and creative participants.

4.3 Big-picture accounting

Financial overview

Preceding sections have described how financial statements appear from the corporate angle. But, as noted earlier, accounting statements for individual participants are properly viewed from a different perspective. This section illustrates the results for typical production, distribution, and exhibition contracts in terms of profit-and-loss statements for individual projects. For the producer, the legal heart of most such projects is the production-financing-distribution (PFD) agreement.

The production section of a PFD concerns the development process of making a feature. It spells out who will be responsible for which steps in bringing the film to completion, who gets paid when, and under what conditions the studio-financier can place the project in "turnaround," that is, abandon the project and attempt to establish it elsewhere.

The financing section of a PFD provides financing-arrangement descriptions and stipulates completion-guarantee details and costs, which might normally average about 6% of total budget. Loan agreements are not finalized until a completion bond is obtained, usually from agencies that specialize in providing such bonds.

But ultimately of greatest importance is the distribution-agreement section. Included here are definitions of distribution fees and specifications

Table 4.3. *Flowchart for theatrical motion-picture revenue: box-office receipts*

Distributor's gross receipts
  less:
    1. Distribution fees
    2. Distribution costs
    3. Third-party gross participations
       ↓

Producer's gross proceeds
  less:
    1. Negative cost
      (a) Direct cost
      (b) Overhead
      (c) Interest on loans
    2. Contingent deferments

First net profits
    ↓

Break-even
    ↓

Third-party net-profit participations (100% of net profits of picture)
    ↓

Producer's share of net profits of picture

Source: Breglio and Schwartz (1980). © John F. Breglio.

concerning audit and ownership rights, accounting-statement preparations, and advertising and marketing commitments.

Table 4.3 provides an overview of revenue flows for a typical theatrical release. In looking at this it helps to keep in mind that the exhibitor's objective is to minimize rentals, but the distributor's objective is to maximize them, and what participants see as their gross is the distributor's rental, not box-office gross as usually reported in the trade papers. For reasons previously discussed, the box-office gross can be much larger than the distributor's gross (i.e., rentals).

A convenient illustration of PFD concepts has been provided by Leedy (1980, p. 1), from which the following descriptions are drawn. Leedy's illustration (Table 4.4) for a major successful picture, while somewhat outdated, is nonetheless useful for illustrative purposes because it includes typical deferred payments to the writer and director, profit participations by the leading actor and actress, and contingent compensation to the financier and producer. It further shows how a $15-million picture (negative cost)

Table 4.4. *Revenues and costs for a major theatrical release, circa 1979*

Gross revenue	
Subject to a 30% distribution fee:	
Theatrical film rental (U.S. and Canada)	$50,000,000
Nontheatrical film rental	1,000,000
U.S. network television	9,000,000
Total	60,000,000
Subject to a 40% distribution fee	
Foreign film rental	35,000,000
Television syndication	4,000,000
Total	39,000,000
Subject to a 15% distribution fee	
Royalty income	950,000
Trailer income	50,000
Total	1,000,000
Total gross revenue	$100,000,000
Distribution fee	
30% × $60,000,000	$18,000,000
40% × $39,000,000	15,600,000
15% × $1,000,000	150,000
Total distribution fee	$33,750,000
Balance	$66,250,000
Distribution expenses	
Cooperative advertising	$20,000,000
Other advertising and publicity	5,000,000
Release prints, etc.	3,000,000
Taxes	2,000,000
Trade-association fees and other	1,500,000
Bad debts	1,000,000
All other expenses	1,750,000
Total distribution expenses	$34,250,000
Balance	$32,000,000
Production cost $15,000,000	
Interest thereon 1,000,000	$16,000,000
Net profit before participations	$16,000,000
Deferments paid	125,000
Participations in gross and net	7,775,000
Total	7,900,000
Net profit to be split 50:50	$8,100,000

Source: Leedy (1980, pp. 1–3).

earning $100 million in distributors' rentals might generate $16 million of profit for financier and producer before participations, and $8.1 million after adjustment for participations and deferments.

As such, however, this model is more suggestive of the situation existing in the late 1970s than currently, because it does not include important revenue contributions from pay-cable and other new-media sources. Nevertheless, the illustration correctly portrays typical domestic theatrical-distribution fees (i.e., United States and Canadian) at about 30%, foreign distribution and television-syndication fees at 40%, and other distribution fees at 15%.[8]

Whereas distribution charges are by long-standing industry practice largely nonnegotiable, limited financing partnerships such as those discussed in Chapter 3 have more recently been able to obtain agreements for below-average rates. Moreover, because these charges have historically been unrelated to actual costs, on occasion they will be adjusted in order to retain the services of important producers. In those cases, a sliding fee scale down to a predetermined minimum – with perhaps a 5% reduction for every $20 million of theatrical rentals generated – is used.

Table 4.4 can also provide an indication of how sensitive profits are to changes in the cost of capital. For example, an assumption of interest rates of 20% for this type of project brings interest cost on the production closer to $3 million than to the $1 million that is shown. If so, $2 million additional interest cost would reduce investors' profits by about 25% from $8.1 million to $6.1 million.[9]

Table 4.5 summarizes how other participants might have fared in Leedy's example of a picture bringing rentals of $100 million. Here it is important to remember that in contrast to the financiers and distributors, the potential profit participants, including the director and lead actors, are at no risk of loss. They generally do not have equity capital invested in the project, and thus their profit participations, if any, should correctly be characterized as salary bonuses.

Participation deals

Participations are limited only by the imagination and bargaining ability of the individuals who negotiate them, but only talents in great demand can command significant participations in addition to fees or salaries.

Pickups Of the several major variants of participation agreements, perhaps the simplest is a "pickup" – a completed or partially completed project presented to studio-financiers or distributors for further funding and support. From the distributor's point of view, pickups are much less risky than are unfilmed projects in their early stages, for which it may be especially difficult to evaluate how all in-process artistic elements fit

Table 4.5. *Fee splits, deferments, and participations for a major motion-picture release: an example based on the results of Table 4.4*

Writer:		
Fee	$250,000	
Deferment	50,000	$300,000
Director:		
Fee	525,000	
Deferment	75,000	600,000
Major lead actor:		
Fee	2,000,000	
Participation[a]	6,875,000	8,875,000
Major lead actress:		
Fee	500,000	
Participation[b]	900,000	1,400,000
Producer:		
Fee	500,000	
Contingency comp.	4,050,000	4,550,000
Financier:		
Interest income	1,000,000	
Contingency comp.	4,050,000	5,050,000
Distributor:		
Fee		33,750,000

[a] Actor participation: Based on $2 million against a participation of 10% of gross revenue less cooperative advertising and taxes before break-even, and an additional 2.5% participation rate on this basis after break-even.
[b] Actress participation (based on 10% of net profits contractually defined as after the deferments and after the participation in gross):

Net profit before participations	$16,000,000
Deferments paid	125,000
Participation in gross	6,875,000
Total	7,000,000
Net profit after participations	$9,000,000
Participation rate	10%
Participation	$900,000

Source: Leedy (1980, p. 3).

together. For this reason, independent filmmakers often find that their best opportunity to distribute through a major is via such pickup agreements.[10]

After seeing what is in most cases the equivalent of a rough draft of the movie, an interested distributor will attempt to forecast a minimum rentals expectation, and then offer an advance toward further production and postproduction costs based on the forecast. Knowing, for example, that distribution expenses for release in, say, the 450 theaters sought by the producer will be $6 million, and taking a standard distribution fee of 30%, the distributor will break even on film rentals of $20 million.

Minimum distribution expense/fee = distributor's break even
$6,000,000/30% = $20,000,000

Given these circumstances the distributor could extend a maximum advance of $14 million to the producer or promoter. However, the amount of advance actually offered by the distributor may be only half of that indicated, because of the following reasons: (a) The distributor requires a cushion against the risk that the rentals forecast may turn out to be too optimistic. (b) The distributor is in business to do better than break even. (c) Not all distribution expenses are included in the minimum figure. (d) This variable-cost example does not reflect the large fixed costs (i.e., overhead at least $25 million per year) of maintaining a major distribution organization, nor does it reflect studio operating expenses (which can easily cost another $25 million).

Coproduction-distribution Distributor-financiers often make coproduction deals with one or more parties for one or more territories so that risks will be shared. For instance, domestic and foreign distributors might each contribute half of a picture's production cost and each be entitled to distribution fees earned in their respective territories. Because distribution costs and box-office appeal often vary significantly in different markets, however, a picture might be profitable for one distributor and unprofitable for another. Also, the results for all distributors may be aggregated, with profits or losses split according to aggregate performance rather than territorial performance.

Talent participations and break-even Writers, directors, or actors may become financial participants if their agents have been able to negotiate for gross "points" – which can be defined on a number of different grosses. Distributors' grosses are what have been called rentals, and participation points defined on this basis are obviously very valuable because a picture does not have to be profitable for such points to be earned. Accordingly, participations of this kind are rare and are assigned to only the very strongest box-office draws.

More usual is a participation based on a designated actual or artificially set break-even level. For example, some talent participants might receive a percentage of distributors' gross after the first $30 million has been generated. In other instances, participations might begin after break-even – defined as distributors' gross minus distribution fees and distribution costs. Additional points might then be earned after, say, rentals reach 3.5 times the production cost. As can be imagined, the variations of this concept are infinite.

However, accounting for the costs of multiple talent participations tremendously increases complexity: What usually begins as a simple agreement between an agent and a studio attorney or business-affairs representative often ends as a complicated financial-accounting document replete with the potential for widely divergent interpretations.

Is star A's participation deducted before that of star B? Is participation based on only domestic rentals or on both foreign and domestic? Which distribution costs are subtracted before artificial break-even? Are both television advertising and national-magazine advertising included or excluded? Those are some of the subjects on which opinions may differ, especially within the context of the tens of thousands of transactions entries that are typically generated in the course of bringing a major feature to the screen. Even in the best of circumstances in which contract terms are sharply defined, it is time-consuming and expensive to follow an audit trail.

Further complications may be introduced with the concept of a *rolling break-even* – defined as the point at which revenues are equal to production costs plus distribution fees and expenses on a continuing basis. In other words, for a picture approaching profitability, a distributor's decision to spend more on advertising will delay or defer breaking even, thereby adversely affecting talent participants entitled to receive points in the picture's "net" profits. As shown in the following formula, the amount of rentals required for a new break-even is found by dividing total expenses exclusive of the distribution fee (i.e., prints and ads plus negative costs) by 1 minus the distribution-fee percentage: Let a = required rentals, b = total expenses, and r = distribution-fee percentage. Then

$$a = b/(1 - r)$$

For instance, if $r = 30\%$ and $b = \$7$ million, then $a = \$10$ million. But if another $1 million is spent on advertising, then $b = \$8$ million, and $a = \$11.43$ million. In this situation, every $1 million of additional expenditure requires an additional $1.43 million of rentals to be generated in order to remain at break-even.

Producers' participations and cross-collateralizations Producers are responsible for a film's production costs, and they often have contractual incentives to keep project expenses down. When costs exceed approved budgets by certain percentages, producers' shares may be penalized by several times the percentage overage. On the other hand, the share of profit, if any, that the producer will receive (in addition to earned production-services fees) can be structured so as to provide a floor or minimum payment that has priority over other (third-party) participations.

Producers are also affected if the financial fate of one picture is tied to that of another, or if the box-office performance of a single picture in one territory is linked to its performance in another. Such *cross-collateralizations* of producers' shares may imply that the profits of one picture must exceed the losses of another in order for there to be anything to share. It is especially frustrating for potential profit participants when profitable picture *A* is cross-collateralized with picture *B* that has perhaps yet to be produced, to be distributed, or to show a profit. In these situations, none of the profit on picture *A* will be credited to participants until picture *B* recovers most of its costs.

Distributor-exhibitor computations

As already indicated, rentals are that portion of box-office receipts owed the distributor. Table 4.6 shows an example in which the exhibitor's nut for fixed overhead is negotiated or set at $1,500, and there is a 90:10 split (90% for distributor, 10% for exhibitor) of box-office receipts after the nut (but not less than the previously agreed 70% of total box-office receipts to the distributor).

In case 1, the distributor will be owed $5,400, whereas in case 2 the distributor will be entitled to $4,200. In neither case will the distributor share in the theater's concession income from candy, beverages, popcorn, and video games (see section 3.4). As can be inferred from Table 4.7, concession sales are a significant profit-swing factor for exhibitors.[11]

Rentals usually are accounted for on a cash basis when collected by the distributor, and expenses are recorded as incurred. In fact, this reporting method – reflecting the normally slow collection of cash and the delayed billing of period expenses such as co-op advertising – is reasonably equitable from all participants' viewpoints.

Co-op advertising is normally calculated on gross receipts and allocated according to the distributor–exhibitor percentage revenue split in effect at the time the advertising appears. The following example indicates the true net percentage:

Box-office gross	$20,000
House expenses	4,000
Net	16,000

Ninety percent goes to the distributor: $14,400 (90:10 split); the true distributor co-op percentage here is 72% (14.4:20.0), not 90%.

In analyzing the corporate accounting statements of exhibition companies, it should also be noted that the mix of owned versus leased real estate, and the methods of accounting for real estate transactions and leasehold improvements, can vary significantly from one company to another, thereby limiting financial comparability.[12]

Distributor deals and expenses

The previous hypothetical example of a film generating $100 million in rentals (Table 4.4) showed a distributor fee, or service charge for the sales

Table 4.6. *Film rentals calculations: examples contrasting floor minimums versus percentages of net box-office receipts*

	Case 1	Case 2
Box-office receipts	$10,000	$8,000
Less deductions for second feature	2,500	2,000
Net box-office receipts	7,500	6,000
Minimum film rental at 70% of net	5,250	4,200
Contractual theater overhead (nut)	1,500	1,500
Net box-office receipts after nut	6,000	4,500
Maximum film rental at 90% of net after nut	5,400	4,050

Table 4.7. *Exhibitor operating revenues and expenses: an example*

Box-office (BO) weekly gross	$3,000
Concession sales (at 15%)	450
Total weekly gross	3,450
Deduct:	
Distributor's share at 50% of BO	1,500
Advertising (10% of BO)	300
Payroll (10% of BO)	300
Food cost (23% of sales)	104
Rent and real-estate taxes at 15% of BO	450
Utilities at $150/week	150
Management fee at 10% of total weekly gross	345
Insurance and employee benefits	100
Repairs and maintenance	100
Miscellaneous (tickets, etc.)	100
Total average weekly expenses	3,449

Source: Lowe (1983, p. 346). From the book *The Movie Business Book* by Jason E. Squire, © 1983 by Jason E. Squire. New York: Simon & Schuster/Fireside.

organization, of $33.75 million. Although much of the fee may in this instance be regarded as profit, it is this very distribution profit on a hit that would be expected to more than offset losses sustained on other releases; 10% of the films released generate 50% of the total box-office receipts (Figure 4.1).

Simplistically, then, it is distribution profit – perhaps for a major distributor averaging at least half (and often much more) of total distribution fees – that provides the positive cash flow for investment in new films. And it is this very profit, derived by subtracting from distribution fees all office overhead costs, compensation for sales personnel, and various other pub-

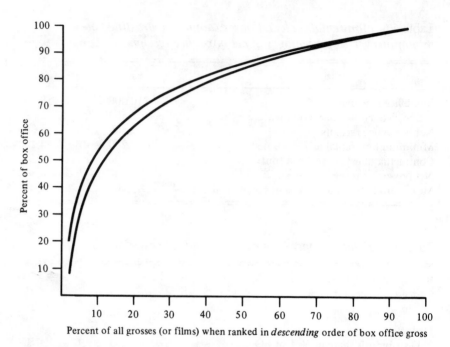

Figure 4.1. Ten percent of films generate 50% of the box office. When film box-office figures are ranked (either by individual weekly grosses or by individual films in order of their box-office grosses), the results fall in the range shown by the plotted curves. *Source: Daily Variety,* July 31, 1984. Copyright 1984 by A. D. Murphy.

licity and promotion expenses *not* recouped through other charges (as described below), which keeps the distributor in business despite the high probability that a picture will *in toto* lose money when *all* input factor costs and expenses are aggregated.

As for the distribution fee itself, it is perhaps best conceptualized as being an access charge or a toll paid to a distribution organization for use of the established turnpikes and bridges that allow direct and efficient access to large audiences. As with all such major access routes or pipelines, there can only be a few, and the up-front capital investment required to establish them is sizable.[13] The tolls or rents charged by distributors for such access are thus normally not especially sensitive to downward pressures, and are, by nature, quasi-monopolistic.

Many, if not most, pictures operate under a "net deal" in which the distributor charges a fixed or graduated percentage of rentals (e.g., 30% in domestic theatrical markets) as a distribution fee, and then makes advances for all other distribution costs, including those for prints, trailers, and national advertising. In addition, there may be charges related to publicity and personal-appearance tours, co-op advertising with exhibitors, taxes (based on rentals) by countries and localities, trade-association and guild fees in the form of residuals (for exhibitions in ancillary markets), and bad debts. The distributor commonly recovers these expenses before making any payments to the producer.

Although the aforementioned net deal predominates, there is also a "gross deal" wherein the distributor is not separately reimbursed for distribution expenses, but instead retains a distribution fee that is considerably higher (50%–70% or more) than normal. Distribution expenses are then recouped out of this higher fee.

For a picture performing poorly at the box office, the producer with a gross deal will have an advantage because overall distribution costs (which can be quite high on a percentage-of-revenue basis) are not chargeable. Contrarily, for a picture doing well at the box office, a producer might prefer a net deal because marketing costs as a percentage of revenues then diminish rapidly, and specific marketing charges become more bearable. Depending on the needs of the distributor and producer at the time an agreement is made, it is also possible to create a structure in which gross-deal and net-deal characteristics are combined as certain performance criteria are met.

In negotiating such formulations, perceived ancillary-market revenue potential has inspired many independent producers to attempt to strip from domestic theatrical-distribution contracts and to retain for themselves the right to exploit cable, videocassette, and other sources of income. Studios are increasingly reluctant to allow these rights to be taken away ("fractionalized") unless compensated through participations or higher distribution fees. Clearly, though, the larger the total up-front studio fee, the less is available for recoupment of production costs – and, ultimately, for profit of the independent filmmaker.

As we have seen, the most important profit center for a studio is found in its distribution activities, where fees range to over 30% of gross receipts, yet expenses are normally covered by 8% to 15% of gross receipts. This cushion of profit is earned in return for taking the risk that a picture will not earn its releasing costs, and it also in effect pays for maintenance and extension of the distribution pipeline. Of course, when a picture is doing well at the box office, distribution profits soar. But on the other hand, theatrical release (as opposed to licensing to home video, pay-cable, syndication, and network markets) is the only area where there is the possibility of a negative cash flow (i.e., where releasing costs can exceed income).

Studio overhead and other production costs

The general characteristics of production-related costs were examined in Chapter 3. From the participants' view, large proportions of those costs are seen as studio overhead charges, which are calculated by applying a contract-stipulated rate to all direct production costs. Such overhead charges may or may not have any close relationship to the actual costs of, for example, renting sound stages or buying props and signs outside of the studio's shops and mills.

Indeed, because it would almost always be less expensive to buy or lease items on a direct-cost basis, participants may question what services and materials are actually covered by the studio rate. If agreements are not clearly written, and thus are open to different interpretations, disputes may arise with regard to contractual overhead charges for everything from cameras and sound equipment to secretarial services. But probably the most important question is whether or not full rates are applicable to location shooting. How these matters are resolved – before, during, or (hopefully not) after production – depends on relative bargaining positions.

Producers are motivated to obtain independent financing in order to avoid or reduce the effects of these charges, which can add between 15% and 25% to a picture's budget and thereby significantly raise the break-even point required to activate participants' share payments. Sometimes it is worthwhile and feasible for an independent producer with outside financing to minimize studio overhead charges by offering the film for pickup in an advanced stage of production. In other instances it is less time-consuming and, in the long run, less expensive to go with the studio.

In brief, although overhead rates generally are not negotiable, the things to which those rates apply (offices, vehicles, etc.) may be, so that it is important for producers to have a clear understanding of what their contracts specify. If a studio wants a project badly enough, the items excluded from the standard rule will be more numerous.

Once production begins, cost accounting then follows a job-order cost procedure whereby time and materials are "charged against" a job or charge number. This is where careful control by the producer (who has final responsibility during the production phase) is essential. Costs can easily get out of hand, because everyone from painters and electricians to cameramen and editors may have at least some authority to charge against the picture's number for materials and services.

Truth and consequences[14]

A synopsis of what usually happens to a dollar that flows from the box office will help clarify the processing thus far described. Assuming that house expenses are 10%, there remains 90 cents, to which (for an important release by a major) a 90:10 split for the first two weeks in favor of the distributor may be applied. That, in turn, leaves a distributor's gross ("rentals") of around 81 cents.

In the United States and Canada, a 30% distribution fee totaling 24 cents is then subtracted, leaving 57 cents. Advertising and publicity costs, which are generally at least 20%–25% of rentals, require deduction of another,

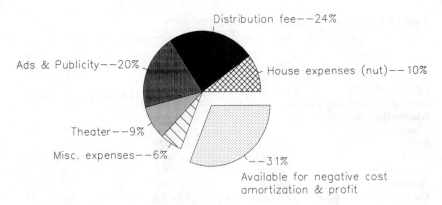

Figure 4.2. Splitting the box-office dollar for a major film.

say, 20 cents. The remainder is now 37 cents, out of which about 6 cents more is required for miscellaneous distribution expenses, including prints, taxes, MPAA seal, and transportation.

Thus, before considering the negative cost of the picture (which can be substantial), there is a residual pool of only 31 cents of the original dollar. Should there also be gross participations, say 10% (of rentals) to a major actor, there would then be 8 cents less with which to recoup the negative cost. And if the picture is studio-financed, half of any profit after recoupment would ordinarily be owed the studio, the other half split among other participants (Figure 4.2).[15] Small wonder, then, that so many firms have found production to be more difficult and less profitable than they had at first thought.[16]

The partial list of high-budget theatrical flops shown in Table 4.8 illustrates that box-office failure is usually congenital: No matter how large ancillary markets grow, they cannot a golden goose of a turkey make. And, there truly is little, if any, correlation between the cost of a picture and the total amount it generates from all markets.

Still, despite the odds against profitability, many people find filmmaking financially attractive, and worth taking a risk on. With a proper combination of luck and pluck, independent producers are sometimes able to arrange financing sufficient to, in effect, end up owning much or all of a possibly valuable negative at little or no direct cost to themselves.

4.4 Television-programming accounting

Television was initially thought to threaten the very survival of movies. The tube's mesmerizing influence and its presence in virtually all households were indeed major reasons that theater admissions decreased from the all-time peak of about 4 billion in 1946 to about 1 billion in the early

Table 4.8. *Selected theatrical winners and losers*

Title	Distributor	Year	Est. neg. cost ($ million)	Est. domestic rentals as of 1989 ($ million)
Winners (high and low budget)				
Jaws	Universal	1975	8.0	129.5
Star Wars	Lucasfilm/Fox	1977	11.5	193.5
Kramer vs. Kramer	Columbia	1979	7.0	60.0
Airplane	Paramount	1980	3.0	40.6
The Empire Strikes Back	Lucasfilm/Fox	1980	32.0	141.6
Raiders of the Lost Ark	Lucasfilm/Fox	1981	22.0	115.6
E.T. The Extra-terrestrial	Universal	1982	12.0	228.6
Return of the Jedi	Lucasfilm/Fox	1983	32.5	168.0
Beverly Hills Cop	Paramount	1984	14.0	80.9
Batman	Guber-Peters/ Warner	1989	35.0	150.5
Losers (high budget)				
Raise the Titanic	ITC/AFD	1980	36.0	6.8
Can't Stop the Music	EMI/AFD	1980	18.0	2.0
The Formula	MGM	1980	15.0	3.7
Heaven's Gate	UA	1980–1	44.0	1.5
Dragonslayer	Disney/Par.	1981	17.0	6.0
Honkey Tonk Freeway	EMI/Universal	1981	24.0	<1.0
Ragtime	DeLaurentiis/Par.	1981	32.0	10.0
Pennies from Heaven	MGM/UA	1981	22.0	3.6
Reds	Paramount	1981	52.0	21.0
One from the Heart	Coppola/Columbia	1982	26.0	<1.0
Inchon	One Way/MGM	1982	46.0	1.9
The Border	RKO/Universal	1982	22.0	5.0
Something Wicked This Way Comes	Disney	1983	23.0	3.0
Howard the Duck	Universal	1986	37.0	10.2
Ishtar	Columbia	1987	45.0	7.5
The Milagro Beanfield War	Universal	1988	18.0	6.5

Source: Variety, January 12, 1983; January 11, 1984, January 11, 1989, January 24, 1990.

1960s. Yet, as it happened, television eventually became the film industry's first major ancillary market and, in the process, probably its savior. But it was a long time before the value of the television market was fully understood by moviemakers.

Today, studios engage in three distinct television-related activities: licensing of features to networks; syndication of features, series, and other programs to local stations; and production of made-for-television movies, series, and programs. Many small firms are also active in these areas.

Feature licensing

The peak demand for network feature-film licenses appears to have been reached in the late 1970s, when pay-cable was still in a relatively early stage of development, and when the American Broadcasting Network, flush with ratings victories and cash, had the wherewithal to bid aggressively for rights to exhibit recent theatrical hits. Many of the major licenses at the time permitted up to five runs for fees that (with escalator clauses based on box-office performance) frequently were in the neighborhood of $20 million.

Bidding fervor cooled, however, when it was gradually recognized that pay-cable was siphoning off the potential for high network ratings through early showings of uncut movies without commercial interruptions. The ratings of all but the biggest box-office hits also diminished relative to those of made-for-television movies. In spite of this, films making their first network appearance in the early 1980s could command an average of perhaps $5 million for two runs. That price reflected expected ratings for the film, the number of weekly hours allotted by the networks for feature-movie programming, and the cost of producing comparable programming in terms of running time and content.

Of course, out of any television-license fees, residual payments to participants have to be made, and other distribution costs deducted, including high-priced legal talent and, on a rainy day, taxi fare up New York's Sixth Avenue. A feature film licensed to network television might thus generate for the studio-distributor a profit margin in the range of 40%–65%.

An important accounting dilemma, nevertheless, appears in the situation in which a package of several features is licensed by a single vendor to one purchaser. According to trade-paper reports,[17] for example, United Artists had followed an allocation formula that

divided the package price by the number of pictures in the package to determine average price per picture,
assigned a value of 1.5 times the average price to the feature with the highest theatrical rentals,
assigned a value of 0.5 times the average price to the feature with the lowest theatrical rentals,
ranked the remaining features by rentals earned and assigned a value in between the range of 1.5 and 0.5 times the average price.

Similar formulas had been used by other distributors with the rationale that over the years "it has been determined that the ratings of the most successful pictures on television, in both domestic and foreign markets, receive no more than three times the rating of the least successful pictures."[18]

Such formulas were legally challenged because they seemed to produce unfair results for some participants, and thus, under current practices, prices for features in a package are supposed to be negotiated separately for each title. But questions concerning the basis for arriving at a specific price may still arise.

For outside participants, probably the easiest way to account for income from television-license fees is on a cash basis as of telecast date, but there can be many variations, to some extent configured by relative negotiating power. As already noted, for purposes of financial reporting, the studio-distributor will recognize revenues at the time the pictures are made available for exhibition. However, actual contract terms might stipulate cash payments of 20% on signing, 50% on availability, and 30% on subsequent runs. (Down payments on old series are smaller.)

Problems as to the timing of cash receipts, allocations, and different reporting requirements frequently arise in situations involving licensing of syndication, pay-cable, and other ancillary-market rights (novelizations, games and toys, character merchandise, and music).

Program production and distribution

Development and financing processes Production of original programming for network television is generally in the form of made-for-television movies ("made-fors") or regularly scheduled series and miniseries, such as "War and Remembrance"[19] or "Roots." Each of these program forms may receive somewhat specialized cost-accounting treatment, with the procedures and methods applied to made-fors being similar to those used in making feature films.

Financing on made-fors and series, however, is provided by the networks on a piecemeal basis. About a year ahead of anticipated play dates, networks and program producers, including the television arms of the major film studios and many large television production independents, sift through hundreds of concepts to select those with the potential to become two-hour movies, miniseries (usually 8–12 hours in length), or one-hour or half-hour series. No more than two or three dozen of these concepts will then be provided with funding, and each will be developed into a "pilot" production that will introduce the major plot and characters.

Pilots allow network purchasers to sense how well the elements in a proposed program will work together on the screen. But they are often loaded with costly production values in an attempt to stimulate the buyers, who make their judgments based largely on first impressions.[20]

Of the 30 or so pilots ordered for the start of the television season, no more than 15 are likely to be accepted for regularly scheduled series programming by the three major networks combined. Acceptance by a network is usually accompanied by a funding commitment to produce 13 episodes initially, and by an option contract for additional episodes (usually 9–11 more) if the program attracts relatively large audiences. For each episode, the network may pay one-third on commencement of filming or taping, another third on completion, and the last third on delivery and clearance (by network censors and others). The percentages at the various steps of a deal occasionally vary, and there may be an additional payment of 10% or so on rerun of an episode.

There are two reasons that producers do not generally profit immediately or directly from series or made-fors developed by the process just described. First, network funding (via license fees, normally for two runs) does not typically cover all the out-of-pocket cash expenditures by the TV program producer. In fact, on the average, such production costs may be only 80% to 85% recouped from the network license fee, with the remainder hopefully covered by revenues generated through licensing in foreign markets.[21] Under these circumstances, even a relatively efficient producer would have difficulty coming out ahead on a cash basis of accounting. But a financial deficit is also virtually assured using the accrual method of accounting, wherein noncash accruals for studio overhead expenses (at 10% or more of the budget) are included. It is thus common for program producers to "deficit finance" their series and made-fors while trusting that the network ratings will be strong enough to carry the show into the potentially more lucrative off-network syndication aftermarket at some future time.[22,23]

Network option clauses, however, are another reason why producers might not immediately profit from a successful series introduction. Option clauses for series usually allow the network to order programs for four to six additional broadcast seasons (with episode fees increasing at least 3%–5%, and more likely 7%–8%, each year), and provide for first right of refusal beyond such a period. This means that even if another network or perhaps a cable channel were to offer the production company more money for a program, the offer could not be immediately accepted. Option clauses thus enable a network to retain a show at a cost below the current market rate in compensation for taking the original risk of placing the show on its crowded schedule before the willingness of an audience to watch the program has been demonstrated.

Nevertheless, with a network contract in hand, a studio or, more likely, an independent producer can obtain additional financial support by borrowing from a bank, other lending institutions, or investors' groups. Cash can also be obtained by selling in advance a program's anticipated syndication rights to distributors. Then, after the initial run (and, presumably, rerun), the production company ends up owning the network-financed program, and can do with it whatever it pleases. The real payoff, if any, however, comes if the series can sustain competitive network ratings for at least three full seasons so that over 60 episodes (typically 22 per season) can be completed. But the probability of this occurring is relatively low; at best, about one in five new series survives the ratings wars that long.[24]

As for movies-of-the-week, first-run syndicated productions (i.e., programming designed for a nonnetwork initial run), prime-time-access shows, and made-for-cable programs, financing is available from well-heeled television-program distribution companies (including, the television divisions of all major movie studios). For exclusive rights, the distributor typically contributes part of the funding in return for profit participations and the opportunity to earn distribution fees.

Syndication agreements Should a series last three seasons on a network,[25] it begins to have significant value for the syndication (used-film) market, because local television stations and cable systems can then obtain enough episodes to "strip" the program into scheduled daily runs over a period of at least several months. Syndication-market licenses, which go to the highest local-station bidder, are conventionally for six consecutive runs of a series in a period of not more than five years[26] and now commonly no longer than three years.

A typical syndication agreement will provide that out of the gross revenues collected, the syndication company will first deduct syndication fees, then deduct out-of-pocket expenses (including costs for shipping, advertising, and prints), and then recoup advances made to producers. Fees for syndication services (i.e., distribution fees) as a proportion of gross income are generally 15%–20% for net stripping sales, 30%–35% for domestic syndication and Canadian theatrical distribution, and 40%–50% for foreign syndication.

Table 4.9, based on syndications typical of a major movie studio, illustrates the profit potential for a distributor and the similarity in structure to the aforementioned gross deal used in theatrical distribution of features. Operating margins for distributors of shows produced by others would normally average 30%, and for long-running self-produced programs around 40%.[27]

Television networks have historically relied on feature films and series to fill most of their prime-time hours. Nevertheless, especially during the 1980s, so-called *first-run* syndication has developed into an important means through which programming for independent (i.e., non–network affiliated) local television stations as well as network affiliates seeking to fill their prime-time access hours (i.e., the hours just before the network's evening schedule begins) can be obtained. First-run syndication, primarily of game or tabloid news shows in recent years, provides television stations with a relatively low-cost, disposable form of programming that is very immediate, and that does not depend on or require a lengthy network run: The programming skips the network entirely, and is syndicated to local stations onward from its first broadcast appearance.

Although an infinite number of variations can be devised to finance and distribute first-run programming, the primary requirement in launching a first-run program series is to have commitments from enough stations so that at least 65% to 70% of the national viewing audience can see the show. These commitments, though, are normally made on the basis of pilots that

Table 4.9. *Network television program production and syndication: a structural example of successful program series, circa 1990*

Production

Network license fee covers 80%–85% of cash outlay.
Foreign sales may recoup remainder of cash outlay on 1-hour shows, but only
   half of remaining cash deficit on ½-hour shows.

Status on accrual basis including overhead and interest
   1-hour shows: 22 episodes/season
                  Cost per episode, $1.2 million
                  Accrued deficit per episode = $250,000
   ½-hour shows: 22 episodes/season
                  Cost per episode, $600,000
                  Accrued deficit per episode = $150,000

Syndication

Distribution fees: domestic 35%, foreign 50%

Assuming 100 episodes are available for syndication

1-hour shows:	Revenues	
	Domestic	$325,000
	Foreign	250,000
		$575,000
	Minus:	
	Residuals, six runs	
	Domestic	65,000
	Foreign	25,000
	Production deficit	250,000
	Distribution costs[a]	65,000
	Studio profit[b]	$170,000
½-hour shows:	Revenues	$1,000,000
	Minus:	
	Residuals, six runs	40,000
	Production deficit	150,000
	Distribution costs[a]	50,000
	Talent profit participations	200,000
	Studio profit[b]	$560,000

[a]Primarily promotion and distribution "bicycling."
[b]Profit would be split if show is independently produced, and does not take account
of losses on shows that fail.

are considerably less elaborately produced than are those for network series proposals. Also, unless a production is a proven ratings winner, it is unlikely that a station would make a syndication agreement that spans more than one year.[28]

Producers and distributors will generally, of course, prefer that stations pay cash for the rights to air the programs. But more often than not, the stations instead prefer to swap, or to barter, some of their advertising time-slots in return for broadcast rights. Such *barter syndication* arrangements, as discussed in more detail in Chapter 6, have grown rapidly into over a $1 billion a year business that, on the margin, reduces revenues available to the networks.[29]

In barter syndication, the key accounting issue concerns the time at which barter revenues ought to be recognized. According to rulings by an FASB task force, such revenues should now primarily be recognized to the extent they are covered by non-cancellable contracts (less an estimated value for "make good" spots), and at the point when a program is available for first telecast.

Costs of production Networks are naturally concerned for their own profit margins, and they attempt to keep their costs under control through tough negotiations on production contracts. The producer's problem is to then live within the budget constraints imposed by those contracts. That is often difficult, given the limited production time and the sharp union-mandated pay escalations for overtime work related to frequent rewriting and rehearsal.

As of the late 1980s, a prime-time one-hour network show such as Lor-imar's "Dallas" required, on the average, some seven days to shoot (many more to edit) and around $1.5 million to produce. But less popular shows with lower-paid performers might have been made for perhaps 70% of that amount.[30]

For a long-running series, the fixed cost for sets, props, and general story concept decreases on a unit basis as more episodes are produced. Everything else being equal, a series will thus over time become more profitable to make. But whether or not this is reflected in cost accounting depends on several additional factors.

First and foremost is the inclination of performers on a highly rated series to begin demanding much higher compensation per episode under threat of resignation. Per-episode compensation for stars has reportedly exceeded $125,000 (in "Dallas", for example), but there have been other instances (e.g., "Three's Company") in which performers' demands have been rejected and their resignations accepted.

Another important determinant of profitability is the rate at which pro-duction costs are amortized. For example, as a producer-distributor like MCA begins to see series-syndication potential, the rate of cost amortiza-tion is reduced (amortization is stretched out over time), so that a portion of expenses can be charged against anticipated future syndication revenues. This treatment of amortization parallels that used in accounting for unam-ortized feature-film residuals, as discussed in section 4.2. In the case of a popular series coming off-network, such syndication revenues can be substantial, as shown by the record $200 million ($1.5 million per episode) initially received by MCA for the one-hour series "Magnum, P.I."[31] But many series, especially hour-longs, do not even come close to the positive results shown in Table 4.9.

First-run production and syndication, however, is relatively attractive to show producers and syndicators because the production costs of such shows are normally much below those of network series, and because the returns from syndication of a successful first-run series materialize much sooner than with syndicated off-network programs. For example, whereas a typical half-hour network comedy series might cost over half a million dollars to produce, a first-run half-hour might cost two-thirds as much. And a week's worth of half-hour game shows (five) can, in fact, be produced for well under a quarter million dollars. But not all first-run series are necessarily low-budget productions: "Star-Trek – The Next Generation" has been the costliest first-run series to date with a per-episode budget of $1.3 million plus $75,000 for special effects.

Costs and problems of distribution Distribution costs for television programming include sales-office overhead, travel, and the important variables of participant residual payments. There are also expenses for retitling episodes, for possible dubbing into other languages, and for print-making – which taken together can become significant. However, the number of prints needed for national syndication is reduced by "bicycling," the swapping of episodes from one station to the next when the sequencing of episodes does not matter. In theory, increased use of low-cost distribution by satellite technology promises that ultimately only one print will be required.

Prior to the advent of "superstations" (local television stations that send their signals via satellite to cable systems around the country), syndicated programs in a local market had been protected from competition through contract exclusivity clauses. But importation of signals from superstations and other long-distance carriers into local markets had largely ended strict exclusivity until the FCC reinstated such exclusivity (with so-called "syndex" rules) in 1990.

As can be seen from Table 4.10, syndication expenditures have grown substantially since the mid-1970s, as both independent and network-affiliated stations have come to depend on programming provided by syndication companies through combinations of cash and time-barter arrangements. Inevitably, the same types of arrangements will also become quite common as private European television markets develop.

But in the 1990s, the greatest changes in program distribution relationships will occur as a result of modifications to the financial interest and syndication rules that had barred television networks from owning any

Table 4.10. *Historical and projected program syndication expenditures among affiliates and independents, 1980–5 (actual) and 1986–90 (projected by INTV);[a] and barter industry revenues, 1982–90[b]*

Year	Independents $ million	Independents % of total	Affiliates $ million	Affiliates % of total	Total program syndication expenditures ($ million)	Barter-syndication[b] revenues ($ millions)
1980	225	42.5	304	57.5	529	—
1981	300	47.5	331	52.5	631	—
1982	389	54.0	332	46.0	721	150
1983	524	58.0	380	42.0	904	300
1984	604	58.9	422	41.1	1,026	450
1985	708	60.6	460	39.4	1,168	550
1986	828	62.3	502	37.7	1,330	650
1987	968	63.9	547	36.1	1,515	775
1988	1,160	64.9	627	35.1	1,787	875
1989	1,330	65.9	687	34.1	2,017	1,050
1990	1,522	66.9	753	33.1	2,275	1,250

Source[a]: Association of Independent Television Stations (INTV), *Estimated TV Syndication Expenditures, 1975–1990,* December 1985.
[b]Advertiser Syndicated Television Association.

syndication interests in shows that they broadcast, and that have placed limits on the number of program hours that a network can self-produce.[32] The rules had originally been promulgated in 1970 to open a way for many independent producers to flourish, and to prevent program domination by the three major networks.[33]

In fact, however, many independents have not flourished. And given the sizable risks and capital investments entailed in the development of television programs, production and distribution have become largely consolidated into the hands of the major movie studios and other media companies with deep pockets. It would thus appear that, ultimately, any rule modifications will have the likely result of finally enabling movie studios and networks to merge with each other.[34]

Revenue-recognition timing and associated controversies Many of the most successful independent producers have established capital bases large enough to support their own distribution systems, and all the major studios have television-program sales subsidiaries. Whenever a distributor owns a program series, revenues and earnings are recognized when the series is made available to stations – a practice identical with that established for feature-film licenses. However, the cash-flow sequence may begin with up to a 10% down payment on signing or on first availability date and be followed by three annual installments of 30% of total revenues due. Following standard accounting procedures, the future cash receivables are then discounted, using an appropriate interest rate, to a present-value receivable that appears on the balance sheet. For series in which only distribution services are being rendered, though, distribution fees would normally be recognized as being earned period-by-period as the episodes are played out, and cash payments might be more evenly disbursed.

Producers, distributor-syndicators, and individual profit participants all have different claims on the television-license income stream, and individuals or corporations may simultaneously function in one or in several of these roles. Moreover, much as on the theatrical side, differences in perspective often lead to great controversies, and to audits. Disputes may occur because the timing of the disbursements and the profits recognized by one participant in a series project may be vastly different from the timing and profits received by another.

Illustrative cases, as discussed in a segment of the CBS show "60 Minutes" (December 7, 1980) and in a *TV Guide* story (Swertlow 1982), have involved actors Fess Parker of the "Daniel Boone" series produced by Twentieth Century Fox and James Garner of the Universal series "Rockford Files." These stars, who had contracted for deferred profit-participation points in addition to or in lieu of greater immediate salary, asserted that the distributors had earned substantial profits totaling many millions of dollars, whereas they had yet to receive any profit on participants' shares.

Parker sued Fox for $48 million, claiming that the one-hour series that ran in prime time for six years on NBC moved into successful syndication and grossed $40 million. Garner claimed that his long-running network series grossed over $52 million from both domestic and foreign sales. How, they asked, is it possible for these series to be reported as unprofitable?

The answer lies in the definition of "profits" used in the contracts. Just as in feature-film participations, a few rare talents may bargain for and be powerful enough to command high fees plus a percentage of gross revenues. Some others may bargain for a high salary and be entitled to only a small (or no) percentage of narrowly defined "profits." And most others are not participants at all; they are fortunate simply to get a job at minimum scale.

Take, for example, a hypothetical situation described by Robert Leeper, a former executive at Universal and Fox, in the *TV Guide* story:

A studio claims a production cost of $10 million for the first year of a one-hour series . . . 70 percent of those are hard, or actual costs for such items as sets, lights and film – but the remaining 30 percent includes studio charges for overhead such as the studio's parking lots and offices.

If the network carrying the $10-million show pays $8 million for the series the first year, then the series has lost $2 million for the year. If the series is a hit and runs for five years on that basis, it means that on the book, technically, the hit series has lost $10 million in production costs alone. There are other charges too. The studio also gives itself 10 percent as a commission for "selling" the series to the network. That's $800,000 a year – an additional $4 million in costs over five years, plunging the series $14 million in the hole on the books. The studio then charges the show interest on these losses. Say that, over the five years, with a fluctuating prime rate, the interest has amounted to $2.2 million. The series is now $16.2 million in the red.

... now, the 125 episodes produced over the five years are sold for a total of $100,000 per episode – a grand total of $12.5 million. The profit participant may think that the series' deficit has now been reduced to $3.7 million, and that he is on the verge of turning a profit. Wrong. Forty percent of the syndication revenue is lost to the distribution fee – the money the studio gives itself for selling the show to stations buying the reruns. In this case, that's $5 million. The remaining $7.5 million is then deducted, leaving the series $8.7 million in the red. The studio then charges the series what are called "actual costs" for distributing the series to syndication. They include costs for editing, making prints and negatives, costs for shipping the series to stations buying the reruns. These "actual costs" may amount to another $1.3 million. So our one-hour series is still $10 million in the red. (Reprinted with permission from *TV Guide* magazine, copyright 1982 by Triangle Publications, Inc., Radnor, Pennsylvania.)

Despite the deficit reported to participants, does the studio make a profit? The answer, in the case of a long-running series, is a qualified yes if it is indeed assumed that "soft" costs (which help to absorb the general overhead costs of running a studio) are embedded in the total production cost figure, if it is understood that the studio is in business to make a profit out of renting its distribution capability (and thus make a profit on the distribution fees charged), and if it is recognized that the studio tends to receive its cash payments a lot faster than do the participants – who might only see a summary accounting such as that shown in Table 4.11.[35]

Studios do not deny that production and distribution of series can be profitable for them even while the statements of individual participants indicate losses. But again, as in feature films, the difference is that the studio places some operating capital at risk with its investments in plant and equipment, sales offices, and other assets required to run the business over the long term. On the other hand, participants are normally paid handsome salaries for their services, and they do not incur such risks.

4.5 Weak links in the chain

Well-publicized financial-accounting disputes in movies and television support an impression that dishonesty and cheating are rampant in entertainment industries. And keen news-media coverage catering to the high level of public interest in industry affairs tends to magnify whatever problems exist. But just as in other segments of the economy, the great majority of individuals and companies in entertainment conduct their businesses

Table 4.11. *Summary profit accounting for the television series
participant; a possible example*

Studio's self-produced series (over five years)
Revenues ($ million):

Network payments for production	50.0
10% selling fee (program to network)	5.0
40% syndication distribution fee (125 episodes at $200,000 per)	10.0
40% foreign-sales distribution fee	5.0
Interest and other	3.0
Total	73.0

Expenses ($ million):

Production costs (including overhead)	65.0
Direct distribution costs	2.0
Residuals and other	6.0
Total	73.0
Studio profit before taxes	0.0

ethically. Indeed, because creation of entertainment products is such a peo-
ple-intensive and people-sensitive process, success may depend as much on
esteem and trust as on ability.

To guard against improper conduct, however, it is necessary to know
where "leakages" in the revenue stream are most likely to occur. In this
section we shall consider how and where people might cheat.[36]

Exhibitors: the beginning and the end

Customers' cash payments at the box office represent both the beginning
of a chain of remittances and the end of a long creative manufacturing
process – with a single, simple idea for a movie eventually generating hundreds of pounds of legal paperwork and hundreds of thousands of feet of
processed film.

Because the precise terms of distributor-exhibitor contracts are rarely
made known to anyone not party to the agreements, both exhibitors and
distributors can, for publicity purposes, sometimes distort the true size of
the box-office gross. In this way, a small picture can for a brief while be
made to look like a modest hit, and a modest hit may be proclaimed as a
virtual blockbuster.

On the next level of the cash stream's cascade, the exhibitor's house
expense (nut) is a negotiated item that can be inflated to ensure a profit to
the exhibitor. In fact, a given theater may simultaneously have different
house-expense understandings with different distributors. The degree of
this inflation can be the result of long-standing tacit agreements, or it may
be subject to momentary relative bargaining strength. Either way, though,

the size of the nut ultimately affects the grosses (rentals) received by the distributor, and thus the incomes of other parties downstream. The incomes of those parties would, of course, also be reduced if theater owners pay their bills slowly, or if there are significant "adjustments" to the allowances for co-op advertising.

Ticket-pricing policies, however, would generally have the greatest effect on what the downstream participants might ultimately receive. Pricing is subject to local competitive conditions, moviegoer-demand schedules, and the exhibitor's interest to make as much as possible from concession sales. Exhibitors who attempt to promote concession sales by setting low admissions prices are in effect diverting and thereby diminishing monies available for downstream disbursements. To prevent abuses in this area, distributors occasionally write contracts specifying minimum per-capita ticket prices (see section 3.4).

Playing the "float" (i.e., the time value of money) is another endemic industry problem. This is somewhat surprising because box-office income is almost always in cash, and, in theory, exhibitors should have absolutely no difficulty in paying rentals immediately due distributors. Moreover, because theater owners normally have an interest in playing a distributor's next film, large distributors have important leverage to encourage prompt remittances. Nevertheless, in practice, playing the float appears at all levels of the industry, and at high interest rates it has a significant cumulative adverse effect on profit participants.[37]

Outright fraud occurs if exhibitors and distributors cooperate to falsely claim national advertising when the advertising is characteristically local. In such situations, national advertising is charged to the producer's share, leaving the exhibitor and distributor a larger profit. It is also sometimes possible for an unscrupulous exhibitor to obtain false invoices for more local advertising (paid on a co-op basis by the distributor) than is actually placed in local papers. Moreover, exhibitors can cheat by conveniently forgetting to inform distributors that after a certain amount of newspaper lineage is placed, a quantity rebate is obtained.

Other unscrupulous practices that can be used to skim rentals properly belonging to the distributor include the following:

Bicycling (i.e., using a single print, without authorization by the exhibition contract, to generate "free" revenues by showing it at more than one location owned by the same management). In multiscreen theaters, for example, a picture that is not playing to capacity might, in violation of day and date (simultaneity) contract terms, be replaced in some showings by another feature that is unauthorized but more popular.
Running the film for an extra showing unauthorized by contract.
Palming tickets (i.e., leaving the ticket untorn and recycling it to the box office, where it can be resold without disturbing the number sequence of the ticket roll).

Changing the ticket roll after a few hundred tickets have been sold. Ticket sales on the substituted roll then go unreported.

Unauthorized reprinting of the negative. Nowadays this includes felonious reproduction of home videotape cassettes, which can result in significant loss of revenues.[38]

"Product-splitting" practices (discussed in section 3.4) that reduce bidding competitiveness and, in turn, the percentage of box office received by distributors.

In addition, distributors might also join with exhibitors in certain actions that further deprive producers and other participants of income that would otherwise be theirs. For instance, this might occur in the area of distributor-exhibitor *settlements* – renegotiations of terms for pictures that do not perform according to expectations.[39]

Distributor-producer problems

As we have seen, the income of profit participants is affected by charges for studio overhead, by publicity and other marketing fees charged for in-house departments, and by deductibles from producer's share that may include dubbing, editing, checking distributor receipts, copyrighting, screenings, censorship clearances, trailer preparation, insurance, tariffs, trade-association dues, print examinations, and print junking costs. If participant contracts are not carefully negotiated, the extent to which these charges are applied in any project is sometimes a source of dispute.

Major profit participants, such as leading performers, can also adversely affect the interests of other participants. For instance, this occurs when special antique furnishings, wardrobes, houses, or cars originally bought for a film are given to performers for personal use after production is completed.

Another version of this occurs when films are being shot in countries that have blocked currency remittances because of foreign-exchange controls. In these instances, it is not uncommon for family and friends of important actors to receive free trips to exotic film locales. Blocked currency earned within a country must be spent within the country of origin.[40]

As already indicated, there is inordinate potential for controversy in allocations of television-license fees, cross-collateralization deals, and studios' accounting for foreign taxes, which may be charged to a picture even though the parent company later receives a credit against U.S. taxes. Also, accounting for remittances from foreign-based sources may be especially difficult because auditing privileges may be contractually restricted to books based in the United States, foreign-exchange rates may be rounded off in favor of the distributor, and foreign collections may be unusually slow.

Producers may attempt to avoid entanglement in these issues by making their own arrangements for independent foreign distribution. This is often done most efficiently by contracting with experienced overseas foreign sales companies, whose service fees are generally in the range of 10%–15% of revenues collected, and are subject to the right of recoupment of direct-sales costs if the film's gross is insufficient.[41]

4.6 Concluding remarks

The essential strength of the major film studios has been derived from their ability to control distribution from the early financing stages to the timing of theatrical release. But new developments in technology are always presenting new challenges and growth opportunities for industry participants.

Such opportunities will allow many smaller companies to carve out profitable niches for themselves. Yet ultimately, the enormous amount of capital required to operate film and television program production and distribution facilities on a global basis presents a significant barrier to entry, and reinforces the trend toward vertical integration of the industry. Because the costs of production are what financial analysts call "sunk" costs, it makes sense for a production to be exposed in as many windows of exhibition – from home video to pay cable to free television – as possible.

That is not to necessarily imply, however, that the emergence of new media markets has eliminated downside risk, or that a flood of eager new entrants will not drive down investment returns for the industry as a whole, or that product appeal cycles have been banished forever. These aspects are part of this business, just as they are for any other business.

Although it is too soon to know whether recent industry consolidation trends will prove viable over the longer run, it is clear that the financial-economic structure of the movie and television production and distribution industry is rapidly becoming more complex, and as such, is providing a more interesting and potentially more profitable arena for investors.

Selected additional reading

Abrams, B. (1984). "Why TV Producers Flock to New York to Just Sit and Fret," *Wall Street Journal*, May 7.

Barnes, P. W. (1987). "How King World Reaps Riches, Fame as a TV Syndicator," *Wall Street Journal*, June 9.

Chambers, E. (1986). *Producing TV Movies.* New York: Prentice-Hall.

"First-Run Syndicators Tune in on TV's Big Bucks," *Business Week* No. 2841 (May 7, 1984):78.

Gottschalk, E. C., Jr. (1972). "Film Makers Struggle with Major Studios for 'Creative' Control," *Wall Street Journal*, December 29.

Gottschalk, E. C., Jr. (1978). "Feud in Filmdom: Movie Studios' System of Splitting Profits Divides Hollywood," *Wall Street Journal*, October 16.

Gubernick, L. (1988). "Miss Jones, Get Me Film Finances," *Forbes*, 142 (14)(December 26):74.

Harmetz, A. (1987). "Now Lawyers Are Hollywood Superstars," *The New York Times,* January 11.

Harwood, J. (1985). "Hollywood Exposing More of Its Ledgers," *Variety,* March 13.

Kopelson, A. (1985). "Presales of Independently Produced Motion Pictures," *The Hollywood Reporter,* March 5.

Landro, L. (1985). "Overseas Distributor Takes on Big Studios By Doing Own Films," *Wall Street Journal,* April 16.

"Lenders Laughing All The Way to The Bank," *Daily Variety,* March 11, 1985.

Meyer, M., and Viera, J. D. eds. (1984). *1984 Entertainment, Publishing and the Arts Handbook.* New York: Clark Boardman Co., Ltd.

Morgenstern, S., ed. (1979). *Inside the TV Business.* New York: Sterling Publishing Co.

Price Waterhouse & Co. (1974). *Accounting for the Motion Picture Industry.* New York: Price Waterhouse.

Sansweet, S. J. (1983). "Even With a Hit Film, A Share of the Profits May Be Nothing at All," *Wall Street Journal,* July 21.

Scholl, J. (1986). "Bad Show: Picture Dims for Syndicators of TV Programs," *Barron's,* December 15.

Schuyten, P. (1976). "How MCA Rediscovered Movieland's Golden Lode," *Fortune* XCIV(5)(November):122.

Sherman, S. P. (1985). "Hollywood's Foxiest Financier," *Fortune* 111(1)(January 7):92.

Tobias, A. (1976). "The Hidden Fight That Finally Made MCA the Greatest," *New West,* April 26.

Trachtenberg, J. A. (1985). "The Other Green Revolution," *Forbes* 135(7)(April 8):101.

Turner, R. (1989). "For TV Comedy Writers, the Money Grows Serious," *Wall Street Journal,* August 2.

5
The music business

Life in the fast lane's no fun if you're running out of gas.

That is exactly what people in the music business discovered toward the end of the 1970s, when after three virtually uninterrupted decades of expansion, recorded-music sales stopped growing. The 1980s, though, have been another story.

Music generates aggregate worldwide revenues of some $30 billion per year. But in accounting for well over half of that total,[1] recorded music is the most audible and visible segment, and as such is most assuredly the economic heart of the business. Accordingly, its analysis will dominate this chapter.

5.1 Feeling groovy

Experimentation with reproduction of moving images can be traced back into the early 1800s. But there was apparently very little interest in reproduction of sound until the venerable Thomas Edison in 1877 developed yet another of his novelty items – a tinfoil-wrapped cylinder that was rotated with a handle. While he cranked the handle and recited the nursery rhyme "Mary Had a Little Lamb" into a recording horn, Edison's voice

130

vibrated a diaphragm to which a metal stylus was attached. And the metal stylus then cut grooves on the surface of the tinfoil. Voilà! When the procedure was reversed, the stylus caused the diaphragm to vibrate and amplified recorded sounds to emanate.

Although early investors indeed tried to popularize the invention through demonstrations in concert halls, country fairs, and vaudeville theaters, the scratchy sound and limited number of times the foil could be used before it deteriorated discouraged enthusiasm for Edison's "phonograph." So it was not until other inventors including Alexander Graham Bell got into the act and improved the original phonograph by using a wax-coated cardboard tube over the cylinder, and until electric power was added, that the popularly called "talking machine" (and also forerunner of the jukebox) finally caught on.

At that stage, people would actually go to a parlor and pay a nickel to listen to these wax cylinders reproduce songs and comic monologues. And ludicrous as it now seems, "a brass band recording a two-minute march had to play that march over and over again, perfectly, to turn out hundreds of recordings."[2]

But already by the 1890s, home phonographs had begun to appear. And by then, a German immigrant, Emile Berliner, had developed a prototype that cut recording grooves onto discs – a modification that within 10 years led to introduction of the gramophone or "Victrola" by the Victor Talking Machine Company.

Technological development, this time of radio and of an electrical recording process, led to further significant sound reproduction improvements and also to conflicts among competing interest groups. Composers encountered tremendous resistance when they tried to collect royalties for performances of their music. And radio station owners insisted that once they had bought a recording, it was theirs to use without any further financial obligation to composers.[3] Throughout the 1920s, but especially in the early half of that decade, it was radio, not phonograph equipment, that experienced the greatest rise in demand.

The Great Depression triggered a collapse of record sales – from $75 million in 1929 to only $5 million in 1933 – and it was not until the late 1930s that recovery became evident. That recovery, however, was naturally slowed in the early 1940s by World War II, and by a protracted musicians' union strike that prevented the manufacture of new records for over a year.[4] By 1945, industry sales were thus still only $109 million.

The next stage of growth was stimulated with the postwar development of tape recordings, which replaced inefficient wax-blank masters, and with introduction of the 12-inch vinyl long-playing (LP) record by Columbia Records in 1948. These LPs, played at 33⅓ revolutions per minute (rpm), could hold 23 minutes of music per side, but did not clearly win out over older 45 rpm and 78 rpm configurations until the late 1950s – when industry sales first exceeded $500 million. But the 1950s were also a time when introduction of new low-cost recording equipment made it possible for many small independent companies to spring up in competition with RCA, Columbia, and Decca – the long-established majors of the time.[5] The independents were the catalysts in bringing traditional jazz, southern rhythm and blues, and gospel-based music styles into the American mainstream.

However, it was not until the mid to late 1960s that the business truly exploded with the universal introduction of truer-to-life hi-fi stereo sound recordings at a time when the postwar baby boomers, then teenagers with lots of money to spend, were becoming ever more attracted to the expanding rock 'n' roll genre. The sixties were also a time in which the record business, paralleling the development of the film business some 30 years earlier, consolidated distribution (and the ownership of "independent" labels) into the hands of a few corporate giants that included RCA, CBS, Warner Communications, and Polygram. This high-growth phase lasted through the 1970s, and was given a powerful boost by introduction of the standardized portable audiotape cassette configuration. By the late 1970s, industry sales at retail list prices hovered at the $4 billion level.

Yet, not all was well with the industry as it entered the 1980s in the fast lane and started to run out of gas. A somewhat older population base with a diminished interest in the new recordings of the time, coupled with poor quality control of vinyl pressings, contributed to a noticeable decline in demand that was not to be reversed until 1983 with the arrival of the compact (4.7-inch) disc (CD). Such digitally encoded (using advanced computer technology) and optically (laser beam) decoded discs provided consumers with distortion-free sound reproduction, and a good reason to go back to buying music. Indeed, by the late 1980s, CDs had already virtually replaced vinyl recordings, and U.S. industry sales had soared to over $6 billion.

CDs, in several different standardized versions and sizes (for use in audio, video, and personal computer applications), are expected to remain the dominant configuration well past the year 2000. And digital audio tape (DAT), a close technological cousin to the CD, will likely soon begin to become the standard audio tape format.

5.2 Inside out

Composing, publishing, and management

The process of creating a musical property and then exploiting it is in many ways similar to property development and exploitation in movies. In both areas, relative bargaining power is a key element. An important difference, however, is that in music an enterprise can be launched with fewer people and with far smaller commitments of capital.

A new composer has several avenues through which work may begin to generate revenues, but the first step is usually publication. The composer can attempt to interest an existing publisher or can establish a new publishing firm. In any case, the normal arrangement is for publisher and composer to share evenly any income from their joint venture.

The publisher's role is to monitor and to promote use of the music through sheet-music sales ("paper" houses specialize in this) and, more important, through live performances and recordings. At each step, royalty income, which may have to be further shared by subpublishers and coauthors, is derived. For a new artist-composer, contract terms are fairly well standardized, but for a recognized talent, many complex variations depending on tax, managerial, and other considerations are negotiated. There are tens of thousands of publishers and self-publishers in the United States.

The services of lawyers and accountants are required in most stages of a composer's career, but if the composer is also a performing artist, as is increasingly common, any degree of success will entail the hiring of a manager and an agent to book concerts, television appearances, and recording schedules. Managers will generally take between 15% and 30% of a performer's income, and talent agents 10%. For a new artist-composer, the functions of manager, legal advisor, and talent agent may be handled by a single individual.[6]

Royalty streams

Performances Assuming that a "demo" (demonstration) record or tape has attracted a publisher's interest, the next step is to work on a full-fledged recorded performance by the composer or to attract the interest of other performers in cutting a so-called cover record of the material. Publishers and performers are always on the lookout for good, fresh material, but only a small fraction of what is offered is accepted, and only a small fraction of what is accepted for publication succeeds in the marketplace. Of hundreds of new works introduced each week, on average not more than 5 to 10 seem to have any chance of receiving widespread recognition.

Whether the music is performed by orchestras, by college bands at football games, by radio stations, by nightclub singers, or by Muzak® speakers in elevators, it is entitled to performance royalties that are collected by two major agencies (and one smaller agency) in the United States. Of the two majors, the oldest and by far the largest in terms of billings is the American Society of Composers, Authors, and Publishers (ASCAP), but the larger, as measured by number of "affiliates," is Broadcast Music Incorporated (BMI). These two agencies combined collect over 95% of all U.S. performance royalties, with the Society of European Stage Authors and Composers (SESAC) receiving the remainder. All three organizations are protectors of composers' rights.

About 60% of performance royalties are derived from use in television, radio, and films, and the major agencies have accordingly developed extensive computerized logging and sampling procedures to assure that composers receive proper remuneration for performances of their works anywhere in the world. To accomplish this, agencies in other countries cooperate with ASCAP, BMI, and SESAC.

The formulas used to determine royalty rates depend on the frequency of use and length of time the music is used, the estimated size of the listening audience, and other factors. For example, classical compositions are accorded more weight than popular jingles. Greater weighting compensates for the relatively greater expenditure of effort in classical composition and for the probable smaller size of audience and lesser frequency of play.

However, the sizes of royalties and the ways in which licenses should be granted to television (i.e., blanket vs. specific performances) have often been subject to proposed legislative changes.[7]

Mechanical royalties Under so-called compulsory licenses, these royalties are derived from publication in sheet-music form (normally at a rate between 3% and 10% of retail price per copy in the United States) and from sales of recordings. But of the two sources, recordings are much more important. As of 1988, the rate for each recorded copy of a song was raised to 5¼ cents for a length of five minutes or less, with 1 cent charged for each additional minute or fraction thereof.

To keep pace with inflation, mechanicals are subject to upward revision over time and as reviewed by the Copyright Royalty Tribunal.[8] Publishers generally split such royalties 50:50 with new writers and 25:75 with more established composers (after deduction of a 4½% collection charge by the Harry Fox Agency).

Synchronization fees In addition to paying a performance fee, anyone using music in films requires a synchronization license. These royalties are individually negotiated by the various parties, but they are normally based on established standards for music length, potential audience, and frequency of use.

Publishers' synchronization and mechanical fees usually are collected from film and record companies by the Harry Fox Agency, which is a wholly owned subsidiary of the National Music Publishers Association. This agency licenses copyrights for commercial recordings, audits the books of record manufacturers, licenses music used in television and movie productions and commercials, and licenses background music used in public places (Figure 5.1).

Copyright The aforementioned royalty streams, including license fees from jukebox and other uses (e.g., wired music services such as Muzak®), were adjusted by Congress in a 1976 revision of the original but technologically outdated 1909 copyright law. The new law grants copyright owners of a musical composition the exclusive right to be the first to record

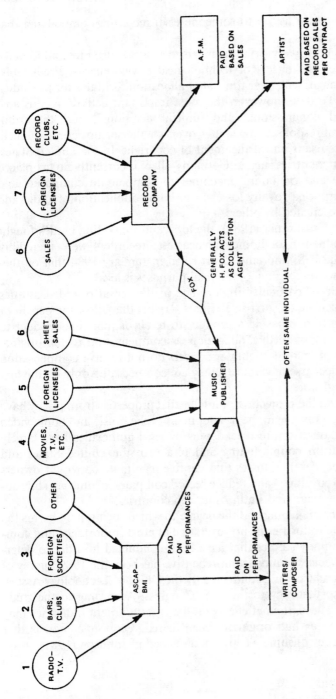

Figure 5.1. Music income flow in the entertainment field. *Source:* Arthur Young & Co. (prepared by E. Cook).

1. Paid on contractual amount based on percentages.
2. Paid on contractual amount based on usage, etc.
3. Paid on usage of songs.
4. Paid on negotiated amount per use.
5. Paid on contractual amount per use.
6. Based on sales of actual units.
7. Based on percentage of sales of product.
8. Based on percentage of sales of product.

and distribute (or to assign to someone else) recordings embodying that composition.[9]

The Copyright Royalty Tribunal meets to arbitrate disputes and to make adjustments for the effects of technological developments. Predictably, many such changes will, over time, alter allocation formulas for the industry's income. To date, however, the most important activity in this area has concerned congressional and judicial decisions[10] and the tribunal's procedural responses to disputes over whether or not home duplication for private use is an infringement of copyright. In the United States, unlike in other countries such as Germany, there is currently no tax placed on blank tape and on taping machines to compensate composers and authors for purported royalty losses from home duplication of audio and visual materials created by others.

As described by Lardner (1987), the legal and marketing battles fought over the introduction of home videocassette recorders were incredibly intense until the U.S. Supreme Court ruled in January 1984 that off-the-air taping of movies for noncommercial purposes is legal.

Another issue of particular importance in the rental of videocassettes involves the doctrine of "first-sale" rights – rights that allow the person or company initially purchasing a product to resell or rent that product to other parties without further obligation or compensation to the original seller. Because of first-sale rights, producers do not receive compensation each time a videocassette is rented; they are compensated only on the first sale to the rental stores.[11]

Copyrights and the protection of intellectual properties from piracy have played an important role in the development of the music and home video businesses. Although severe crackdowns by legal authorities have largely curbed losses from counterfeiting and piracy in the United States and Western Europe, revenue losses that deprive legitimate copyright owners of their entitled royalties[12] and reduce record company income are still substantial in some Asian and Latin American countries.

The issue of home taping and the degree to which such taping harms the video and music industries is, however, one of great importance and complexity. Of the many studies that have been conducted in order to determine the net effects, the most comprehensive has been the 1989 Survey of Home Taping and Copying conducted by the Office of Technology Assessment, an advisory agency to the U.S. Congress. According to the study (U.S. Congress 1989), the net effects on the entertainment industries may not be as severe as had originally been feared. Economic models that explain why some consumers copy are discussed in Johnson (1985).

Guilds and unions

The effects of labor-union contracts, primarily those of the American Federation of Television and Radio Artists (AFTRA) and the American Federation of Musicians (AFM), extend to virtually every area of the music-making business. Singers, soloists, and choral ensembles are generally represented by AFTRA, whereas other musicians, including conductors, arrangers, copyists, and instrumentalists, are members of the AFM. However, opera, ballet, and classical concert and recital performances may be covered by the American Guild of Musical Artists (AGMA), and other representations may be made through the Actors Equity Association or the Screen Actors Guild. The New York Dramatists Guild is a trade association representing lyricists, composers, and writers for the Broadway musical theater (see also Chapter 11).

As in the business of filmed entertainment (see section 3.3), labor unions certainly help their employed membership by bargaining for higher wages and pension benefits. But it can also be argued that if it were not for the high production costs inherent in using union performers, there might be many more productions in which musicians could find work, albeit at lower average wages. It is not unusual for new artists and new record companies to attempt to circumvent the use of union labor, or for background-music recordings to be made in Europe, where labor costs are much lower.

Both AFTRA and AFM have tried to maintain strict union shops, but right-to-work laws in various states have reduced union influence, especially in the rock, country, and R&B segments. However, if a record master copy is transferred from a nonunion independent producer to a record company that is party to AFM agreements (which most record companies of any significance are), then union control over wages is reasserted. This control also appears in areas such as voice overdubbing, a situation in which a union contractor will charge a producer for an additional voice even though it is only electronically mixed.

Royalty artists, who are entitled to AFTRA scale plus royalties based on the number of records sold, must also conform to union-negotiated rules. And for musicians who participate in making broadcast commercial spots, there are, of course, extended repetitive payments. Whenever an AFTRA member performs on tape for one medium and that tape is used in another medium, the performer receives additional payments.

Concerts, theaters, and "serious" music

Concerts by popular performers (in which an advance against a percentage of anticipated gate receipts may be obtained) are often profitable for their organizers if they are skillfully budgeted and well planned. Concert tours can provide significant income for performers and, more important, can leverage sales of records and other licensed merchandise.[13]

Much less likely to turn a profit are theater presentations on Broadway, summer musical theater, classical-music concerts, and opera. In fact, it has been estimated that, on average, performing-arts organizations, including symphonies, operas, and ballet companies, earn less than 40% of their costs of operation (Baumol and Bowen 1968). Raising ticket or subscription prices, or increasing the number of performances, often further increases operating deficits (see Chapter 11). Thus, financial support from municipal and private sources is normally required to sustain these activities, and Congress, through creation in 1965 of the National Endowment for the Arts (NEA), has provided support by allocating federal funds to match local contributions. Some 1,500 orchestras and 600 opera companies, plus individual artists, are eligible for grants. (The NEA's legislative mandate is limited to support for individuals and organizations that are tax-exempt.)

5.3 Making and marketing records

Record markets

The experience in the United States and Canada since World War II suggests that development of a strong and rapidly growing market for recorded music requires conjunction of several elements. First and foremost is an expanding teenage/young-adult population within a thriving middle class. It is essential, moreover, that there be national advertising media in which large and cost-efficient marketing campaigns can be placed and that retail outlets be well stocked. And it helps to have steady price and performance improvements in audio hardware and recording technology.

All of these elements were present in the postwar period, and, not surprisingly, the recorded-music business grew from $100 million to almost $6 billion in domestic retail sales in the space of 40 years (Table 5.1). Because many of the same factors were present in other developed countries, sales of recorded music outside the United States have grown similarly – currently exceeding domestic sales by an estimated 35%.

In the United States unit shipments of albums increased at a compound annual rate of 3.9% between 1971 and 1980 (Figure 5.2). But in the early 1980s, the combination of economic recession, higher prices, more off-the-air taping, and other factors caused shipments to decline. Over this period, however, the prerecorded-cassette format gained steadily against the vinyl, eight-track, and open-reel tape configurations – and by 1984, cassettes accounted for over half of total album units. Interest in off-the-air taping of music also generated demand for blank audiocassettes; shipments of these rose from an estimated 150 million units in 1978 to 366 million units in 1988 (Table S5.4).

The largest group of record buyers, according to surveys (see Table S5.1) in the early 1980s, were young adults, not teenagers. Teens of the 1950s and 1960s apparently carried an interest in music well into their twenties and thirties, and they thereby broadened the market's demographic boundaries. In addition, there was a substantial increase in the number of new households as the relatively large post-World War II population cohorts

Table 5.1. *Music industry shipments in millions of units and dollars,*
1973–88

Year	Total	LPs/EPs	Cassettes	CDs	Singles	8-track and other
Units shipped (net after returns)						
1973	614.0	280.0	15.0		228.0	91.0
1974	592.0	276.0	15.3		204.0	96.7
1975	531.8	257.0	16.2		164.0	94.6
1976	590.9	273.0	21.8		190.0	106.1
1977	698.2	344.0	36.9		190.0	127.3
1978	726.2	341.3	61.3		190.0	133.6
1979	701.3	318.3	82.8		195.5	104.7
1980	683.7	322.8	110.2		164.3	86.4
1981	635.4	295.2	137.0		154.7	48.5
1982	577.7	243.9	182.3		137.2	14.3
1983	578.0	209.6	236.8	0.8	124.8	6.0
1984	679.8	204.6	332.0	5.8	131.5	5.9
1985	653.0	167.0	339.1	22.6	120.7	3.6
1986	618.3	125.2	344.5	53.0	93.9	1.7
1987	706.8	107.0	410.0	102.1	82.0	5.7
1988	761.9	72.4	450.1	149.7	65.6	24.1
Dollar value						
1973	2,001.0	1,246.0	76.0		190.0	489.0
1974	2,186.4	1,356.0	87.2		194.0	549.2
1975	2,378.3	1,485.0	98.8		211.5	583.0
1976	2,732.0	1,663.0	145.7		245.1	678.2
1977	3,500.8	2,195.1	249.6		245.1	811.0
1978	4,131.4	2,473.3	449.8		260.3	948.0
1979	3,685.4	2,136.0	604.6		275.4	669.4
1980	3,862.4	2,290.3	776.4		269.3	526.4
1981	3,969.9	2,341.7	1,062.8		256.4	309.0
1982	3,641.6	1,925.1	1,384.5		283.0	49.0
1983	3,814.3	1,689.0	1,810.9	17.2	269.3	27.9
1984	4,370.4	1,548.8	2,383.9	103.3	298.7	35.7
1985	4,387.8	1,280.5	2,411.5	389.5	281.0	25.3
1986	4,651.1	983.0	2,499.5	930.1	228.1	10.4
1987	5,567.5	793.1	2,959.7	1,593.6	203.3	17.8
1988	6,254.8	532.3	3,385.1	2,089.9	180.4	67.1

Source: Recording Industry Association of America.

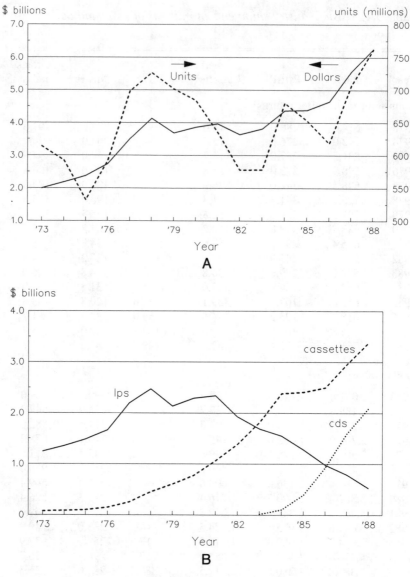

Figure 5.2. Recorded-music industry, 1973–88. (a) Manufacturers' shipments. (b) Sales by configuration (at suggested list price). *Source:* RIAA.

matured. Major improvements in semiconductor technology had, by the late 1970s, also brought down the prices of stereo components for home and car. And during this period, the emergence of FM stereo radio as the popular music medium of choice cannot be overestimated.

Nevertheless, these trends were not strong enough to overcome the generally deteriorating economic conditions that appeared in the early 1980s. Because of the much higher costs of petroleum-based products such as vinyl, record prices were sharply raised, and there was a noticeable decline in the quality of vinyl pressings. Indeed, for a while it was not uncommon for consumers with top-of-the-line stereo receivers located in strong-signal areas to make off-the-air recordings whose quality matched or surpassed that of some store-bought records.

But changes in the system of distributing music products also had an important effect on the industry's sales. Until the late 1970s, records were essentially distributed on consignment – with unsold units returnable for full (or nearly full) credit against new albums. This meant that many stores could be opened on shoestring financing. Rampant inflation and a slowing in unit growth, however, led to a breakdown of the system as undercapitalized retailers began paying their bills with "plastic" (i.e., returned records) instead of cash.

To end these abuses, the major distributors sharply curtailed their returns policies. This meant that for the first time, retailers were faced with a significant inventory risk, and they reacted accordingly by becoming much more cautious and selective in their purchases. That, in turn, made manufacturers and distributors less willing to risk large sums on unproven new artists.

Great success up to the mid-1970s also led to sloppiness in budgeting and cost control, mostly in the areas of artists' royalty guarantees and marketing. Bidding for star performers reached unreasonable heights, as many large record companies subsequently found that even stars could not consistently generate the ever-increasing "megaton" record shipments needed to underwrite large royalty advances. Once the growth of unit shipments stalled, major cost reductions had to be implemented throughout the industry.

By 1983, the industry's financial situation had stabilized. But more importantly, the advance of technology once again – as it had so often before – caused the music industry's growth rate to accelerate. The catalyst this time was the development of low-cost, high-speed microprocessor and memory devices: In brief, the era of cheap computing power had arrived. And with this power came the ability to digitalize sound, that is, to reduce sound to equivalent numerical data through frequent sampling and processing. Such digitalization eliminates undesired noise while providing a marked improvement in fidelity over analog reproduction techniques.

Immediately, the ability to digitalize sound led to the introduction of music synthesizers – computers capable of producing and mixing sounds in a manner not possible with traditional instruments – and to compact discs.[14] These developments stimulated new interest in music as fresher, cleaner sounds became available, and as consumers also then decided to upgrade their libraries of favorite music into the compact disc configuration.

Yet that is not all. By the early 1980s, as low-cost videocassette machines became available, a whole subindustry of music video recordings sprang up. And the advent of satellite-delivered cable television channels allowed the introduction, in 1981, of Music Television (MTV), a 24-hour network that bases its programming on a mixture of rock-music videos, music news, and specials.

Deal maker's delight

Production agreements As seen in previous chapters, creativity is not limited to finished products; it also appears in financial and manufacturing arrangements. And if anything, the scope for deal making in records as compared to movies is increased because of the relatively smaller capital commitments and fewer people involved in making a recorded-music product. Still, most record companies are highly selective in signing talent, and fancy deal making is a privilege mostly reserved for already established artists.

Whereas in the early days of the business the record companies simply signed an artist and had an in-house producer known as an artist-and-repertoire (A&R) man guide the project, today there is a tendency for artists to work with independent producers. Like record-company A&R people, these independents will help the artist select material and a music style, decide where and how the recording is to be made, and generally watch over budgets for studio recording and rehearsal times, mixing, and editing. Sometimes they also become involved with the design and artwork for album liner notes.

Variations in financial arrangements usually develop as independent producers and independent "labels" (companies) work with the artist as subcontractors for the major record companies.[15] But as Baskerville (1982, p. 300) notes, deals are typically structured in one of the following ways:

1. The label signs the artist, and an in-house producer, compensated through salary plus perhaps some royalties, handles the project.
2. Talent is already under contract with a label, and the label retains an independent producer or company to deliver a master tape. The outside producer will intially receive a production fee and also negotiate a royalty of 1% to 5% based on retail sales. The record company will normally set the budget to which the independent will adhere.
3. Independent artists and producers make a master tape and then try to sell the master to a label. If accepted, the label compensates the artist-producer team through royalties perhaps earned against an advance.
4. A label may form a joint venture with an independent producer or artist. Royalties will then be shared in proportion to the size of financial commitments.
5. An artist may form a production company to make and deliver a mas-

ter tape to a label. A free-lance producer may then be hired by the artist's production company.

6. An artist may be employed by a corporation that then sells the artist's services to a label in return for royalty considerations.

Within this context, many "independent" labels emerge. But few are truly independent because the initial financing and manufacturing and distribution of the final product are much more efficiently handled by large record companies that are able to diversify their risks over many different labels and take advantage of economies of scale.

Independent labels and producers may also negotiate adjustments when, as is often the case, a given individual functions in several different capacities. The producer may be trained in both music and audio engineering; the performing artist may be a co-producer and fund-raiser. In the end, however, whether the producer or artist receives the most compensation depends on relative bargaining strengths. Important producers may receive from the label several percentage "points" in addition to production fees between \$25,000 and \$100,000 (half paid on signing) that are nonrecoupable against royalties. In total, this may be more than what the artist receives.

Talent deals Talent royalty rates depend on the degree to which the artist is in demand. Major artists often can command over 15% of retail price, which would amount to well over \$1.00 per album, but minor players will be signed at a rate of 10% or less of retail. A sliding scale may be used whereby the first 100,000 units sold are at 9%, and for every 100,000 units thereafter the royalty rate is scaled upward by one or two percentage points. In most cases, record companies will estimate the artist's annual royalties and then advance about one-half that amount.

An important reason for the decline in record-industry profitability during the late 1970s was excessive royalty bidding by major companies for popular artists whose contracts were up for renegotiation. Significant losses ensued when large royalty advances were not covered by subsequent album sales. To at least partially protect themselves from such potential losses, companies may sign an artist to deliver several albums over a certain period of time and then, as in films, partially cross-collateralize royalty advances over those albums.

Production costs

Once the deal-making phase is completed, musicians and producers begin a long process that leads to delivery of a completed master. Decisions concerning the time and place of recording and the numbers of backup singers and musicians must be made. Rehearsals must be scheduled.

Production costs for a popular album generally are budgeted for at least

$125,000, and if a lot of studio time is used to "fine-tune," costs can soar well past $300,000. As production costs rise, it of course becomes progressively more difficult for the record company to make a profit from the album.

Having delivered a master tape mixed down to two-channel stereo and formatted for an album, the producer will generally be paid the remaining half of the production fee, or an advance on royalties. But for the record company, other expenses are just beginning: A marketing campaign must be planned, album-cover artwork must be commissioned, and a timetable for pressing must be established. This last point is sometimes of particular importance because release strategies have occasionally been hampered by production bottlenecks in the pressing stage.[16]

As previously noted, rapidly rising prices for raw materials, particularly petroleum-based vinyl, had affected retail record prices in the late 1970s. But by the mid-1980s, increases in raw-materials costs for cassettes and compact disc composites, for album covers and liners, and for outer plastic shrink-wrapping had moderated along with the overall rate of inflation. The costs of manufacturing a typical CD or cassette album as of 1990 are shown in Table 5.2 (a) while the costs associated with production and shipment of a traditional vinyl album are shown in Table 5.2 (b). As can be seen, the profitability of the CD configuration compared to the others is most impressive.

Marketing costs

Marketing campaigns for albums can be very costly because they frequently involve concert tours, cooperative advertising with local retailers,

Table 5.2 (a) *Manufacturing costs for compact discs and cassettes, circa 1990*

	Compact discs	Cassettes
Revenues/unit	$8.75	$5.50
Cost/unit		
Raw media	$0.90	0.45
Pressing/recording costs	0.80	0.35
Jewel box/plastic case	0.40	0.25
Package	0.35	0.25
Printed material	0.10	0.10
	$2.55	$1.40
Gross profit/unit[a]	$6.20	$4.10

[a]Gross profit before royalties and overhead (including writedowns of unsuccessful albums) and marketing costs.

Table 5.2. (b) *Costs for vinyl LPs*[a]

A. Financial commitment also called "investment" or "risk" of record company
    1. Recording costs of LP: $125,000 to $250,000
    2. Promotion, advertising, initial pressing: $100,000 to $300,000, plus video – formidable costs for no return
    3. Advance to artists
B. Profit structure: the following structure is based on a wholesale selling price of records, about $4.30 on an $8.98 suggested retail list price
    1. Costs
        (a) Pressing and jacket: $.75 to $.80
        (b) Royalties to artists and producers: $0.82 (12% royalty, all-in, beginning artist – all records shipped); each 1% increases rate by about 6.8 cents
        (c   Copyright royalties: 35 cents (average)
        (d) AFM: $0.08 to $0.09
        (e) Freight: $0.10 or more
        (f) Costs of distribution: $0.60, some costs not readily available on a per-unit basis.
        (g) Approximately $1.60 to $1.65 profit on these figures before the following (varies widely with structure):
             (i)   Promotion advertising: Uncertain figure per unit, e.g., $100,000 over 200,000, LPs = $0.50 per unit
             (ii) Overhead
             (iii) Returns, obsolescence, write-offs
    2. Compare, however, profits where millions of units, as opposed to 100,000 units, were involved
    3. Breakdown of cost for singles: $1.99 retail

Cost:	$0.21
Copyright:	0.08
AFM:	0.02
Shipping:	0.01–0.50
Royalty:	at $1.99, at 11% royalty rate, $0.17 each record shipped

---

[a] *Source:* L. Lee Phillips, Esq. of Manatt, Phelps, Rothenberg, and Tunney (Los Angeles). From Biederman and Phillips (1980); data updated to 1984.

in-store merchandising aids (possibly including stand-alone displays, posters, and T-shirts), radio and television commercials, and "promo" press kits. Free records are also sent to hundreds of radio stations. For most albums, marketing costs might average $75,000, but for a release by a major artist, costs might exceed $300,000.

Promotional efforts are generally aimed at the most influential reporting stations, that is, some 200 to 300 stations monitored by tip sheets and trade papers such as *Cash Box* and *Billboard.* Indirect spending for promotional purposes also used to include significant sums for bribery of station managers and program directors until such so-called "payola" was publicized and outlawed in the 1960s. Nowadays, virtually any station of importance is extremely careful to set policies limiting the size and frequency of gifts or favors that employees are allowed to accept.[17]

But to aid in promotions, record companies also have staffs of "trackers" whose job it is to know which songs and albums radio stations around the country are adding or deleting on their play lists. With popular-music stations able to add at most three or four new cuts per week to their lists, competition for airplay is intense, as can be seen from the fact that every year an estimated 2,600 albums, averaging some 10 cuts per album, are released.

This enormous "wastage," where perhaps as little as 10% of new material must make a profit large enough to offset losses on the majority of releases, is even worse than in films, where, on average, 7 of 10 projects are losers. However, the most popular recordings – especially those by new artists – are immensely profitable, and again, as in other entertainment industry segments, a small part of the product line will generate a large part of the profits.

Distribution and pricing

With wastage so high, and with all but the most successful recorded-music products having a relatively short life cycle, lasting at most a few months, there is no room for distribution inefficiences. And because efficiency in this area requires that retailers located over a wide geographic swath have their inventories of hits quickly replenished, most records are distributed by large organizations with sufficient capital to stock and ship hundreds of thousands of units on a moment's notice.

The two major record distributors in the United States are WEA, the distribution arm for the Time Warner Inc. labels (Warner Bros., Elektra, Atlantic, Asylum, Nonesuch, Geffen), and CBS (Columbia, Epic, Masterworks), which was bought by the Sony Corporation of Japan in a 1987 transaction described by Boyer (1988).[18] Together, these companies handle about half the records sold in North America, and about 35% of the total elsewhere.

Somewhat smaller in the United States, but still important distributors on a worldwide basis, are the Dutch-owned Polygram Group (Deutsche Grammophone, Decca, Mercury, Polydor, London, A&M, Island) and the German-owned BMG or the Bertelsmann Group (RCA, Ariola, Arista). MCA records (MCA, Motown) and the English-owned EMI (Capitol, Angel, Manhattan, Blue Note) are also significant, but operate on a lesser scale. For the most part, the market shares of these major distributors tend to be fairly stable over long periods.[19]

Success in distribution depends on the size of capital commitment and on the ability to quickly sense where and how well new music is selling. To this end, distributors employ large staffs of sales and promotion people and rely extensively on outside intelligence-gathering sources. But whereas this structure works well in large regions, major distribution organizations are less efficient in servicing smaller stores and out-of-the-way territories. Thus, there exists a second tier of smaller independent distributors, known as one-stops, who handle all labels, including those of the majors. One-stops evolved in the 1940s to accommodate the needs of jukebox operators; today they also handle orders from small stores.

Another significant distribution channel for records is through clubs and *rack jobbers*. CBS owns the largest record club in the United States, and RCA the second largest. Clubs account for about 10%–12% of total dollar volume.

Rack jobbers, primarily Handelman and Lieberman Enterprises, now a subsidiary of LIVE Entertainment, have also substantially contributed to the growth of the music business since 1950, and more recently to the growth of the home video industry.[19] "Racks" may operate record departments in space leased from department stores. Or, for maintaining inventories and promotion displays in record departments owned and operated by other parties, they may earn fees based on a percentage of sales. Agreements with rack jobbers can take many different forms and may include diverse retailing environments such as drugstores and supermarkets, but the main attraction is always that the jobber can obtain quantity discounts and can provide expertise in selecting and maintaining inventory for products with a relatively short life cycle.

Rack jobbers, in effect, thus absorb the nonspecialized retailer's risk of purchasing too much of the wrong product or too little of the right product. In return, jobbers operate on the spread between large-quantity discount prices of major distributors and their own higher quasi-wholesale prices. Generally, the jobber's risk of guessing wrong on the order size for a particular item is reduced through diversification over many titles, and also through some return privileges. The margin for error, though, is not too large, especially when changes in musical tastes become abnormally volatile.

Last in the distribution chain is the cutout wholesaler, who buys, for prices at or below cost, records that have been returned to the distributor. *Cutouts*, which appear as secondary merchandise in discount stores, are the industry's errors in judgment as to production quantity and/or quality. They often provide real bargains for patient and knowledgeable consumers.

However, cutouts and overstocks have been an area of dispute and litigation between artists and record companies because contracts are normally written in terms of royalties on the number of recordings *sold,* not the number manufactured. Such excess recordings may be used in barter for other goods and services, or can be used to raise cash for the record company. Only major artists have the bargaining power to negotiate that excess inventories be destroyed rather than sold as cutouts.

Table 5.3. *Music industry retail-trade census data by selected segments, 1958–87[a]*

Year	No. of establishments with payroll	Receipts ($ thousand)	Receipts ($) per Employee	Establishment
Total retail trade				
1987	1,503,593	1,493,308,759	83,988	993,160
1982	1,421,988	1,037,917,920	71,838	729,900
1977	1,303,621	696,959,644	53,653	534,634
1972	1,264,922	440,221,656	39,267	348,023
1958	1,180,641	187,089,900	23,649	158,465
% change				
1958–87	27.4%	698.2%	255.1%	526.7%
Musical-instrument stores				
1987	4,690	2,321,197	90,151	494,925
1982	5,213	1,877,397	68,505	360,136
1977	5,748	1,602,001	50,880	278,706
1972	4,939	1,054,816	39,638	213,569
1958	3,197	410,280	21,938	128,333
% change				
1958–87	46.7%	465.8%	310.9%	285.7%
Record shops				
1987	6,272	3,930,403	88,507	626,659
1982	4,778	1,903,625	73,604	398,415
1977	3,655	1,122,210	58,914	307,034
1972	2,590	391,133	36,378	151,017
1958	1,859	123,997	22,386	66,701
% change				
1958–87	237.4%	3,069.8%	295.4%	839.5%

[a]Data for 1982 are not entirely consistent with figures from previous years. To obtain greater consistency, slight adjustments have been made to accommodate revisions.
Source: Census of Retail Trade, U.S. Department of Commerce.

As might be expected, major-distributor pricing policies have an important effect on firms farther downstream in the distribution chain. There is, nevertheless, no easy method by which to analyze such policies because all major companies now have different scales for quantity discounts and return-privilege limits. However, the sizes of discounts are normally proportioned according to order quantities, which means that rack jobbers and one-stops operate in wholesaler price niches.

Although wholesale pricing is relatively straightforward, in retail pricing, there is often an interesting economic anomaly in that the newest products in strongest demand may be priced lower than older items in less demand.[21]

For small music retailers forced by marketing considerations to add new video and audio product lines, rapid technological developments are at best a mixed blessing. Proliferation of different cassette and disc formats has substantially magnified capital requirements, and each format introduction multiplies the number of relatively high value stockkeeping units (SKUs) that must be carried in inventory. This is ultimately hastening the consolidation of music and home video software retailing into stronger and larger specialty chain stores (Table 5.3).

5.4 Financial accounting

As might be expected, the corporate financial-accounting perspective is different from that of the artist. From the corporate view, enough profit must be generated to compensate shareholders with a competitive return on investment and simultaneously to underwrite development of as many new talents as possible. Individual artists, of course, are concerned primarily with their own financial statements.

Artists' perspective

Among the major issues that need to be negotiated between artists and record companies are the date of contract expiration, the number of albums committed, exclusivity, foreign-release intentions, and royalties and advances. For example, a contract may require that three master tapes be delivered within three years of signing and may stipulate penalties to be paid if for some reason the albums are not released.

With the possible exception of contracts in the jazz field, labels generally require their artists to provide exclusive services, which may extend to music-video performances on cassettes and discs. Artist contracts may also delineate the foreign countries or territories for which album release is planned. This can be significant in that a major portion of sales may occur outside the United States (sometimes at royalty rates 75% of the domestic rate).

Greatest attention, however, is usually focused on negotiations for artist royalties and advances. Ten percent of retail price is normally a starting point, and percentages are often scaled upward from this level in proportion to sales. Payout increments are frequently contingent on attainment of an RIAA-certified (Recording Industry Association of America) gold-record sales level (500,000 unit sales for albums, 1 million for singles) or platinum-record sales level (1 million albums, 2 million singles).

Contract discussions may furthermore involve issues of creative control, ownership of masters, publishing-rights ownership, production-budget

Table 5.4. *Artist's financial perspective, first gold album*

Album units at $7.98 list price	$7.98
− 10% breakage	−0.80
− 10% packaging fee	−0.80
	$6.38
Royalties:	
10% on first 150,000 units	95,700
12% on next 350,000 units	267,960
15% on all additional units	
Gold-record-album royalties	$363,660
− advance	100,000
Royalties payable by label	263,660

minimums, conditions under which a contract can be assigned to another person or company, the artist's right to audit the firm's books, the label's minimum commitment to spend on promotion, and charge-back items, such as production expenses that the record company has the right to recoup before paying royalties beyond the negotiated advance. Default and arbitration-procedure clauses are also included in many contracts in case of unforeseen disagreements or problems.

Disagreements and problems are especially likely to arise if the label and artist do not have a clear understanding of the royalty base to which the aforementioned royalty rates are applied. The record company may limit the royalty base to 90% of actual sales to allow for "breakage" (damage) of records in shipment. There may also be specifications for discounting royalties by up to 15% for free goods (i.e., promotional copies that are given away). Other discounts to royalties might include 10% for packaging (cover artwork) or 50% for record-club sales. In addition, clauses involving tape sales, merchandising, and cross-collateralizations (see section 4.3) affect the royalty base.

How a relatively new artist with a first gold album might fare financially can be seen from the hypothetical example of Table 5.4, in which significant leverage for sales above 500,000 units is apparent.

Company perspective

Record companies may earn a profit at many different levels of activity, ranging from production fees and breakage charges to distribution. But, as previously indicated, large profits from a few winners must more than offset the many losses. Financial statements of the large, publicly owned recorded-music firms in aggregate provide the best window from which to understand the corporate financial-accounting perspective.

Table 5.5 *Recorded-music industry, revenues and earnings[a]: composite of three companies, 1984–8*

Year	Revenues	Operating income	Operating margin (%)	Assets	Operating cash flow
1988[b]	5,278.2	694.5	13.2	3,060.1	785.8
1987[b]	3,556.0	464.7	13.1	2,357.8	520.0
1986	3,014.3	346.4	11.5	1,650.3	392.7
1985	2,468.4	255.0	9.1	1,440.6	262.5
1984	2,357.8	224.5	9.5	1,340.4	259.0
CAGR[c]	22.3	32.6		22.9	32.0

[a]In millions of dollars, except margin (%).
[b]CBS operating income, assets, and cash flow are estimated for 1987 and 1988, MCA data also includes fees for domestic distribution of home video products.
[c]Compound annual growth rate, 1984–8 (%).

Pretax operating profits and margins for distributors of major labels have historically fluctuated unpredictably (Table 5.5), and steady growth for even the largest organizations is far from assured. Although the basic financial operating structures are similar for all of the major distributors, there are, nevertheless, differences in how interest and overhead expenses are charged to music divisions, and also differences in "return reserves." Such reserves are set aside as a fixed percentage of sales, and are closely related to recent experiences with records returned by retailers. For example, during the late 1970s – when return privileges were still almost unlimited and when retailers beset by high interest rates and declining sales trends sent back unusually large numbers of records – some distributor companies found their reserves inadequate. Losses, instead of profits, began to appear.

The following excerpt from the 1982 Warner Communications annual report illustrates return-reserves accounting policies:

Inventories other than motion picture inventories are stated at the lower of average cost or estimated realizable value. In accordance with industry practice, certain products are sold to customers with the right to return unsold items. Revenues from these sales represent gross sales less a provision for future returns. It is general policy to value returned goods included in inventory at estimated realizable value but not in excess of cost.

Industry practices in this area are delineated by Financial Accounting Standards Board (FASB) statement 48, which specifies how an enterprise should account for sales of its products when the buyer has a right to return the (nondefective) product. The key condition that must be met for applicability of this statement is that the amount of future returns must be reasonably estimable. In the case of music products, there is generally enough volume and historical experience with which to make such estimates.

Royalties earned by artists, as adjusted for anticipated returns, are charged to the expense of the period in which sale of the record occurs. And advance royalties paid to an artist are reported as assets if the past performance and current popularity of that artist provide a sound basis for forecasting recoupment of the advance.

Accounting for license agreements, minimum guarantees, and advance royalties, however, is governed by FASB statement 50, which specifies that licensors should initially report minimum guarantees as a liability, and then recognize the guarantees as revenue as the license fee is earned under the agreement.

Tax treatments

Prior to the 1976 tax-code revisions, recording costs could be treated as totally current expenses deductible from current income, or they could be capitalized and subject to regular depreciation deductions. As of the 1976 revisions, however, for noncorporate producers, the costs attributable to the production of a sound recording, film, or book are deductible – on a flow-of-income basis – pro rata over the period in which the property generates income. This "flow of income" method of cost amortization for noncorporate producers also applies to record master costs and uses the same approach as in the film business, where estimates as to the total amount of income to be received over the economic life of the asset must also be made. Corporate producers, on the other hand, may have the option to treat recording costs as current expenses deductible in the year incurred.

In practice, record masters that have a useful commercial life of more than a year from date of release are rare. However, according to Shemel and Krasilovsky (1985, p. 362), "the costs incurred in preparing master recordings, used for substantially more than one year to produce records for sale, are required to be depreciated over the period that the master recordings are utilized for that purpose."

5.5 Strike up the band

No discussion of the music business would be complete without at least a brief overview of the musical instruments segment. So in closing this chapter, we strike up the band.

Although an estimated 40 million Americans play musical instruments, aggregate industry sales have not grown in real terms since the early 1970s – when unfavorable demographic, economic, and social trends first appeared. Indeed, the percentage of personal-consumption expenditures going to this segment (including sheet music and accessories) has declined noticeably (from 0.21% in 1974 to 0.12% in 1988) as interest in learning to play has declined, and as the availability of equipment and instruction in schools has been significantly reduced.[22]

Shrinking school enrollments – a trend that will reverse in the 1990s – as well as municipal and state funding problems, have had the greatest effects in retarding sales growth. But young people's fascination with video games and computers has also diverted spending that might have otherwise been directed to this area.

Although prior to 1985 there had been several major publicly held instrument manufacturing companies, many of the brand-name divisions of those companies have been restructured into smaller privately owned firms, and financial operating data on the industry are thus now largely unavailable. Census of manufactures data for 1987, however, indicate that the value of shipments in that year totaled $838 million, which was actually (due to an increase of imported goods) below the $925 million shipped ten years before.

5.6 Concluding remarks

The 1980s have been a period of tremendous change for the music industry. For one, the industry has taken on a truly global dimension, which has in part manifested itself in the purchase of two great American record companies, CBS and RCA, by foreign interests.

But just as significantly, there has been a technological revolution in the way music is produced and reproduced. Until the computers of the 1980s, sound was recorded and replayed using embellishments of the processes discovered by Thomas Edison a hundred years before. Yet thanks to recent technological developments, listeners and musicians can be assured that the potential for creation, for enjoyment, and for use of music has never been greater.

Selected additional reading

Baig, E. (1984). "The Can-Do Promotor of the Jacksons Tour," *Fortune* 110(4)(August 20):160.

Brownstein, S. (1986). "Music Videos Hit a Sour Note," *New York Times,* July 6.

Cieply, M. (1986). "A Few Promotors Dominate Record Business," *Wall Street Journal,* April 18.

Kerr, P. (1984). "Music Video's Uncertain Payoff," *New York Times,* July 29.

Knoedelseder, W., Jr. (1985). "Cut Rate Albums Hit Sour Note," *Los Angeles Times,* May 18.

Landro, L. (1985). "Producers, Artists Push Music-Video Sales as Market for VCRs Expands and Changes," *Wall Street Journal,* March 20.

Miller, M. W. (1987). "High-Tech Alteration of Sights and Sounds Divides the Arts World," *Wall Street Journal,* September 1.

Newcomb, P. (1988). "Waiting for the Next Elvis," *Forbes* 142(10)(October 31):122.

Newcomb, P. (1989). "Welcome Back, Grace Slick," *Forbes* 143(10)(May 15):56.

"Now Playing: The Sound of Money," *Business Week,* No. 3065 (August 15, 1988).

Sherrid, P. (1983). "Beautiful Model Meets Sumo Wrestler," *Forbes* 132(6)(September 12):38.

Trachtenberg, J. A. (1984). "The Middleman," *Forbes* 134(2)(July 16):127.

Zaslow, J. (1985). "New Rock Economics Make It Harder to Sing Your Way to Wealth," *Wall Street Journal,* May 21.

6
Broadcasting

Programs are scheduled interruptions of marketing bulletins.

Marketing bulletins, in fact, are the essence of commercial broadcasting in the United States.

This chapter is concerned with the economics of radio and television broadcasting – a topic that is closely tied to developments in the movie, recorded-music, sports, and other entertainment-distribution businesses. By the end, it should be evident that maybe Marshall McLuhan was onto something when he said, "the medium is the message."

6.1 Going on the air

Technology and history

Broadcasting began the twentieth century as a laboratory curiosity; it will end the century as a business generating over $50 billion per year. But monolithic the industry is not. In fact, many subsegments compete vigorously with each other.

Strictly speaking, commercial broadcasters sell time that is used for dissemination of advertising messages. In actuality, though, what is sold is

155

access to the thoughts and emotions of people in the audience. Companies selling beer prefer to buy time on sports-events programs, whereas toy and cereal manufacturers prefer time on children's shows.

To distribute commercial messages to audiences, or, conversely, to deliver audiences to advertisers, four basic broadcasting media have evolved over the last 50 years: AM (amplitude-modulation) and FM (frequency-modulation) radio and VHF (very-high-frequency) and UHF (ultra-high-frequency) television. All of these technologically defined media operate under identical macroeconomic conditions, but different microeconomic conditions.

AM radio was the first medium to gain widespread popularity, during the 1920s. But television (VHF) was well into development at that time, and by the early 1930s the National Broadcasting Company (NBC) had begun transmitting experimental telecasts from the Empire State Building. Nevertheless, not until the 1939 World's Fair did NBC begin regular program service (then regarded as a nearly miraculous technological feat) to those few receivers then in existence. Yet, despite strong early consumer interest in this new medium, receivers did not begin to appear in significant numbers of households until the early 1950s: Economic restraints and contingencies related to World War II and the Korean War and the high initial prices of receiving equipment bridled the industry's progress.

But it was not until the late 1960s and early 1970s, that FM radio (with its high-fidelity stereo-signal capability) and UHF television became financially viable. FM radio achieved this through a shift to album-oriented popular music appealing to a rapidly expanding population of teens and young adults, and UHF television was helped along by the emergence of a third major network (American Broadcasting), more powerful UHF transmitters, and a congressional mandate to manufacture equipment with tuners able to receive UHF.

Indeed, throughout the history of broadcasting, the economic values of television and radio properties have been closely related to the technological characteristics of the means of transmission.

Consider AM radio stations. AM signals bounce off the ionosphere at nighttime and thereby can cause interference with other stations operating on the same frequency hundreds or thousands of miles away. To prevent such interference, the Federal Communications Commission (FCC) does not permit many small stations to transmit, or to transmit at full power, once the sun sets. That obviously limits audience size and reduces a station's value. On the other hand, so-called clear-channel stations are permitted to transmit at a maximum of 50,000 watts (W), and can be heard at all times of the day and night over broad regions of North America.

FM radio, however, is essentially a local medium because signals can rarely be well received beyond a 60-mile radius from the transmitter. And VHF television signals, which have the same travel characteristics as FM,[1] must be boosted by relay stations in order to reach beyond about 100 miles.

Table 6.1. *U.S. broadcasting facilities, 1989*

Service	On air	CPs[a]	Total[b]
Commercial AM	4,957	261	5,218
Commercial FM	4,210	753	4,963
Educational FM	1,398	252	1,650
Total radio	10,565	1,266	11,831
FM translators	1,769	318	2,087
Commercial VHF TV	547	23	570
Commercial UHF TV	527	213	740
Educational VHF TV	122	5	127
Educational UHF TV	218	26	244
Total TV	1,414	267	1,681
VHF LPTV	300	205	505
UHF LPTV	324	1,508	1,832
Total LPTV	624	1,713	2,337
VHF translators	2,722	121	2,843
UHF translators	2,133	443	2,576

[a]Construction permits.
[b]Includes off-air licenses.
Source: Broadcasting, September 4, 1989.

All other things being equal, UHF signals travel even less distance than VHF signals, and thus UHF requires significantly greater electric power for transmission, often more than 1 megawatt (MW). Not suprisingly, then, UHFs were the last to be commercially developed.

Finally, as of the late 1980s, low-power VHF television stations (LPTV) have been introduced. LPTV can meet many strictly local programming needs at minimal cost and can be established complete with satellite earth station and origination equipment for about half a million dollars. With a 1-kilowatt (1 kW) transmitter and a high-gain antenna, a signal can then extend as much as 18 miles from the transmission point.

As of September 1989, there were 4,957 authorized commercial AM radio stations, 4,210 commercial FM stations, and 1,074 VHF and UHF commercial television stations in the United States. In addition, there are hundreds more educational installations and television-signal translators (relay stations) (Table 6.1).

Basic operations

The success of a television or radio station in attracting an audience is measured by *ratings points* – the percentage of households able to receive the signal that are actually tuned to the signal. If, for example, in an area where 100,000 households own radios there are 12,000 listening to a certain station, then that station's *rating* is 12.0.

A station's *share,* however, is measured as the percentage of all households that are actually using their sets and are tuned to a certain program. Assume that a signal area contains 100,000 households with televisions, that 60,000 of those sets are turned on, and that 20,000 are watching channel 2. Then channel 2's share is 33.3.

Regular measurements of ratings and share figures are offered by two major services: Nielsen (A.C. Nielsen Co.) and Arbitron (American Research Bureau). Arbitron takes its measurements over a signal's area of dominant influence (ADI), which essentially coincide with the U.S. Census Bureau's standard metropolitan statistical areas (SMSAs). Nielsen's equivalent is a designated market area (DMA).

In the so-called sweeps months (each November, February, May, and July), local-station advertising rates for upcoming periods are established with the assistance of the ratings measured by these two services. But programming battles are particularly intense in the months of November and February, during which there is a strong seasonal tendency toward stay-at-home viewing and listening. Many appealing "specials" are aired in those months in an attempt to boost ratings.

The methods used by the two services to sample homes using television (HUT) vary to a degree, but will generally provide consistent trend results over time. Nielsen measurements for national network prime-time television shows, that is, programs broadcast in the period 8–11 PM for the East and West coasts (one hour earlier for Central Time and Mountain Time), are made through devices called People Meters that are connected to a scientifically selected sample of over 4,000 homes. The Nielsen television index (NTI) that is so derived then provides advertisers with significant data on the audiences for various programs, and thus forms the basis for how much a network can charge for the commercial time breaks within those programs. For local program and station evaluations, however, the Nielsen station index (NSI) is derived from a combination of People Meters and viewers' diaries.[2]

Advertisers naturally want their messages to be delivered to audiences that will most likely be interested in purchasing their products or services. Advertising agencies accordingly attempt to find programs or stations attracting the best target audience, defined by demographic, income, and ethnic mix: Razor-blade commercials appear regularly on sports/action programs; ads for laundry products appear on the daytime soap operas.

Further distinctions are made between national (network) ads, national spot ads, and local ads. Large brand-name companies with national distribution often find that purchases of national-network time through agencies (which normally receive fees of 15% of their gross billings) are the most efficient (least expensive on a cost-per-viewer basis) means of communicating with potential customers.

Table 6.2. *National advertising expenditures index, 1975–88.*

Year	Network TV	Spot TV	Magazines	Newspapers	Radio	Outdoor	CPI[a]
1975	100	100	100	100	100	100	100
1976	124	133	122	117	118	114	106
1977	150	136	148	131	133	125	113
1978	172	161	177	148	154	139	121
1979	199	177	200	168	167	161	135
1980	222	201	215	180	187	173	153
1981	240	231	241	201	214	194	169
1982	266	269	253	215	236	215	179
1983	302	297	289	250	263	237	184
1984	361	338	337	286	294	260	191
1985	350	370	352	306	328	282	198
1986	362	405	363	328	351	294	201
1987	369	422	383	357	364	306	208
1988	398	440	414	379	394	318	216

[a]Consumer price index.
Source data: Robert J. Coen, McCann-Erickson Worldwide, New York.

However, for some nationally distributed products, a particular local audience can often be reached more effectively through so-called national spot purchases on local outlets, and as arranged with station representatives (reps). Reps are familiar with the various rate cards (prices) and program research demographics, and provide a conduit for time sales for their own broadcasting companies or (if independently organized) for groups of other stations. In 1989, commissionable spot billings for the 13 national TV rep firms were over $7 billion, or more than 90% of all spot time sales. (At an average commission rate of 7% to 8%, estimated rep firm revenues were thus around $500 million in that year.)

On a local level, of course, smaller businesses buy time directly from local stations. Many of these transactions are at unpublished prices.

Broadcasters sell time to advertisers using the concepts of gross rating points (GRP), reach, and frequency. Because a rating point is the estimated percentage of households or of target audience potentially exposed to a commercial, *gross rating points* are the sum of all the ratings figures. *Reach* is the percentage of households (or of target audience) exposed to a message at least once over a predetermined span. It is also called cume, short for cumulative audience. *Frequency* is simply the number of times an ad is used during a period of time. Thus, GRP is reach multiplied by frequency.

Advertisers generally assess the relative expense and efficiency of delivering a message via different media (Table 6.2) on the basis of cost per thousand households (CPM). These figures can be determined from a sta-

Table 6.3. *Annual U.S. advertising expenditures, 1965–88 (in $ billion)*

	1965	1970	1975	1980	1985	1988
Newspapers	4,426	5,704	8,234	14,794	25,170	31,197
Magazines	1,161	1,292	1,465	3,149	5,155	6,072
Farm publications	71	62	74	130	186	196
Television, total	2,515	3,596	5,263	11,469	21,022	25,686
Three networks	1,237	1,658	2,306	5,130	8,060	9,172
Cable networks	—	—	—	45	594	942
Syndication	—	—	—	50	520	901
Spot (national)	892	1,234	1,653	3,269	6,004	7,147
Spot (local)	386	704	1,334	2,967	5,714	7,270
Radio, total	917	1,308	1,980	3,702	6,490	7,798
Network	60	56	83	183	365	425
Spot (national)	275	371	436	779	1,335	1,418
Spot (local)	582	881	1,461	2,740	4,790	5,955
Yellow pages	—	—	—	2,900	5,800	7,781
Direct mail	2,324	2,766	4,124	7,596	15,500	21,115
Business publications	671	740	919	1,674	2,375	2,610
Outdoor	180	234	335	578	945	1,064
Miscellaneous	2,985	3,848	5,506	7,558	12,107	14,531
Total[a]						
National	9,340	11,350	15,200	29,815	53,355	65,610
Local	5,910	8,200	12,700	23,735	41,395	52,400
Grand total	15,250	19,550	27,900	53,550	94,750	118,050

[a]Total is sum of major categories.
Source: Robert J. Coen, McCann-Erickson, Inc., New York.

tion's rate card or schedule, which, as posted with the Standard Rate and Data Service (SRDS), indicates how much half a minute will cost during a specific part of the day, day of the week, and season. Aggregate spending on various media since 1965 is presented in Table 6.3.

As in any other business, discounts for purchases in quantity are normally available. But in addition, because unsold time is lost forever, prices become increasingly negotiable as the broadcast date approaches. Advertisers, stations, and program producers also sometimes engage in *barter,* a practice in which time is swapped for goods and services, or, more commonly, for programming. Barter-syndication deals, which amounted to about $1 billion in 1989 and have risen by over 15% a year in the 1980s, provide advertisers with time that is generally at least 15% less expensive than on the networks.[3]

The microeconomic considerations in commercial advertising, broadcasting operations, and government regulation have been formally inves-

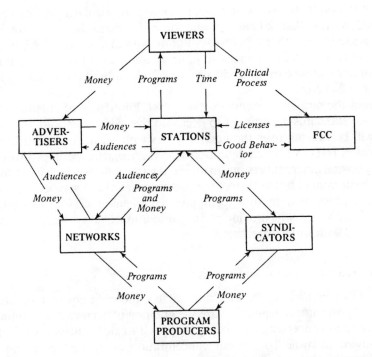

Figure 6.1. Organization of the television industry. *Source:* Owen et al. (1974). ©
1974 Bruce M. Owen.

tigated in a wide variety of studies, several of which will be noted in section
6.2. The organization of the television industry is illustrated in Figure 6.1.

Regulation and technology

Broadcasting is one of the few entertainment sectors heavily regulated by
the government. Such regulation is an outgrowth of the need to allocate
scarce space in the broadcast frequency spectrum according to constraints
imposed by technological factors and world political considerations.[4] Periodic meetings of the World Administrative Radio Conference (WARC)
determine frequency allocations so that international frequency interference is minimized. Politics and historical precedents have also helped
determine which of several available television transmission systems a
country has adopted.[5]

The United States was the first country to develop television into a mass
medium, and in the process the United States standardized the earliest
(now technologically inferior) system, known as NTSC (National Television Systems Committee), with a 525-line scan. The same system is used
in Canada, Mexico, Japan, and 23 other countries. Elsewhere around the
world, however, there are different standards with 625-line scans. The

SECAM (sequential color and memory) system originated in France and is used in more than 20 nations, and the PAL (phase-alternation line) system is used in 37 others. Picture resolution with SECAM and PAL is superior to that with NTSC because of more scanning lines per frame, but their use of alternating current of 50 Hz (vs. 60 Hz in the United States) leads to more flickering.[6]

From the business-economics standpoint, knowledge of different transmission standards is pertinent to decisions that consumers and broadcasters will be making over the next 10 years with regard to high-definition television (HDTV). High-definition television signals, perhaps broadcast using several different versions in different parts of the world, will undoubtedly be dominant by the turn of the century as television sets become much more sophisticated in their computerized signal-processing capabilities. New HDTV sets will provide picture resolution quality nearly as fine as film, and with wider aspect ratios.[7]

Organizational patterns and priorities

Networks and affiliates In the United States, the most obvious manifestations of government regulation are the granting of licenses and promulgation of rules concerning how many stations a single business organization is allowed to own. To prevent concentration of ownership in too few hands, prior to 1985 the FCC had permitted one corporation to own a maximum of seven AM and seven FM radio stations, and a maximum of five VHF television stations (plus two UHFs). Since then, the limit has been lifted to 12 stations each, so long as the total audience does not exceed 25% of the national television audience.[8] However, other significant rules pertaining to cross-media ownership and foreign ownership are less likely to be eased: Newspaper and cable concerns are forbidden to own television and radio stations in the same communities; a single company is prohibited from holding two broadcast properties in a market; foreigners are limited to ownership positions of less than 25% of a holding company with broadcast licenses, or 20% of a license directly.

As of 1989, the three major national television corporations (the networks) – Columbia Broadcasting (CBS), National Broadcasting (NBC), and American Broadcasting (ABC) – owned and operated (O&O) five large-city television stations each, including local "flagships" in New York, Chicago, and Los Angeles. Also, Fox Broadcasting has recently emerged as a competitor to the three majors.[9]

Television networks were established in the late 1940s and early 1950s (and radio networks in the 1920s) by attracting independently owned affiliates to carry regularly scheduled programming produced by the network itself or by outside contractors. Except for news and sports programs, networks currently do not significantly participate in the ownership of productions, but this situation may ultimately be changed through future modifications of the financial interest and syndication rules (see section 4.4).

Each of the three webs, as they are often called in the trade press, now has approximately 200 affiliates that normally receive compensation to carry scheduled national programming. Affiliate compensation in the period 6–11 PM generally is 30%–33% of the station's hourly rate, and the percentage is lower at other hours. Many factors, including physical coverage, number of competing UHFs and VHFs, and long-standing relationships, determine compensation rates.[10]

Although the networks appeared near the beginning of television's history, it was not until the early 1970s that ABC became financially viable. An important catalyst for this change was government regulation that allowed local affiliates access to prime time (7:30 to 8:00 PM) through the so-called prime time access rule. Such reversion of several hours per week to affiliates reduced the networks' inventories of evening time and drove prices up.[11]

By the mid-1980s, general trends toward economic deregulation also began to affect the broadcasting industry: Capital Cities Communications, a group station owner, acquired ABC; NBC was acquired by General Electric; CBS became a target of several takeover attempts; and Twentieth Century Fox and Metromedia merged most of their operations to form a *de facto* fourth network. Moreover, in terms of program content, the traditional distinctions between network affiliates and independent stations (discussed in a subsequent section) had begun to blur.

Outside of the United States, the organization and regulation of broadcasting varies substantially from country to country, but the most common arrangement is to have a mixture of public and private enterprises placed under the supervision of a government agency. However, as privately owned, advertiser-supported networks become significant, they typically begin to assume many of the operating features that have characterized the American television system.[12] Key comparative data concerning television in eleven major countries are provided in Table 6.4, and additional relevant data are presented in Table S6.4.

Ratings and audiences By definition, the network with the most popular shows attracts the largest audience. The ratings leader can command prices at higher than average CPMs because advertising time (spots) on the most popular programs is normally in short supply relative to advertiser demand. Advertisers are interested in shows with high ratings because of their reach, their consistency, and their potential for creation of numerous merchandising opportunities.

In addition, the ratings leader garners higher prices because advertising-campaign managers who buy large quantities of time well in advance of use (so-called "up-front" buyers) often bid aggressively in order to ensure that spots on programs attracting desired targeted audiences are obtained.

Table 6.4. *Television outside the United States, selected countries, 1990*

	TV households (million)	Estimated TV advertising expenditures[a] (US$ billion)	Approximate VCR penetration (%)	TV ad $s per HH
Austrialia	6.2	1.1	62.0	177
Canada	9.8	2.5	60.0	255
France	20.9	2.2	33.0	105
Germany	20.5	1.2	47.0	59
Italy	24.4	3.5	30.0	143
Japan	59.0	11.0	70.0	186
Netherlands	5.6	0.4	46.0	71
Spain	10.8	1.9	35.0	176
Sweden	3.1	0.1	40.0	32
Switzerland	2.3	0.1	35.0	61
United Kingdom	21.0	4.2	60.0	200
Total	183.6	28.2	—	—
Average	—	—	47.1	133
United States	91.0	30.0	70.0	330

[a]For all forms of TV advertising including cable and satellite. See also Table S6.4.

The remaining spots, sold on a "scatter" basis, are normally lower-priced because they are sold closer to broadcast time and may not provide advertisers with optimal reach or frequency. However, exceptions can occur with late-breaking campaigns, or during periods of greater scarcity, when scatter prices can rise despite close proximity to the broadcast date.[13]

Moreover, as we have seen in the case of ABC, the network that leads the ratings also has the potential to attract new affiliates. The addition of affiliates further boosts total network revenue because the percentage of the national population reached by an advertising message is thereby increased.

Except for programming-related outlays, which are the dominant expense components, the costs of network operations remain relatively fixed regardless of ratings performance or number of affiliates. The ratings laggard, however, has proportionately greater total expenses because many new shows must be ordered and then extensively promoted on introduction, and because advertisers disappointed by poor ratings performance often must be compensated with additional "free" time through so-called make-goods (more formally, they are audience-deficiency announcements).

In contrast to television, radio networks are much more varied and numerous, and they are more specifically targeted in terms of local-market demographic, ethnic, and other factors. But whether in television or in radio, it is clear that significant leverage on profits accrues to the ratings leader. Indeed, in network television, a prime-time ratings point won or lost is worth at least $60 million in pretax profits. To place that in perspective, the ABC network had estimated 1989 billings of $2.5 billion, and pretax profit of $165 million. Comparable estimated billings and profits for CBS were $2.3 billion and $85 million, and for NBC $2.9 billion and $300 million, respectively.

Because of the tremendous importance of ratings performance to the profitability of a broadcast enterprise, there has been much research to determine the kinds of programs certain demographically targeted audiences prefer to view. Only recently, however, has there developed a substantial body of research that investigates the behavioral characteristics of television audiences in general. As noted in a comprehensive review by Barwise and Ehrenberg (1988), two important behavioral features have been observed: The *Duplication of Viewing Law,* and the *Double Jeopardy Effect.*

In brief, the Duplication of Viewing Law states that "the percentage of the audience of program B which also watches program A simply varies with the rating of program A, with only small deviations." And, "for pairs of programs on different days and different channels, the duplication of program B with A generally equals the rating of A."[14]

The Double Jeopardy Effect is another interesting phenomenon that "occurs when people have to choose between broadly similar items that differ in popularity. The less popular items are not only chosen by fewer people but are liked somewhat less by those who choose them."[15] In other words, viewers of programs with low ratings are less loyal than viewers of programs with high ratings.

The Double Jeopardy Effect has probably been felt most acutely at the networks, where ratings have been significantly eroded by the increasing competition from cable, independent stations, and videocassettes (Table 6.5). Yet, as noted in Flax (1982) and illustrated in Figure 6.2, for profit-maximizing organizations, there comes a point at which a trade-off of profit for extra market share does not make economic sense.

Inventories Network prime-time inventories used to be limited to six minutes per hour (seven minutes during movies, sporting events, and specials) by voluntary adherence to unofficial guidelines of the National Association of Broadcasters (NAB). But there has been anti-trust controversy regarding how closely networks should adhere to such guidelines, and in the future there will be more flexibility in the number of commercial minutes a network sells during different times of day.[16] Indeed, ABC and CBS began to gradually expand commercial availability in 1982, with ABC adding one minute per evening. All other things being equal, an increase in the supply of time will, of course, cause prices to decline.

For network programs, of the nine minutes per hour set aside for prime-time nonprogram material, affiliates might normally retain 2.5 minutes (60

Table 6.5. *Network television and its competition, 1980 and 1990*[a]

	1980	1990[b]
Prime-time TV households		
Network share	85	65
Network ratings	50.5	37.7
Average rating per network	16.8	12.6
Average households per network (thousand)	13,400	11,500
TV households (thousand)	79,900	91,400
Penetration of new media (% of TV households)		
Basic cable	22.0	57.0
Number of independent stations	119	355
Pay-cable	11.0	47.0
Videocassettes	2.0	70.0

[a]Projected.
[b]Approximations based on standard industry estimates

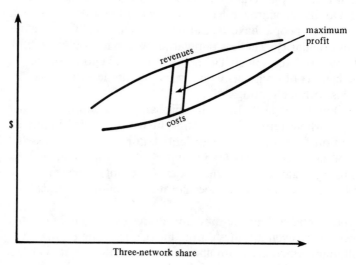

Figure 6.2. Curves for network profit-maximization strategy. *Source:* Flax (1982).

seconds at the start and end, 30 seconds in the middle), with 30 seconds of this used for network and station promos, teasers, identification, and program titles and credits. This compares with 4 to 12 minutes that affiliates retain (weekends at least 7 minutes) in daytime.

Affiliates are motivated to provide broadcast clearances for network shows. The shows are provided to them without expenditure of cash and without the headaches of production financing and creation. In effect, 2.5 minutes per hour on a popular network show usually can generate substantially greater profits for the affiliate than a full nine minutes accompanying a program the local station has either self-produced or acquired elsewhere for cash or barter of time.

Independent and public broadcasting stations Television stations not affiliated with one of the three major networks are known as independents, and in recent years these stations have become serious competitors for network audiences. Independents try to counterprogram against network affiliates by offering news at times earlier or later than the networks, by providing viewers with more material of local interest, and by rerunning popular programs that were previously shown on networks. As such, these stations are the bulwark of the syndication market – into which shows canceled by the networks are sold if there are enough episodes to allow *stripping* (continuous use of episodes over several days per week).

Although independent stations may purchase first-run programs and to a limited extent self-produce programming, they normally rely on syndicated products to fill prime-time schedules. Consequently, in cities with more than one independent station, there may be aggressive bidding to obtain rights to the most popular series coming off the networks. Because rights to a half-hour episode (the most efficient length) of a popular series may sell for upward of $75,000 in a major city, producers often can aggregate substantial sums from all markets (see section 4.4). Stations, however, have in recent years been increasingly inclined to conserve cash through the use of barter-syndication arrangements such as those discussed in Chapter 4 (e.g., see Table 4.10). These arrangements have also been used to good effect by independents known as *superstations* that send their signals via satellite to cable systems around the country.[17]

Syndicated (usually first-run) radio programs generally follow a unified theme (e.g., "The History of Rock 'n Roll") or use a personality (e.g., "Larry King"). In payment for such programming, stations may make various arrangements, including combinations of cash, bartered goods and services, and time. The major independent time-barter company in radio is Westwood One.

Considerably different in temper and means of funding are the television and radio stations affiliated with the Public Broadcasting Service (PBS). These stations receive government subsidies, and additional financial support is funneled to them from corporations and individuals through the nonprofit Corporation for Public Broadcasting, which was set up by act of Congress in 1967. Programs on these stations are distributed by the PBS, and are not interrupted by commercial announcements. However, series programs are usually "sponsored" (supported) by one or several corporate grants.[18]

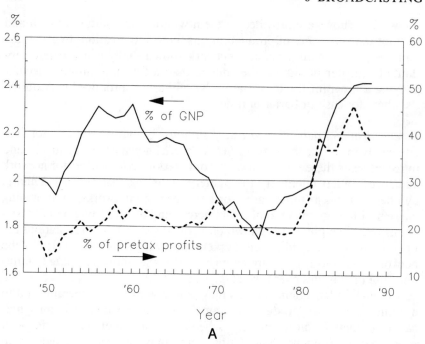

A

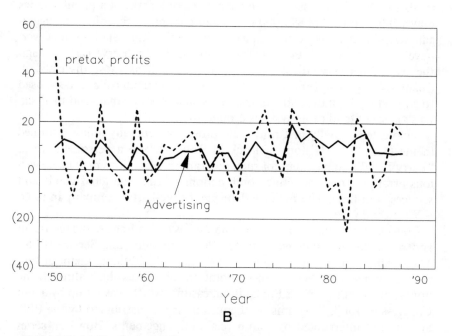

B

Figure 6.3. (a) Total advertising expenditures as a percentage of GNP and pretax corporate profits (excluding IVA adjustment), 1949–88. (b) Pretax corporate profits and spending for advertising, year-over-year percent changes, 1950–88.

6.2 Economic characteristics

Macroeconomic relationships

Broadcasting industry growth inevitably traces a path similar to that of the U.S. economy. Although factors such as presidential elections and Olympic Games every four years noticeably affect supply and demand for the commercial-time inventory, macroeconomic trends are of overriding importance to the industry's secular financial performance.

Corporate profits, though, are perhaps the most important influence on how much companies will spend on advertising through newspapers, magazines, billboards, direct mail, and commercial broadcasting services. During periods of economic duress, many companies find that advertising budgets are tempting and expedient targets for cost-cutting. But there are also many firms, primarily those selling "soft" consumer products (e.g., soap, cosmetics, hamburgers), for which market-share and consumer-awareness considerations make it all but impossible to significantly trim advertising spending except under the most adverse of circumstances. This relationship between expenditures on advertising and corporate profits is illustrated in Figure 6.3.[19]

Nevertheless, because some firms must inevitably reduce advertising budgets during a recession, there is always a decline (unevenly apportioned) in overall demand for broadcasting services when the economy weakens. Large, nationally known brands continue to be advertised on network television with approximately the same degree of intensity regardless of general economic conditions; but prices for network time do soften to the extent that major, highly cyclical consumer-products companies, such as automobile manufacturers, reduce budgets.

Smaller local businesses, however, normally feel a recession much more immediately, and thus may more sharply curtail advertising expenditures on local independent stations. In other words, in an economic downturn, network and *national spot* (regional/local ads for national brands shown on local-station time) advertising may hold up much better than local advertising. The one mitigating factor for stations is that as their spot rates decrease relative to those charged for network time, some ads normally going to networks may instead be placed locally.

Figure 6.4 illustrates various trends and economic relationships in broadcasting, including the quadrennial influences of presidential politics and Olympic Games. Since 1960, television revenues have, on the average, risen 15.2% in major election years and 9.0% in the others. And over that span, advertising as a percentage of personal consumption expenditures has generally held to the range of 3.0% to 3.7%.

Microeconomics considerations

Broadcasting services, like national-defense services, are public goods: The cost of production is independent of the number of consumers who enjoy

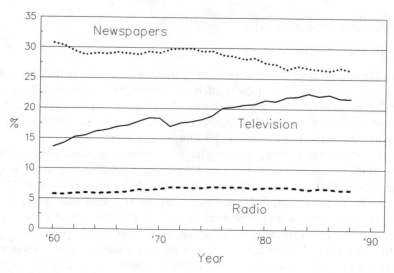

Figure 6.4. Percent shares of total advertising: television, radio, and newspapers, 1960–88. *Source:* Based on data by Robert J. Coen, McCann-Erikson, Inc.

benefits, and one person's consumption does not reduce the quantity available to others.[20] Moreover, broadcasting is a highly regulated industry in which public-welfare and government-policy questions frequently arise. Attempts to resolve such matters have quite naturally involved professional economists.

In fact, economic studies have been especially influential in setting the course of regulation in broadcasting and cable on the following issues: prime-time-access rules, network financial-interest and programming-syndication activities, funding for public broadcasting, distant-signal-importation guidelines for cable systems, and proposals for low-power VHF "drop-ins" (small stations that do not interfere with standard stations on the same frequency in other communities). But because of the public-good characteristics of broadcasting services and the requirement that service providers sometimes be granted monopoly powers, in most studies it has been difficult to evaluate the relative efficiencies of alternative market structures.

Against this background, several microeconomic analyses, including theories of program choice and models of network behavior, have appeared (Noll, Peck, and McGowan 1973). As Owen, Beebe, and Manning (1974, p. 101) noted, in many of these models,

competition under advertiser support tends to produce less diversity and more "wasteful duplication" than is socially optimal. This is a direct parallel to Hotelling's [1929] famous spatial competition example of "excessive sameness." This duplication occurs because there is a tendency for a decentralized system of broadcasting, with limited channel capacity, to produce rivalry for large blocks of the audience with programs that are, if not identical, at least close substitutes.

The economic literature on issues pertaining to broadcasting and advertising has by now become quite broad and sophisticated. Many such analyses have appeared in the *Journal of Business* or in the *Bell Journal of Economics.*[21]

6.3 Financial-performance characteristics

Variable cost elements

Because operating costs are relatively fixed, growth in broadcast revenue is the key variable behind changes in industry profitability. In other words, if demand for commercial time is high, prices for spots rise, but everything from the cost of powering the transmitter to the cost of programming does not vary, at least over the short run.

That does not, however, imply that the rate of increase in operating costs is to be ignored. In fact, profitability can be especially sensitive to changes in the general and administrative (G&A) and programming expense areas.

For networks, programming cost increases have been particularly steep, growing at a compound annual rate of 14.4% between 1971 and 1980, and at an estimated rate of 8.0% annually between 1980 and 1990. Although much of the more than $6 billion that the networks spend each year is for programs that are licensed from the television production divisions of movie studios, a considerable part of their budgets is also allocated to self-produced programming in the form of news, sports, and daytime serials.

News, in fact, costs each network an average of around $300 million a year. But daytime serials (soap operas) can be shot for less than $30,000 per half hour, and game shows for not much more because of relatively low performers' salaries, fixed studio locations, and greater use of videotape. These production cost figures are, of course, significantly below those for regular prime-time network series, in which the production cost per hour is now generally above $1 million an hour.[22]

For networks and some stations, daytime television is therefore the most profitable schedule segment. Program costs are lower, and there are more commercials in each hour than in prime time: Twelve network minutes per hour in daytime versus six minutes per hour in prime time, with local stations having at least three minutes of "adjacencies" plus three minutes of promos in each period. The availability of more minutes thus compensates for a smaller audience base. With networks often deriving about half their profits from daytime, there is always a strong incentive to increase, or to at least maintain, daytime ratings.

Aggregate financial-performance numbers for television and radio stations as compiled by National Association of Broadcasters (NAB) annual surveys, and by the FCC prior to 1980, show that G&A is the largest expense category for affiliated television stations, but programming is the largest and probably most rapidly growing cost of operations for independents. Table 6.6 indicates revenue and expense category proportions for

Table 6.6. *Typical television station revenues (total time sales) and expenses in percent by major categories*

Total time sales (revenues)	%	Expenses	%
Network compensation	7.5	Engineering	11.5
National and regional		Program and production[a]	25.5
advertisements	47.5	News	13.5
Local advertisements	45.0	Sales	12.5
	100.0	Advertisements and promotion	4.0
		General and administrative	33.0
			100.0

[a]The typical independent station spends a far greater percentage (perhaps up to 50% of all expenses) on program acquisition, but much less (perhaps 6% of all expenses) on news. Because of such programming cost, the pretax margin of profit for independents is on average no more than one-half to two-thirds that of the typical affiliate.

what might be a typical station.[23] Aggregate industry data are then presented in Table 6.7.

Financial-accounting practices

The timing of recognition of programming expense by a station and network is usually different from that for the producer-distributors discussed in section 4.4. Stations or networks will not charge the expense when the product becomes "available," but rather when it is broadcast. Using

Table 6.7. *Radio and television broadcasting, revenues and earnings:[a] composite of 64 companies, 1984–8*

Year	Revenues	Operating income	Operating margin (%)	Assets	Operating cash flow
1988	16,614.6	2,657.0	16.0	24,192.2	3,462.6
1987	15,206.6	2,552.1	16.8	23,552.9	3,320.3
1986	14,087.3	2,153.9	15.3	19,645.8	2,786.6
1985	13,117.4	2,178.3	16.6	12,921.0	2,736.0
1984	12,672.5	2,070.5	16.3	11,069.8	2,552.6
CAGR[b]	7.0	6.4		21.6	7.9

[a]In millions of dollars, except for operating margin (%).
[b]Compound annual growth rate, 1984–8 (%).
Source: Communications Industry Report, 1989. New York: Veronis, Suhler & Associates, Inc.

accrual accounting, about two-thirds of the total program expense of a continuing (old) series usually will be recognized on first run, and the remaining third on re-run. Cash payments, however, may vary in response to producer requirements and relative beginning strengths.

Prior to 1975, accounting practices for program materials varied widely. Some broadcasters recorded neither program rights nor related obligations on their balance sheets. In that year, however, an AICPA position paper on this subject brought greater uniformity to the industry's procedures, which were finally formalized in 1982 by issuance of Financial Accounting Standards Board statement 63.

According to this statement, a broadcaster (licensee) will account for a license agreement for program material as a purchase of a right or group of rights. The licensee will then report an asset and a liability for the rights acquired and the obligations incurred when the license period begins and the following conditions have been met:

1. The cost of each program is known or determinable.
2. The program material has been accepted by the licensee in accordance with the agreement.
3. The program is available for its first showing or telecast.

In addition, the asset will be segregated on the balance sheet between current and noncurrent based on estimated time of usage, and the liability segregation will be based on payment terms. The asset and liability is then reported either on a present-value basis in accordance with APB opinion 21 (which describes the general accounting treatment for discounting payables and receivables) or at the gross amount of the liability.

Capitalized costs of program-material rights are carried on the balance sheet at the lower of unamortized cost or estimated net realizable value on a program-by-program, series, package, or day-part basis, whereas network-affiliation agreements are presented as intangible assets.

Costs are then to be allocated to individual programs within a package on the basis of the relative value of each to the broadcaster. As determined earlier, capitalized costs are to be amortized on the basis of estimated number of future showings (or, when this is not possible, over the period of the agreement).

More specifically, feature programs are to be amortized on a program-by-program basis or approximation thereof for a package, whereas program series and other syndicated products are to be amortized as a series. Straight-line amortization may be used if all showings are expected to generate similar revenues (Table 6.8).

6.4 Valuing broadcast properties

Although there are no absolute formulas for valuing broadcast properties, stations change hands often enough[24] that at any given time the going rate

Table 6.8. *Recognition of acquired-program material assets, liabilities, and expenses: an illustration*

Asset and liability recognition[a]

Film	License period		Year of asset and liability recognition		
	From	To	19X1	19X2	19X3
A	10/1/X1	9/30/X3	$8,000,000		
B	10/1/X1	9/30/X3	5,000,000		
C	9/1/X2	8/31/X4		$3,750,000	
D	9/1/X3	8/31/X5			$2,250,000

Expense recognition[a]

Film	Year of expense recognition[a]				
	19X1	19X2	19X3	19X4	19X5
A		$4,800,000[b]	$3,200,000[c]		
B		3,500,000[d]	1,500,000[e]		
C			2,813,000[f]	$ 937,000[g]	
D				1,463,000[h]	$787,000[i]
		$8,300,000	$7,513,000	$2,400,000	$787,000

[a]Under the gross approach, all costs under a license agreement are recorded as amortization of program cost.
[b]$8,000,000 × 60%.   [f]$3,750,000 × 75%.
[c]$8,000,000 × 40%.   [g]$3,750,000 × 25%.
[d]$5,000,000 × 70%.   [h]$2,250,000 × 65%.
[e]$5,000,000 × 30%.   [i]$2,250,000 × 35%.
Source: FASB statement 63. © Financial Accounting Standards Board, High Ridge Park, Stamford, CT 06905, USA. Reprinted with permission, Copies of the complete document are available from the FASB.

in the market can be fairly easily determined. In addition to current profitability, other important variables to consider include the following:

Interest rates
Regional location (fast-growing sun-belt states are preferable to depressed
    areas in industrialized snow-belt states)
Changes in regulatory stringency
Place on the radio dial (in tuning, center is passed most frequently and is
    thus most desirable)
Allotted signal power and time of operation
Surrounding terrain (e.g., mountains and tall buildings may block signals)
Current program style and format relative to other local stations

Real estate value alternatives at transmitter and/or studio site
Amount of debt to be assumed
Short-term and intermediate-term potential effects of cable and other new
  local distribution services

The significance of interest rate levels is no different here than elsewhere. High real rates (i.e., as adjusted for the rate of inflation) not only undercut profits via macroeconomic effects on revenues, but also reduce the number of buyers who can obtain loans and service debt without strain. High rates also diminish the alternative-use value of any real estate that is included in a station transaction and, more significantly, reduce the net present value of future expected cash flows.[25]

In determining station values, the second most important consideration after taking interest rates into account is often whether or not a significant improvement in profits can be effected through alterations in program content and style. In television this may entail changes in local news and sports personalities or changes in prime-time access programs. In radio, changing from "top 40" style to country and western, to all news or all talk, to adult/contemporary (A/C), to middle-of-the-road (MOR), to current hits (CHR), or to album-oriented rock (AOR) might be involved. Indeed, the rise of FM versus AM properties was initiated by format alterations that appealed to young, free-spending audiences.

Of course, all other things being equal, sales of stations with similar characteristics ought to command about the same multiple of *operating cash flow,* which is defined as operating income before depreciation and amortization, interest, and taxes. This cash-flow definition is used because price and value comparisons may be more accurately determined prior to consideration of widely varying debt-financing arrangements and tax circumstances.[26]

So-called leveraged buy-outs – in which money is borrowed against a station's assets (in reality, cash flow) – have also been used to help finance purchases of broadcast properties.[27] But as noted in Newcomb (1989), such leveraged transactions have not always worked according to plan. In the mid-1980s, cash flow multiples rose to 14 or more in response to changes in an FCC rule (in 1984) that permitted corporations to own as many as 12 television, 12 AM, and 12 FM outlets (but in markets collectively containing no more than 25% of the nation's TV homes) instead of 7 each, the previous limit.

A station's *cash flow margin,* that is, its operating cash flow taken as a percentage of its revenue, will generally average in the range of 25% to 45% for a healthy television and radio property. Typically, however, the higher end of the range is only seen at larger stations.

To approximate the value of a broadcast (and, similarly, a cable) property: Assign a multiple of cash flow – say in the range of 8 to 12 times (a higher or lower figure depending on prevailing interest rates). Then subtract from the product of the assumed multiple times the cash flow a figure representing "net debt" – long-term debt minus net current assets. To then arrive at a per-share figure, divide the resulting difference by the number of shares outstanding.

value = (assigned multiple × projected cash flow)
$$- \text{(long term debt} - \text{net current assets)}$$

Such calculations have recently helped to focus attention on the difference in the value of broadcast (and cable) properties as measured by the going multiple of cash flow (i.e., the so-called private market value), and the value of the underlying publicly traded shares. Indeed, the very existence of such discrepancies within an environment of deregulatory political trends has given rise to a spate of corporate takeovers. Even so, however, it is not particularly easy to determine what a reasonable discount to private market value should be. On the one hand, private market prices reflect the powers that derive from total control over an asset. But on the other hand, at least in theory, this positive attribute is somewhat diluted if consideration is given to the taxes that will have to be paid by the seller on liquidation of the asset. In all, then, because of normal uncertainties about the direction of interest rates and the course of economic growth, there is usually a significant speculative element involved, and public-share discounts to private market values are often 30% or more.

6.5 Concluding remarks

The potential for broadcast-industry profitability in any one year depends more directly on the overall condition of the economy than on anything else. But over the long run, growth will most likely be affected by several new developments that will challenge the preeminence of television and radio broadcasting as evolved since the late 1940s. As of the mid-1980s, the major challenges have come from cable and cable-related services, and from proliferation of videocassette recorders.

Of these, cable is probably the more important because new or upgraded systems are able to distribute up to 100 channels without interference from tall buildings and hilly terrain, and without constraint in transmission power. In fact, cable has already significantly eroded network viewership from about 84% of homes in 1980 to an average share of under 65% in 1990. Network audience levels are being sustained only because of expansion in the number of television households to an estimated 91.4 million in 1990 from 79.9 million in 1980.

Although advertisers do not yet use it as a major medium, cable moreover has the potential to eventually expand time inventories and therefore to mitigate price increases for commercial television spots. In addition, although most cable channels undoubtedly will be devoted to video programming, data-transmission and cable-radio services with no advertising may begin to supplant commercial FM radio.

Widespread use of home audio and video recording and playback devices also affects broadcasting. In both audio and video there is an indirect loss of audience through substitutional programming, as, for example, when owners of videocassette recorders (VCRs) play rented movies instead of watching a local station. But the VCR's potential to eliminate commercial messages when recording a program for later use further confounds the best-laid corporate advertising plans.[28] With VCRs and disc players already in some 70% of households by 1990, these problems can only worsen.

Although they are of somewhat lesser significance, video games and other computerized-entertainment software offerings (see Chapter 8) also divert audiences by providing alternative programming for the television screen.

These elements have reduced the growth potential for broadcasting profits, as compared with growth in the 1965–80 period. But the industry is nonetheless far from enervated; few businesses can regularly generate the high relative cash flows and pretax margins of over 20% that are common in broadcasting. And many advertisers will continue to be attracted to network television because of its great efficiency in reaching the mass of consumers. Even at a cost per thousand (CPM) averaging around $8 (in 1990) for a 30-second spot, network television compares favorably against newspapers ($10–$20 CPM).

In addition, many local businesses also still tend to underutilize local-television services, and thus may represent another source of secularly rising demand. Especially at the local level, it will be difficult to replace the strong news- and sports-programming capability of commercial stations.

In summary, broadcasting is a multifaceted, regulated industry now entering a period of maturity in which expansion will be slower and the challenges greater. However, it remains a business in which profit margins are well above average, and in which cash generation is unusually high. As such, broadcasting will, for a long time, continue to be a major source of entertainment.

Selected additional reading

Abrams, B. (1984). "CBS Program Chief Picks Entertainment for 85 Million Viewers," *Wall Street Journal,* September 28.

   (1985). "TV 'Sweeps' May Not Say Much, But for Now That's All There Is," *Wall Street Journal,* February 28.

Berman, S., and Flack, S. (1986). "Will the Network Take It Out of Hollywood's Hide?" *Forbes* 138(4)(August 25).

Botein, M., and Rice, D. M. (1980). *Network Television and the Public Interest.* Lexington Mass.: Lexington Books, Heath.

Brown, P. B. (1983). "Where Else Can You Go?" *Forbes* 131(13)(June 20):48.

Bylinsky, G. (1984). "High Tech Hits the TV Set," *Fortune* 109(8)(April 16):70–81.

Carnegie Corporation (1979). *A Public Trust: The Landmark Reports of the Carnegie Commission on the Future of Public Broadcasting.* New York: Carnegie Corporation and Bantam Books.

Cherington, P., Hirsch, L., and Brandwein, R. (1971). *Television Station Ownership: A Case Study of Federal Agency Regulation.* New York: Hastings House.

Coase, R. H. (1966). "The Economics of Broadcasting and Government Policy," *American Economic Review* 56(May):440–66.

Colvin, G. (1984). "The Crowded New World of TV," *Fortune* 110(6)(September 17):156.

Donlan, T. G. (1983). "Clear Signal: Deregulation Touches off a Wave of Bids for TV Stations," *Barron's,* July 11.

"Estimated U.S. Advertising Expenditures, 1935–1979," *Advertising Age,* April 30, 1980, p. 260; September 14, 1981; May 30, 1983; May 6, 1985.

Fabrikant, G. (1987). "Not Ready For Prime Time?" *New York Times,* April 12.

Foster, E. S. (1978). *Understanding Broadcasting.* Reading, Mass.: Addison-Wesley.

"Has the FCC Gone Too Far?" *Business Week* No. 2906 (August 5, 1985):48–54.

Head, S. W. (1976). *Broadcasting in America: A Survey of Television and Radio,* 3d ed. Boston: Houghton Mifflin.

Kagan, P. (1983). "Broadcasting Bonanza: TV Stations Are Fetching Record Prices," *Barron's,* October 17.

Kneale, D. (1988). "'Zapping' of TV Ads Appears Pervasive," *Wall Street Journal,* April 25.

    (1989). "CBS Frantically Woos Hollywood to Help It Win Back Viewers, *Wall Street Journal,* February 9.

    (1989)."Seeking Ratings Gains, CBS Pays Huge Sums for Sports Contracts," *Wall Street Journal,* October 10.

    (1990) "Duo at Capital Cities Scores a Hit but Can Network Be Part of It?" *Wall Street Journal,* February 2.

Landro, L. (1984). "TV Networks Are Again Producing Films for Release in Movie Theaters," *Wall Street Journal,* December 5.

    (1984). "Independent TV Stations Assume Bigger Role in Broadcast Industry," *Wall Street Journal,* May 11.

Leinster, C. (1985). "NBC's Peacock Struts Again," *Fortune* 112(3)(August 5):26–30.

Levin, H. J. (1980). *Fact and Fancy in Television Regulation: An Economic Study of Policy Alternatives.* New York: Russell Sage Foundation.

Mathewson, G. F. (1972). "A Consumer Theory of Demand for the Media," *Journal of Business* (April)45(2):212–24.

Mayer, J. (1983). "Putting Ads on Public TV Angers Few," *Wall Street Journal,* March 24.

Moore, T. (1986), "Culture Shock Rattles the TV Networks," *Fortune,* 113(8)(April 14).

Newcomb, P. (1989). "Negative Ratings," *Forbes* 143(3)(February 6):138.

Peterman, J. L. (1979). "Differences Between the Levels of Spot and Network Television Advertising Rates," *Journal of Business* 52(4)(October):549.

Poltrack, D. F. (1983). *Television Marketing: Network/Local/Cable.* New York: McGraw-Hill.

Routt, E. (1972). *The Business of Radio Broadcasting.* Blue Ridge Summit, Pa.: TAB Books.

Saddler, J. (1984). "Push to Deregulate Broadcasting Delights Industry, Angers Others," *Wall Street Journal,* April 16.

(1985). "Broadcast Takeovers Meet Less FCC Static, and Critics Are Upset," *Wall Street Journal,* June 11.

Schmalensee, R., and Bojank, R. (1983). "The Impact of Scale and Media Mix on Advertising Agency Costs,"*Journal of Business* 56(4)(October).

Sellers, P. (1988). "Lessons From TV's New Bosses," *Fortune,* 117(6)(March 14):115.

Shames, L. (1989). "CBS Has Won the World Series . . . Now It Could Lose Its Shirt," *New York Times Magazine,* July 23.

Sherman, S. P. (1985). "Are Media Mergers Smart Business?" *Fortune* 111(13):98–103.

Simon, J. L. (1970). *Issues in the Economics of Advertising.* Urbana: University of Illinois Press.

"Television Ratings: The British Are Coming," *Fortune* 111(7)(April 1, 1985):109.

"Television Turns 50," *Broadcasting,* May 1, 1989.

Telser, L. G. (1966). "Supply and Demand for Advertising Messages," *American Economic Review* 56(May):457.

"The Networks Produce Some Panic in Hollywood," *Business Week* No. 2854 (August 6, 1984):90.

Traub, J. (1985). "The World According to Nielsen: Who Watches Television – And Why," *Channels,* January/February.

Waters, H. F. (1988). "The Future of Television," *Newsweek,* (October 17): 84.

Weisman, J. (1987). "Public TV in Crisis," *TV Guide,* (31, 32)(August 1, August 8).

"Why Television Stations Are Such Hot Properties," *Business Week* No. 2795 (June 20, 1983).

Wirth, M. O., and Allen, B. T. (1980). "Crossmedia Ownership, Regulatory Scrutiny, and Pricing Behavior," *Journal of Economics and Business* 33(1)(fall):28–42.

7
Cable

You cannot plan the future by the past. – Edmund Burke

Though said some 200 years ago, this might well be a slogan for executives of fast-growing cable-TV and other new video-media companies in which managements are in a never-ending scramble for franchises, for funding, and for subscribers. In this chapter, the historical and economic relationships among broadcasting, cable,[1] and other new media are explored.

7.1 From faint signals

In the late 1940s, the technological marvel of wireless broadcasting was still in an early phase of development when the first community-antenna television (CATV) systems were being built in mountainous or rural regions where over-the-air television signals were difficult, if not impossible, to receive. CATV was an eminently logical idea, developed, according to legend, by a television set retailer who wanted to sell more sets: With a good antenna atop a nearby mountain and a clear signal as retransmitted by wire (cable), a burgeoning number of new television households would be created.

But until the 1960s, with broadcasting expansively dominant, CATV remained a backwater of the video-communications business. Broadcasters' aggressive lobbying against competition from cable was manifest in arcane FCC regulations limiting the number of distant signals that could be imported into large markets, and prohibiting (in 1970) pay-cable systems from showing movies less than 10 years old and sporting events that had been on commercial television during the previous 5 years.

Pay services evolve

The dreams of pioneers notwithstanding, high and rising interest rates, inability to attract sufficient capital funding, and excessive rates of "churn" (i.e., household connects and then disconnects) plagued the industry well into the 1970s. By 1975, however, FCC restrictions on cable's distant-signal-importation and programming options began to ease. And, more significantly, Time Inc., the giant magazine-publishing company with interests in electronic communications, started a pay-TV movie-distribution organization known as Home Box Office (HBO). In contrast to over-the-air commercial-broadcast television services that provided viewers with ostensibly "free" signals, pay-TV required that a subscribing household make monthly cash payments for programming.

In and of itself, offering of a *pay cable* service as opposed to *basic cable* service, which simply brought a clearer signal from over-the-air broadcasts into the home, was not revolutionary. What made the difference was that pay-TV service was for the first time able to be nationally and simultaneously distributed to local franchises via space-satellite transponders. This technological advance, in effect, now made it possible to simultaneously provide households with several specially programmed movie and sports channels. Basic services thus became only the first of many pay "units" or tiers that the so-called *multiple system operators* (MSOs) – companies that operated more than one cable system – could offer viewers.

Although it was largely unrecognized at the time because of HBO's heavy start-up costs and losses, so was born not only a major new national television network, but also the first serious threat to the movie industry's strong grip on distribution and pricing of its product. Five years elapsed before the filmed-entertainment companies fully understood what had happened, and before a subsequently ill-fated attempt was made at launching Premiere, a pay-channel service owned by four leading studio-distributor companies.[2]

Proliferation of pay services was by then well in progress, and by the late 1970s there were several major national film and special-entertainment offerings in competition to HBO. The most important of these were "Showtime," owned by the former Teleprompter and Viacom, and the Warner-Amex-sponsored "The Movie Channel."[3] However, at least 50 other enterprises catering to disparate groups of viewers had also sprung up.[4]

Table 7.1. *Top 15 cable networks*[a]

Rank	Cable network	Start-up date	Systems	Subscribers (million)
1	ESPN	September 1979	19,000	50.1
2	Cable News Network	June 1980	8,200	47.9
3	TBS	December 1976	12,885	45.6
4	USA Network	April 1980	10,100	45.2
5	CBN	April 1977	8,225	42.7
6	MTV	August 1981	5,050	42.6
7	Nashville Network	March 1983	7,510	42.0
8	Nickelodeon	April 1979	6,245	41.4
9	Lifetime	February 1984	4,200	39.9
10	C-Span	March 1979	2,950	39.0
11	Nick at Nite	July 1985	3,335	37.1
12	Weather Channel	May 1982	3,200	36.0
13	Arts & Entertainment	February 1984	2,600	36.0
14	Discovery Channel	June 1985	3,700	35.8
15	Headline News	January 1982	3,200	32.6

[a]The subscriber number does not represent the actual viewing audience, but rather the total universe that can receive the network in question.
Source: Channels, March 1989.

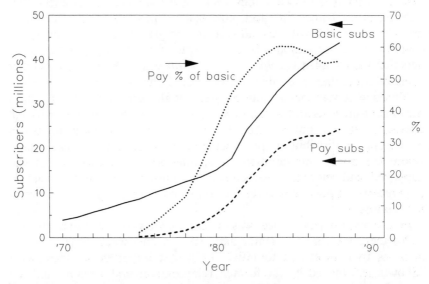

Figure 7.1. Cable industry trends, 1970–88. Number of basic-cable subscribers (solid line) and pay-cable subscribers (dashed line), and pay-cable subscribers as a percentage of basic-cable subscribers (dotted line).

However, the great eagerness with which new cable households embraced the plethora of pay channel offerings misled many MSOs into bidding too aggressively for the then unbuilt large city franchises that had come up for proposal in the late 1970s and early 1980s: Later on, many financially overextended MSOs had to renege on their promises as construction and operating cost estimates soared well beyond the points at which reasonable returns could be expected.

Also, despite enormous industry growth, many services during this time continued to experience substantial losses as revenues from subscriptions and other sources were insufficient to cover operating expenses, including those for program production and acquisition, for marketing to system operators and consumers, and for leasing of time on satellites.[5] The current survivors of the great cable network competition of the last fifteen years are listed in Table 7.1.

Still, though, with over 50% of all television homes subscribing to at least a minimal basic cable service, cable had by the mid-1980s become the dominant signal-delivery system in the United States and Canada (Fig. 7.1). Congressional passage of the Cable Communications Policy Act of 1984 that allowed for deregulation (in 1987) of service pricing clearly marked the industry's coming of age in terms of both political and economic power.

7.2 Cable industry structure

Operational aspects

Coaxial cable has the capability of bringing into each home over 100 interactive channels of entertainment and other services. But construction projects are very capital- and politics-intensive, and years may elapse from the point of conceptualization to the stage of operational profitability. Such delays provide the more rapidly deployed and less expensive noncable alternative programming services with opportunities for expansion.

In the days when the business was primarily a CATV service, not much more than a well-located large antenna, a couple of signal amplifiers, and a few miles of wire were needed for operations to begin. However, proliferation of pay services, rapid growth in the number of urban-based customers, demands for upgrading or rebuilding of older 12-channel one-way systems, and requirements for subscriber addressability have substantially increased the complexity of equipment and the size of capital investment needed to provide efficient service.

For instance, advances in electronics have made it possible for coaxial-cable channel capacity to increase: New systems can now handle frequency bands upwards of 400 MHz, versus 300 MHz or less in older systems. And new fiber optic systems can provide further substantial performance improvements. But many millions of previous-generation signal

Table 7.2. *U.S. cable systems by subscriber size and channel capacity, 1988*

	Systems	% of total	Subscribers	% of total
Size by subscribers				
50,000 & over	168	1.86	15,771,313	34.65
20,000–49,999	379	4.20	11,722,327	25.75
10,000–19,999	495	5.49	6,951,078	15.27
5,000–9,999	662	7.34	4,650,464	10.22
3,500–4,999	387	4.30	1,608,433	3.53
1,000–3,499	1,644	18.25	3,134,569	6.89
500–999	1,272	14.12	909,400	2.00
250–499	1,265	14.04	456,280	1.00
249 & under	2,225	24.70	304,875	0.69
Not available	513	5.70	—	—
Total	9,010	100.00	45,508,739	100.00
Channel capacity				
54 & over	682	7.57	9,371,921	20.60
30–53	4,489	49.82	30,128,970	66.20
20–29	1,418	15.74	4,022,687	8.84
13–19	293	3.25	277,111	0.61
6–12	1,175	13.04	954,570	2.10
5 only	30	0.33	6,398	0.014
Sub-5	7	0.08	1,333	0.002
Not available	916	10.17	745,749	1.64
Total	9,010	100.00	45,508,739	100.00

Source: Television Factbook, No. 57. Washington D.C.: Warren Publishing Inc., 1989.

converters (which adapt cable-frequency transmissions so that they can be seen on an ordinary television receiver) must still be replaced at considerable cost.

Computers and transportation vehicles are two other major capital items. At the head-end facilities (from where signals are sent to subscribing households), computers monitor the system's wires and amplifiers for any breakdowns that may occur, and keep track of what each household is receiving. And they are, of course, used to update records of connections, disconnections, monthly billings, and program-guide shipments.

Yet, in addition, field-service personnel (whose salaries are a major operating expense) also require extensive fleets of trucks and other mobile equipment in order to connect and disconnect homes, install converters, and repair and maintain wires. Especially in large cities, where installation is complicated by the density of population and the need to construct underground conduits (instead of renting the use of telephone utility poles as in rural regions), the problems of maintenance, of customer service, and of signal piracy can be so severe as to noticeably reduce a system's profit potential. Table 7.2 shows a breakdown of U.S. cable systems by subscriber size and channel capacity as of 1988.

Franchising

Cable systems constitute a natural monopoly. It is therefore not surprising that government regulation has become a prominent part of the industry's economic landscape. And despite considerable easing of federal regulation since the early 1970s, the FCC retains authority, even (as the Supreme Court ruled in 1984) to preempt city and state controls.[6]

Nowhere, however, have the regulatory features been historically more visible than at the local community level, from which franchises are originated and administered. Municipalities may receive up to 5% (normally 3% as a base) of system revenues and may negotiate strongly for other special benefits in return for granting a local monopoly.[7] And until recently, they had governed increases on fees for basic services.[8]

In order to bid successfully for a franchise that is yet to be constructed, cable companies must carefully forecast potential revenues and costs of operation over the typical 15-year franchise period.[9] Franchise bidders also often promise to contribute to the community fully equipped television studios, libraries, and several "free" local-access channels.

Construction proposals (so-called requests for proposals or RFPs) obviously require large expenditures of time and money without any assurance that a bid will be successful. Furthermore, in the event of a successful bid, several years will elapse between the time the franchise is awarded and the time the new system becomes fully operational (is "energized") and profitable. In the interim, financing and construction expenses may rise substantially over the original estimates, and the cream of the market may be skimmed by other technologies (discussed in Section 7.4) that can be implemented more rapidly at lower capital investment and with much less red tape. It can be seen from Table 7.3 and Figure 7.2 that the peak of annual investment in plant and equipment occurred in the early 1980s.

Revenue relationships

As already noted, the introduction of pay cable services on a nationally distributed basis was crucial in launching the industry on a high-growth path. Ultimately, though, the willingness of consumers to continue to subscribe to such services depends on the quantity and quality of the programming that is provided. For that reason alone it is important to understand the economic relationships between program suppliers, program wholesalers, and MSOs.

Table 7.3. *Cable construction data*

Year	Miles of construction			Cost	
	New	Rebuild	Total	Total ($ 000)	Per mile ($)
1988	39,377	62,765	102,142	1,612,889	15,791
1987	21,875	42,880	64,755	1,253,146	19,352
1986	27,132	28,926	56,058	985,515	17,580
1985	36,678	28,057	64,735	1,306,048	20,175
1984	39,954	28,758	68,712	1,139,374	16,582
1983	68,975	27,150	96,125	1,488,100	15,481
1982	85,168	31,459	116,627	1,818,461	15,592
1981	71,615	23,952	95,567	1,403,878	14,690
1980	56,332	10,070	66,402	1,187,744	17,887
1979	31,914	8,143	40,057	651,853	16,273
1978	22,126	8,157	30,283	241,607	7,978
1977	18,793	7,458	26,251	194,795	7,420
1976	12,458	3,100	15,558	168,952	10,859
1975	11,175	3,255	14,430	126,822	8,789

Source: CableVision, March 27, 1989, and prior-year construction estimate issues.

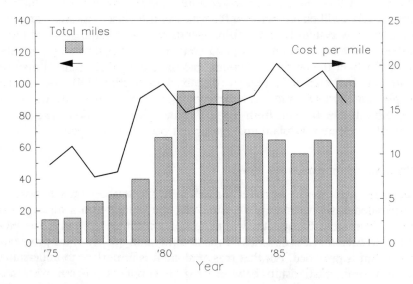

Figure 7.2. Cable system construction trends, 1975–88. Miles and costs in thousands.

MSOs are, of course, perfectly capable of self-producing low-budget programs of local interest. But by and large, that is not what the paying customers want to see. And so a situation developed in which it became convenient for the MSO to purchase from wholesalers like HBO or Showtime the rights to play movies, or to obtain special interest programming by making arrangements to join with other MSOs in support of a specialized network like CNN (Cable News Network) or ESPN (Entertainment and Sports Network). In establishing such specialized cable networks, the costs of expensive productions could be covered by small charges to each subscriber, and in the case of movies, there would be no need for each small MSO to inefficiently deal with the large Hollywood studios on a picture-by-picture basis.

For the filmed entertainment programming wholesalers – HBO and Showtime and The Disney Channel, for example – relationships with MSOs on one side and the program suppliers on the other may be rather complex. Since over 300 titles a year are normally required in order to fill out a channel's schedule, wholesalers will commit to spending hundreds of millions of dollars to license in advance a full (or nearly full) slate of a studio's output (sometimes exclusively) for a three- to five-year period. Such arrangements provide studios with a solid base of production financing, while assuring wholesalers of a programming schedule that can retain the allegiance of their immediate customers, the MSOs. The license fees thus negotiated will typically be calibrated to the theatrical box-office performances of the films in these packages, and if averaged over all new titles in a package, might generally work out to a cost of under 20 cents a subscriber (but possibly more, depending on the popularity of the films included and exclusivity arrangements).

In purchasing from the wholesaler, the MSO, in turn, abides by a rate card that sets a standard monthly minimum per household and certain sliding-scale surcharges that are used by the wholesaler as an incentive for the MSO to sign up as many subscribers as possible.

A summary of a representative rate card prior to volume discounts, which can substantially lower the total cost to the MSO, might be as follows:

If the system charges over $12.00 a month, the wholesaler is to receive $6.25 + 50% of any amount over $12.00; systems at $11.00–$12.00 pay $6.50 flat, and those under are scaled down $0.25 for each dollar until a floor rate of $5.00 flat is reached for systems charging under $6.50.

Thus, the wholesaler will normally receive a little over half of what the retailer (the MSO) charges the average household for the pay channel service. And then, on average about one-half of what the wholesaler receives (or around 25% of the retail price) is used to pay the program suppliers, be they movie studios or other production and/or distribution entities.[10]

Considerably simpler to describe, however, are the revenue-sharing relationships for cable networks. Although the types of arrangements between

Table 7.4. *Advertising expenditures on cable, 1980–8*

Year	Ad expenditures ($ million)
1980	58
1981	124
1982	230
1983	396
1984	594
1985	806
1986	951
1987	1,171
1988	1,450

Source: Cable Advertising Bureau.

MSOs and the specialized cable networks may vary considerably from one situation to another, it is common for each MSO to compensate the network for its programming on the basis of at least 5 or 10 cents a month per subscriber. The network may then also derive half or more of its total revenues from the sale of national or regional advertising.[11] Nevertheless, it is still an open question how much advertising on cable viewers will tolerate as the price of basic services, as shown in Figure 7.3, rises.[12]

Estimated advertising expenditures on cable services in the 1980s are shown in Table 7.4; these figures can be compared with network television advertising of approximately $9.1 billion in 1988, and national spot and local spending in that year of around $7.2 billion each. Whereas it remains to be seen how tolerant of commercials cable viewers will be, there is no doubt that commercial sponsorship of such programming will become increasingly attractive to advertisers as audiences for network television stop growing, and as demographic and income characteristics of cable audiences improve.

Thus, unlike broadcasting, financial support for cable programming can come from viewers, from advertisers, from cable operators, or from a combination of all three sources. In 1989, cable industry revenues were approximately $15.0 billion, with estimated pretax profits of $2.0 billion – thereby placing the cable industry at virtual financial parity with the commercial broadcasting industry.

7.3 Financial characteristics

Capital concerns

The industry's tremendous thirst for capital to upgrade old systems and construct new ones ("new builds," in industry parlance) has led to concentration into fewer, but financially stronger, ownership entities. As can be seen from the data in Table 7.5, major publicly owned companies now control the largest subscriber groups.

Because capital costs for system expansions have been so large, it was not until the late 1980s that the industry could begin to show significant aggregate operating profits after deduction of interest expenses. But just as in broadcasting, however, the more relevant measure of financial performance for cable industry companies is not operating profit, but operating cash flow before taxes, depreciation, and interest expense. As in broadcasting, this definition of cash flow is used to avoid comparative distortions that may arise as a result of financing and tax variations.

Cable operating margins, calculated by taking operating cash flow as a percentage of revenues, also provide a handy means of comparison among different operating systems. Such margins would normally fall into the range of 35% to 50% for most financially strong companies.[13]

For many analytical purposes, however, the most convenient way to understand the profitability and cash-flow potential of a system is through use of population-density and penetration figures. Much of a system's operating cost is fixed and independent of subscriber numbers, and construction cost per mile may in some instances be essentially the same whether there is one subscriber or a thousand subscribers along that mile.[14] "Drop" charges (the cost of attaching a home to the main feeder cable) and the cost of installing converters (used to enable an ordinary 12-channel VHF TV tuner circuit to display more than 12 signals) are the only major variable expenses related to subscriber density.[15]

A simple exercise, with the following assumptions, will illustrate:

A new 1,000-mile system costs an average of $15,000 per mile, or $15 million to build.
Both basic and pay monthly service charges are $10.00.
Penetration of the 10,000 homes along the 1,000-mile route is 50%, and the ratio of pay to basic subscribers is also 50%.
The cable operating margin is 40%.

Thus, annual revenues from basic service would be $600,000 ($10/ month × 12 months × 5,000 subscribers), pay-service revenues would be $300,000, and total revenues $900,000. Applying a 40% operating margin, profits would then be $360,000, which is a 2.4% (360/15,000) return on total capital investment before accounting for depreciation, interest, and taxes.

The return on capital (ROC) in this example appears to be surprisingly inadequate for two reasons. First, the number of homes passed per mile of plant (viz., the density) is far too low to support a new build. The density of 10 homes per mile in this example compares with an average of about 80 homes per mile for all systems in the United States. Were this hypothetical system to contain the average homes per mile, and with all other things equal, the ROC would be 19.2%.

Table 7.5. *Top 25 multiple-system operators, 1988*

Rank	System operator	Number of subscribers	Pay-cable units	Homes passed by cable	Homes in franchised areas	Miles of plant
1	Tele-Communications Inc.	5,977,000	4,485,500	10,187,500	10,600,000	103,000
2	American TV & Communications Corp.	3,212,000	2,660,000	5,446,000	6,800,000	40,300
3	Continental Cablevision Inc.	2,302,000	2,537,000	4,275,000	4,600,000	41,000
4	Storer Cable Communications	1,516,623	1,258,478	2,555,158	2,756,159	31,475
5	Warner Cable Communications Inc.	1,488,720	1,298,330	2,830,044	3,350,250	25,750
6	Cox Cable Communications	1,465,245	1,268,887	2,557,130	2,611,992	23,527
7	Comcast Cable Communications Inc.	1,410,000	1,234,000	2,549,000	2,654,000	26,700
8	United Artists Cablesystems Corp.	1,276,000	1,144,000	2,108,000	2,200,000	13,455
9	United Cable TV Corp.	1,251,884	963,471	2,209,966	2,343,000	21,581
10	Newhouse Bcstg.	1,123,634	1,068,298	1,689,042	1,701,321	22,728
11	Viacom International Inc.	1,114,500	815,700	1,847,000	1,869,000	15,714
12	Cablevision Systems Corp.	1,099,421	2,284,363	1,905,434	2,520,888	14,650
13	Jones Spacelink Ltd.	1,088,828	792,374	1,689,683	1,708,430	20,478
14	Heritage Communications Inc.	1,078,085	816,779	2,036,848	2,173,299	22,233
15	Times Mirror Cable TV	976,385	684,788	1,660,197	2,311,000	16,600
16	Sammons Communications Inc.	853,868	969,279	1,356,789	1,356,789	15,500
17	Century Communications Corp.	774,439	444,292	1,386,127	1,409,000	14,308
18	Cooke Cablevision	692,790	337,027	1,103,159	1,103,159	14,394
19	Adelphia Communications Corp.	682,000	497,400	1,018,961	1,018,961	10,795
20	Paragon Communications	678,000	495,000	1,271,000	1,403,000	12,100
21	Falcon Cable TV	630,000	369,295	992,924	992,924	14,105
22	Cablevision Industries Inc.	601,596	501,998	948,622	1,142,569	13,677
23	TeleCable Corp.	560,859	261,913	859,849	870,000	10,660
24	Centel Cable TV Co.	553,123	379,347	921,238	921,238	13,141
25	Rogers Cablesystems Inc.	516,626	510,000	940,000	940,000	9,718

Source: TV Digest, December 5, 1988.

Table 7.6. *Typical investment per subscriber, circa 1990*

Fixed	
Plant (including labor)	$700
Head-end, vehicles, etc.	100
Origination, studios and equipment	75
Other	75
Total fixed	950
Variable	
Converters	75
Drops	75
Total variable	150
Total per subscriber	$1,100

But second, in a modern system, the ratio of pay to basic subscribers would almost certainly be well over 50%. And any incremental pay revenues (as well as higher penetration levels) would significantly boost returns; once a system is in place, the cost of adding subscribers or tiers of service beyond the basic service is minimal. (In most instances, the returns to equity investors would also be noticeably higher than in this example because most of the capital needed to build the system would be borrowed.)

Another interesting aspect is revealed by relating the total investment required to provide service to a subscriber to the minimum average monthly charge the system needs in order to stay in business over the long run. Assume, for example, that a 54-channel addressable system were to be built starting in 1990. Estimated investment per subscriber typical of the industry might then appear as in Table 7.6. If interest rates were around 14% per year, and the system were depreciated over the usual 15-year franchise period at 6% per year, then just to recover interest and depreciation, the minimum average monthly charge to each subscriber household would have to be $18.33, that is, $[(0.14 + 0.06) \times 1,100]/12$.

As of the end of 1988, total borrowing by the cable industry was probably around $35 billion, which implies an average of about $760 of debt per subscriber, backed by perhaps another $340 or so (per subscriber) in equity. But with new builds costing at least $1,100 per subscriber, it is easy to see how billions of dollars more will have to be raised largely through issuance of high-yield ("junk") bonds, bank loans, and limited partnerships, or be funded out of cash flows in order to maintain, to upgrade, and to expand systems. Recent industry operating data are shown in Table 7.7.

Accounting conventions

In the life-cycle development of a cable company there are three distinct stages for which special accounting treatments have evolved and been cod-

Table 7.7. *Cable, system operators, revenues and earnings*[a]*: composite of 44 companies, 1984–8*

	Revenues	Operating income	Operating margin (%)	Assets	Operating cash flow
1988	7,469.3	1,372.1	18.4	26,741.6	3,205.5
1987	5,921.4	1,071.5	18.1	19,345.7	2,497.0
1986	4,256.3	815.8	19.2	14,724.8	1,713.4
1985	3,322.4	598.6	18.0	7,495.4	1,442.5
1984	2,836.7	407.5	14.4	6,533.8	1,139.7
CAGR[b]	27.4	35.5		42.2	29.5

[a]In millions of dollars, except for operating margin (%).
[b]Compound annual growth rate, 1984–8 (%).
Source: Communications Industry Report. New York: Veronis, Suhler & Associates, Inc.

ified – first by a March 1979 AICPA position paper, and then by subsequent issuance in 1981 of Financial Accounting Standards Board (FASB) statement 51. The three distinct stages are as follows:

1. Start-up: the time between construction start and receipt of service by the first subscriber.
2. Prematurity: usually less than two years and coincident with construction completion; it is the time between first subscriber activation and maturation of the system.
3. Maturity: the system at maturity.

Before the AICPA guidelines, major cable franchises generally capitalized all start-up expenses until the system was profitable. But under FASB statement 51, construction, labor, interest, and other start-up expenses are normally capitalized only during the first phase. In effect, the prematurity period now bears a significant amount of cost, while installation-fee revenue accruals are not as high as they were prior to implementation of FASB statement 51. More specifically (and paraphrasing the rules established by FASB statement 51):

In the second phase, most subscriber-related operating expenses are not capitalized, although plant costs may continue to be capitalized. Systemwide costs – such as for local programming, pole rentals, property taxes, and so forth – may be partially capitalized and partly expensed, the amounts depending on the ratio of the number of current subscribers to the expected number at the end of the prematurity phase. This formula is also used for depreciation and amortization, which must be over the same period, and not longer than the life of the franchise.

In addition, the amount of interest cost to be capitalized during prematurity is determined in accordance with FASB statement 34, which indicates that the amount of interest cost capitalized shall not exceed the total amount of interest cost incurred by the system in that period.

The initial costs of subscriber installations, however, are capitalized and depreciated over the period used for the whole system. Similarly, the costs of successful franchise application are capitalized and amortized according to standards for intangible assets as delineated in APB opinion 17.

Except for installation fees – which can be accrued as revenues only to the extent offset by direct selling costs incurred – revenues from monthly subscriptions are recorded as income. If installation fees exceed marketing costs, the difference is capitalized and recorded as income over the expected average period during which the subscriber is expected to be active.

Although accounting rules for system operations are obviously very precise, for cable systems that are being acquired there have been questions concerning how the excess price over book or fair value paid by the acquirer should be amortized – 15 years over the contract life of the franchise, or over a maximum of 40 years. It is also uncertain whether such amortization is a tax-deductible item or nondeductible goodwill. The IRS has naturally argued that amortization of excess price over book is not deductible, but questions on both issues yet remain, and treatments vary.[16]

7.4 Development directions

Pay-per-view

It is fair to say that were it not for the introduction of pay movie and sports channels beginning in the 1970s, the cable industry today would be far smaller than it is. But clearly, the next step, along with the replacement of coaxial cable by optical fibers and the introduction of high-definition pictures, is the burgeoning of pay-per-view (PPV) services. Throughout most of the 1980s, an average of less than 15% of all cable converters were capable of being directly addressed from a system's head-end, and subscription to pay *channels* rather than to specific program offerings was the only technologically practical means of sending several pay signals into the home.

With the number of addressable households and the availability of low-cost computer power increasing rapidly, however, it is a virtual certainty that PPV services will become much more significant contributors to industry revenues at the same time that they (to some extent) cannibalize subscriptions to the more traditional pay channel services and adversely affect videocassette rentals. That PPV has the potential to be an extremely profitable service for cable systems to offer, even if half or more of the revenues collected are remitted to program originators or distributors, can be seen from the following simple example. Assume:

A universe of 25 million addressable homes
A response rate of 4%, or 1 million households
A PPV price of $10
That the MSO and movie company or other program supplier each retain 40% of the PPV price to the viewer
That a program wholesaler/distributor retains 20% in return for setting up marketing and distribution.

Then both the cable companies and the program suppliers will each generate $4 million of revenue in one night. For the movie company in this hypothetical situation, the amount would compare very favorably with what would ordinarily be obtained through licensing to a pay channel (or through theatrical exhibition). And for the cable company, the potential exists for substantially enhanced profitability if the subscribing household makes more than one PPV selection a month, or if the response rate is higher than 4%.[17]

Cable's competition

Cable has been, and will long continue to be, the major alternative distribution system to over-the-air broadcasts. Cable, nonetheless, continues to be challenged by a veritable alphabet soup of competitors (or potential competitors) that include MMDS, SMATV, DBS, and a few smaller variants.

MMDS Microwave multipoint distribution of signals via stright-line microwave has the tremendous advantage of not requiring streets to be dug up or telephone poles to be rented. The line-of-sight signals for such "wireless" cable systems can be distributed locally to apartment or office clusters.[18]

SMATV Satellite master antenna television is an extension of this concept, except that the master community antenna is actually a receiving dish that can pull pay-channel signals from satellite transponders and distribute them locally to homes and apartments located nearby. In densely populated areas, SMATV can often circumvent the extensive and expensive politicking that usually accompanies cable-franchise bidding, and can skim some of the cable franchise's cream years before a cable system is built.

DBS Direct broadcast satellites can send pay channel signals to small receiving dishes owned or leased by viewers. Thusfar, DBS has not been a viable competitor to cable in the United States (mainly because cable got into the home first). But in Japan and in Europe, DBS presents a potentially strong challenge to the growth of cable systems.[19]

STV Subscription television using scrambled over-the-air UHF broadcast signals was an early competitor to cable in the United States, but could not provide the programming and visual quality to compete over the long run.[20]

These alternatives to cable have not developed into major competitors, and altogether, they do not account for more than a small fraction (under 5%) of the total number of households that subscribe to a pay television service.[21]

7.5 Valuing cable-system properties

Although transfer prices are popularly and casually measured in terms of price per subscriber, with recent (1989) market prices averaging about $2,500 per subscriber, this measure can be misleading. Some factors that ought to be considered when making comparisons on the basis of per subscriber averages are the following:

Long-term interest rates, which affect projected cash flows, construction costs, and perhaps consumers' willingness to take extra pay services.

New-household formation expectancy and demographic and income mix, which depend on the location of the system.

Franchise agreements, which may have widely differing terms.

The quality and quantity of off-the-air signals, which influence the willingness of consumers to pay for television programming.

The condition of a system's physical plant, which includes the number of miles of plant yet to be built, current channel capacity, and previous maintenance and repair policies.

Prospects for changes in government regulation, especially with regard to subscriber pricing policies.

The probabilities that potential new competition from telephone companies or others might be permitted.

An illustration of how a few of these points might be included in evaluating a specific cable system appears in the following example: If both basic-cable and pay-cable service rates are $12.00 per month, and the penetration of pay into basic is 50%, then, on the average, subscribing households will annually generate $216 ($144 basic, $72 pay). Further assuming that the operator's margin on basic is 50%, and on pay 40%, profit before depreciation interest and taxes will be $100.80. A potential buyer of such a system would then weigh all of the aforementioned factors and decide upon an appropriate valuation multiple of this "cable cash flow," as it is called. Typically, such a private market multiple will range between 10 and 15 times *projected* cash flow. And so, given that both basic prices and pay penetration rates could probably be substantially raised in this hypothetical system, it is quite possible that an acquirer might be willing to value it at $2,000 per subscriber.

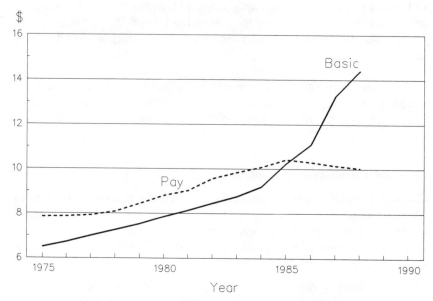

Figure 7.3. Basic and pay cable estimated average monthly rates, 1975–88.
Source: data © Paul Kagan & Associates, Inc., Carmel, California.

As in other capital-intensive businesses, projected cash flow is the critical element that enables system maintenance and expansion, pay-down of debt, and diversification. But, just as with broadcasting properties, private market values are normally significantly higher than are seen in public market transactions (see section 6.4).

To estimate what the implied value per subscriber is for publicly traded shares, the number of shares outstanding for a company should be multiplied by the price of a share. Then the amount of debt should be added, and the result divided by the number of subscribers[22]:

$$\frac{\text{value per}}{\text{subscriber}} = \frac{[(\text{stock price} \times \text{shares outstanding}) + \text{debt}]}{\text{subscribers}}$$

Before the blossoming of pay-cable services, system transfers among public companies averaged about six to eight times "cable" cash flow. But during periods of exuberant bidding, the multiple has on occasion risen to over 15 times.

7.6 Concluding remarks

Significant advances in signal distribution technology[23] combined with generous applications of capital and several doses of deregulation have enabled the cable business to grow into a $20-billion-a-year giant in the space of 25 years. Now that cable reaches into almost 60% of U.S. households, however, it is showing signs of maturity: The thirst for capital to upgrade into fiber optics and to maintain plant is still present, but the growth rate as measured by the net addition of new subscribers and pay services is inevitably slowing.

The great cash-flow and wealth-generating machine that is cable has also inevitably attracted the attention of other participants in the broadly defined telecommunications business; that is, the attention of the much dreaded telephone companies, or telcos, as they are handily called in the cable industry. With fiber optics and the appropriate digital switching devices, there is no reason, at least in theory, that telcos – over their *own* fiber optic wires into the home – could not provide telephone services in addition to the same types of services that cable companies provide. The legislative and regulatory battles[24] between the telcos and the cable industry are likely to extend over decades, and the ultimate resolution of this epic political and economic power struggle is by no means clear as of the early 1990s.

What is clear, however, is that television sets are no longer passive devices. As indicated in the next chapter, they can even play games with you.

Selected additional reading

Block, A. B. (1985). "Fat, Wired Cats," *Forbes* 135(4)(February 25):84–9.

"Captain Comeback: Ted Turner is Back From the Brink," *Business Week,* No. 3115 (July 17, 1989):98.

Cleaver, J. (1983). "The Medium Is Potent, if the Message Is Clear," *Advertising Age,* June 13.

Cooney, J. (1983). "Cable TV's Costly Trip to the Big Cities," *Fortune* 107(18)(April 18):82–8.

Emshwiller, J. R. (1989). "Prying Open the Cable-TV Monopolies," *Wall Street Journal,* August 10.

Holsendolph, E. (1982). "Tougher Times for Cable TV," *New York Times,* July 11.

Landro, L. (1983). "MTV Music Channel Rocks Teen-Agers, but Big Advertisers Haven't Tuned In," *Wall Street Journal,* August 24.

Lee W. E. (1984). "A Regulatory Lock Box on Cable TV," *Wall Street Journal,* October 15.

Mahar, M. (1988). "Captain Courageous and the Albatross," *Barron's,* July 11 and"The Baby Bells vs. the Big Gorilla?" *Barron's,* August 1.

Mahon, G. (1984). "Fine-Tuning Cable TV," *Barron's,* July 16.

Marcom, J., Jr. (1989). "TV de Triomphe," *Forbes,* 144(8)(October 16):124.

O'Connor, J. J. (1984). "Where's That Promised New World of Cable?" *New York Times,* November 24.

O'Donnell, T., and Gissen, J. (1982). "A Vaster Wasteland," *Forbes* 129(11)May 24):109–16.

Park, R. E. (1971). "The Growth of Cable TV and Its Probable Impact on Over-the-Air Broadcasting," *American Economic Review* 61(May):69.

"Pay-TV: Even HBO's Growth Is Slowing," *Business Week,* No. 2850 (July 9, 1984):40.

Russell, S. (1984). "Will VCRs KO Pay Cable?" *CableVision,* June 25.

Seiden, M. H. (1972). *Cable Television U.S.A.: An Analysis of Government Policy.* New York: Praeger.

Sloan Commission (1971). *On The Cable: The Television of Abundance,* Report of the Sloan Commission on Cable Communications. New York: McGraw-Hill.

Smith, R. L. (1972). *The Wired Nation.* New York: Harper & Row.

"Subscription Television," *Broadcasting,* August 16, 1982.

"The HBO Story: 10 Years that Changed the World of Telecommunications," *Broadcasting,* November 15, 1982.

Trachtenberg, J. A. (1985). "Here We Go Again," *Forbes* 136(5)(August 26):108–14.

(1988). "Diary of a Failure," *Forbes,* 142(6)(September 19):168.

U.S. Department of Commerce (1988). *Video Program Distribution and Cable Television: Current Policy Issues and Recommendations,* NTIA Report 88–233, June 1988.

Waldman, P. (1990). "New Fees Alter 'Basic' Idea of Cable TV," *Wall Street Journal,* January 23.

Williams, M. J. (1984). "Slow Liftoff for Satellite-to-Home TV," *Fortune* 109(5)(March 5):100.

Woodward, C. C., Jr. (1974). *Cable Television: Acquisition and Operation of CATV Systems.* New York: McGraw-Hill.

8
Toys and games

It's not whether you win or lose, but how you play the game.

In the age of computers, that statement takes on new meanings: Only a few people in the world can beat the best computerized chess-playing machines, and video games cannot ever really be defeated because no matter how high the score, it is always the human who tires first or makes the fatal error.

This chapter, largely focusing on computerized toys and games, will show how microelectronic-chip technology has enabled game designers to conveniently and inexpensively transform plain television screens into playfields of extraordinary capability. And we shall see how from a small kernel there evolved in only 10 years a business that at its short-lived peak in 1982 was larger in terms of domestic retail sales than the movie and recorded-music industries combined.

First, however, we gain important perspective by examining the more traditional toy and game sectors.

8.1 Not just for kids

Toys are the quintessential entertainment products. Indeed, it is the very potential for entertainment – play aspect, if you will – that makes something a toy instead of a merely nondescript object composed of plastic or wood or fiber or metal. The key additional ingredient, of course, is the imagination of the player. A toy, virtually by definition, alters a person's psychological state – diverting the attention in the same way that (as noted in Chapter 1) all entertainment products and services do. Thus the toy business is an integral part of the entertainment industry: It's not just for kids.

Financial flavors

In recent years, in fact, the toy industry has evolved into a rather sizable business in the United States that annually generates over $10 billion of sales at wholesale and about $15 billion in retail sales as of the early 1990s. Worldwide, the figures are probably two to three times as great, with thousands of companies involved in the manufacture and distribution of toy and game products of all kinds.

It is, in brief, still a highly fragmented industry, but is now at the beginning of a significant movement toward consolidation as it becomes increasingly apparent that true economies of scale (on a global basis) in manufacturing, and in marketing and advertising (in pursuit of scarce retailer shelf space), can only be achieved through mergers and acquisitions. In this respect, it is therefore not surprising to see the toy industry following the patterns established in other entertainment subsegments. Nor, for that matter, is it surprising to see many of the major entertainment companies either owning or taking an interest in toys.

By the early 1990s, the industry in the United States was dominated by five major manufacturer/distributor organizations which accounted for an estimated half of total sales. Those companies include Hasbro, Mattel, Tonka, Fisher-Price (Quaker Oats), and Nintendo. On the retail level, however, the business is dominated by Toys 'R' Us, with a leading 25% share, and several smaller national retailers.

Because it is a rare manufacturer indeed who will refuse to help an important retailer out of an inventory problem, it usually falls to the manufacturer to provide the costly incentives, sometimes in the form of rebates or price cuts, that are required to clear the shelves. And it is in such situations that investors would do well to remember the one unwritten rule of financial accounting for toy manufactuers: Receivables are really just inventories held in storage by the retailer. Disregard of this rule can lead to harsh earnings surprises.

As can be seen from Table 8.1, toy revenues grew by 6.3% over the 1984–1988 span, but with considerably greater variance of resulting earnings performance than in any of the other classified entertainment industry segments. Such variance becomes even more visible in Table 8.2, which tracks the sales pattern of major industry product categories over a similar period. The volatility is enough to make Santa dizzy.

Table 8.1. *Toy industry financial composite (12 companies),[a] 1984–8*

Year	Revenues	Operating income	Operating margin (%)	Assets	Operating cash flow
1988	5,130.8	357.3	7.0	4,050.9	514.1
1987	4,935.7	30.9	0.6	5,063.9	192.4
1986	5,283.6	456.0	8.6	4,012.3	608.2
1985	4,783.2	546.8	11.4	3,173.1	649.4
1984	4,020.6	556.1	13.8	2,805.9	648.8
CAGR[b]	6.3	−10.5		9.6	−5.6

[a]In millions of dollars except for operating margin (%).
[b]Compound annual growth rate, 1984–8.

Table 8.2. *Toy industry factory shipments of leading categories, 1983–8[a]*

Category	$ million						CAGR[b] (%)
	1983	1984	1985	1986	1987	1988	
Infant/preschool	508	739	824	860	776	867	11.3
Dolls	660	1,524	1,562	1,088	867	966	7.9
Plush	360	544	585	1,062	1,174	687	13.8
Figures	376	622	840	861	702	523	6.8
Guns	54	64	68	151	96	80	8.2
Vehicles	707	784	695	651	971	1,276	12.5
Ride-ons (excluding bikes)	255	285	283	288	632	608	19.0
Games and puzzles	684	1,094	642	808	830	950	6.8
Building/construction sets	97	141	189	183	196	187	14.0
Educational/scientific	21	30	58	37	65	48	18.0
Crayon/chalk/drawing	110	113	118	127	158	164	8.3
Model kits	71	89	86	80	129	144	15.2
Total[c]	3,903	6,029	5,950	6,196	6,596	6,500	10.7

[a]Shipment figures are for first U.S. billing in dollars.
[b]Compound annual growth rate 1983–88.
[c]Total excludes TV video games and other miscellaneous toy categories.
Source: Toy Manufacturers of America.

Building blocks

As noted by Owen (1986), the roots of the giant American toy companies are humble indeed. Yet even today, with all the sophisticated market research that these companies can so readily command, the reasons for the success or failure of particular toy lines are often not well understood. Sometimes a toy line like the popular Strawberry Shortcake of the early 1980s can be successfully created out of thin air; at other times all the pre-planning[1] and advertising in the world cannot move a product – movie and television show tie-ins notwithstanding.

So-called trademarked *staple* products like the board game Monopoly or like Lego blocks, or Mr. Potato Head, or the Barbie doll, however, seem to have an almost timeless, evergreen, appeal. As might be expected, such products produce abnormally high profit margins for the companies that make them. But staples – though they are to the toy industry what film libraries are to the studios – are not sufficient in and of themselves as fuel for growth. For that, toy companies require luck, pluck, and lots of spending on product development and television marketing. In this respect, the development process for new toy products is similar to that in film and music. And as in film and music, it is often the singularly profitable hit that pays for the many new product introductions that flop.

But the parallels between toys and other entertainment industries should not be stretched too far. The highly compressed seasonal pattern of retail demand, and the enormous amount of physical inventory handling that is required to service this demand, intensifies short-term delivery pressures on both manufacturers and retailers.[2] More often than not, these pressures lead to inventory imbalances (of too many unsold products) that must be corrected before retailers are again "open-to-buy" (that is, are able to order, in both a fiscal and physical sense) new toys for the spring season.

Although demographic arguments are frequently invoked to favorably portray the industry's growth potential, most such generalized arguments should be carefully analyzed. For instance, it is usually more important in forecasting changes in industry demand to know the number of first-births than it is to know the projected total number of children in the population: Parents tend to buy more toys for a first child than for any other. But in launching a marketing campaign, it may be even more important to know the income level distribution of couples expecting a first child.

8.2 Chips ahoy

Toys may be differentiated from other entertainment industry segments, not so much because demand for them tends to be so volatile and faddish as because a relatively high percentage of their cost components (value added) is tied up in the manufacture and movement of physically bulky inventory. For most entertainment products and services, in contrast, the proportionately greatest amount of value added is to be found in the organized bits of information (that we call programming or software) stored on inherently inert media such as compact discs or magnetic tapes, or relayed through cables, or broadcast over the air.

Because video games are again really no more than organized bits of information storable on inert media or capable of being electronically transmitted, they are indeed close technological cousins to many other entertainment industry products. The only difference with video games, then, is that you need a computer to play them. As we shall see, both branches of the video game industry grow from the same roots, and share a future influenced by the rate of innovation in electronic-component and software[3] design.

Slots and pins

The history of coin-operated machines, which precedes that of home video by about 85 years, can be traced to 1887, when a San Francisco inventor, Charles Fey, introduced the first nickel-in-the-slot machines in the gambling halls of his city. The checkered and colorful saga of their use in the United States follows closely the development pattern of the gaming industry, which is the topic of the next chapter. For now it is sufficient to note that during the Great Depression of the 1930s there began to emerge amusement-only machines – the forerunners of today's sophisticated pinball and video gadgets.

One of the most important early pin models was the Ballyhoo, introduced by a struggling Chicago-based company, Lion Manufacturing. Lion was predecessor to today's Bally Manufacturing which, along with several other Chicago companies including Gottlieb, Williams and Stern, had by the early 1970s become the leading worldwide producers of such machines.[4]

But in the mid-1970s there were two critical events: Bally replaced electromechanical pinball components with new electronic circuitry, and large cities such as Los Angeles, Chicago, and New York legalized placement of pins in general public locations. The effects were to catapult Bally to a position of industry leadership, and to dramatically expand the demand for state-of-the-art electronic models with enhanced features.

Pong: pre and après

As we now know, the market for coin-op machines was not limited to pinballs, and video games were already on the horizon by the end of the 1960s. In fact, their technological roots can be traced back to 1962, when MIT graduate student Steve Russell demonstrated *Spacewar,* a science-fiction fantasy game played on a PDP-1 mainframe computer and a large-screen cathode-ray tube. That game attracted a wide cult following among computer buffs.

The next important step came in 1968, when Sanders Associates engineer Ralph Baer developed a console that could be used to display games on ordinary television sets. Sanders[5] patented this idea and sold the rights to Magnavox, now a division of Philips, the large Dutch consumer electronics conglomerate.

But it was not until the early 1970s that a young University of Utah engineering graduate, Nolan Bushnell, came to realize that the price of electronic computing power (integrated circuits) had declined to the point that adaptation of *Spacewar* from a large computer into coin-op form was becoming economically feasible. Bushnell and associates began working on such a machine in a converted bedroom workshop and emerged with a version they called *Computer Space*.[6]

Following this, Bushnell wanted his design company, Syzygy, to develop a driving game.[7] Yet for a tiny outfit with limited resources and experience, that was a rather ambitious goal. And so, to gain the necessary skills, Bushnell had the company start by building a prototype that could simulate the simplest game he could think of: tennis. Much to the surprise of its designers, the game was fun to play. Still, manufacturers were not interested in producing it, and Syzygy had no choice but to assemble the product itself. *Pong,* as it was known, became an instant rage in bars and restaurants where pinball was popular.

In all, Syzygy – by early 1973 renamed Atari after a term (meaning prepare to be engulfed) from the Japanese game of go – sold about 10,000 units, and 90,000 or so copies or adaptations from other manufacturers flooded the market. Pong was truly the first major coin-operated video hit.

It did not, however, take long for commercial Pong-style home video games to appear. Consoles dedicated to playing only a few variations of one or two games introduced in 1972 under the Magnavox Odyssey® label. And soon thereafter, Magnavox was joined by Atari, Coleco, Fairchild Instrument, National Semiconductor, and RCA. Yet despite early enthusiasm, consumer interest in this area proved much more fleeting and fickle than had been anticipated, and as price competition and losses mounted, most of these manufacturers withdrew from the field.

Profits proved just as elusive at Atari, where a rapidly growing market presence in coin-op and home video required greater infusions of capital and more professional management than the company could readily muster. By the end of 1976, the founders of Atari had sold their holdings to Warner Communications for about $28 million, a value approximating their sales in that year.[8]

Fortunately, just as the industry was subsiding, the Japanese coin-op manufacturer, Taito, introduced through U.S. national distributor Bally-Midway its *Space Invaders* arcade model. The game immediately captured the public's fancy with its graphics and quick-response shoot-'em-up play features, and was the first popular machine to highlight the emerging capabilities of microelectronics and of software design: *Space Invaders* was instrumental in raising coin-op-industry unit-volume expectations well beyond the 20,000 or so that was considered exceptional in the heyday of pinball.

There soon followed a flurry of popular videos that employed the same or better hardware and even more imaginative software. The hit parade (see Table S8.1) included *Asteroids* and *Missile Command* developed by Atari, *Defender* from Williams Electronics, and the ubiquitous *Pac-Man* and *Ms. Pac-Man* games designed by the private Japanese company Namco (distributed in coin-op version by Bally, and in cartridges by Atari).

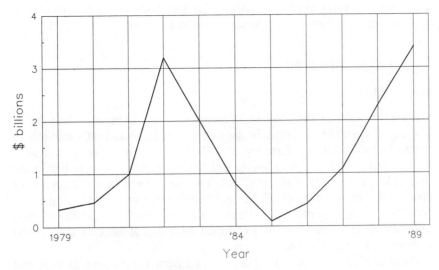

Figure 8.1. Home video game sales at retail in the United States, 1979–89.
Source: Nintendo of America Inc.

Pac-Man was especially significant in that it was the first to attract women video-game players in large numbers.

Of course, the same software improvements and technological advances (faster microprocessors and larger memories) that permitted designers to produce spectacular aural and visual effects for coin-op machines were also at the same time being applied to home video units. And so it was only a short while before the programmable consoles that had been languishing for lack of software suddenly began to sell in large numbers: Consumers had finally discovered they could play a reasonable facsimile of their favorite arcade games at home.

The effect on industry revenues was electrifying. Atari, for example, had been unprofitable for the first three years under the aegis of parent Warner Communications. But by the end of 1979 it had hit its stride – either self-designing or licensing the most popular arcade concepts for cartridge format. Sales, which had been $28 million in 1976, rose to over $2 billion in 1982, and over the same span, annual operating income went from a loss of several million dollars to profits of more than $320 million. Indeed, at one point along the way, Atari had captured some 80% of the worldwide market for home video games.

By 1980, the industry's potential also looked good enough for Mattel, then the largest toy company in the United States, to introduce its Intellivision® brand of consoles.[9] And so, for a while, at least, it was a great party. It seemed that the more the supply of software and hardware increased, the more demand there was. As shown in Figure 8.1, industry sales of consoles and cartridges rose from practically zero in 1977 to over $2 billion at wholesale ($3 billion at retail) in 1982.[10] And in that year, video-game hardware and software sales accounted for approximately one-third of total U.S. toy manufacturers' shipments. Pong had pinged.

8.3 Structural statements

Home video

But all this was too good to last. Whereas the coin-op business had developed a fairly stable structure, home video as of the mid-1980s was still in a considerable state of flux. By late 1982 the public's fascination with arcade games had begun to wane, and fewer hit concepts were becoming available for conversion to cartridges. The market was being flooded with hardware and software of all kinds. And inexpensive microcomputers[11] were beginning to capture the attention of consumers on the basis of their entertainment value plus the presumed educational benefits they could provide to an average family.

As saturation became more evident to all participants, price cutting and wholesale dumping of excess hardware and software inventories accelerated – thereby producing aggregate industry losses that amounted to an astounding $1.5 billion in 1983 alone.[12] And it was not until the late 1980s that the industry's previously amorphous structure, at least on the software side, had stabilized and had in many respects become rationalized along the lines of the recorded-music and book-publishing businesses.

Also by this time, the hardware side of home video had settled considerably. Japan-based Nintendo started around 1986 to introduce a more technologically sophisticated but easier to use game console, and with tight control of software development and marketing, was able to capture up to 80% of a once-again booming market.[13]

Coin-op

Coin-op has had a far more rigid industry structure than home video. But that has not prevented it from experiencing boom-and-bust type swings in demand (Figure 8.2). Unlike home video, however, the industry has been historically dominated by a few large companies that are now to a great extent vertically integrated in the four activities that define a presence in the coin-op business. Those activities include:

Game design, which in the early years of video was dominated by private Japanese firms and their American-based affiliates. As evidenced by the introduction of *Space Invaders* and by the success of *Pac-Man,* Japanese firms have been in the forefront of design, which can in some cases cost up to $1 million per model.

Manufacturing and assembly, in which component producers of monitors, printed circuit boards, and memory and microprocessor chips participate. In this area, the computerized-entertainment business in both coin-

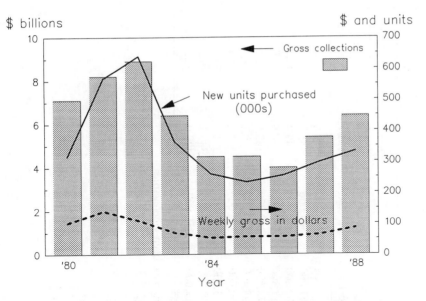

Figure 8.2. Coin-operated video games, 1980–8. Source: *Play Meter* data.

op and home segments consumes a significant portion of worldwide electronic-component production.[14]

Distribution, through which machines of various manufacturers are wholesaled, serviced, and sometimes exchanged. This part of the business also requires considerable capital and is relatively concentrated as compared to home video distribution. Distributors supply credit to smaller operators to finance purchase of machines, and generally encourage newmodel purchases by accepting trade-ins of used equipment. They and others may, moreover, supply conversion kits, primarily new circuit boards, that enable existing cabinets and monitors to be adapted for new games.

Operation or ownership of locations, either arcades or a string of smaller locations in which the machines are placed. The approximately $6.4 billion[15] (Table 8.3) that *Play Meter* estimates was collected in 1988 by the coin-op business begins with the operators of arcades (where many machines are congregated), or of routes comprised of a variety of street locations (each with only a few machines). Operators and location owners will normally split revenues on a 50:50 percentage or some ratio close to that after a certain minimum payment or guarantee to the route operator has been assured.[16]

Profit dynamics

A hit game, like hit a movie or record, will generate extraordinary returns, whether in arcade or home versions. If, for example, the game is one like

Table 8.3. Coin-op games in the United States[a]

Year	Gross collections ($ billion)	Weekly gross ($)		Operator population	Games on location	Locations	New game purchases	Average	
		Video game[b]	Pinball					Games per operator	Locations per operator[c]
1980	7.1	102	63	7,500	NA	NA	315,000	NA	NA
1981	8.2	140	66	9,000	780,000	245,000	567,000	86.7	27.2
1982	8.9	109	55	12,000	1,793,000	409,200	640,000	149.4	34.1
1983	6.4	70	38	11,000	1,876,000	417,300	363,800	170.6	37.9
1984	4.5	53	41	9,000	1,652,000	378,500	260,300	183.6	42.1
1985	4.5	57	52	6,000	1,501,000	293,400	233,200	250.1	48.9
1986	4.0	57	51	4,500	1,450,000	350,000	255,000	322.2	77.8
1987	5.4	64	60	4,700	1,510,000	375,000	298,000	321.3	79.8
1988	6.4	86	54	5,100	1,750,000	460,000	333,000	343.1	90.2
1989	7.0	68	70	5,000	2,100,000	413,000	350,000	420.0	82.6

[a]About 85% of the coin-up industry game purchases in the 1980s are estimated to have been video games.
[b]Weighted average of kits and dedicated games in 1988.
[c]Estimated number of locations in 1981.
Source: Play Meter.

Nintendo's huge late 1980s success, *Super Mario Brothers 2,* in which at least one-third of Nintendo's 15 million console owners bought a copy, then direct gross profit can be estimated to have amounted to at least $45 million according to the following assumptions: Actual manufacturing and shipping costs were probably well under $5 a unit; the basic development and/or licensing costs were $1 million dollars; advertising and promotion were $4 million; and the average wholesale price was about $15.

Of course, most games will not be nearly as profitable. And a large installed base of compatible consoles or computers is an essential pre-condition for achieving such impressive results.[17] Nevertheless, it is this kind of potential profitability – especially as ultimately projected on a global scale – that continues to attract consumer electronics companies and software developers to the business.[18]

The coin-op side will also profit greatly from a hit game, but generally not to the same order of magnitude as is seen in home video. Manufacturers need a production run of at least 5,000 units in order to cover development and fixed costs, but rarely would there be a demand for more than 30,000 units.

From the operators' perspective, once a machine is on location, it is in competition with other machines for players' time and money, and so receipts per square foot per unit time therefore becomes an appropriate measure for comparing one machine's performance with that of another. At the height of the *Pac-Man* or *Asteroids* frenzy of the early 1980s, for example, some locations were taking in $400 or more per week on a machine that cost $2,400. However, under more normal conditions, collections will average significantly below $100 a week on machines that have been out for a while.[19]

Be it in coin-op or home video though, the most profitable games are simple to understand and to play on an elementary level, but are compellingly difficult – and forever impossible – to fully master.[20]

8.4 Concluding remarks

This chapter has told a story of boom and bust: of delight in transforming a television screen into a magnificent fantasyland, and of despair in discovering that losses can often come easier than profits.

As we have seen, the toy and game manufacturing business generally tends to be as volatile as it is faddish. But especially in the computerized-entertainment subsegment, there can no longer be any doubt that we will continue to be charmed in ways we can only begin to imagine. For instance, computerized games will increasingly incorporate artificial intelligence (and artificial "reality") capabilities, and will evolve away from those requiring only simple hand-eye coordination skills to those in which thinking strategies and abstract reasoning are helpful factors. Thus will be provided challenging interactive role-playing "experiences."

Even more promising, but still further in the future, are personal robots – surely the ultimate purveyors of computerized-entertainment services. Robots will be able to perform a wide variety of tasks: Sentry duty and housekeeping, for example. Perhaps their most important characteristics, however, will be derived from interchangeable personality modules. As Frude (1983) has noted:

> The scene is set for entirely new dimensions of human simulation. And the preposterous notion that a future "personal friend" might be purchased off the shelf now has to be seriously considered. . . . [But still,] getting a machine to laugh is easy. Getting it to laugh at a joke is very, very difficult.

Selected additional reading

Churbuck, D. (1990). "The Ultimate Computer Game," *Forbes* 145(3)(February 5):154.

Cohen, S. (1984). *Zap: The Rise and Fall of Atari.* New York: McGraw-Hill.

Coll, S. (1984). "When the Magic Goes," *Inc.,* October.

Deutsch, C. H. (1989). "A Toy Company Finds Life After Pictionary," *New York Times,* July 9.

Diamond D. (1987). "Is the Toy Business Taking Over Kids' TV," *TV Guide,* 35(14)(June 13).

Flax, S. (1983). "The Christmas Zing in Zapless Toys," *Fortune* 108(13)(December 26):98–108.

Hector, G. (1984). "The Big Shrink Is on at Atari," *Fortune* 110(1)(July 9):23–36.

Hubner, J., and Kistner, W. F., Jr. (1983). "What Went Wrong at Atari," *Info-World,* November 28 and December 5.

Nocera, J. (1984). "Death of a Computer: How Texas Instruments Botched the 99/4A," *InfoWorld,* June 4 and June 11; see also *Texas Monthly,* April.

Palmer, J. (1989). "'Joy Toy' Nintendo's Future Not All Fun and Games," *Barron's,* June 26.

Pereira, J. (1989). "As Ghosts of Yules Past Haunt the Toy Shelves, 'Gottahaves' Are Gone." *Wall Street Journal,* December 12.

Ressner, J. (1982). "Atari Celebrates First Decade of Record-Breaking Growth," *Cash Box,* November 20, p. 62.

"Software Publishing: Now the Agents Are Moving in," *Business Week* No. 2854 (August 6, 1984):84.

U.S. International Trade Commission (1984), *A Competitive Assessment of the U.S. Video Game Industry,* Washington, D.C.: USITC Publication 1501.

Wojahn, E. (1988). *Playing By Different Rules: The General Mills/Parker Brothers Merger.* New York: American Management Association.

Zachary, G. P. (1990). "Computer Simulations One Day May Provide Surreal Experiences," *Wall Street Journal,* January 23.

Part III
Live entertainment

9
Gaming and wagering

It's better to be born lucky than to be born rich.

In the gamer's world, strange things happen: Kings and queens play amidst snake eyes and wild jokers. This chapter will take a look at gaming and wagering activities – on which, in the aggregate, consumers spend more than for any other forms of entertainment.

9.1 From ancient history

At first

Interest in betting on the uncertain outcome of an event is not a recently acquired human trait. As noted by Berger and Bruning (1979, p. 10), "archaeologists believe that cave men not only beat their wives, they wagered them as well." Evidence of mankind's strong and continuing interest in gambling is found in the following historical examples:

In biblical times, the selection of Saul to govern the Hebrew kingdom was determined by lot.

In the tomb of Egyptian pharaoh Tutankhamen was found an ivory gaming board.

213

Palamedes, according to Greek mythology, invented dice and taught sol-
diers how to play with them during the siege of Troy. Ancient Greek
worshippers played dice games and bet on horse races.

The Romans invented the lottery, and they wagered on the outcomes of
chariot races. The emperor Nero was said to be addicted to such racing.

The earliest playing cards were of Chinese origin and were derived from
Korean playing sticks. Cards similar to those of today were used by the
French in the fourteenth century and are descended from tarot decks
used for fortune telling. France's Louis XV had a deck made of silver,
and England's Henry VIII was a notorious gambler.

The sailing of the *Mayflower* to plant a colony in the New World was
financed by a lottery. So were some great educational institutions
including Harvard, Yale, and Dartmouth. So was the colonial army that
helped create the United States.

Gaming in America

Preliminaries Wagering had a long and colorful history thousands of years
before the United States came into being. But, as Findlay (1986) describes,
despite often ambivalent public attitudes toward legalization of such activities, in the process of its development the United States added a few exciting chapters of its own.

Even in colonial times there appears to have been some pretty fast
action: Consider that four years after the *Mayflower* landed, the Virginia
Assembly passed a law against gambling. And legislation passed in Boston
in 1630 also decreed that "all persons whatsoever that have cards, dice, or
tables in their houses shall make away with them before the next court
under pain of punishment" (Berger and Bruning 1979, p. 17).

Then there was the country's first lavish casino, referred to as a "rug
joint," that opened in New Orleans for 'round-the-clock operation in 1827.
And a similar place – no doubt frequented by many of the fledgling
nation's politicians – was opened in Washington, D.C., on Pennsylvania
Avenue in 1832.

The year 1850 saw San Francisco, with its gold-rush mentality and 1,000
assorted establishments, become the gambling capital of the West. And the
cowboy's midwestern equivalent was Dodge City, Kansas. But all kinds of
wagering and card playing were also common at that time on Mississippi
riverboats, in the terminal port city of New Orleans, and in New York and
Chicago. New York, for instance, had an estimated 6,000 gambling locations in the 1850s. And by the 1920s, Miami had become the place where
serious bets were accepted.

Although gambling is certainly not unique to the American character,
this country has contributed to the development of games such as poker
and craps, and toward rationalizing the marketing and operating proce-

dures used in modern casinos and lotteries. Gaming and wagering activities are today a regular part of life for all income classes and ethnic groups.

The Nevada experience Nevada's history as a center for betting goes back to the mid-1800s. There, as in San Francisco, a boom in precious-metal mining attracted many rough-and-ready customers for gambling and affiliated services, including liquor sales and prostitution. Nevertheless, the territory's attitude toward legalization of gaming fluctuated – depending on the perceived degree of corruption and cheating – for over half a century before the state of Nevada finally legalized, in 1931, what could not in practice be stopped.

Curiously, before World War II, Reno was a more important gaming center than was Las Vegas, a town first settled in the mid-1800s, "founded" in 1905 by sale of some Union Pacific railway-junction property to private interests, and incorporated in 1911. Yet it was not until the 1930s that the growth of Las Vegas began to accelerate. Construction of Hoover (alias Boulder) Dam, a major Bureau of Reclamation project located in Boulder City about 30 miles away, apparently was the major catalyst of change. Completion of the dam brought water and electrical power to the region, and spurred the development of commerce. Also, many itinerant construction workers who had bought their supplies and spent their free time gambling in Las Vegas eventually became permanent residents.

Las Vegas, however, only began to emerge as a world-famous entertainment capital after the second World War, in 1946. The city's proximity to the burgeoning population of Los Angeles and the increasing availability of low-cost air travel contributed significantly to its growth. But, in addition, there was Benjamin "Bugsy" Siegel. As Skolnick (1978, p. 111) indicates,

> It had been Siegel's ambition to build a luxurious complex that would offer gambling, recreation, entertainment, and other services catering to the area's increasing tourist trade . . . Siegel had persuaded the crime syndicate that he could transform Las Vegas into a legal gambling oasis for organized crime, and received their backing in 1943. With their support, he started to work on his initial venture – really the first of the major Strip hotels – the Flamingo.[1]

Nevada's decision (in 1946–7) to establish and to fund – through taxes on gross casino winnings[2] – regulation and enforcement agencies that would ensure fair and honest conduct of the games and of casino operations was of further importance. The irony, of course, was that at the start of legalized modern gaming in Nevada, often the only operators with enough expertise to run the games fairly were people previously affiliated with illegal organizations.

As might be expected, the "connections" of some of those operators created law-enforcement problems that surfaced most noticeably in the 1950s,

as attempts at state licensing and gaming-control functions came into conflict with mob interests in a lucrative and rapidly growing business. Indeed,
it was not until the mid-to-late 1960s that organized crime's grip on the
industry's finances began to be loosened as a result of pressure from the
Department of Justice and other federal-government investigative agencies, and as a result of the large-scale investments by billionaire Howard
Hughes.

This process was further speeded by passage in 1969 of the Corporate
Gaming Act, which allowed companies with publicly traded shares to own
and operate casinos in the state of Nevada. Ownership by large corporations provided an important means of financing casino-hotel expansions,
of attracting middle-class and convention-related customers, and of developing an untainted corps of professional managers.

Enter New Jersey New Jersey's involvement in casino gaming, however,
began much differently than Nevada's. New Jersey's Atlantic City had been
a popular ocean resort in the early 1900s. But gradually, because of neglect
and because of the increasingly availability of low-cost air travel, it decayed
into what was euphemistically called an economically depressed area. It
was always clear, though, that with its proximity to dense population centers in Philadelphia and New York, the town would make an especially
attractive location for casinos. And so – with the promise of stimulating
urban renewal and providing extra funding for senior citizens' programs –
began the efforts of developers to legalize gambling. Voters rejected the first
referendum for statewide gambling in 1974, but in 1976 they approved a
second one limiting casinos to Atlantic City.

Public reaction to New Jersey's legalization was awesome. Immediately
on opening the first Atlantic City casino in 1978, Resorts International was
overwhelmed by enormous crowds betting huge stakes. And over the
immediately following years the early momentum continued. Despite having only one-tenth as many first-class hotel rooms (5,000 as of 1984) as its
Nevada counterpart, Atlantic City began to compete effectively with Las
Vegas as a major center for entertainment and gaming (Figure 9.1 and
Table 9.1). By 1984, for example, table-game and slot revenues in New
Jersey were within 3% of the Las Vegas total of around $2 billion, and
annual visitor arrivals in Atlantic City were 28.5 million, compared with
about 12.8 million in Las Vegas.[3]

Horse racing Casinos, though, are only part of the story of gaming and
wagering in the United States. Horce racing has a particularly interesting
history, with direct antecedents of the American experience traceable to
England, where a public racecourse was opened in Smithfield, London, in
1174. By the eighteenth century, racing had developed into an important
English sport (governed by the Jockey Club), and records of breeding and
race results began to be published (in the *Racing Calendar).*

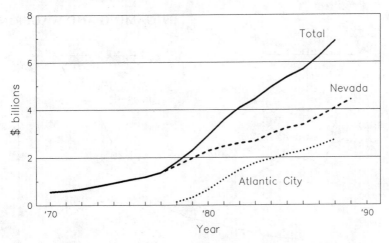

Figure 9.1. Annual casino revenues in Nevada and Atlantic City, 1970–88.

Table 9.1. *Gaming win in Atlantic City and Nevada*

Year	Total U.S. casino revenues ($ billion)	Nevada total June fiscal year taxable gaming revenues ($ billion)	Las Vegas (Clark County) Gross winnings ($ billion)	Visitors (million)	Atlantic City Gross winnings ($ billion)	Visitors (million)
1970	0.560	0.560	0.369	6.8		
1971	0.608	0.608	0.399	7.4		
1972	0.683	0.683	0.476	8.0		
1973	0.804	0.804	0.588	8.5		
1974	0.937	0.937	0.685	8.7		
1975	1.066	1.066	0.770	9.2		
1976	1.188	1.188	0.846	9.8		
1977	1.380	1.380	1.015	10.1		
1978	1.805	1.671	1.236	11.2	0.134	7.0
1979	2.306	1.980	1.424	11.7	0.325	9.5
1980	2.917	2.274	1.617	11.9	0.643	13.8
1981	3.563	2.463	1.676	11.8	1.100	19.1
1982	4.093	2.600	1.751	11.6	1.493	23.0
1983	4.454	2.683	1.887	12.3	1.771	26.4
1984	4.943	2.991	2.008	12.8	1.952	28.5
1985	5.367	3.228	2.233	14.2	2.139	29.3
1986	5.647	3.366	2.393	15.2	2.281	29.9
1987	6.205	3.710	2.738	16.2	2.496	31.8
1988	6.809	4.074	3.003	17.2	2.735	33.1
CAGR[a]:						
1970–88	14.9	11.7	12.3	5.3		
1978–88					35.2	16.8

[a]Compound annual growth rate (%).
Source: Las Vegas Convention/Visitors Authority and Atlantic City Casino Association.

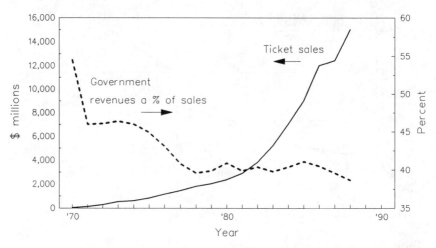

Figure 9.2. Lottery ticket sales and net government revenues as a percent of sales in the United States, 1970–88. *Source: Gaming and Wagering Business,* compiled by T. La Fleur.

The first American racetrack with regularly scheduled meetings was founded in Hempstead (Long Island), New York, in 1665, and tracks soon appeared in several other colonies. It was not until 1821, however, that the first thoroughbred racecourse was built. Just after the Civil War, the sport began to achieve wide popularity because of the development of pari-mutuel ("between ourselves") betting. Prior to that time, betting had been handled by bookmakers, who had posted arbitrary odds. But with a pari-mutuel system, bets could be pooled and the odds determined by the opinions of bettors as measured by amounts wagered on each horse.

Racing has grown into a business that generates annual gross revenues similar in magnitude (about $3 billion) to those generated from casino table games (Table 9.3), and by the late 1980s, horse racing (including thoroughbred, quarter-horse, and harness varieties) had gradually been legalized in over 40 states.[4] But in recent years, growth of interest in racing has been minimal.

Lotteries In contrast to racing, however, growth of interest in lotteries has been explosive. Lotteries have been common throughout the history of the United States. In fact, according to Scarne (1974, pp. 150–2), there were half a dozen of them operating in each of the 13 colonies before the American Revolution, and by 1831 there was an average of one major drawing per week in New York City alone. However, with many of the lotteries of that time privately owned and subject to little or no control, abuses and irregularities began to appear, and public opinion gradually turned against them. An act of Congress in 1890 finally forbade the sending of lottery tickets through the mails, and by 1894 the Louisiana Legislature phased out the last of the legal lotteries.

Some 70 years would elapse before the state of New Hampshire (in 1964) revived the lottery as a fund-raising mechanism. The popularity of this approach to balancing state budgets was such that by 1990, lotteries had been legalized in over 30 jurisdictions (and also in all Canadian provinces), and the gross ticket sales exceeded $16 billion, or almost $70 per capita[5] (Table S9.3 and Figure 9.2).

Other wagering Bingo, too, has developed into an important legalized activity that generates gross wagering of at least $1.1 billion in the 46 states where it is played.[6] Indeed, bingo attracts some 40 million participants and is the most widespread of all legalized wagering games.

Still smaller, but rapidly growing grosses are generated in public poker clubs, which have long been legal in certain counties in California. And blackjack games with small maximum bets ($2) are operated for charities all over North Dakota. There the state receives 5%, the charity 65%, and the location owner 30% of the casino's gross win.[7]

9.2 Money talks

As can be seen from Table 9.2, at the end of the 1980s, gaming and wagering in the United States was a $28 billion business. This is the total amount of revenue (before expenses) that gaming business operators retained (or won), and it represents the *net* amount that players *lost*. Of this total, lotteries (at around $8 billion) and casinos ($7.5 billion) have been the two fastest growing major components (Table 9.3).[8] By comparison, domestic movie ticket sales in 1989 were $5 billion, and recorded music sales about $7 billion.[9]

Macroeconomic matters

The rate of growth of legalized gambling, which comprises approximately 80% of the sums indicated, has been well above that of the economy as a whole for virtually the whole post–World War II period. For example, net public spending (losses to operators of casinos, pari-mutuels, and bingo) on gaming and wagering accounted for around 0.2% of disposable income in 1960. But with the additions since then of lotteries and of casinos in Atlantic City, and with the tremendous expansions in Nevada, the share of disposable income devoted to these activities had about doubled by 1990. A similar story can, of course, also be seen in looking at personal consumption expenditure data (Figure 1.9).

Because casinos are nowadays often highly leveraged in both a financial and an operating sense, there is always a question with respect to the sen-

Table 9.2. *Gross handle and revenues in the United States, 1982–8*

Year	Total	Legal	Illegal
Gross wager (handle), $ billion			
1988	252.73	210.71	42.02
1987	218.13	183.82	32.31
1986	198.78	166.47	32.31
1985	190.80	159.16	31.65
1984	177.05	146.97	30.08
1983	160.93	132.14	28.79
1982	151.25	125.76	25.50
CAGR[a]	8.9	9.0	8.7
Gross revenues (win), $ billion			
1988	27.99	21.27	6.63
1987	24.01	18.38	5.63
1986	22.55	16.92	5.63
1985	20.89	15.34	5.55
1984	18.86	13.62	5.25
1983	16.85	11.84	5.01
1982	14.93	10.41	4.52
CAGR[a]	11.0	12.6	6.6
Gross margin (retention rate or win rate), %			
1988	11.1	10.1	15.8
1987	11.1	9.9	17.4
1986	11.3	10.2	17.4
1985	10.9	9.6	17.5
1984	10.7	9.3	17.4
1983	10.5	9.0	17.4
1982	9.9	8.3	17.7

[a]Compound annual growth rate, 1982–8 (%).
Source: Gaming and Wagering Business (Christiansen, 1989).

sitivity of gaming and wagering activities to adverse business cycle fluctuations in the overall economy. Unfortunately, it is not easy to provide a definitive answer.[10] Certainly, convention-trade travel to Atlantic City and Nevada would normally be curtailed in any economic downturn as businesses attempt to pare expenses. But many other factors, among which the following are most important, may also be decisive:

Air fares and the cost and availability of gasoline
Recent number of room additions as a percentage of total industry capacity
Dollar-exchange rates against major Asian and European countries
Projected rates of inflation and factory unemployment

Funding functions

Gaming and wagering in the United States are governed by a hodgepodge of state and local laws that reflect the ambivalence of the population toward these activities. On the one hand, most jurisdictions have few if any qualms about permitting church or social bingo – a game which, as Cook (1979) notes, has a high cost to the player. Nor do people seem to object to lotteries – a game with even higher costs to the player than bingo. Yet, people often rise up in moral indignation against casinos and race tracks (in which the operators' percentage is much lower). Moreover, other anomalies, as Rose (1986) discusses, have sprung up in communities such as those near Los Angeles, where only card games of a precisely defined type are allowed to be played. Yet, in Nevada, the acknowledged sports and race book and gaming capital of the world, a state lottery is *illegal*.

The logic concerning when and where gaming establishments may advertise is also peculiar. The Federal Communications Commission, for example, follows a set of anti-lottery laws passed before the year 1900. However, states are exempted from the rules. And so states regularly promote their lotteries on radio and television. But casinos can only advertise on cable: On regular television, they are only allowed to mention their non-casino attractions such as golf courses and restaurants.

It is not surprising, then, that all of this amibivalence and confusion spills over into the politics of regulation and legalization. Legalization in a state or city is always easier to achieve if, by reason of history and culture, the dominant population groups favor such activities. But what usually precipitates a move toward legal sanction is a need for more social-welfare funding than can be comfortably raised via direct taxation.

And it is in this regard that the public may sometimes be fooled into thinking that legalization is a costless way to raise net additional revenues. As demonstrated by Abt, Smith, and Christiansen (1986) or Skolnick (1978, 1979) or Mahon (1980), legalization of gaming is not a taxpayers' panacea. It should be a step taken carefully, and legislators would be wise to consider that the amount of revenue raised from legalization of lotteries, off-track betting, and casinos is often relatively small compared to what can be raised through other forms of taxation. In addition, as Sternlieb and Hughes (1983) and others have noted, such legalizations tend to spawn huge and politically powerful bureaucracies that may ultimately operate against the public interest.

Regulation

Government regulation is more visible in gaming than in any other entertainment industry segment. It has developed from historical experience with a cash business that has often nourished the coffers of organized

Table 9.3. *Total estimated legal gambling in the United States, 1982–8[a]*

| | Casinos | | | Parimutuels | | | |
| | | | | Horse racing | | | |
Year	Slots	Table games	State lotteries	Track	OTB	Dog racing	Jai alai
Gross wager (handle), $ billion							
1988	37.3	126.2	17.1	11.4	2.2	3.3	0.6
1987	32.8	112.0	13.1	11.1	2.1	3.2	0.7
1986	28.5	101.4	12.5	10.4	1.9	3.0	0.7
1985	26.2	99.6	10.2	10.5	1.8	2.7	0.7
1984	23.8	92.9	8.1	10.4	1.8	2.5	0.7
1983[d]	18.8	87.2	5.2	9.9	1.7	2.3	0.6
1982[d]	14.4	87.0	4.1	10.0	1.7	2.2	0.6
CAGR[e]	17.2	6.4	26.9	2.3	4.7	6.7	0.3
Gross revenues (win), $ billion							
1988	4.0	3.1	8.4	2.3	0.5	0.6	0.1
1987	3.6	2.8	6.6	2.2	0.5	0.6	0.1
1986	3.2	2.6	6.3	2.0	0.5	0.6	0.1
1985	2.9	2.5	5.2	2.0	0.4	0.5	0.1
1984	2.7	2.4	4.2	2.0	0.4	0.5	0.1
1983[d]	2.4	2.3	3.0	1.9	0.4	0.5	0.1
1982[d]	2.0	2.2	2.2	1.9	0.4	0.4	0.1
CAGR[e]	12.3	5.6	25.4	3.3	4.1	6.5	1.7
Gross margin (retention rate or win rate), %							
1988	10.8	2.4	49.4	19.7	22.7	19.3	19.6
1987	10.9	2.5	50.1	19.8	22.9	19.5	19.5
1986	11.1	2.6	50.8	18.9	23.3	19.5	19.5
1985[f]	11.1	2.6	51.0	18.9	23.3	19.5	19.5
1984	11.1	2.6	51.0	18.7	23.2	19.5	18.3
1983[d]	12.5	2.6	58.9	18.7	23.4	19.5	18.0
1982[d]	13.9	2.5	53.1	18.5	23.4	19.5	18.0

[a]Some figures may not be precise due to rounding.
[b]Excluding Nevada.
[c]Excluding bingo.
[d]Prior to 1984, sports books, horse books, and sports cards were combined into "other" category.
[e]Compound annual growth rate, 1982–8, (%).
[f]The previous 1985 estimate of $582 million in gross revenues for charitable games has been subsequently reduced to $525 million.
[g]Not meaningful.
Source: Gaming and Wagering Business (Christiansen, 1989).

Legal bookmaking	Card rooms[b]	Bingo	Charitable gambling[c]	Other Indian reservation	Non-casino gaming devices
1.73	3.5	4.1	2.3	0.4	0.3
1.38	3.1	4.0	2.0	0.3	
1.19	1.1	3.6	1.8	0.3	
1.13	1.1	3.4	1.7	0.3	
1.11	1.1	3.2	1.5	—	
0.85	1.1	3.1	1.4	—	
0.54	1.0	3.0	1.2	—	
21.5	22.9	6.7	11.8	NM[g]	
0.10	0.3	1.1	0.7	0.1	0.1
0.09	0.3	0.9	0.6	0.1	
0.08	0.1	0.9	0.5	0.1	
0.06	0.1	0.9	0.5	0.1	
0.05	0.1	0.8	0.5	—	
0.04	0.1	0.8	0.5	—	
0.03	0.1	0.8	0.4	—	
26.1	33.0	5.2	10.3	NM[g]	
6.0	8.0	23.9	30.4		
6.2	8.0	23.1	30.8		
6.8	5.0	25.6	30.4		
5.4	5.0	26.5	31.2		
4.7	5.0	25.9	35.0		
5.1	4.9	26.0	33.1		
4.8	5.0	26.0	33.0		

crime, deprived government of tax revenues, and plainly cheated ordinary players.

Regulative power usually rests in the state legislatures, which formally legalize gaming activities (lotteries, tracks, and casinos) and also establish agencies to oversee that those activities are conducted honestly and competently, and with full accounting of tax revenues to the state. To achieve these ends, legislatures establish regulatory enforcement, investigation, and licensing agencies that, in conjunction with local-community interests, promulgate specific standards and rules of conduct.

In racing, for example, there is the New York State Racing and Wagering Board, which institutes measures to safeguard the integrity of racing and compiles statistical and other information concerning New York Racing Association tracks and off-track betting (OTB) parlors. More widely known, however, are the Nevada and New Jersey gaming commissions, which oversee licensing and regulation of casino gaming and slot-machine operations in those states. New Jersey's regulatory bodies are to a great extent patterned on those earlier developed in Nevada, where there is a two-tier structure: the Gaming Control Board works at the staff level on investigation and audit, and the Gaming Commission acts as a quasi-judicial body that deliberates on licensing, revocations, and other related matters.

Agents and investigators representing the Federal Bureau of Investigation (FBI) and the Internal Revenue Service (IRS) have generally played a role ancillary to that of the state commissions. But should any of the state bodies prove ineffectual, it is likely that the federal government would immediately become more actively and visibly involved in industry affairs. The most direct influence would then probably be felt through augmentation of tax-reporting requirements. (As of 1985, for example, cash transactions above $10,000 have had to be reported to the Treasury Department.)

The difficulty of designing regulation that balances the needs of the business with that of the public's interest can be seen in the case of New Jersey, where in zeal to ensure that casinos would be impervious to influence by organized crime, the legislature in that state incorporated particularly detailed instructions in bills to legalize Atlantic City gaming. All employees (initially including restaurant busboys, hotel bellhops, and parking attendants far removed from gaming-transactions areas) had to submit detailed license applications.[11]

As Atlantic City gaming matured, many of these early regulations proved to be unnecessarily stringent, if not outright detrimental to industry growth and profitability. Those standards were then somewhat relaxed as the commission and its enforcement division began to concentrate on licensing of people who directly handle gaming activities and grant credit (dealers, pit bosses, cage personnel, and casino managers), of top executives, of companies supplying the industry with goods and services (linen, liquor, food, etc), and of slot machines.

Without close scrutiny at the financial-accounting and operational levels, there is a natural tendency for illegal activities to arise, and despite such safeguards, frauds and tax evasions are still occasionally discovered in lotteries (e.g., irregular printing of tickets), in horse racing (e.g., substitution by "ringers," use of illegal drugs on animals, and fixing of races), and in casinos (e.g., skimming money before reporting to the state). But with a strong regulative mandate and sufficient enforcement and licensing personnel, these problems can be largely avoided, and the public assured that the games are fairly conducted and that the government is receiving full tax revenues.

Regulation is initiated and designed to support the commonweal, and thus the legalized-gaming industry – even when not directly owned or operated by a state – always has a close and lasting relationship with regulatory bodies established and controlled by elected officials. However, as Skolnick (1978) suggests, there is always the potential for gaming interests to become so politically powerful that they circumvent the spirit, if not the actual letter, of the law.

Financial performance and valuation

The variety of companies that derive some or all of their income from operation of legalized gaming and wagering activities is surprisingly broad.[12] In addition to the relatively well known casino-hotel concerns, there are the manufacturers of computer components and the designers of software used in lottery systems management. There are companies that manufacture sophisticated slot and poker machines. And then there are the plastics and paper companies that make dice and playing cards, and the breeding and real estate companies that are involved in racing. However, of all these categories, the most readily definable and investable grouping is that of the casino-hotel operators.

Although casino returns on investment (ROI) have varied greatly from company to company, and over time, and although casino and other gaming properties have been known to fail[13] despite having the mathematical odds of the games in their favor, the casino industry has generally prospered in the 1980s.

A review of the casino industry's financial performance, as shown in Table 9.4, indicates that in recent years revenues, assets, and operating income have all grown at around the same rates, and it has been this remarkable stability as compared to other industry subgroups that has in the aggregate enabled the industry to borrow heavily against a relatively small equity base.[14]

It is thus not surprising that most investors or lenders today would find that the most appropriate way to value a gaming enterprise is (just as in cable or broadcasting) by analyzing its potential in terms of operating cash flow before taxes, interest, and depreciation are taken into account. The multiple that would then be applied to such a projected "casino" cash flow

Table 9.4. *Casino-hotel revenues and operating earnings: composite for 19 companies, 1984–8*

Year	Revenues	Operating income	Operating margin (%)	Assets	Operating cash flow
1988	6,323.7	1,107.3	17.5	8,288.3	1,479.2
1987	5,755.4	939.7	16.3	7,615.5	1,291.0
1986	5,156.3	880.4	17.1	7,034.0	1,197.9
1985	4,921.7	803.9	16.3	6,556.1	1,092.7
1984	4,639.2	767.4	16.5	5,914.2	1,024.3
CAGR[a]	8.1	9.6		8.8	9.6

[a]In millions of dollars, except for operating margin (%)
[b]Compound annual growth rate, 1984–8 (%).

figure would be a function of: interest rates, buyer enthusiasm, competitive considerations, the worth of underlying real estate for alternative uses, and general economic conditions.[15] Private market value would then be determined by subtracting net debt (long term debt minus net current assets) from the aforementioned multiple of projected cash flow. The concept (and also the existence of normally deep public market discounts to private market values) is the same as is described for broadcasting or cable properties in sections 6.4 and 7.5, respectively.

9.3 Underlying profit principles and terminology

There are uncountable variations on the thousands of card, dice, and numbers games that have been invented by mankind over the millennia, but of these, only a few have been standardized for use in today's legalized-gaming environment. This section presents a framework for understanding how games generate profits on the transactions level.

Principles

A governing principle behind the conduct of every profit-making betting activity is to pay less than true odds to the winner. But because there is a general impression that profits come only out of the collective hide of the losers, this notion is often surprising. However, it is indeed payment of *less* than true odds to winners (out of the losers' pool) that provides the casino with its "edge" (Table 9.5), the racetrack with its "take," and the lottery with its "cut." In other words, losers' money is used to compensate winners, but not as adequately as game mathematics would require. Hence, profits are, in a sense, derived from both losers and winners. Pari-mutuel betting, in which various taxes, track fees, and "breakage" charges (see

Table 9.5. *Characteristics of casino games*

Games	Edge[a] (%)	Frequency of play (min.)
American roulette	1.4–2.7	0.75
French roulette	1.4–2.7	1.5–2
Blackjack	At least 0.6	2–3
Punto banco	1.25	2–3
Craps	1.4–5.6	1.5–2
Baccarat banque	0.9–1.5	2–3

[a]In a rational world it might be expected that the edge would be inversely proportional to the frequency with which the game is played, but this is clearly not so in the actual casino world. In any case, many players are under the illusion that the more often they can play, the more likely they are to win.
Source: Royal Commission on Gambling (1978, p. 451). Final Report, London, July 1978, Vol. 2, p. 451.

Appendix B) are deducted from the pool of funds contributed by winners and losers, provides a clear example of this.

With a statistical advantage established, operating profitability is then affected by the number of decisions, or completed betting events per unit time. A second governing principle is thus found in the steady pressure to raise or to maintain the rate of decision as high as possible so that statistical advantages are compounded as much as possible over time. That is, if winners are shortchanged of true odds by even a small percentage often enough, then the aggregate amount kept by the game operator (the "house") can be substantial.

For this reason, when management attempts to assess the profitability of, for example, "junkets" (in which travel, hotel, and other expenses are paid by the casino-hotel in return for a promise to gamble a certain minimum over a few days' time), it should use a formula including an estimate of the house edge, the average number of decisions per hour, and the average size of betting units. Similar criteria should be used in determining whether or not a bettor qualifies for "comps" (complimentaries), which may include any or all of free drinks and meals, shows, rooms, and transportation.

A third governing principle in the operation of games of chance is applied when betting limits (the maximum amount permitted to be wagered on each decision) are imposed. Murphy (1976), for example, notes that in a game with 50:50 odds – tossing pennies and betting double or nothing – the usual assumption is that over a long period of time the outcome will be even. This, however, is untrue if one player has limited capital and the other has infinite capital: The expected outcome for the player with limited capital is total loss. The imposition of a betting limit (which, in effect, artificially constrains the player's capital relative to that of the game operator), in and of itself, practically guarantees that over an extended period the operator will win all, even without benefit of a house edge.[16] Thus, in such cases it is not the edge, but the limit, that defeats the gambler.

In practice, players have the highest probability of winning if they make just one large bet, rather than dividing their stake into many smaller units and rebetting. With one large bet, the edge has minimal opportunity to grind down the player's capital. However, because most people would not enjoy going to a casino or track and making only one bet, they trade off the probability of winning for entertainment value derived through extended playing time. An excerpt from *Gambling Times*[17] illustrates:

> In playing red or black on roulette with one $100 bet, the house edge is 5.26% (there are 18 reds, 18 blacks, and 2 greens – so odds are 20 to 18 against) and a bet may be expected to be won 47.37% of the time – almost an even chance. Now suppose $5 units are bet until $100 are either won or lost. Out of 1,000 trials, on average 873 times there would be a loss of $100, and only 127 times a win of $100. The average amount to bet to obtain a decision would be $1,451 compared to $100 with one large bet.

Terminology and performance standards

A positive expected return to the game operator is realized over many betting events – be they dice rolls, card flips, slot-machine pulls, races run, or lottery tickets sold. The total amount bet is called the *handle,* and the amount that remains for the game organizer after the betting-event result has been determined is the *win.*

In casino table games, cash or cash equivalents, such as credit slips, called *markers,* are collected (dropped) into sealed boxes under the tables. The dollar-equivalent aggregates in the boxes have thus become known as the *drop* – a term that also applies to the coins (and/or tokens) fed into slot machines. The *win rate,* expressed as a percentage, is then the total win (over time) divided by the total drop. This percentage is usually referred to as the *hold.*[18] In contrast, at tracks, states charge a fixed percentage of the handle as a "fee" for participation.

Although the operator's positive-expected-return percentage produced by trials over many betting events is generally small (ranging from almost nil at some points in a blackjack game to over 15% for some bets in craps, at the Big Six wheel, in lotteries, in bingo, and at the track), win rates normally range between 10% and 22% of the drop in casinos, 17% or more of the handle in racing, and ~50% of the handle in lotteries.

Nevertheless, the similarity of conversion of cash at the track into tickets and cash at the casino into chips does not mean that the handle at tracks and lotteries can be compared to the drop in a casino. In casinos, handle is many times the drop because (a) it is unusual for all chips (cheques) purchased and counted in the drop to be immediately "invested" in the game, and (b) "reinvestment" of chips won or retained in the course of play may increase the handle without correspondingly increasing the drop through additional chip purchases. Of course, such is not the case with pari-mutuel tickets, where there is no fractional retention of the ticket's value. The full face amount of the ticket is bet in each race.

The following numerical example, assuming a one-roll-decision dice game in which the casino edge is 2%, should help clarify the terminology. Say there are five bettors, each betting $10 on a throw of the dice. The handle is then $50. Assume further that the players are not using cash, but instead cheques or chips issued by the casino and bought at the table for cash. The drop will then also be $50 at the start of the game. Theoretically, for each decision, the casino ought to expect to win 2%, or $1, of the total amount bet. Of course, this may or may not happen over the short run, but it will, on average, occur over the long run (i.e., over many betting decisions).

Now assume for a moment that on the first roll the players as a group come out even, and then they bet the second roll identically as the first. The handle at that table has now risen to $100, while the drop has remained $50 (no player had to buy more chips).[19]

Another hypothetical situation can be examined to illustrate how the hold is over 10% even when the house's edge may be 1%. Suppose that a player beginning with a $100 stake, and buying $100 worth of chips, on each decision happens to experience the long-run average loss specific to that game of 1% per decision. On the first deal of the cards, the casino wins $1, and the player has $99 left over. On the second deal, the casino wins another $0.99, and the player has $98.01 remaining. Extrapolating, after 11 decisions the player has less than $90, and the casino more than $10 – and at this stage, the win as percentage of the drop (the hold) is over 10% (with the handle over $1,000).

Most games have win rates that over time are characteristic and thus can be used as benchmarks to see how the performance of a specific table (or of a casino with many tables) measures against long-term statistical norms. Nevada characteristic win-rate averages, for example, are shown in Table 9.6. From this, it can be seen that baccarat is the most volatile (i.e., has the highest variance) of all games in terms of gross win fluctuations. Indeed, there have been occasional instances in which casinos have had losing months at their bacarrat tables.[20]

Analysis of casino game performances can also be extended well beyond the rudiments just presented. Detailed knowledge of the probability for each betting-decision result (and of the average number of events per final decision) is required to calculate cost as a percentage of money bet (see, for example, Table S9.5). And such knowledge may then be used to determine the true cost to the casino of player junkets and comps. An interesting rule of thumb mentioned by Kilbey (1985), for example, is that a casino has earnings potential of around one average bet per hour. That is, if the average bet is $25, then the casino can expect on average to win that amount in each hour of play.

With slots often accounting for over half of a casino's activity, managers

Table 9.6. *Hold (% win to drop) for Nevada, 1975–89*[a]

| Year | Major table games | | | | | Keno |
	Blackjack	Craps	Roulette	Baccarat	Avg.	
1975	19.7	18.1	31.2	18.8	22.7	28.2
1976	19.6	18.3	29.7	21.0	23.0	28.1
1977	19.9	18.7	30.1	18.4	22.4	27.8
1978	20.0	19.0	29.4	20.9	23.1	28.2
1979	19.8	18.7	32.6	20.9	24.1	28.4
1980	19.7	18.6	29.4	22.6	23.5	28.7
1981	19.2	18.3	26.8	21.6	22.2	28.1
1982	18.8	18.8	28.5	26.3	24.5	28.7
1983	18.3	18.4	26.4	21.9	22.2	28.8
1984	18.2	18.1	25.5	21.4	21.7	28.7
1985	18.0	17.4	27.3	20.8	21.8	28.5
1986	17.6	17.7	25.4	18.8	20.6	28.2
1987	17.6	17.3	28.5	23.2	23.0	28.0
1988	17.6	17.2	27.2	26.1	23.5	28.5
1989	17.4	17.1	26.7	25.4	23.1	28.0
Mean	18.7	18.1	28.3	21.9	22.8	28.3
Variance	0.9	0.4	4.1	5.8	0.9	0.1

[a]Fiscal years ended June 30 beginning in 1984.
Source: Nevada Gaming Control Board

are also motivated to compare ROI performances of various machines. A utilization model that can be used for such purposes is described by Johnson (1984, p. 62). As illustrated in the following, it includes variables for coin denomination, hold, average coins played, and cycle time:

Equations

1. denomination × hold × average coins played = win per game
2. average daily drop ÷ win per game = games played
3. games played × cycle time ÷ hours operated daily = utilization rate

Sample calculation

1. $0.05(denomination) × 0.15(percentage hold) × 2.2(average coins played) = $0.0165.
2. To win $25, this machine must be played 1.515 ($25/$0.0165) times.
3. Assuming an average cycle time of 10 seconds, it will take 15,152 seconds (4.21 hours) or a 17.5% utilization rate over 24 hours to reach these earnings.

Table 9.7. Atlantic City market share by casino, 1979–88

Opening sequence	Total sq. ft. Dec. 1988	Market share (%)									
		1979	1980	1981	1982	1983	1984	1985	1986	1987	1988
1. Resorts	59,857	63.7	33.2	17.0	14.4	14.3	13.1	11.4	10.3	9.6	8.9
2. Caesars	59,617	35.8	32.5	17.6	13.0	12.1	11.4	11.6	11.4	11.6	11.2
3. Bally Park Pl	59,996	0.5	28.1	17.2	13.2	13.0	12.2	10.5	10.0	10.0	9.8
4. Sands	50,090		4.2	8.4	9.8	8.8	8.2	8.4	8.3	7.7	7.5
5. Harrah's	59,718		1.2	13.0	11.8	11.4	10.8	10.1	10.4	9.9	10.3
6. Bally Grand	45,442		0.8	14.3	12.4	14.8	12.9	11.2	11.0	9.7	8.1
7. Atlantis	50,601			8.5	9.5	8.1	7.5	6.5	4.5	2.9	3.1
8. Claridge	43,054			3.0	6.0	6.2	6.3	5.6	5.3	5.0	4.9
9. Tropicana	87,760			1.0	10.0	11.2	11.2	9.9	9.4	8.5	8.5
10. Trump Plaza	60,000						6.4	9.5	9.6	9.8	11.0
11. Trump Castle	60,000							5.4	9.9	9.6	9.0
12. Showboat	59,388									5.9	7.7
Total	695,523	100.0	100.0	100.0	100.0	100.0	100.0	100.0	100.0	100.0	100.0
Total gross win ($ million)		$325.5	$642.7	$1,099.8	$1,493.2	$1,770.9	$1,951.8	$2,138.7	$2,281.2	$2,495.7	$2,734.8

Source: New Jersey Gaming Control Commission.

9.4 Casino management and accounting policies

Marketing matters

One way to understand the business of a casino (or that of any other wagering establishment) is to visualize it as a retailer, ostensibly of betting opportunities, but in actuality, of experiences that are stimulating, exciting – *entertaining*. That such experiences have an inherent value to the customer is proven time and again by the fact that – although they receive nothing tangible in return for the money they (on-balance) spend – the customers tend to come back for more than one visit. The marketing challenge is to get customers into the store through advertising, marketing, and publicity, and to then keep them shopping in the store for as long as possible.

Casinos in particular have found it necessary to create marketing images that most appeal to the core of players they are likely to attract. For example, Circus Circus casino-hotels have long and very profitably catered to low and mid-budget players who do not require extensive credit-granting facilities or lavish meal and entertainment services. On the other hand, both Caesars World and the Golden Nugget have profitably exploited – without sacrificing the important and vastly broader upper-middle-income player group – the so-called high-roller niche, in which practically any whim of the free-spending gamer is indulged.[21] And several casinos still also attract players by developing tour and travel discount packages and junkets.[22]

Even with all this, of course, market shares for individual companies do not remain static (Table 9.7), and it is crucial for managements to accommodate the shifting demands of players by accordingly altering the mix of their games over time. In recent years, for instance, technological advances in the design of video slot (including poker and blackjack) machines have made them so popular that they have come to account, at the expense of table games, for a steadily rising share of overall industry revenues (Figure 9.3).

Cash and credit

Large casinos will often have millions of dollars in cash and equivalents either in play or ready for play at the tables and slot machines. Also, in order to attract and to retain business, most casinos extend credit and comps (free goods and services) to their better customers. The short-run management problem is to oversee and control the flow of cash, credit, and comps – preventing the abuses by employees and by customers that can naturally be anticipated when there is regular and close contact with sizable amounts of money.

Achievement of such control requires implementation of highly detailed and regimented rules of conduct. And enforcement of the rules must be accompanied by a strong commitment from upper management to subject

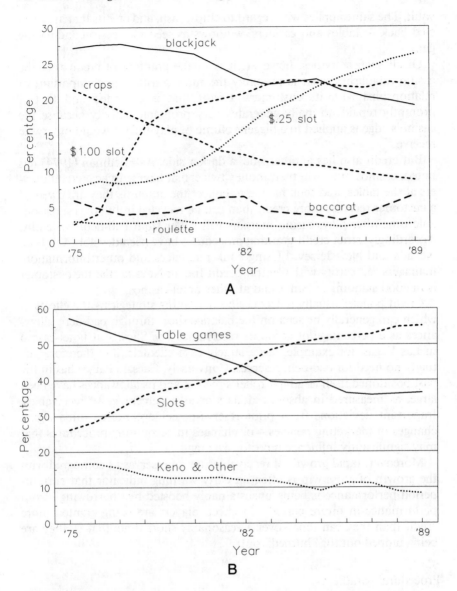

Figure 9.3 Percentage of revenue derived from table games versus devices in Nevada, 1975–89: (a) major game categories; (b) table games and slots. *Source:* Nevada Gaming Control Board.

any deviations and irregularities to close scrutiny. In practice, this means that operating procedures are broken into many small and well-defined steps: Many people must watch many people as credits and comps are granted, and as the cash moves from the pockets of the players into the tables and slots, into the counting rooms, and then finally into a bank vault. The same applies with regard to chips, cash, and credits that are recycled back to tables and cashiers' windows as seed money to conduct the games.

Of all such activities, however, it is in the granting of credit that the casino establishes what is probably the most sensitive and important of relationships with its customers. Credit that is extended and that is promptly repaid normally generates very profitable activity because the casino's edge is applied to a bigger volume of play than it would otherwise receive.[23]

But credit also has another side, a darker side. As Friedman (1974) has noted, casinos must win their money twice; first having to beat credit players at the tables, and then having to collect the amounts they are owed. If a customer receives more credit than can be recycled in full over a reasonable time after play, casino margins will suffer from bad-debt write-offs. Accordingly, strict credit-granting procedures have been developed in both Nevada and New Jersey.[24] Using bank references and other information, managers can certify with Central Credit Inc. in Nevada that the customer is in good standing at banks and at other hotel-casinos.

Credit policies usually reflect casino marketing strategies – the effects of which can generally be seen on the balance sheet through bad-debt allowances as a percentage of accounts receivable. The Showboat hotel-casino in Las Vegas, for example, has a largely cash clientele, and therefore virtually no need for bad-debt reserves. Conversely, Caesars Palace has in the past positioned itself as a high-roller's mecca, and its allowances have been large, as measured in absolute dollars or as a percentage of receivables. Important deviations from prior reserve-percentage norms often signal changes in marketing policies – or changes in accounting procedures that may significantly influence reported earnings.

Moreover, rapid growth of receivables net of reserves as compared with the growth of gross win is often an early warning indicator that current-period performance is being unsustainably boosted by "borrowing" from performance in future periods. In effect, players are being granted more credit than they can repay over a reasonably short time; that is, they are being tapped out (or "burned" out).[25]

Procedural paradigms

Fill slips record the value of the bills, coins, and chips the cashier's cage issues to the gaming tables, and credit slips record the value of these items returned to the cage. Nevada Gaming Commission Regulations [number 6.040(5)] indicate the method that must be used to transfer cash and equivalents between tables and the cage.

According to the regulations [and following Friedman's (1974) presentation], "all fill slips and credit slips shall be serially numbered in forms prescribed by the board," and the serial numbers must include letters of the alphabet "so that no gaming establishment may ever utilize the same number and series ... All series numbers that are received by the establishment must be accounted for. All void slips shall be marked 'VOID' and shall require the signatures of the 2 persons voiding the slip."

In addition, there are several detailed regulations as to how drop boxes are unlocked with two different keys – one issued by the cage, and the other by the accounting department at the time the count is scheduled. Once the drop box is opened, regulations specify that the contents of each box or bag be counted and verified by three counting employees, and that the count be supported by all credit and fill slips taken from the box.

The count team notes shift win, shift currency drop, shift fill and credits, and shift IOUs to the cage and typically sorts a box's contents into (a) currency, (b) chips, (c) fill slips, (d) chip credit slips, and (e) name credit slips. A table shift's records will then include the table's opening chip bank as a fill slip and the shift's closing chip bank as a chip credit. Calculations by shift can then be made as follows:

currency + chips + name credits + chip credits + closing bank
    = table income
opening bank + fills = table fills
table income − table fills = table win

More specifically, the win or loss at each table in each shift may, as illustrated in AICPA (1984, p. 7), be computed as in the following example:

Cash in the drop box		$6,000
Credit issued and outstanding		3,000
Total *drop*		9,000
Less: Beginning table inventory	$14,000	
Chip transfers		
Fills	5,000	
Credits	(1,000)	
	18,000	
Ending table inventory	(11,000)	7,000
Win		$2,000

Of course, all accounts, including cash, hold IOUs (a customer's check that a casino agrees not to process until some time in the future), and others, are verified and balanced according to standard journal-entry procedures. But, in addition, table-game and slot results are regularly analyzed by shift, using statistical tests to signal possible significant deviations in win and drop figures from previously established averages. In this way, casino management can detect where there might be any fraud by employees or customers. When aggregated over longer periods, such as a week or a month, these statistics are also analyzed to indicate trends in win per square foot. Similar to sales-per-square-foot calculations used in the retailing industry, these figures permit relative-efficiency comparisons to be made to experiences in prior periods, and to the performances of other

Table 9.8. *Nevada gaming revenue analysis, fiscal year 1987*

Category	Statewide	Las Vegas Strip
Revenue per square foot[a]		
Pit[b]	$1,637	$2,559
Coin-operated devices[c]	1,098	1,233
Poker and pan	897	1,097
Race and sports	382	380
Total casino	$1,205	$1,541
Casino department % of revenues from:		
Pit[b]	40.5%	50.5%
Coin-operated devices[c]	55.4	44.8
Poker and pan	1.9	2.0
Race book	1.3	1.6
Sports pool	0.9	1.0
Total revenue	100.0%	100.0%

[a]Statewide includes 155 locations, Las Vegas Strip 38 locations.
[b]Includes keno and bingo.
[c]Primarily slot machines.
Source: Nevada Gaming Abstract, State Gaming Control Board.

casinos. Table 9.8, for example, shows Nevada revenues and average win per square foot data by game category.

9.5 Gambling and economics

The psychological roots of the desire to gamble are complex and not completely understood. In fact, some psychologists (e.g., Halliday and Fuller 1974) view gambling as a neurosis rather than a form of entertainment.

Economists, however, deal with the demand for gaming services through utility-function models. In such models, consumers express their preferences by making purchases according to the utility they expect to derive from the goods or services bought.

To see how this line of thinking evolved, we have to go back over 200 years. At that time, some mathematicians were concerned about resolving the so-called St. Petersburg paradox, which was presented in the form of a coin-tossing game. In theory, because the expected value (payoff, or return) of the game was infinite players should have been willing to pay an infinite amount to participate, yet no one was willing to do so. Mathematicians Daniel Bernoulli and Gabriel Cramer resolved the paradox by rejecting the principle of maximum expected return, and substituting the concept of expected utility in its place. Because of the diminishing marginal utility of

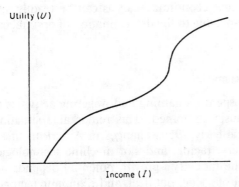

Figure 9.4 An individual's utility function. *Source:* Friedman and Savage (1948).

money (the additional utility derived from additional money increments decreases as the money value of the prize increases), participants would determine the amount they were willing to play in a St. Petersburg type of game according to the game's expected utility, not its expected monetary returns.

Significant further work on the nature of utility functions was done in the 1930s, when it was demonstrated that unless the function is bounded, new paradoxes can be constructed. But it was not until the 1940s that Von Neumann and Morgenstern (1944), in their classic work on game theory, showed how the expected-utility hypothesis leads to optimal decisions under conditions of uncertainty.

Friedman and Savage (1948) then later published an important study discussing the application of the expected-utility concept to choices made by individuals. Why, they asked, would many people purchase insurance (pay a premium to avoid risk) and also gamble (undertake risk)? To answer, they postulated (as shown in Figure 9.4) that over some range, the marginal utility of wealth increases, which means that the utility functions of individuals contain both concave (risk-aversion curves graphically represented as outward-bending from the origin) and convex (risk-affinitive) segments.

In contrast to the theoreticians just cited, however, other economists have examined the gaming industry through a variety of standard econometric modeling approaches. Eadington (1976), for example, estimated for the Nevada economy the coefficients in a production function of the form $Q = f(K, L, M)$, and was able to draw conclusions concerning economies of scale, the marginal productivity of various games and devices, and the optimal mix of games and devices. And still others (e.g., Asch, Malkiel, and Quandt 1984) have suggested that certain betting situations and the securities markets are behavioral analogs that can be studied through market-efficiency theories.

In all, the academic literature on gambling and economics has developed rapidly because gaming and wagering activities have so many quantifiable

aspects, and because economic analysis can be readily applied to everything from game-playing to the determination of optimal casino comp and
credit policies.

9.6 Concluding remarks

In total, more is spent on gaming and wagering activities than on movies
and recorded music combined. This remarkable situation has, in part,
reflected since the early 1950s changes in American lifestyles as well as
advances in lottery, racing, and slot machine technologies. As we have
seen, however, the industry's growth potential depends on an unusually
broad assortment of social, political, and economic factors that cannot be
easily forecasted far into the future.

Yet, as economists Ignatin and Smith (1976) have noted, the one constant throughout is that gambling possesses both consumption and investment characteristics; it provides direct utility with the hope of financial
gain. In other words, people do not gamble only for money; they also gamble because it is entertaining.

Selected additional reading

Barron, J. (1989). "States Sell Chances for Gold as a Rush Turns to a Stampede,"
    New York Times, May 28.
    (1989) "Has the Growth of Legal Gambling Made Society the Loser in the Long
    Run?" *New York Times,* May 31.
Bass, T. A. (1985). *The Eudaemonic Pie.* Boston: Houghton Mifflin.
Bassett, G. W., Jr. (1981). "Point Spreads versus Odds," *Journal of Political Econ-
    omy* 89(4):752–68.
Blum, H., and Gerth, J. (1978). "The Mob Gambles on Atlantic City," *New York
    Times,* February 5.
Clotfelter, C. T., and Cook, P. J. (1989). *Selling Hope: State Lotteries in America.*
    Boston: Harvard University Press.
Cook, J. (1980). "The Most Abused, Misused Pension Fund in America," *Forbes*
    126(10)(November 10):69–82.
Cook, J., and Carmichael, J. (1980). "Casino Gambling: Changing Character or
    Changing Fronts," *Forbes* 126(9)(October 27):89–104.
Cordtz, D. (1990). "Betting the Country," *Financial World,* 159(4)(February 20).
Crist, S. (1989). "Race Tracks Step Lively to Keep up With Bettors," *New York
    Times,* May 29.
Curry, B. (1984). "State Lotteries: Roses and Thorns," *State Legislatures,* March.
Demaris, O. (1986). *The Boardwalk Jungle.* New York: Bantam.
Epstein, R. A. (1967). *The Theory of Gambling and Statistical Logic.* New York:
    Academic Press.
Hamer, T. P. (1982). "The Casino Industry in Atlantic City: What Has It Done for
    the Local Economy?" *Business Review.* Federal Reserve Bank of Philadel-
    phia, January/February, pp. 3–16.
Hannon, K. (1987). "Post Time?" *Forbes,* 140(7) (October 15): 74
Harris, R. J., Jr. (1984). "Circus Circus Succeeds in Pitching Las Vegas to People
    on Budgets," *Wall Street Journal,* July 31.

Klein, F. C. (1983). "Horse Racing Gives Bush-League Owner Thrills, Little Profit," *Wall Street Journal,* August 31.

Lancaster, H. (1985). "Investing in Horses Is a Lot Like Betting: Some Luck, Some Skill, Maybe a Payoff," *Wall Street Journal,* March 15.

Lancaster, H. (1980). "Casino 'Hosts' Pamper High-Rolling Bettors to Keep Them Rolling," *Wall Street Journal,* September 3.

Liebau, J. (1983). "Tearing Up the Turf," *Barron's* August 8.

Longstreet, S. (1977). *Win or Lose: A Social History of Gambling in America.* Indianapolis: Bobbs-Merrill.

Messick, H., and Goldblatt, B. (1976). *The Only Game in Town: An Illustrated History of Gambling.* New York: Crowell.

Morehead, A. H., and Mott-Smith, G., eds. (1963). *Hoyle's Rules of Games.* New York: Signet Books, New American Library.

National Association of State Lotteries (1989). *Annual Report.* Rockville, Md.: Public Gaming Research Institute.

Nevada Gaming Control Board (1989). *Nevada Statistical Abstract.* Carson City: NGCB.

New York State Racing & Wagering Board (1981). *Annual Report.* New York: NYSRWB.

Paher, S., ed. (1976), *Nevada Official Bicentennial Book.* Las Vegas: Nevada Publications.

Painton, P. (1989)."Boardwalk of Broken Dreams," *Time* 134(13)(September 25).

Pollock, M. (1987). *Hostage to Fortune: Atlantic City and Casino Gambling.* Princeton (N.J.): Center for Analysis of Public Issues.

Reinhold, R. (1989). "Las Vegas Transformation: From Sin City to Family City," *New York Times,* May 30.

Ross, I. (1984). "Corporate Winners in the Lottery Boom," *Fortune* 110(5)(September 3):20–5.

Scheibla, S. H. (1984). "Good Horse Sense?" *Barron's,* December 31.

Seligman, D. (1975). "A Thinking Man's Guide to Losing at the Track," *Fortune* XCII(3)(September):81 and;

   (1987). "Turmoil Time in the Casino Business," *Fortune* 115(5)(March 2).

Swartz, S. (1985). "New Jersey Casino Commission Stirs Controversy With Rulings," *Wall Street Journal,* March 11.

Thorp, E. O. (1962). *Beat the Dealer.* New York: Random House (Vintage Books paperback, 1966).

Treaster, J. B. (1982). "Mob Alliance to Share Casino Riches Reported," *New York Times,* September 1.

Turnstall, J., and Turnstall, C. (1985). "Mare's Nest: The Market in Thoroughbreds Is a Mess," *Barron's,* July 15.

Vinson, B. (1986). *Las Vegas Behind the Tables!* Grand Rapids (Michigan): Gollehon.

Wells, K. (1988). "Philip Anderson Has a Feeling He Knows What's in the Cards," *Wall Street Journal,* January 13.

Yoshihashi, P. (1990). "More States Like Odds on Sports Betting Despite Fierce Opposition to Legalization." *Wall Street Journal,* February 1.

Ziemba, W. T., and Hausch, D. B. (1984). *Beat the Racetrack.* New York: Harcourt Brace.

10
Sports

It ain't over 'til it's over. – Yogi Berra

In sports today, chances are the game's not over 'til there's another television commercial.

This chapter concentrates on sports – as much an entertainment business as any thus far discussed. The exposition underscores the importance of links to broadcasting, cable, and wagering segments and shows why tax-law considerations are at the core of many sports business decisions.

10.1 Spice is nice

Economic characteristics

Since 1929, spectator sports have accounted for approximately 2.1% of personal-consumption expenditures on recreation, with the most recent peak of 2.7% attained in 1971. As can be determined from Figure 1.9 (p. 22), spending in this area naturally declined during both World War II and the Korean War. However, considerable long-run variation in the sports percentage of PCE does not suggest any clear pattern of sensitivity to ordinary business-cycle fluctuations.

240

Table 10.1. *Attendance at professional-sports exhibitions, 1960–88[a]*

| Year | Attendance (thousand) | | | |
	Baseball	Basketball	Football[b]	Hockey[c]
1988	53,799	12,654	17,024	12,118
1985	47,742	11.491	14,058	12,742
1980	43,746	10,697	14,092	11,511
1975	30,373	7,591	10,769	10,306
1970	29,191	7,113	9,992	6,454
1965	22,806	2,750	6,547	3,127
1960	20,261	1,986	4,154	2,574

[a]Includes regular season, playoff, and championship attendance. The number of teams in 1988 was 26 in baseball, 25 in basketball, 28 in football, and 21 in hockey. Two new teams were added to basketball in 1988 and two more in 1989. In 1961, the number of teams was 16 in baseball, 9 in basketball, 14 in football, and 6 in hockey.
[b]National Football League.
[c]National Hockey League.
Source: Statistical Abstract of the United States, 1989, U.S. Department of Commerce, Bureau of the Census.

Nor, for that matter, does a look at trends in admissions to major professional sports contests. Attendance at football (NFL), major-league baseball (NL and AL), basketball (NBA), and hockey (NHL) games grew at an average annual rate of around 5.2% from 1960 to 1980; however, as indicated in Table 10.1, attendance at basketball and hockey games has changed relatively little since the mid-1970s.

Because team franchises are essentially local monopolies that are created and controlled by the owners' associations, they are relatively unaffected over the short-run by normal competitive pressures. In fact, franchises can report operating losses year after year yet still maintain a high or rising valuation upon transfer. Nevertheless, there is an underlying sensitivity to changes concerning player contract standards and tax and antitrust laws.

The broadcast and cable connection

The most striking feature of modern sports business is how dependent it has become on the broadcasting and cable industries. Indeed, in the absence of this electronic-media coverage and the fees generated therefrom, many fewer professional teams, and probably many fewer fans would have been created.

Sales of transmission rights for sporting events are still heavily weighted toward over-the-air broadcasters, but as the cable subscriber base has

Table 10.2. *Hours of network TV sports events, 1988*

Sport	Hours	Percent of total
Baseball	184	10.6
Basketball	263	15.2
Football	423	24.4
Golf	218	12.6
Multi-sports	138	8.0
Olympics	270	15.6
Tennis	90	5.2
Other	146	8.4
Three network total	1,732	100.0

Source: Nielsen Media Research.

Table 10.3. *Three-network sports sponsor payments, 1981–8*

Year	Network hours	Gross advertising ($ million)	Average payment per hour ($)
1988	1,844	1,466	795,011
1987	1,593	1,396	876,334
1986	1,513	1,294	855,254
1985	1,542	1,230	797,665
1984	1,825	1,295	709,589
1983	1,514	1,270	838,838
1982	1,434	925	645,049
1981	1,390	841	605,036

Source: Capital Cities/ABC

grown to over half of all television homes, cable has become much more important as a source of team revenues. In fact, by the mid-1980s, major boxing events had already become the province of pay-per-view cable, and other sports offerings had become the mainstay for primarily advertiser-supported cable networks. By the mid-1990s, cable is expected to be an important licensee of rights to major sporting events including the Olympics, the World Series, and the Super Bowl.

The significance of the electronic-media/sports linkage can be inferred from examination of the number of network hours (Table 10.2) allocated to sports events, and network sponsor payments for sports programming (Table 10.3).Network spending for quadrennial broadcast rights to the Olympic Games is shown in Table S10.1.

The wagering connection

Wagering has always been an integral part of sports because a contest is always more exciting when spectators are personally involved in the outcome. Indeed, betting on virtually any type of match, from baseball through boxing, is legal and well developed in Nevada (and also in England). Everywhere else in the United States, however, legal sports betting is largely limited to racetracks (horses and dogs) or to jai alai (in Connecticut and Florida).

Illegality, however, has not stopped people from risking billions of dollars each year on the results of football, baseball, basketball, hockey, boxing, and automobile racing. According to Christiansen (1989), for instance, the illegal gross handle for such activities was about $26.3 billion in 1988, with the largest portion wagered on football games (Table S9.7).

But that is not all. The spice that wagering adds to spectator sports is also immediately reflected in increased demand for coverage by electronic and print media. The potential for high ratings leads sponsors to pay high prices for commercial time, and leads stations, networks, and cable systems to then bid aggressively for rights to distribute the signal. Because revenues generated from sales of these rights are essential to the operation of spectator-sports enterprises, wagering indirectly provides important financial underpinnings by creating demand for information that otherwise would be of limited interest.

10.2 Operating characteristics

Revenue sources and divisions

Although each professional sport or team has its own special problems and opportunities, they are all concerned with the potential for tax-shelter benefits for franchise owners, and with the prices received for broadcast and cable rights. Nevertheless, each of the three major sports (football, baseball, and basketball) has evolved differently with regard to these fundamentally shared concerns. Football, however, appears to be the advanced prototype after which the others will eventually pattern themselves.

Football's lifeblood is network-television money: In the early 1980s, for example, the National Football League signed a $2-billion, five-year contract with the networks that for the first time was sufficiently large to provide each club with a profit before counting gate receipts.[1] This financial cushion from sale of broadcast rights (and ultimately cable rights) permits revenues to be shared amongst all teams, and it insulates owners from the normal adverse financial consequences of prolonged mismanagement or incompetence or even competition.[2] The result is that – despite considerable disparity in on-field performance – the richest team generates only about 20% more gross revenue than the poorest. That is not yet the case,

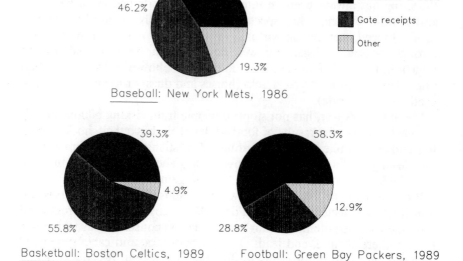

Figure 10.1. Operating-revenue sources for football, baseball, and basketball in percent: three recent examples. *Source:* Durso (1986), *Amusement Business* (July 1, 1989), and Celtics Annual Report.

however, in baseball and basketball, in which the size of the local market and the degree of competence demonstrated are much more highly correlated to the total amount of television, cable, and stadium-admission revenues that can be attracted.

Football's allocation arrangement – which contains an element of immunity or exemption from antitrust laws also seen in baseball – tends to reduce aggressive bidding for star athletes and to diminish the general usefulness of free-agency status for players.[3] This is in contrast to the traditional situation in baseball and basketball: Free-agency status in those sports has been generally effective and has produced many multimillion-dollar-per-year contracts.

In baseball and basketball, most revenues have not been shared, and market size and gate receipts have historically been much more important determinants of profitability.[4] As Figure 10.1 illustrates, in both sports, ticket sales have typically accounted for approximately 50% of total revenues, with concession income from parking fees, advertising, and beer, peanut, and hot-dog sales accounting for only a small part of total income.

But although local-broadcasting license fees have perhaps recently averaged about 25% of a baseball team's total revenues, such fees are likely to become proportionately much more important as a source of income in reflection of up-trending prices for local television and radio broadcast rights.[5] In brief, then, it would appear that increasingly valuable television and cable rights in national, local, and international markets (and not prospects for immediate profitability) are what make investments in professional sports especially attractive for wealthy private investors who can take advantage of favorable tax treatments.[6,7]

Labor issues

The stormy and well-publicized labor relationships that characterize modern professional sports can be best understood in the context of several landmark legal decisions – the most significant of which was *Federal Baseball Club of Baltimore* v. *National League,* argued in the U.S. Supreme Court in 1922. At the time, big league baseball was essentially operated as a cartel in which teams agreed not to hire away each others' players. And it was this case that provided baseball clubs with continued immunity from antitrust laws, and thus with the ability to hold onto young players as team property for the duration of their playing careers. Under these conditions, players had no choice but to accept whatever salaries the team owners decided was fair.

Toolson v. *New York Yankees* in 1953 presented the court with yet another opportunity to correct the obvious economic imbalances, but again the justices decided that baseball was entitled to a special status, and they passed the responsibility for any changes on to a reluctant Congress.

However, legal challenges by players against the owners' finally began to succeed in the 1970s, with what in late 1975 came to be known as the Messersmith Decision. Prior to this decision, a team would sign a contract with a player for a brief period, usually one season, and under the so-called reserve system the team could hold onto the player for much longer by exercising options to extend contract terms. But after this decision, an athlete could, under much less restrictive conditions, become a free agent.[8]

Football and basketball, of course, were never granted the special antitrust immunity of baseball. Yet as Michener (1976, p. 482) has noted, both sports often acted as if they were immune. Indeed, in both sports, although an athlete could in theory become a free agent after "playing out his option" on a reduced salary, an indemnity system (wherein the player's new team had to compensate his previous team) effectively reduced the player's value to a prospective new owner of his contract.[9]

The court decisions of the 1970s have given athletes the right to negotiate for higher compensation with teams other than their own, and contract terms are no longer necessarily or automatically extended beyond an initial period. As a result, in all major sports (but especially in baseball), the implementation of free agency has significantly raised the level of player compensation (Table 10.4 and Figure 10.2).[10] Another consequence, how-

246

Table 10.4. *Average player salaries, 1977–88[a]*

Year	Baseball	Basketball	Football[b]	Hockey
1988	430,700	600,000	255,714	188,000
1987	402,600	510,000	247,000	172,000
1986	410,500	440,000	230,000	158,000
1985	369,000	375,000	202,000	145,000
1984	325,900	325,000	163,145	145,000
1983	298,000	275,000	130,000	130,000
1982	245,000	249,000	105,000	124,000
1981	196,500	212,000	90,102	120,000
1980	146,500	171,000	78,635	108,000
1979	121,900	170,000	68,893	101,000
1978	97,800	148,000	62,585	92,000
1977	74,000	139,000	55,288	96,000
CAGR[c]	17.4	14.2	14.9	6.3

[a]May not include all deferred compensation benefits, and salaries for each sport may not be directly comparable.
[b]Football figures reflect average base salary, plus average incentives earned during the season. Player benefits under the collective bargaining agreement are not reflected in these numbers, but the average cost to the club per player per year was over $60,000. Prior to 1982, data are from NFL Players Association.
[c]Compound annual growth rate, 1977–88 (%).
Source: NFL Management Council, NBA, National League of Professional Baseball Clubs, National Hockey League, and players' associations in each sport.

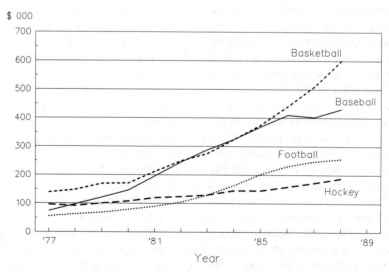

Figure 10.2. Player compensation in major sports, 1977–88.

ever, is that sports unions have become much more vociferous and aggressive.[11]

Tax-accounting and valuation treatments

Historical development Even assuming substantial growth in cable and broadcast revenues, it would in many cases be difficult to justify investment in a professional-sports franchise if such investment did not include the tax benefits that accrue to high-income owners. In recent years, tax-law revisions and court interpretations have made this an exceedingly complicated subject, most of which is beyond the scope of this book. Nonetheless, because expansions in professional sports are so dependent on tax and accounting treatments, it is worthwhile to outline the major concepts (Horvitz and Hoffman 1976; Raabe 1977; Ambrose 1981; Harmelink and Vignes 1981).

Prior to 1954 there was a uniform practice of signing players to one-year contracts and then expensing the acquisition costs of player contracts during the year of play. In 1954, however, the IRS made a distinction between purchase of a single player's contract and purchase of substantially the entire roster of a baseball club's contracts acquired at one time. In the former case, expensing the cost over one year would remain appropriate; but in the latter, the aggregate amount assignable to players' contracts was to be capitalized, and then expensed over the useful life of the assets.

These rulings remained in effect until 1967, when the IRS reconsidered treatment of individual player contracts in light of baseball's so-called reserve clause that effectively tied a player to a team for his entire career despite the one-year term of his contract. A team's effective long-term control over its athletes implied, according to the IRS, that the cost of individual players' contracts ought also to be capitalized and then expensed over the useful life of the asset.

Then, in the early 1970s, guidelines pertaining to professional-football expansion agreements provided favorable tax treatment to franchise owners. Of greatest importance was the IRS allowance that payments to established teams from new teams could be allocated between the franchise cost and the cost of player contracts for the veterans picked in the expansion draft. Because proceeds allocated to franchise cost were to be treated as capital gains, while proceeds allocable to player contracts were subject to recapture (of tax benefits by the IRS), owners were naturally provided with incentive to allocate as much as possible to franchise costs.

Further IRS rulings indicated that the "option clause" in football-player contracts would be regarded as similar to baseball's "reserve clause," that television revenue did not constitute "passive investment income" (and would therefore not adversely affect election of subchapter S treatments), and that franchise proceeds received in return for relinquishment of exclusive territorial rights would be granted favorable capital-gains treatment.[12]

Because most clubs were (and still are) owned by private individuals or by a small number of partners, owners' income from other sources could then be sheltered as long as the franchise was held as a sole-proprietorship, partnership, or so-called subchapter-S corporation (or subsidiary of a profitable privately held corporation). All that needed to be done was to buy a franchise and to then allocate a large percentage (say 80%–90%) of the purchase price to player contracts. The resulting large write-downs and reported losses would provide substantial tax savings, and after a few years, the franchise could be sold (Table 10.5).

In effect, prior to the mid-1970s, player-contract depreciation deductions would be converted into capital gains, because sellers would allocate most of the purchase price to the franchise asset and very little to player contracts, and buyers would allocate a large portion of the purchase price to depreciable player contracts.

Current treatments By 1976, concern about potential abuses of professional-franchise ownership had risen to the point that Congress felt it necessary to take corrective action against overstating the basis for depreciation, claiming large tax losses despite positive cash flows, and avoidance of depreciation recapture on players who had retired or were otherwise eliminated from the roster. The new law specified that franchise buyers and sellers would have to agree on an allocation formula, that no more than 50% of the purchase price of a franchise would be allocable to player contracts, and that there would be special recapture provisions designed to prevent the stocking of a team with new players possessing substantially undepreciated contracts just before sale of a franchise.

Several important court decisions[13] have further defined the tax and accounting ramifications in this area since 1976, but issues involving the amortizability of television, and especially of cable rights, still appear somewhat unsettled.

Asset-evaluation factors At a minimum, valuation of a professional-sports franchise would require detailed knowledge of the following:

Demographic composition and size of the local market, and degree of competing professional-sports activity in that market, so that ticket pricing and local-broadcast/cable-revenue potential can be determined
Stadium real-estate development potential, if any
Player-contract status and union-contract stipulations
Potential for network-broadcast, international, and regional-cable revenues
IRS treatments of deductions for player contracts and broadcast/cable rights
As always, the current level and forecasted trend of interest rates

Table 10.5. *Franchise-cost example: rapid write-off and high purchase price attributed to player contracts prior to 1976*

Franchise cost:	$10,000,000
(10% cash, 90% long-term debt)	
Cost allocation:	
Player contracts: 80%, useful life 5 years	8,000,000
Depreciation: $8,000,000/5 = $1,600,000/year	
Franchise: 15%, nondepreciable	1,500,000
Equipment: 3%, useful life 10 years	300,000
Depreciation: $300,000/10 = $30,000/year	
Stadium lease: 2%, useful life 10 years	200,000
Depreciation: $200,000/10 = $20,000/year	
Income statement	
Revenues	
Gate receipts	$2,900,000
Television revenue	1,400,000
Parking concessions	345,000
Other income	80,000
Total revenue	$4,725,000
Expenses:	
Player salaries	$1,700,000
Coaching salaries	350,000
Administration	1,050,000
Training camp	175,000
Interest	900,000
Lease rental	100,000
Total expenses	$4,275,000
Net income	$450,000
Depreciation:	
Player contracts	$1,600,000
Equipment	30,000
Lease acquisition	20,000
	$1,650,000
Loss reportable for partners' tax filings	$1,200,000

Source: This table appeared originally in Horvitz and Hoffman (1976, p. 178), the March 1976 issue of *TAXES – The Tax Magazine,* published and copyrighted 1976 by Commerce Clearing House, Inc., in Chicago. It appears here with their permission.

10.3 Sports economics

Analyzing economic efficiency in sports is no different than in any other field, and typically, a slew of statistics can be employed to measure performance from angles that might be of little interest to fans, but of great interest to investors and economists. The following is a brief review of some of the more prominent studies in this field.

A most comprehensive collection of economics analyses of sports has been presented by Noll (1974), including, for example, a mathematical model by Quirk and Hodiri of a professional league. This model employs concepts such as a team's inventory of playing skills and cost per unit of playing skills acquired. Assuming that a league is in steady-state equilibrium (the stock of playing skills of each team remains fixed over time) and that franchise owners are motivated solely by profits from operations, Quirk and Hodiri (1974, pp. 36–7) reached the following conclusions:

a) Franchises located in areas with high drawing potential have stronger teams than franchises in low drawing-potential areas.

b) On balance, franchises in low drawing-potential areas sell players to franchises in high drawing-potential areas.

c) If local television revenues are ignored, the distribution of playing strengths among teams is independent of the gate-sharing arrangements.

d) The higher the share of television and radio revenues accruing to the home team, the higher the costs of players and the smaller the chance of survival for low drawing-potential franchises.

Also in the same collection is an inquiry by Noll concerning demand for sports contests. Among the factors that, a priori, can be expected to influence demand are ratios of skillful to unskillful players, a winning as opposed to a losing home team, population size and characteristics of the city in which a game is played, amount of competing entertainment available, and ticket prices (e.g., average price per seat). Noll's regression results for baseball attendance in the 1970 and 1971 seasons indicated that:

1. A negative correlation between attendance and income gives the impression that baseball is a working-class sport.
2. There is a strong positive effect on attendance from winning a pennant.
3. The drawing power of baseball is substantially enhanced if a team has star players.
4. The demand for baseball appears relatively price-inelastic, which means that teams could raise ticket prices without significant loss of paid attendance.

Conclusions similar to these were also drawn by Demmert, who found a strong positive correlation between economic performance and athletic performance, and found that "institutional restrictions on the economic mobility of professional athletes ... serve as a rent transfer mechanism, assuring the economic viability of the league at the expense of the players" (Demmert 1973, p. 96).

The aforementioned studies suggest how standard economic theories and techniques might be applied to this subject. Additional analyses might, for example, include such variables as player costs per point scored or yard gained, and calculations of relative-productivity ratios.

10.4 Concluding remarks

Sports will continue to be a highly visible and important part of entertainment tightly linked to the broadcasting, cable, and wagering industries. As such, the tools and methods of economic analysis used in those sectors can be readily applied in the study of sports economics. Some major trends include the following:

Movement toward greater sharing of network-broadcast and cable revenues by professional baseball, basketball, and hockey teams

Emergence of large local and regional cable networks that support collegiate and individual athletic events

Greater emphasis on player mobility and player rights as reserve-clause control by owners is weakened

Significantly increased bargaining power of pay-cable networks and pay-per-view promoters relative to television networks in obtaining distribution rights to major sporting events.

Selected additional reading

Abrams, B. (1984). "How Networks Vied in Grueling Bidding for '88 Winter Games," *Wall Street Journal,* February 22.

(1985). "Cost of TV Sports Commercials Prompts Cutbacks by Advertisers," *Wall Street Journal,* January 15.

"Baseball Strike Issues," *New York Times,* August 1, 1981.

Behar, R. (1987). "Spreading the Wealth," *Forbes,* 140(3)(August 10).

Blustein, P. (1983). "Are Baltimore Orioles Best Team in Baseball, Or Just the Best Run?" *Wall Street Journal,* October 5.

Bulkeley, W. M. (1985). "Sports Agents Help Athletes Win – And Keep Those Super Salaries," *Wall Street Journal,* March 25.

Chakravarty, S. N. (1983). "Character Is Destiny," *Forbes* 132(8)(October 10):114–23.

Chass, M. (1985). "Baseball Strike Is Settled; Games to Resume Today," *New York Times,* August 8.

(1988). "7 in Baseball Collusion Case Win Free Agency," *New York Times,* January 23.

"Fourth and Long. But the USFL Goes for It," *Business Week* No. 2830(February 27, 1984):108.

Fishof, D., and Shapiro, E. (1983). *Putting It on the Line: The Negotiating Secrets, Tactics & Techniques of a Top Sports and Entertainment Agent.* New York: William Morrow.

Frank, A. D. (1983). "How Bad Can You Hurt?" *Forbes* 131(4)(February 14):42–3.

Friedman, R. (1984). "Holmes-Coetzee Bout, A Promoter's Dream, Becomes a Nightmare," *Wall Street Journal,* May 22.

(1985). "They Get Little Ink. But 15 Other People Also Own Yankees," *Wall Street Journal,* April 16.

(1985). "Playing Basketball In the Minors Offers Only Minor Rewards," *Wall Street Journal,* February 26.

Harris, D. (1986). "New Troubles in the N.F.L.," *New York Times Magazine,* September 7.

Hart-Nibbrig, N., and Cottingham, C. (1986). *The Political Economy of College Sports.* Lexington Massachusetts: D. C. Heath.

Harwood, S. J. (1983). "Valuation of Player Contracts When Acquiring a Professional Baseball Team – An Analysis of *Selig v. United States,*" *Taxes* 61(10):670–7.

Helyar, J. (1984). "More Cities Plan Domed Stadiums. But Returns May Prove to Be Small," *Wall Street Journal,* May 17.

  (1984). "Green Bay Packers Are Threatened by Football's Changing Economics," *Wall Street Journal,* December 14.

Klatell, D. A. and Marcus, N. (1988). *Sports For Sale: Television, Money, and the Fans.* New York: Oxford University Press.

Klein, F. C. (1985). "Sports Teams Are Losing Their Bet That Fans Will Pay for TV Events," *Wall Street Journal,* February 19.

Krise, S. A. (1975). "Certain Tax Implications of Professional Sports," *CPA Journal,* April.

Lancaster, H. (1985). "USFL Facing a Fourth-and-Long As It Staggers Into Third Season," *Wall Street Journal,* February 26.

  (1987). "Timeout: Despite Success of Celtics Sale, Doubts Remain About Sports Offerings," *Wall Street Journal,* May 8.

  (1988). "Baseball Owners Found in Collusion in Free-Agent Case," *Wall Street Journal,* September 1.

Lineberry, W. P., ed. (1973). *The Business of Sports.* New York: H. W. Wilson Co.

Lueck, T. J. (1987). "Baseball Entrepreneurs Score in Bush Leagues," *New York Times,* August 24.

Merwin, J. (1982). "The Most Valuable Executive in Either League," *Forbes* 129(8)(April 12):129–38.

  (1983). "Big League Baseball's New Cash Lineup," *Forbes* 131(7)(March 28):168–9.

  (1984). "It's Show Time," *Forbes* 133(4)(February 13):102–10.

Mieher, S. (1985). "Sports Teams Hardly Ever Score Big Bucks, But Who Cares?" *Florida Trend,* February.

Moldea, D. E. (1989). *Interference: How Organized Crime Influences Professional Football.* New York: Morrow.

Moore, T. (1985). "Baseball's New Game Plan," *Fortune* 111(8)(April 15):16.

  (1986). "It's 4th & 10 – The NFL Needs the Long Bomb," *Fortune,* 114(3)(August 4):160.

"Nothing Sells Like Sports," *Business Week,* No. 3014 (August 31, 1987).

"Professor Hardball," *Business Week,* Vol. 3098, April 3, 1989.

Rader, B. G., (1984). *In Its Own Image: How Television Has Transformed Sports.* New York: The Free Press.

Revzin, P., and Russell, M. (1985). "To Mark McCormack, Business Success Is Mostly Fun and Games," *Wall Street Journal,* June 27.

Robichaux, M. (1989). "Dallas Cowboys Face Financial Predicament Spreading in the NFL." *Wall Street Journal,* October 23.

  (1990). "If Baseball Hurls Shutout, Many Will Be Losers," *Wall Street Journal,* January 23.

Rosen, S. (1981). "Economics of Superstars," *American Economic Review* 71(December):845.

Saporito, B. (1987). "The Life of a $725,000 Scab," *Fortune,* 116(9)(October 26):91.

Sobel, R. (1985). "Baseball Rights Fees in 1985 to Remain at $275 Million," *Television/Radio Age* 32(16)(February 18).

Stavro, B. (1985). "It's a Classic Turnaround Situation," *Forbes* 136(1)(July 1):66–70.

"The Man with the Golden Arm," *Newsweek,* CXIII(15), April 10, 1989.

"The NBA Is Paying Out Like There's No Tomorrow," *Business Week*, February 5, 1990, No. 3144.

Weber, B. (1986). "The Man Who Built the Mets," *New York Times Magazine,* August 3.

Wermiel, S. (1984). "NCAA Pacts to Televise College Football Violate Antitrust Law, High Court Rules," *Wall Street Journal,* June 28.

"Who Says Baseball Is Like Ballet?" *Forbes* 107(7)(April 1, 1971).

11
Performing arts

Break a leg!

The performing arts traditionally generate more psychic than pecuniary income, and they operate under somewhat different economic assumptions than the other entertainment industries thus far discussed. In fact, many organizations in this segment are nonprofit – for their very existence requiring substantial subsidization from government and private-foundation grants, and from contributions by individuals.

As we shall see, the fundamental creative processes in the performing arts have remained essentially unchanged for centuries, but technological developments have been important in mitigating the pernicious effects of inexorably rising costs. Fortunately, it still doesn't cost anything to wish performers well by telling them to "go break a leg."

11.1 Audiences and offerings

The potential widespread appeal of live performances notwithstanding, there are severe time and financial constraints that limit audience size and scope. As Baumol and Bowen (1968) indicated in their seminal study, the audience for high culture is dominated by highly educated individuals in high income brackets (Figure 11.1). Attendance at live performances usually requires a relatively large allocation of time, and often entails substantial expenditures on tickets and on incidentals such as for restaurants and parking (Figure 11.2).

Another hypothesis as to why the audience for live performances seems to become ever more exclusive was offered by Linder (1970), who noted that as economic growth increases our incomes and the available array of consumption goods, there is a tendency toward more "goods intensity" at the expense of time spent on cultural activities. Time to consume goods does not increase commensurately with the number of goods available.

Trends in demand for the major performing arts categories may be inferred from the selected data of Table 11.1.

Commercial theater

On and off-Broadway Professional drama became an important entertainment medium during colonial times, but not until the nineteenth century was theater organized into a stock system of local resident companies permanently engaged at a particular location. However, accomplished performers soon thereafter began to form touring companies, which by the late 1800s had mostly replaced resident stock companies.

By the early 1900s, syndicates owning chains of theaters and controlling bookings and fees had become dominant. The famous Shubert chain was, for example, formed in this period. But this was largely a passing phase, as commercial theater further evolved into the current structure, in which producers select a play, raise funds, and hire a director and cast, while theater owners generally handle box-office personnel and stagehands, advertising and sales functions, and sometimes musicians. As Poggi (1968, xv) has noted:

Like so many of our social and economic institutions, the commercial theater has become highly centralized ... At the beginning of the century there were usually 250 to 300 productions touring the country at the height of each season; now there are about 20. In the late 1920s there were usually more than 250 productions opening on Broadway in a single season; now there are seldom more than 60.

Still, however, it is Broadway – essentially the theater district in New York City – that attracts the bulk of commercial theater receipts in the United States. Broadway attendance and ticket-price trends are illustrated in Figure 11.3, from which it can be seen that the number of tickets sold did not change significantly during the 1980s.[1] In that decade, admission trends for off-Broadway performances were probably quite similar, but data on this is not reliable.

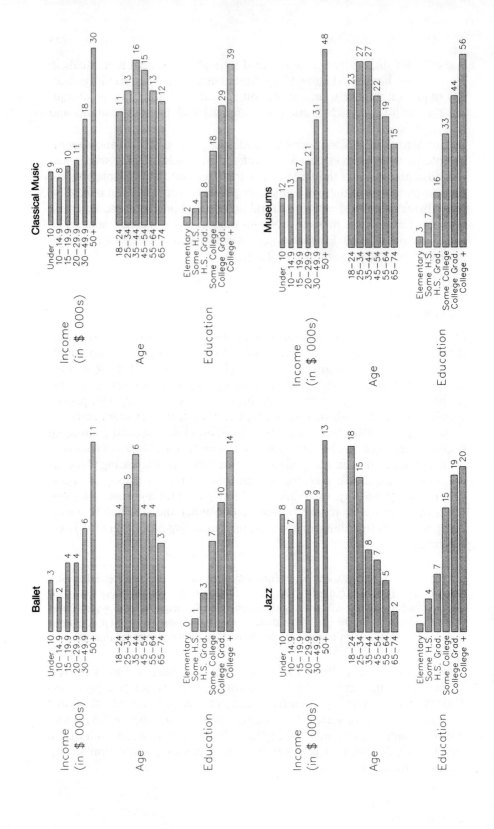

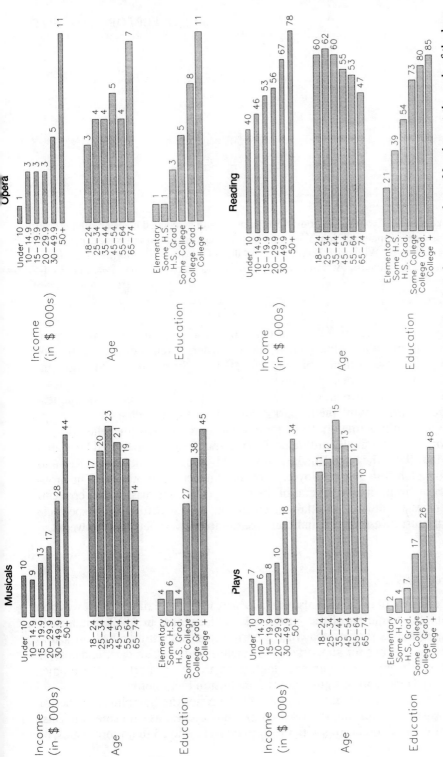

Figure 11.1. Characteristics of the culture audience by income distribution, educational attainment, and age. Numbers at the ends of the bars show the percentage of respondents participating. *Source:* U.S. NEA survey (1985).

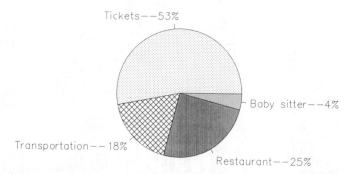

Figure 11.2. Cost of going out: ticket expense and associated costs of attendance at live performances. New York City (percentage distribution of total expenses by type). *Source:* William J. Baumol and William G. Bowen, *Performing Arts: the Economic Dilemma.* A. Twentieth Century Fund Study, © 1966, Twentieth Century Fund, New York.

Circus Circus is generally considered one of the major performing arts in Europe, but not in the United States – where circus companies are not government-subsidized, but are operated by private for-profit organizations. As such, circus companies are best categorized as a permanent traveling form of commercial theater having some of the same economic features as amusement/theme parks, the topic of the next chapter.

Of the approximately 10 major domestic circuses, few are believed to be more than marginally profitable. For instance, even when owned by Mattel in the 1970s, the huge Ringling Bros. and Barnum & Bailey units (Red and Blue, each with 350 employees) were not financially impressive. The problem in circus, like in several of the other performing arts, is that cost efficiencies are difficult to attain given the size and structure of the spectacle that must be assembled and then disassembled every few days or weeks.[2]

Orchestras

The history of orchestras also extends back to colonial times, but it was not until the founding of the New York Philharmonic in 1842 that formal organizations proliferated. In the early years, orchestras relied on a few wealthy patrons for support: J. P. Morgan, Andrew Carnegie, and Joseph Pulitzer were important contributors to the New York Philharmonic; Henry Higginson was guarantor of the Boston Symphony.

Today, orchestras are categorized by the American Symphony Orchestra League into three major classes: community orchestras with small budgets, metropolitan orchestras with medium budgets, and 25 major orchestras, of

Table 11.1. *Selected data for U.S. legitimate theater, opera companies, and symphony orchestras, 1960–87 (receipts and expenditures in millions of dollars; for season ending in year shown, except as indicated)*

Item	1960	1965	1970	1975	1980	1985	1987
Legitimate theater:							
Broadway shows:							
New productions	58	67	62	59	67	31	40
Playing weeks[a,b]	1,156	1,250	1,047	1,101	1,541	1,062	1,031
Number of tickets sold (thousands)	NA	NA	NA	NA	9,380	7,156	6,968
Gross box-office receipts	45.7	50.5	53.3	57.4	143.4	208.0	207.2
Road shows:							
Playing weeks[b]	728	643	1,024	799	1,351	993	901
Gross box-office receipts	27.3	25.9	48.0	50.9	181.2	225.9	224.2
Opera companies[c]	754	732	648	807	986	1,123	1,224
Major	NA	27	35	54	109	168	174
Expenditures	NA	NA	36.5	NA	133.6	256.5	321.1
Other companies	403	296	266	335	458	576	658
Workshops	351	409	347	418	419	379	392
Opera performances	4,232	4,176	4,799	6,428	9,391	10,642	11,794
Operas performed	287	331	341	387	497	578	622
Musical performances	NA	NA	NA	NA	1,397	4,983	7,759
Musicals performed	NA	NA	NA	NA	104	242	278
World premiers	NA	NA	17	16	79	121	129
Attendance (millions)	NA	NA	4.6	8.0	10.7	14.1	16.4
Symphony orchestras[d]	1,226	1,385	1,441	1,463	1,572	1,572	1,572
College	250	290	298	300	385	371	365
Community[e]	933	1,032	1,019	1,003	926	946	936

Table 11.1. (cont.)

Item	1960	1965	1970	1975	1980	1985	1987
Urban	—	—ᶠ	24	41	85	89	92
Metropolitan	18	38	72	90	115	96	102
Regional	—ᵍ	—ᵍ	—ᵍ	—ᵍ	29	40	45
Major	25	25	28	29	32	30	32
Concerts	NA	5,558	6,559	14,171	22,229	19,969	20,059
Attendance (millions)	NA	11.6	12.7	18.3	22.6	23.7	25.1
Gross income	NA	52.0	72.3	124.5	246.3	435.4	523.6
Earned income	NA	NA	43.1	70.9	141.2	250.7	305.9
Contributed income	NA	NA	30.2	53.6	105.1	184.7	217.7
Gross expenses	NA	53.0	76.4	129.5	252.1	441.8	525.4

Note: NA, not available.

ᵃAll shows (new productions and holdovers from previous seasons).

ᵇEight performances constitute one playing week.

ᶜMajor companies have annual budgets of $100,000 or more and issue American Guild of Musical Artists (AGMA) contracts to soloists. Workshops are primarily college and university opera groups.

ᵈFor years ending Aug. 31. Orchestras other than college groups are principally defined by their annual budgets: As of 1983, community, under $115,000; urban, $115,000–250,000; metropolitan, $250,000–900,000; regional, $900,000–3,400,000; and major, over $3,400,000. Prior to 1983, other budget classifications were in effect.

ᵉBeginning 1978, includes youth and chamber groups with budgets under $70,000.

ᶠClassification began in 1967.

ᵍClassification began in 1976.

Sources: for theater, *Variety*, various early June issues, *Central Opera Service Bulletin*, New York, various issues; American Symphony Orchestra League, Washington, D.C.

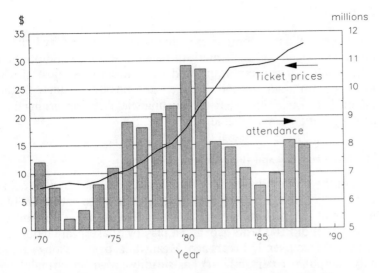

Figure 11.3. Broadway theater price and ticket sales trends, 1970–88 seasons. *Source: Variety* and League of American Theatres and Producers.

which those in Boston, Cleveland, New York, and Philadelphia are the most important. Major orchestras account for well over half of the total attendance at concerts staged by professional groups.

Opera

Opera is drama set to music, and the development of opera has closely followed that of drama. The roots of opera can be traced to ancient Greek theater presentations and to the religious plays of the Middle Ages that illustrated biblical stories with action and music. However, not until the 1600s did opera evolve into a distinctive form using complicated plots and more varied orchestral arrangement. This form flourished in Europe over the next 200 years.

Opera seems to have come of age in the United States with organization in New York City in 1883 of what was to become known as the Metropolitan Opera Company. Yet, as a reflection of the complexity and cost of staging grand opera, there are currently only four major opera companies in the United States: the Metropolitan, the New York City Opera, the Chicago Lyric Opera, and the San Francisco Opera.

The economic problem is that when all lead and supporting singers, chorus, ballet, orchestra, and extras are included, there are 200 or more professionals on a payroll sustained by at most 4,000 seats per performance. Thus, it is understandable that even some fairly large cities do not have permanent grand-opera companies.

Dance

Major professional dance companies include the New York City Ballet, the San Francisco Ballet, and the American Ballet Theater. In addition, there are at least half a dozen important modern dance groups, most of which are dependent on a single choreographer, and possibly a single financial benefactor. Because of this, relatively few financial data concerning dance-company operations are available.

11.2 Funding sources and the economic dilemma

The core of the economic dilemma, as originally outlined by Baumol and Bowen (1968), is that it is virtually impossible to raise substantially the productivity of live performances. It takes as long to play a Brahms concerto today as it did 100 years ago, and a play by Shakespeare requires the same time as it did over 350 years ago. Meanwhile, over the long run, productivity (output per person-hour) has steadily grown in virtually every other segment of the economy. As it happens, a live performance is unique in itself being an end product.

The economic dilemma becomes ever more pronounced as productivity in other sectors increases, as real-income growth makes society more goods-intensive, as operating costs rise in line with overall inflation, and as ticket prices rise in an attempt to cover "income gaps."

More specifically, ticket prices for live performances have consistently risen at a rate higher than the consumer price index, and there is evidence from studies such as that of Baumol and Bowen that higher ticket prices reduce demand – especially from less well-to-do and younger segments of the population. This effect may become more visible in periods of economic recession, when even upper-income consumers may reduce spending in this area.

Yet there can be few educated people who would argue that live performing arts should be allowed to wither. From a purely practical viewpoint, traditional theater, opera, and dance forums provide a training ground for performers in the mass-entertainment media; however, perhaps more important, they greatly enrich the surrounding society, making it more interesting and more "human." In a world constantly in budget crisis, the problem is how to finance such cultural activity. The answer both in the United States and abroad has been to fund through philanthropy and subsidy (Table 11.2).

As would be expected, the likelihood of regular contribution to the arts rises substantially with income, and contributions by individuals and estates are estimated to be the largest single source of voluntary funding; combined contributions from corporations and foundations account for only about 10% of all private philanthropic support. Nevertheless, major orchestras and opera appear to receive proportionately more regular con-

Table 11.2. *Sources of funding for the performing arts, percentage distribution of total operating income by source, 1965–6 and 1973–4*

Source of income	Theater companies		Metropolitan Opera		Other operas		Symphonies		Dance companies		All, except Metropolitan Opera	
	1965–6	1973–4	1965–6	1973–4	1965–6	1973–4	1965–6	1973–4	1965–6	1973–4	1965–6	1973–4
Government sources[a]	4	13	—[b]	5	2	10	5	15	11	11	5	13
Ticket income	68	52	52	44	50	40	38	30	42	27	44	35
Services income, nongovernment	1	2	11	11	3	5	9	9	8	19	7	9
Recordings, radio, TV, films		—[b]	3	2		—[b]	3	2	—[b]	2	2	2
Nonperformance earned income[c]	6	7	5	10	5	3	11	5	5	6	9	5
Other unearned income[d]	21	26	28	28	39	41	33	40	34	34	33	37
Number of organizations covered	27	31	1	1	30	28	91	78	17	15	165	152

Note: Because of rounding, detail may not add to 100%.

[a] Includes services income from government sources and government grants.

[b] Less than 0.5%.

[c] Income from performances of other groups, school income, and receipts from concessions, program advertising, facilities rentals, etc.

[d] Unearned income other than government grants, that is, individual, business, and foundation contributions and grants and endowment earnings.

Source: Netzer (1978, p. 101).

Table 11.3. *Financial support for the arts from the NEA, 1970–85 ($ million)*[a]

Type of fund and program	1970	1975	1980	1985
Funds available[b]	15.7	86.9	188.1	171.7
Program appropriation	6.3	67.3	97.0	118.7
Matching funds[c]	2.0	7.5	42.9	29.5
Grants awarded (number)	556	3,071	5,505	4,801
Funds obligated	12.9	81.7	166.4	149.4
Music	2.5	14.9	13.6	15.3
State arts agencies	1.9	14.7	22.1	24.4
Museums	NA	10.8	11.2	11.9
Theater	2.8	6.4	8.4	10.6
Dance	1.7	6.1	8.0	9.0
Public media	0.2	5.4	8.4	9.9
Challenge[d]	—	—	50.8	20.7
Visual arts	1.0	3.2	7.2	6.2
Other	2.8	20.1	36.6	41.3

Note: NA, not available; dash indicates not applicable. *Source:* NEA.
[a]For years ending June 30 in 1970 and 1975; for years ending September 30 in later years.
[b]Includes other funds, not shown separately. Excludes administrative funds. Gifts are included through 1980 and excluded thereafter.
[c]Represents federal funds appropriated only on receipt or certification by endowment of matching nonfederal gifts.
[d]Program designed to stimulate new sources and higher levels of giving to institutions for the purpose of guaranteeing long-term stability and financial independence. Program requires a match of three private dollars to each federal dollar. Funds for Challenge grants are not allocated by program area because they are awarded on a grant-by-grant basis.

tributions than theater or dance, although some private-institution grants (foundations, corporations, and labor unions) are regularly directed toward specific support of other organizations and projects including those in museums, music, architecture, and literature.

Performing arts often are also subsidized by government funding through state and local arts councils and through federal participation in matching-grant programs of the National Endowment for the Arts (Table 11.3). However, in Europe, national-government support has a much longer and deeper tradition than in the United States – where emphasis has often been on construction of cultural centers tied to urban-renewal projects, rather than on reduction of operating deficits. Table 11.3 illustrates the relative importance and the diversity of various sources of funding for the arts.

Although on purely economic grounds it can be argued that taxpayers' financial support for money-losing arts programs enjoyed by an elite few is a waste of resources better spent elsewhere, justification of some government subsidy can be made:

Support for the arts opens opportunities for development of talented individuals from nonaffluent backgrounds.

Such support has educational benefit, exposing young people to cultural activities that they might not otherwise encounter.

Arts are public goods, which when provided to individuals, automatically become available to and benefit other members of the community.

In this respect, arts are goods with both public and private characteristics, and, like education, they can justifiably be supported by a combination of public and private contributions. For private corporations, sustenance of cultural activities often stimulates local commercial activity and provides new business opportunities that have positive feedback on prospects for employment and for profits. And for individuals, in addition to purely aesthetic pleasures, there are often substantial tax advantages that accompany support of the arts.

11.3 The play's the thing

Production financing and participations

Financial support for the arts, whether from public or private sources, is usually dedicated to the development of specific facilities, or to sustenance of fixed dance, orchestral, and opera groups: Usually, no direct financial return on investment is expected. But when it comes to funding of theater, the motives for support are often much more speculative and entrepreneurial than in any of the other arts. In fact, the financing and development process for new commercial-theater productions most closely resembles that used in movies.

To start, a producer normally acquires through agents the rights to a play or other literary property that is to be adapted for stage.[3] Then, an option contract is used for the interim period in which all the artistic and financial elements ultimately needed to mount a stage production are assembled.

In acquiring rights to a play, the producer adheres to Dramatists' Guild option-contract stipulations that provide the playwright with a nonrefundable deposit to be forfeited if the play is not produced within a year or some shorter period. In addition, the dramatist is entitled to royalties on a sliding scale, between 5% and 10% of the box-office gross, and to the bulk of receipts from ancillary rights, including film, cable-television, and foreign productions.

Once an option is acquired, the producer then approaches prospective investors known as *angels,* to provide financing. Angels must indeed love

Table 11.4. *Typical financial participations in
theater productions*

Gross participation (%)	
Playwright	10
Lead performer	5
Director	2
Theater manager	25
Profit participation (%)	
Playwright	5–10
Director	5
Lead performer	5–10
Other performers and show manager	10
Producer	15
Investors	50–60

theater because tax sheltering is much more effective in oil, real estate, and professional sports franchises than on Broadway, where depreciation aspects are limited. An angel must also have enough income to afford a tax loss (write-off); historically the odds against ever seeing a return on investment are over 2 to 1. Yet, angels continue to be attracted: Every so often a show will provide spectacular returns on investment, especially when sales of cable-television, movie, record-album, and other rights are included.[4]

Dismal statistics, however, seem not to damp enthusiasm for investment in theater. Although financing is occasionally in the form of sale of stock in a corporation organized for production of a play, it may also be in the form of a large development investment that is granted by film studios in return for eventual movie rights. More typically, though, an offering prospectus describing anticipated running and start-up costs of a show is circulated to interested individual investors, who are offered in return for their capital a share of potential profits in a limited partnership. These partners are usually guaranteed half of any profits earned by the production (Table 11.4).

Other investors may include the play's director, leading performer or performers, and the theater owner. Directors and lead performers will usually receive a small percentage (e.g., perhaps 5%) of the play's earnings in addition to salary or fee, whereas theater owners may (depending on season, theater quality, and the producer's reputation) receive 20%–30% of the box-office gross. As noted by Baumol and Bowen,

the locus of control of a production is sharply divided between the producer and the owner of the theater in which the play is performed.

While the producer selects his play, controls the artistic standards of the production, raises the funds invested in it, hires the director and the cast, sets wages and decides on outlays on costumes and scenery, there are other matters which he normally does not control completely. A powerful producer can obtain a contract giving him a substantial voice in what may be termed the marketing of a play, but usually this is left largely in the hands of the theater owner, who often supplies, in addition to box office personnel and ushers, several stagehands and, where appropriate, several musicians. He bears part of the cost of advertising, has a voice in the setting of ticket prices, and supplies tickets to brokerage agencies. He has complete control of the box office, into which a producer may even be refused admittance . . .

The theater owner normally receives a percentage of the weekly gross of a play so that, aside from the advantages of length of run it is in his interest to house a successful play. Since the contract usually provides that he can eject a play from his theater when the weekly gross falls below a pre-specified figure, it is alleged that box office personnel have sometimes been instructed to refuse to sell tickets to potential patrons, stating that all the seats were already sold. (Baumol and Bowen 1968, pp. 20–1)

As in movie deals, variations from fairly standardized percentages are based on the bargaining power of participants. A major star in a small play can receive weekly guarantees plus increasing percentages of gross after receipts reach certain levels. Directors may receive fairly large up-front fees and smaller percentages of weekly grosses. Playwrights normally earn at least a minimum author's royalty of 10% weekly, and the show's general manager will receive a fee plus weekly salary, and perhaps a small percentage of net profits, if any.

Operational characteristics

A private placement memorandum will estimate the weekly break-even and weekly net profit at capacity for a show that is up and running. But even relatively modest productions require extensively detailed budgets and forecasts because of the many small items that when added together make for significant running costs.

The estimates in Table 11.5 are for a $500,000 Broadway production staged in 1982. As can be seen, advertising expenses constitute a major proportion of total runnning costs. In this example, the weekly break-even, including all royalties, was calculated at $84,500 per week, and at capacity, weekly receipts and net profits were estimated at $200,000 and $80,000, respectively.

The high fixed costs of operation naturally create a large leveraged effect on profits, and in effect, there is a tendency to have either a bona fide hit with substantial profit, or an outright failure – with little likelihood of anything in between the extremes. A graph can be used to illustrate the sensitivity of profits to changes in box-office receipts for a play with running costs of $100,000 per week, average ticket prices of $30, and seating of 500 (Figure 11.4). Here it is assumed that the production does not garner additional revenues from cable-television or movie-rights sales or from any

Table 11.5. *Budget estimtes for a $500,000 Broadway stage production: an example, circa 1982*[a]

Scenery	$36,500
Props	5,400
Costumes	7,400
Electrics and sound	17,000
Fees	36,000
Rehearsals	46,700
Advertising	134,000
Other costs	77,000
Total production costs	$360,000
Pre-New York (rehearsals, hauling)	$38,000
Bonds (AEA, IATSE, ATPAM, theater)	57,000
Reserve for contingency and preview losses	45,000
Total capitalization	$500,000

[a]During the 1983–3 season, average Broadway production costs were as follows: comedies/dramas, $666,000; musicals, $2,144,563; low-budget musicals, $324,375 (according to New York State attorney general's office).

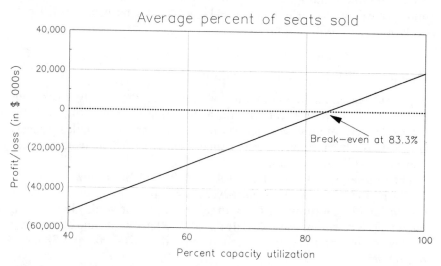

Figure 11.4. Break-even-capacity utilization: an illustration.

other such ancillary sources, and that royalties and other payments are not scaled (usually they are).

Break-even example:
Running cost per week: $100,000
Seating: 500 persons

Average ticket price: $30
Performances per week: 8

Under these conditions, break-even requires an average capacity utilization of 83.4% (417 seats); figures consistently below that level will cause losses to mount rapidly.[5] Yet, as noted by Lawson (1983), levels of 70% or less are not uncommon.

Last but not least in budgeting for a show, investors should have a solid grasp of labor union contract stipulations. Relationships with the Actors' Equity Association, the Dramatists' Guild (playwrights), the Society of Stage Directors and Choreographers, and the International Alliance of Theatrical Stage Employees may have important financial ramifications on performing-arts productions.[6]

11.4 Economist echoes

Studies of the economics of the performing arts are relatively recent; a large literature in this area has not yet evolved. But several important works including those of Baumol and Bowen (1968), Blaug (1976), Netzer (1978), and Throsby and Withers (1979), can be cited. Some tentative general conclusions from these studies (Hendon, Shanahan, and MacDonald 1980, p. 21):

According to economic theory, art goods themselves are not public goods. In economic theory, a necessary but not sufficient condition for a pure public good is that it can be jointly consumed perfectly. The exclusion principle says that a product, though jointly consumed, can be provided in separable units to various consumers. Because admission to an artistic event (or right to use) can be provided in separable units, the exclusion principle is operable in the arts.
The more definitive externalities generated by the arts usually flow to special-interest groups.

Hansmann (1981) is also especially insightful in exploring the reasons for the preponderance of nonprofit-institution involvement in the high-culture performing arts. He notes that high fixed production costs relative to marginal costs and overall demand force performing-arts groups to engage in price discrimination if they are to survive without subsidy. However, because opportunities for effective ticket-price discrimination are limited, the nonprofit-organization structure seems best suited for encouraging voluntary donations.[7]

11.5 Concluding remarks

Performing-arts organizations seem always to live on a financial precipice. This condition is, of course, a function of live-audience size limitations, the great expense of coordinating an effective production, and the perpetually high cost of money for risky ventures. From an economist's view, however, the most important and ineluctable element is that productivity cannot be raised significantly in the performance of performing arts.

As suggested by Baumol and Baumol (1984), not even the development of new electronic delivery and storage systems can in the long run provide an escape. On the programming-cost side, an hour of performance still takes an hour, whether it is done before a camera for distribution on television, cable, or videocassette, or for a live audience.

In reference to the network-television business, for example, the Baumols noted that there will be

an initial period of decline in total costs (in constant dollars) followed by a period in which . . . costs begin to behave in a manner more and more similar to the live performing arts. The reason is that the cost of the highly technological component (transmission cost) will decline, or at least not rise as fast as the economy's inflation rate. At the same time, the cost of programming increases at a rate surpassing the rate of inflation.

If each year transmission costs decrease and over-the-line or programming expenses increase, eventually programming cost will begin to dominate the overall budget . . . One of the major networks reports . . . that while over-the-line costs comprised 30 to 35 percent of a dramatic presentation ten years ago, they now constitute 50 percent of the budget. (Baumol and Baumol 1984, p. 36)

Of course, on the positive side, advances in technology enable much larger audiences to enjoy performances. As a consequence, revenues derived from the new media are gradually becoming much more significant considerations in financing the arts, and backers of commercial-theater productions may look increasingly to cable-television license fees or home video presentation formats to enhance profits or to reduce losses.[8] Furthermore, although the culture audience is not proportionately large even among such viewers, it is likely that the convenience and relatively low cost of home-video devices will encourage frequent sampling by devotees while stimulating greater interest from others. At a minimum, then, the spread of new-media technologies should help retard financial decay in performing-arts organizations.

Cultural achievements reflect not only the discipline, devotion, and intelligence of individuals, but also the most basic values of the society. That is why, for example, the free expression inherent in two distinctly American art forms, jazz and modern dance, would not thrive in an authoritarian environment.

No matter what the politics, however, the economic dilemma for performing arts cannot be circumvented. In a free society, some manner of subsidy – usually a combination of government support and tax incentives for private individuals and corporations – is normally required to sustain or to expand high-culture activities.

Selected additional reading

Andresky, J. (1983). "So You Want to Be an Angel?" *Forbes* 131(3)(January 31):92–7.

Baumol, H., and Baumol, W. J., eds (1984). *Inflation and the Performing Arts.* New York: New York University.

Biddle, L. (1988). *Our Government and the Arts: A Perspective from the Inside.* New York: American Council for the Arts.

Brockett, O. G. (1979). *The Theater: An Introduction,* 4th ed. New York: Holt, Rinehart and Winston.

Clark, L. H., Jr. (1985). "Why Can't the Arts Be More Businesslike?" *Wall Street Journal,* June 11.

Cox, M. (1984). "Orchestra Thrives by Playing the Music People Didn't Want," *Wall Street Journal,* July 19.

Duka, J. (1982). "Cable TV Turns Hungrily to the Theater," *New York Times,* June 27.

Dunning, J. (1986). "Dance as Big Business May Pose a Threat to Dance as Art," *New York Times,* March 30.

Farber, D. C. (1981). *Producing Theatre: A Comprehensive Legal and Business Guide.* New York: Drama Book Specialists.

Feld, A., O'Hare, J., and Schuster, J. M. D. (1983) *Patrons Despite Themselves. Taxpayers and Arts Policy. A Twentieth Century Fund Report.* New York: New York University.

Godley, W. (1977). "The Economics of the Arts," *Economic Journal 87* (September):578–80.

Goodman, W. (1984). "Scholars Debate Need to Aid Arts," *New York Times,* May 2.

Hoelterhoff, M. (1987). "New York City (Opera) on $112,452 a Day," *Wall Street Journal,* August 18.

Honan, W. H. (1989). "Arts Dollars: Pinched as Never Before," *New York Times,* May 28.

Kroeger, B. (1987). "Raising a Million for 'Les Mis.'" *New York Times,* July 19.

Langley, S. (1980). *Theatre Management in America, Principle and Practice,* Rev. Ed. New York: Drama Book Publishers.

Larson, G. O. (1983). *The Reluctant Patron.* Philadelphia: University of Pennsylvania.

"London's West End Fights Off an Attack of the Glums," *The Economist Magazine,* May 17, 1986.

Lynes, R. (1985). *The Lively Audience: A Social History of the Visual and Performing Arts in America, 1890–1950.* New York: Harper & Row.

Mayer, M. (1883). "The Big Business of Grand Opera," *Fortune* 108(8)(October 17):146–60.

Moore, T. G. (1966). "The Demand for Broadway Theatre Tickets," *Review of Economics and Statistics* 48(1)(February):79–87.

Mulcahy, K. V., and Swain, C. R., eds. (1982). *Public Policy and the Arts.* Boulder, Colo.: Westview Press.

Murray, M. (1956) *Circus!* New York: Appleton-Century-Crofts.

National Endowment for the Arts (1981). *Conditions and Needs of the Professional American Theater.* Washington, D.C.: NEA.

Revzin, P., and Patner, A. (1989). "Conductor Barenboim Survives Tough World of Orchestral Music," *Wall Street Journal,* May 2.

Silk, L. (1978). "The Metropolitan Opera – The High Price of Being Best: The Books Reveal the Cost Squeeze," *New York Times,* February 12.

Snyder, L. (1977). "How to Lose Less on Broadway," *Fortune* XCV(5)(May):147.

Taylor, F., and Barresi, A. L. (1984). *The Arts at a New Frontier: The National Endowment for the Arts.* New York: Plenum.

Wickham,G. (1985). *A History of the Theatre.* New York and Cambridge: Cambridge University Press.

12
Amusement/theme parks

Mickey is the mouse that roared.

The industry of themed amusement parks – begun in July 1955 by Mickey Mouse, the famous Disney character – has evolved into a multibillion-dollar entertainment segment. In this chapter we shall sketch the ecomonic out-lines of amusement/theme-park operations.

12.1 Flower power

Gardens and groves

The roots of this business extend to seventeenth-century France, from where the concept of pleasure gardens with fountains and flowers gradually spread throughout Europe. London's Vauxhall Gardens, for example, were established in 1661. And by the eighteenth century, as Kyriazi (1976) has noted, entertainment and circus acts, including trapeze and tightrope, and ascension balloons and music were added. Meanwhile, in England affiliations with nearby taverns or inns became common. Yet it was not until

273

the 1873 Vienna World's Fair held at The Prater, that mechanical rides and fun houses were introduced. As Mangels (1952, p.4) describes it,

for more than three hundred years, elaborate outdoor amusement centers have existed in several European countries. Known usually as "pleasure gardens" they were remarkably similar to those of today in their general layout and variety of entertainment. Some of the larger parks provided events and devices which thrilled their visitors as keenly as present-day attractions. Queens of the slack wire and dare-devils of the flying rings brought gasps of facinated terror, much as they do beneath the Big Top today ... free balloon ascensions, and parachute jumps held crowds spellbound as far back as the seventeen-nineties.

In the United States, however, amusement areas did not begin to appear until the late 1800s, when streetcar companies began to build picnic groves to attact weekend riders. Soon thereafter, food and rides came to be emphasized, and major facilities such as New York's Coney Island sprang into national prominence. But although by the 1920s there were some 1,500 such parks in the United States, the Great Depression, the develop-ment of movies, television, and automobiles, and the decay of inner-cities eventually led to the demise of most.

Modern times

Walt Disney, first a struggling cartoonist and then filmmaker, liked spend-ing time with his children. Trouble was, there were few bright, clean parks where all members of the family could have fun. So being an extraordi-narily imaginative and entrepreneurial soul, he envisioned creation of such a park modeled in part after the famous Tivoli Gardens that he had seen in Copenhagen (Thomas 1976, Chapter 20).

As the legend goes, he brought his plans for an amusement park con-taining themed areas before a rather skeptical and reluctant group of bank-ers. But somehow – with perseverance, bank loans supplemented by bor-rowing on his life-insurance policies, and sale of concession rights to the young American Broadcasting Company – he managed to open Disney-land in 1955[1] amidst the Anaheim California, orange groves. The rest, as they say, is history.

Disneyland's immediate success led to numerous expansions. But not until the late 1960s did other large public companies begin to invest heavily in this business.[2] And it was not until 1971 that Disney itself extended into the swamplands of Florida to construct, for an estimated $300 million, the core of Disney World.[3]

As of the early 1990s, theme parks in the United States – including about 30 majors, and a host of smaller ones – generate over $4 billion a year from over 125 million visitors (Table 12.1).[4] Yet in a somewhat ironic twist, the American-style theme park concepts of the late twentieth century are now being exported back to Europe and to elsewhere around the globe.[5] A com-pilation of such major theme parks and annual visitor estimates appears in Table 12.2.

Table 12.1. *Estimated attendance (thousands) at major theme park facilities in the United States, 1975–88*[a]

Year	Total	Disneyland (Anaheim)	Disney World (Orlando)	Total excluding Disney parks
1988	107,291	12,161	26,731	68,399
1987	106,389	12,841	28,227	65,321
1986	98,582	11,979	25,453	61,150
1985	91,418	11,744	21,755	57,919
1984	86,934	9,869	21,121	55,944
1983	93,566	9,980	22,712	60,874
1982	80,749	10,421	12,560	57,768
1981	82,718	11,343	13,221	58,154
1980	81,731	11,522	13,783	56,426
1979	80,461	10,760	13,792	55,909
1978	80,504	10,807	14,070	55,627
1977	73,159	10,676	13,057	49,426
1976	68,286	10,211	13,107	44,968
1975	60,948	10,062	12,515	38,371
CAGR[b]	4.4	1.5	6.0	4.5

[a]Fiscal years.
[b]Compound annual growth rate, 1975–88 (%).

12.2 Financial operating characteristics

Operating a theme park is very much like operating a small city: The streets should frequently be swept clean and occasionally repaved; sewer and sanitation systems should be efficient yet invisible; police, fire, and health departments should be trained and available at a moment's notice. Those elements alone are difficult for most cities to handle well. But, in addition, a park also issues its own currency in the form of ticket books, and it provides visitor-transportation systems, live-entertainment services, and sometimes extensive shopping, hotel, and car-care facilities.

Furthermore, parks – subject as they are to seasonal and circadian rhythms of attendance and to rapidly changing weather patterns – usually depend on a seasonal and largely unskilled work force that has inherently high turnover. In all, it is not easy to juggle those elements and consistently generate significant earnings growth (see Table 12.3). For a specific park, operating-margin performance, thus may be uneven and volatile: One year the problem is gasoline shortages; the next it may be abnormally hot summer temperatures, rainy spring weekends, or, as in 1982, competition from a World's Fair.

Table 12.2. *Selected major theme park facilities*

Facility	Year opened	Approximate number of annual visitors (millions)
North America		
Disney World, Florida	1971	30.0
Disneyland, California	1955	13.5
Sea World, Florida	1973	4.6
Universal Studios Tour, Florida	1990	5.0[a]
Universal Studios Tour, California	1964	3.8
Knotts Berry Farm, California	1940	4.0
Busch Gardens, Florida	1959	3.9
Sea World, California	1963	3.4
Six Flags/Magic Mountain, California	1971	3.1
Kings Island, Ohio	1972	3.0
Cedar Point, Ohio	1870	2.9
Six Flags/Great America, Illinois	1976	2.6
Six Flags/Texas	1961	2.5
Six Flags/Georgia	1967	2.4
Great America, California	1975	2.3
Opryland, Tennessee	1972	2.3
Canada's Wonderland, Toronto	1981	2.3
Kings Dominion, Virginia	1975	2.2
AstroWorld, Texas	1968	2.1
Busch Gardens, Virginia	1975	2.1
Six Flags Great Adventure, New Jersey	1973	2.0
Six Flags/Mid-America, Missouri	1971	1.5
Boardwalk & Baseball, Florida	1987	1.5
Hersheypark, Pennsylvania	1907	1.8
Europe		
EuroDisney	1992	12.0[a]
Tivoli Gardens, Denmark	1843	4.5
Grona Lund, Sweden	1883	1.4
Alton Towers, U.K.	1924	2.3
De Efteling, Netherlands	1951	2.3
Europa Park, W. Germany	1975	1.5
Duinrell, Netherlands	1935	1.1
Thorpe Park, U.K.	1979	1.1
Mirapolis, France	1987	1.0
Bellewaerde, Belgium	1969	0.6
Other		
Tokyo Disneyland, Japan	1983	12.0
Sea World, Australia	1971	1.2

[a]Projected.

Table 12.3. *Theme parks, revenues and earnings: composite of 4 companies,[a] 1984–8[b]*

Year	Revenues	Operating income	Operating margin (%)	Assets	Cash flow
1988	2,901.8	702.3	24.2	4,279.8	935.7
1987	2,609.8	666.5	25.5	3,554.9	876.5
1986	2,248.5	525.1	23.4	3,087.2	703.5
1985	1,901.9	355.4	18.7	2,867.5	519.2
1984	1,752.3	279.4	16.2	2,858.9	430.5
CAGR[c]	13.9	25.9		10.6	21.4

[a]Industry data are heavily weighted by Disney park performance. Excluding Disney, aggregate operating income for the remaining sample of theme companies was $86.7 million, $99.7 million, $121.4 million, $117.6 million, and $137.5 million, in 1984 through 1988, respectively.
[b]In millions of dollars except for operating margin (%)
[c]Compound annual growth rate, 1984–8 (%).

No matter what the uncertainties, however, operating leverage – familiar in the airline and hotel business – is a constant feature. The costs of labor, electricity, insurance, and so forth remain relatively fixed, and once the break-even point is reached, every additional admission ticket sold produces a high marginal profit.[6]

Such is the case until the park becomes crowded. At that point, long lines at popular attractions reduce opportunities for impulse spending, crimp the initial good mood of the visitors, and entail additional labor and materials costs. Most parks will find that in analyzing daily results, marginal-profit curves as a function of attendance would probably appear similar to Figure 12.1.

On the other hand, Table 12.4 demonstrates how sensitive operating profits are to changes in two key variables: visitor-days (attendance equivalent to the number of separate visitors times the number of days of operation) and average per-capita spending. In this example it is assumed that because of climatic factors, a park has an effective operating season of 100 days per year, that on an average day there are 25,000 visitors, and that average per-capita spending on admissions, rides, foods, beverages, and trinkets is $20. With a relatively stable operating expense of $30 million, operating earnings, as shown in column A, will be $20 million.

Assuming that the number of visitors increases by 20% to 30,000 per day and that expenses remain largely unchanged, operating profit will increase by 50% to $30 million, as indicated in column B. And if attendance holds constant and per-capita spending rises by 20%, the same 50% increase in operating profit will appear as in column C. Finally, assume, as in column

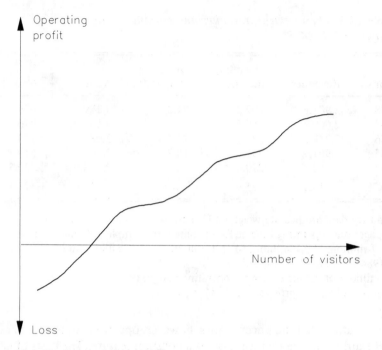

Figure 12.1. Profit as a function of attendance: an illustration.

Table 12.4. *Theme-park operating leverage: an example*

	A	B	C	D
Visitors, avg./day	25,000	30,000	25,000	30,000
Visitor-days (att.)	2,500,000	3,000,000	2,500,000	3,000,000
Per-cap. spending ($)	20.00	20.00	24.00	24.00
Total annual revs. ($)	50,000,000	60,000,000	60,000,000	72,000,000
Operating expenses	30,000,000	30,000,000	30,000,000	30,000,000
Operating profits ($)	20,000,000	30,000,000	30,000,000	42,000,000

D, that per-capita spending and attendance each rise by 20%. Then operating profit will increase to $42.0 million – a gain of 110% over that shown in column A.

Of course, in the real world, operating expenses will rise along with attendance, per-capita spending will tend to decrease as attendance rises near capacity (i.e., the crowds are immobilized), and the gains in profit will not be as large as indicated in this simplistic example. But substantial operating leverage will still be visible in actual results.

Because compounding of changes in both attendance and spending has such great impact on profits, park managers devote much of their time to figuring how each input factor can be increased without adversely affecting

Table 12.5. *Selected service industry census comparisons for amusement parks, 1972–87*

Year	No. of establishments with payroll	Receipts ($ thousand)	Receipts per: Employee ($)	Receipts per: Establishment ($)	Payroll as % of receipts
Total selected services[a]					
1987	1,624,622	752,474,203	47,964	463,169	37.6
1982	1,339,229	426,981,971	38,446	318,827	37.1
1977	724,203	164,219,449	25,913	226,759	34.1
1972	683,614	95,675,519	18,034	139,955	34.9
% change					
1972–87	137.7	686.5	166.0	230.9	
All amusement & recreation services (incl. motion pictures)					
1987	74,293	52,807,943	56,839	710,798	27.0
1982	72,976	33,114,974	41,199	453,779	26.6
1977	61,761	19,756,133	29,919	319,880	26.7
1972	66,064	12,660,113	19,386	191,634	30.4
% change					
1972–87	12.5	317.1	193.2	270.9	
Amusement parks					
1987	744	3,469,836	57,434	4,663,758	23.6
1982	491	1,823,728	39,250	3,714,313	33.1
1977	663	1,172,419	31,675	1,768,354	30.1
1972	682	467,718	22,928	685,804	34.0
% change					
1972–87	9.1	641.9	150.5	580.0	

[a]Except hospitals
Source: Census of Selected Services, U.S. Department of Commerce.

the other. Toward this end, many fancy mathematical modeling techniques (linear programming, production-function, and queuing-system estimators, etc.) can be used to improve the efficiency of park operations. Norms for average daily attendance conditioned on weather, line waiting times, and price elasticities can be established and tested much as though parks were production-line factories.[7]

Nevertheless, because there really is no such thing as a typical theme park – operations depend so much on region, weather patterns, number of season days, local demographic and income characteristics, and age and amount of capital invested – it is difficult to establish a representative statistical composite. Each facility must develop its own set of standards.

12.3 Economic sensitivities

A sense of how this industry's operating performance compares with those of other economic segments can be derived from Table 12.5, which is a

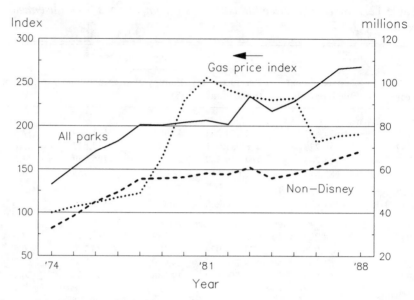

Figure 12.2. Theme-park attendance in the United States versus index of average gasoline prices, 1974–88.

condensed version of the census of selected service industries (Table S1.4). What we see is that between 1972 and 1987, park receipts grew almost as fast as the total service economy and faster than the whole amusement-and-recreation services subsegment. But, in addition, the numbers suggest that the park industry has in the aggregate not been especially able to mitigate the inherent labor intensity of operations: Receipts per employee between 1972 and 1987 increased by about the same percentage for amusement parks (150.5%) as for all services (166.0%)

Unfortunately, there are also difficulties in correlating theme park admissions trends with important economic time series such as GNP or real disposable income. For instance, an economic recession could be expected to adversely affect admissions growth trends. But ticket pricing, the opening of new park attractions, availability and pricing of gasoline, airline fares, and demographic changes are among some of the other variables to be considered. Major theme park admissions trends are compared to an index of gasoline prices in Figure 12.2.

12.4 Valuing theme-park properties

Real estate – the key asset of any park – normally has the potential to provide the extraordinary long-term returns on investment that plainly are not obtainable from day-to-day operations. But for this to occur, a park must be located in the path of suburban expansion, where it will ultimately be worth more dead than alive. In such instances the land is a true hedge against inflation, and operation of a park may be seen as merely an interim holding action in anticipation of development of higher-value alternative uses.

Assuming, nevertheless, that a park will continue to be operated, the usual established methods for valuing other entertainment properties may also be applied here. As in the broadcasting and cable industries, for example, theme park asset values are taken as a multiple of projected operating cash flows before taxes, interest, and depreciation. Such multiples would, of course, normally he expected to vary inversely to interest rates. Other factors affecting the multiple of cash flow would naturally include:

Age and condition of the park's rides and attractions
Demographic and income trends in the surrounding region
Potential for expanding ride and admissions capacity
Potential for raising prices and/or per capita spending
Prospects for development of nearby transportation facilities
Proximity of other similar attractions[8]

Again, as in other entertainment industries, public market valuations are often only one-half to two-thirds of what private market valuations based on a multiple of cash flow might be. Thus, well-situated theme parks with proven operating characteristics are often attractive candidates for leveraged buy-outs in which banks or other large institutions will lend a major percentage of the required funding for the buy-out based on the security of the park's cash flow.

12.5 Concluding remarks

In the United States admissions growth trends have been fairly stable and somewhat above the rate of growth of real GNP over long periods. Because of this, many of the larger parks have been able to generate cash flows significantly in excess of their capital needs, and have appropriately attracted the attention of investors.

Although the industry seems to be rather mature in North America, where it has developed into an entertainment form dominated by a few large companies that have the marketing expertise and capital to continually upgrade and expand their facilities, it seems to be on the verge of substantial growth in other parts of the world. In whatever location, though, the degree of success will have as much to do with intangible elements – quality of design, efficiency of service, and public fancy – as anything else.

Selected additional reading

Braithwaite, D. (1967). *Fairground Architecture: The World of Amusement Parks, Carnivals, & Fairs.* New York: Praeger.

Finch, C. (1975). *The Art of Walt Disney: From Mickey Mouse to the Magic Kingdoms.* New York: Harry N. Abrams.

Hannon, K. (1987). "All Aboard!" *Forbes,* 140(3)(August 10).

Mosley, L. (1987). *Disney's World: A Biography.* Briarcliff Manor (N.Y.): Stein and Day.

Mrowca, M. (1983). "Amusement Park in Ohio Has Its Ups and Downs But Continues to Draw Crowds after 114 Years." *Wall Street Journal,* July 8.

Schickel, R. (1968). *The Disney Version: The Life, Times, Art and Commerce of Walt Disney.* New York: Simon & Schuster.

Part IV
Roundup

13
Epilogue

Time flies when you're having fun.

Entertainment is a big and rapidly changing international business, and the study of its economic characteristics is still at an early stage. As a platform for such studies, this book has attempted to convey a sense of the industry's dynamics in relation to the financial and economic features that enduringly characterize entertainment enterprises. This closing chapter provides a review and summary of those features.

13.1 Common elements

As seen in Chapter 1, leisure time – which can be grossly defined as time not spent at work – has been expanding very slowly, if at all, in recent years. Indeed, over the long run, the potential to expand leisure time depends on the rate of gain in economic productivity, which is in turn affected by the rate of technological development.

After deducting life-sustenance activities from nonwork time, we have what is known in the vernacular as free time. But time is never really free in an economic sense because there are always alternative-opportunity costs. Entertainment, defined as that which has the effect of pleasurably

285

diverting the psyche, thus competes for – and is ultimately limited by – the amount of free time available.

Beyond these generalities are several frequently observed industry characteristics.

Many are called, but few are chosen:

Perhaps the most noticeable tendency of entertainment businesses is that in the steady-state growth phase (i.e., after a segment has attained a size at which long-run domination by several large companies has been established), *profits from a very few highly popular products are generally required to offset losses from many mediocrities.* This is evident in movies, production of network-television shows, toys and video games, and recorded music. But it appears to a much lesser extent in the performing-arts category; there, even a few occasional hits cannot counterbalance chronic operating deficits.

Ancillary markets provide disproportionately large returns:

Another key characteristic is that *entertainment products often derive a very large proportion of their returns from ancillary or secondary markets.* Films, for instance, now on an average derive over half their revenues from cable and home video rather than from theatrical release. But spin-offs of character licenses ("Annie" from the theater, and before that the comic strip, for instance) are also in this category. Additional examples include spin-offs of popular TV series and sequels and novelizations of popular movies.

Marketing expenditures per unit are proportionately large:

Many entertainment products or services have unique features that must continuously be brought to the attention of potential consumers. In addition, the life cycle of an entertainment product may be very brief. Therefore, be it gaming casinos in Atlantic City, theme parks in Florida, or a new video game, *per-unit marketing expenditures tend to be large relative to total unit costs of operation or production.* As an example, it may be recalled that marketing typically adds at least 50% to the cost of the average major feature-film release.

Capital costs are relatively high; oligopolist tendencies are prevalent:

As happens in many other industries, once beyond the very early stages of a segment's developement, *the cost of capital and the amount of it required for operations becomes a formidable barrier to entry by new competitors.* Most entertainment industry segments thus come to be ruled by large companies with relatively easy access to large pools of capital. Such oligopolistic tendencies can, for example, be seen in distribution of recorded music and movies, and in the gaming, theme-park, cable, video-game, and broadcasting industries.

Many products and services are not standardized (which is good for entrepreneurs, and bad for relative-productivity gains):

There are four important consequences of such nonstandardization:

1. Despite the oligopolistic framework, *there is considerable freedom for the entrepreneurial spirit to thrive.* That is, operas, plays, movies, ballets, songs, and video games are uniquely produced and are normally originated by individuals working alone or in small groups, and not by giant corporate committees. One can become rich and famous as a direct result of one's own creative efforts.

2. *The entrepreneurial spirit and thus importance of the individual to the productive process is accommodated by means of widely varying, uniquely tailored financing arrangements.* This is especially evident in movies, recorded music, and sports.

3. *Where the production is the product itself* (e.g., live performance of music or dance), *it is difficult to enhance productivity.* To some extent this feature also appears in areas as diverse as filmmaking, sports, and casino gaming.

4. Under the aforementioned conditions, *the costs of creating and marketing entertainment products such as movies and television programs tend to rise at above-average rates.*

Technological advances provide the saving grace:

Fortunately, ongoing *technological development makes it ever easier and less expensive to manufacture, distribute, and receive entertainment products and services.* Over the long run, this leads to more varied and more affordable mass-market entertainment.

Entertainment products and services often have strong public-good characteristics:

With pure public goods, the cost of production is independent of the number of consumers; that is, consumption by one person does not reduce the amount available for consumption by another. Although delivered to consumers in the form of private goods, *many entertainment products and services, including movies, records, television programs, and sports contests, have public-good characteristics.*

Entertainment products and services have universal appeal:

Demand for entertainment cuts across all cultural and national boundaries, and many cravings (for laughter, for music, or for gambling) have deep-seated psychological roots. This means that many entertainment products have worldwide market appeal, and that incremental revenues from international sources can have an important effect on profitability.

13.2 Guidelines for evaluating entertainment securities

The preceding chapters provide a background for analysis of entertainment industry investments. But many factors not explicitly treated here – Federal Reserve Bank policy, overall economic trends, and investor psychology – also influence investment performance (Figure 13.1).

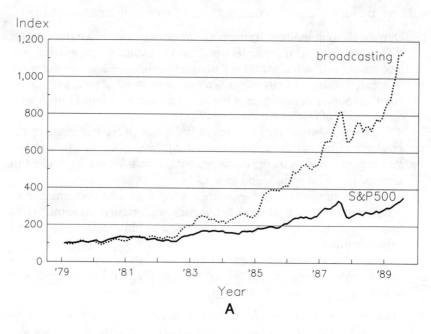

A

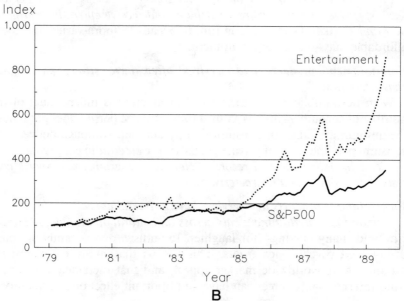

B

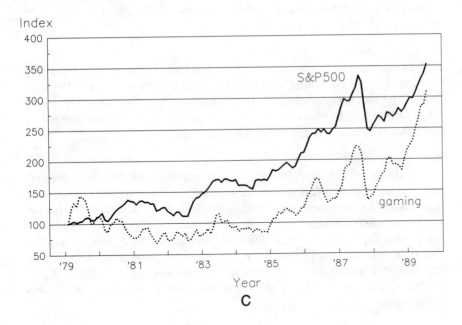

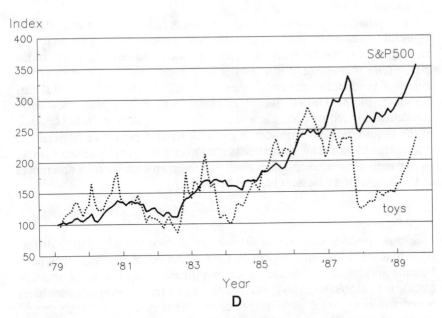

Figure 13.1. Standard & Poor's stock price indices for (a) broadcast media, (b) entertainment, (c) casinos, and (d) toys versus the S&P 500 stock composite index, 1979–89. Based on month-end prices.

Happily, it is not necessary to delve into those subjects to extract a few basic investment decision guidelines.

Cash flows and private market values:

Most entertainment companies are first analyzed in terms of what a private buyer might be willing to pay for the right to obtain access to the cash flow of the enterprise. Public market valuations are often typically in the range of one-half to two-thirds of the private values, which are derived as multiples of projected cash flow (minus debt).

Debt-equity ratios:

The ability to service debt varies widely among entertainment companies, but it is always a function of the volatility of projected cash flows. The less volatile the cash flow, the higher is the debt level relative to equity that can be comfortably accommodated on the balance sheet. Casino industry companies, for instance, would generally be expected to experience far less cash flow volatility than companies in the toy and game industries. And by and large, the major movie and record companies, relying on libraries and catalogs as they do, would usually fall somewhere in the middle of the volatility range.

Price/earnings ratios:

For entertainment stocks, the price/earnings ratio has lost a great deal of its usefulness as an investment tool. In movies and television, for example, earnings trends can be easily distorted because of accounting conventions that require management forecasts of anticipated revenues, and by recognition of syndication earnings when a series is made available. But furthermore, in the United States (as opposed to Britain and elsewhere), accounting for acquisitions has a major effect on reported earnings because of the requirement to write-down goodwill (over a period of 40 years). If price/earnings ratios are nonetheless used to compare entertainment stocks to alternative investments, then obviously, adjustments for such differences in the accounting practices have to be made.

Price/sales ratios:

Because price-to-sales ratios do not suffer from the accounting distortions that are frequently present in the calculation of earnings, they have become increasingly popular as an investment tool. For entertainment stocks, the price/sales ratio (price per share divided by revenues per share) is perhaps most useful, as a "reality-check." However, adjustments should be made to smooth or normalize sales over several periods if, for example, there is evidence that sales are far above or below trend. In the former situation, this could be caused by release of an unusually popular movie, or toy, or record, and in the latter by an economic recession.

Book value:

This traditional yardstick for financial analysis normally has little relevance in the evaluation of entertainment company stock prices because the key earnings power may reside – as in the case of film libraries or song catalogs – in assets that have already been largely or completely written down. Also, in the case of real estate assets – studio backlots, theme-park facilities, transmission tower sites – the historical cost basis is usually far below what a property might currently be worth. Brand names and relative market positions may also have considerable value, yet not be reflected in the stated book numbers.

13.3 Final remarks

Entertainment has proven to be one of life's essentials – perhaps just behind food, shelter, and clothing in its importance to many people. Indeed, once a society develops to the point that there is what economists call discretionary income, a substantial portion of such discretionary income can be expected to be spent on entertainment products and services.

As we have also seen, technological development has been the driving force behind the growth of the entertainment industries. Development of technology leads indirectly to an increase in leisure time availability through economic productivity enhancements, and leads directly to qualitative improvements and reductions in the costs of manufacturing and distribution.

Current trends suggest that the entertainment industries will in the aggregate continue to grow at faster than average rates, and that they will continue in the process of integrating vertically and globally. But no matter how large or widespread the corporate entities become, entertainment industries will remain dependent on the vitality and creativity of individuals. In this respect, they will not have changed at all.

Notes

Chapter 1

1. Also, as De Grazia (1962, p. 13) notes, it is obvious that "time on one's hands is not enough to make leisure," and free time accompanied by fear and anxiety is not leisure.

2. As Smith (1986, p. 8) has futher noted, such surveys indicate that for full-time day-shift plant workers, the average workweek decreased by 0.8 hour between 1973 and 1985, but that over the same period, "the schedule of full-time office workers in the private sector rose by 0.2 hour, with the result that the workweek of these two large groups converged markedly."

Also see Supplementary Table S1.2 in Appendix C, which shows that hours for full-time service workers declined faster than for white-collar and blue-collar employees between 1968 and 1979.

3. The Harris nationwide cross-section sample survey of 1,501 adults found that the estimated hours available for leisure have been steadily decreasing from 26.2 hours per week in 1973 to 16.6 hours per week in 1987. Apparently, Harris argues, a combination of economic necessities and choices by women who want to work has increased the number of families in which both husbands and wives hold jobs. Also see Gibbs (1989).

4. Robinson (1989, p. 35) found, for example, that "people aged 51 to 64 have gained the most free time since 1965, mainly because they are working less. Among people in this age group, the proportion of men opting for early retirement increased considerably between 1965 and 1985."

5. According to Curran (1984), on a "multifactor" basis, including capital and labor, productivity growth averaged 2% per year from 1948 to 1973, and 0.2% in the subsequent eight years.

6. There are many fine texts providing full description of these tools; see, for example, Henderson and Quandt (1971).

7. In Linder (1970), standard indifference-curve–budget-line analysis is used to show how the supply of labor is a function of income and substitution effects. The standard consumers' utility function is $V = f(Q, T_c)$, where Q is the number of units of consumption goods, and T_c is the number of hours devoted to consumption purposes. Two constraints are $Q = pT_w$, and $T = T_w + T_c$, where p is a productivity index measuring the number of consumption goods earned per hour of work (T_w), and T is the total number of hours available per time period.

To maximize utility, V now takes the Lagrange multiplier function

$$L = f(Q, T_c) + \lambda[Q - p(T - T_c)]$$

which is then differentiated with respect to Q, T_c, and multiplier λ.

8. See Trost (1986) and *Monthly Labor Review,* U.S. Department of Commerce, Bureau of Labor Statistics, November 1986, No. 11.

9. Owen's (1970) exhaustive study of these issues leads to a model supporting the hypothesis of a backward-bending labor-supply curve and suggesting that demand for leisure activity has positive income and negative price elasticities consistent with economic theory.

10. Utility can often be visualized in the form of a mathematical curve, or function. For instance, the utility a person derives from purchase of good x might vary with the square root of the amount of x; i.e., $U(x) =$ square root of x. Also see section 9.5 and Levy and Sarnat (1972).

11. The number of people who are net consumers (children and senior citizens) divided by the number of net producers; see, for example, Burton and Toth (1974).

12. The table, however, does not do justice to the cable television and lottery spending categories, which are the largest and fastest growing segments, but are unfortunately lumped into the "other" section.

13. Both Figure 1.6 and Table S1.1 are based on NIA data series.

14. Official data on entertainment industry exports is sketchy. To derive a rough approximation of United States net entertainment exports for 1990, assume that exports of movies and television programs account for about $1.0 billion each, recorded music $1.5 billion, theme parks $0.5 billion, and casinos $0.5 billion. Imports in related categories probably aggregate to around $1.0 billion. So net U.S. entertainment exports thus might total at least $3.5 billion.

Chapter 2

1. This and other aspects of the industry's long and colorful history are recounted in books such as those by Stanley (1978), Knight (1978), and Balio (1976).

2. Most of the recent industry consolidation, in which approximately 4,000 of some 21,000 screens changed hands, occurred between 1985 and 1988, but especially during 1986 before the 1986 Tax Reform Act took effect.

Values in this business as in the others related to entertainment are calculated in terms of cash flow multiples (pretax, preinterest, and predepreciation). At the height of the bidding, most of the multiples for properties in large cities were in the range of 10 to 14 times based on projected cash flows for the following year. But many properties in smaller cities are priced at five or six times. Also, although many big-city purchase prices averaged well over $1 million per screen, including big and small cities together, transfer prices per screen averaged just below $500,000 during the 1980s.

3. Tri-Star Pictures was a new studio formed in 1982 by Columbia (Coca-Cola), CBS, and Home Box Office (see Sansweet 1983), with equal initial capital contributions totaling $50 million. Prior to a public stock and debt offering in 1985, the principal shareholders contributed another $50 million. CBS soon thereafter, however, sold its interest, while Coca-Cola increased its share of ownership. Nonetheless, in late 1987, Coca-Cola merged the former Embassy Pictures and Merv Griffin Enterprises television properties into Tri-Star, and renamed the whole package Columbia Pictures while retaining a 49% interest in the total entity. All of Columbia was then bought by Sony, the Japanese electronics giant in November 1989.

4. Two large companies that made feature films, CBS and ABC, reentered production (but not distribution) in the early 1980s after a hiatus of about 10 years. Both companies had produced movies in the late 1960s and early 1970s, but after sustaining substantial losses they had withdrawn from the field. CBS originally distributed its Cinema Center Films (e.g., *My Fair Lady*) through National General Corp., and American Broadcasting's ABC Pictures used a now-defunct subsidiary of Cinerama (Cinerama Releasing). By 1984, however, both companies again withdrew from theatrical production after again sustaining losses.

5. From the time prior to when national distribution networks had become fully operational.

6. Spectral analysis is a statistical technique often used in signal-processing applications (in this case, economic time series) to determine whether or not cyclical patterns exist. Details of how such statistical evaluation is done are beyond the scope of this book. References that explain the technique include Bloomfield (1977), Koopmans (1974), and Gottman (1981).

7. Regression models attempt to explain via statistical testing based on probabilistic assumptions the extent to which some variables affect others. For example, a first naive attempt at constructing such a mathematical relationship might be in the form of an equation indicating that aggregate industry profit (the dependent variable) is a function of the number of admissions and the number of releases (the independent variables).

8. The number of films rated by MPAA is published each year in *Variety*. See, for example, the issue of November 29, 1989.

9. In addition, though, major studio distributors have not been able to fully participate in the profits generated by the new media sources. For example, in pay-cable, Time Warner, Inc.'s cable program wholesaler, Home Box Office (HBO), emerged in the 1970s as a powerful, almost monopsonistic (a market with one buyer and many sellers) middleman for Hollywood's products. In its position as dominant gatekeeper to the nation's wired homes, HBO was able to bargain effectively for retention of an important part of the revenue stream derived from sale of pay cable services (also see Chapter 7). And by 1981, HBO had already surpassed the large theater chains to become Hollywood's single largest customer, licensing in excess of $130 million in that year. Indeed, it was not until the alternative Movie

Channel and Showtime pay-cable services merged, and until videocassette recorder (VCR) penetration rates reached over 20% of television households (in 1984), that HBO experienced significant competition. Prior to merging, Showtime was owned by Viacom, and The Movie Channel was jointly owned by Warner Communications and American Express. Ownership of Showtime/TMC was split 50% Viacom, 40.5% Warner, and 9.5% American Express until 1985, when Viacom bought it all. In 1989 half of Showtime was then sold to Tele-Communications Inc.

The preceding history is that around 1980, the major studios finally recognized that they had lost control of unit pricing and distribution in the important new medium of pay-cable, and they attempted to reassert themselves by launching their own pay channel called Premiere. The studio consortium participants, however, encountered great difficulty in arriving at consensus decisions – especially under threat of antitrust litigation aimed at preventing films from being shown exclusively on Premiere.

Showtime, meanwhile, was able to formulate exclusive five-year license agreements with Paramount. This $500 million agreement signed in 1983 has subsequently been followed by other exclusive arrangements between cable wholesalers and film producers, who generally would like to see Showtime/The Movie Channel survive as a competitor to HBO. Were Showtime and the third important pay channel, The Disney Channel (begun in 1983), to disappear, film licensing prices would likely decline. The history of HBO and its competitors is covered in Mair (1988).

10. See, for example, Brown (1984).

11. As the excellent review of this controversial issue by Linfield (1987), however, notes, colorization does not destroy the original black and white negatives or prints, which remain available for viewing by future generations. As of 1988, the cost of colorizing a minute of film was approximately $2,000.

12. The most important transfer of the early 1980s was MGM's 1981 purchase of the United Artists subsidiary of Transamerica for $380 million (including UA's worldwide distribution organization and library of over 2,200 titles, many of Academy-Award-winning best-picture stature). However, a subsequent (1985) transaction then again split MGM/UA Entertainment into separate pieces. The whole company including MGM/UA's distribution arm and a combined total of about 4,600 features was sold to Turner Broadcasting for $1.5 billion, which was only the first of several subsequent transactions of great complexity. Ultimately, in 1989, United Artists' 1,000-feature library, distribution arm, and television business again came up for sale.

In 1981 and 1982 there were two other notable transfers involving more than just film libraries and distributing organizations. The 1981 takeover of Twentieth Century Fox for $722 million included extensive real-estate properties and several profitable divisions (a soft-drink-bottling franchise, an international theater chain, Aspen Ski Corporation, five television stations, and Deluxe Film Laboratories). Likewise, the 1982 purchase of Columbia Pictures (for about $750 million) by the Coca-Cola Company included some broadcasting properties, part of the Burbank Studios real estate, and an arcade-game manufacturing subsidiary.

Also of historical interest, Warner Bros. sold 850 features and 1,500 shorts to PRM, an investment firm, and Associated Artists Productions, a television distributor, in March, 1956. Through its purchase of Associated Artists Productions in late 1957, United Artists, for about $30 million, then gained control of some 700 pre-1948 Warner films and several hundred other features, short subjects, and cartoons.

13. Significant changes in studio real estate included the early 1970s combination of the Columbia Pictures and Warner Bros. lots (at a time when Columbia was in great financial distress), and MGM's decision in 1973 to reduce production and to thus sell 130 out of 175 acres in Culver City. More recently, the former MGM Culver City property was bought by Lorimar, which was subsequently merged into Warner Communications (now Time Warner Inc.). In 1989, Columbia (Sony) then swapped its Burbank holdings for the Culver City property held by Warner. Also, eighteen acres of the Columbia studio were purchased by developer Saul Pick in 1977 for $6.1 million, while MGM's early 1970s sale of the Culver City assets brought $12 million. Lorimar's 1987 purchase from Turner Broadcasting of the remaining Culver City property was for over $50 million, but it is impossible to attribute an exact price because other assets were included in the transaction.

14. In fact, the demand for production space had become so strong that other parts of the country were able to effectively compete against Hollywood with so-called runaway studios by promising more accommodating shooting schedules or lower overall costs (Bagamery 1984). See also Harris (1981).

Chapter 3

1. In order to preclude excessive charges ("double-dipping") on the talent packages put together for television, agencies have devised alternative compensation approaches for themselves. The alternative, in its simplest form, and as described by Davis (1989), is to receive "the equivalent of 5 percent of the money paid the show's production company by the network, 5 percent of half the profit, if any, the production company gets from the network, and 15 percent of the adjusted gross – basically, syndication sales less the costs not picked up by the network. . . . An agency like [William] Morris can expect to make anywhere from $21,000 to $100,000 from every episode of a network show, and the eventual take from the syndication of a hit can be staggering. The Cosby show, a Morris package, is expected to give the agency an income of $50 million from reruns alone."

2. With the exception of Josephson International, their financial statements are not public, and it is thus difficult to rank agencies by size. However, an important new competitor is Creative Artists Agency, formed in 1975 by former William Morris agents. CAA is known as the most powerful movie packager in Hollywood. See Akst and Landro (1988), Gubernick (1989b), and especially Davis (1989). In 1988, CAA's revenues were estimated to have been $65 million.

3. As of 1987, domestic rentals, according to *Variety,* were $6.7 million.

4. This, despite the fact that presales for domestic home video may be payable 25% upon commencement of principal photography, 25% upon delivery of an answer print, 25% three months after initial theatrical release, and the remainder on availability in home video markets.

5. Until the Tax Reform Act of 1986, which caused the gradual withdrawal of investment tax credits (ITCs) for the entertainment industry, such credits had been one of the most important sources of cash for movie and television-series producers. Feature films – recognized in the tax code as capital assets having useful lives of over three years – had been eligible for ITC treatment. Such qualification had resulted from the industry's lobbying efforts directed at Congress, and from precedents set in tax litigation involving Disney and MCA. In the 1970s, both companies won ITC benefits in appeals-court rulings. Dekom (1984, p. 194) discussed the ITC options available to filmmakers under Section 48K of the pre-1986 IRS code.

6. From the investors' perspective, the interest-free loan contains a not-so-obvious cost of inflation; i.e., the guaranteed return of capital is in absolute dollars, not inflation-adjusted dollars. Moreover, because HBO retains pay and syndication rights, major theatrical distributors would normally be reluctant to distribute Silver Screen features – perhaps unless offered a juicier-than-average distribution fee.

7. As may be inferred, this type of partnership arrangement, and HBO's other participations (e.g., in Tri-Star Productions and in Orion Pictures) have made HBO a major force in feature-film production, as well as in distribution on pay-cable systems. HBO's interest in filmmaking stems from a simple economic fact: With such a large subscriber base, it often costs less (some $3 million to $6 million) to produce a feature directly for cable than to buy rights on a per-subscriber basis from the other studios. Also see Mair (1988).

8. According to Securities Exchange Commission 10-K filings, as reported in *Variety* of May 10, 1989, Silver Screen Partners (SSP) I through IV were all profitable in 1988. SSP IV ended 1988 with net income of $16.15 per unit. Each unit was sold for $500 in June of 1988. In the same year, SSP III, which raised $300 million and invested in 19 pictures – including *Good Morning Vietnam, Three Men And A Baby,* and *Who Framed Roger Rabbitt* – netted $61.63 per unit. Roughly, that would suggest that the return for the year, including these three extraordinarily popular films, was 12.3% on the base of $500 a unit.

9. Under Regulation D, accredited individual investors (as of 1986) are those with at least $1 million of liquid net worth and $200,000 of annual income in each of the two most recent years. Rules for a Regulation D offering are differentiated for issues of over and under $5 million.

10. As in modern portfolio theory applied to stocks and bonds, diversification over many projects reduces overall risk. However, systemic risk, i.e., risk inherent to investment in the movie industry as a whole, cannot be diversified away; see, for example, Hagin (1979).

11. The emergence of new distribution media, including cable, videodiscs, and cassettes, supposedly increases the demand for feature-film programming. Actually, it has required many years for this increased demand to have a noticeable financial impact. Taken in aggregate, the supporting income derived from pay-cable, disc, and cassette license fees has merely prevented the motion-picture industry from suffering substantial deficits. Also see section 2.4.

12. It is estimated that labor fringe benefits add 20%–30% to above-the-line costs and 30%–40% to below-the-line costs.

13. To therefore prevent major financial losses in case of natural or other catastrophe, and to secure the positions of major lenders on a picture (be they studios or banks), completion-bond guarantees must normally be obtained from specialty insurers. Usually, such contracts cost about 6% of a film's budget, but there is some variation that depends on the riskiness of the location, on the previous experience of the director and producer, and on the size of the production budget. As a practical matter, lending institutions do not provide interim financing for projects whose completion is not assured. In order to activate loan agreements, independent producers must always obtain completion bonds in conjunction with signed distribution contracts from creditworthy organizations.

14. Troma was featured in the work of Schumer (1982) and Trachtenberg (1984). See also Cox (1989b). EO Corporation was described in *Variety,* July 23, 1980, in *Esquire,* November 1980, and on the CBS "60 Minutes" program of August 8,

1982. Rosen and Hamilton (1987) also describe low-budget independent feature marketing and financing in more detail.

15.   A settlement was ultimately reached on a formula with elements similar to those used for television-license residuals – originally negotiated in the early days of television by SAG's then-president, Ronald Reagan.

In outline, the writers agreed to 2% of producers' revenues after the producer had recouped $1 million per hour of taped programming and $1.2 million per hour of filmed programming from any combination of sales to pay-television systems, videodiscs, and cassettes. Actors received residuals for original programming made for pay-television and received 4.5% of a distributor's gross after a program had played for 10 days within a year on each pay-television system. In the 1983 SAG–AFTRA settlement with the AMPTP there was an increase from 4.5% to 6% of distributors' gross (4.95% to 6.66% counting pension and welfare contributions), and no change in the terms requiring sales of 100,000 videocassettes before compensation begins.

In 1984 the Directors' Guild won an increase in the share of residuals from films distributed on videocassettes. Directors had been entitled to 1.2% of producers' revenues on cassette sales, but under the 1984 contract this rose to 1.5% of the first $1 million and 1.8% thereafter. In contract discussions, the directors initially had sought to link home-video royalties to the much larger base of distributors' revenues. Also, under the previous agreement, directors are entitled to receive a fraction of a cent for each subscriber to pay-television systems until a production has recouped $2 million per hour of programming. They are then entitled to 2% of gross receipts.

16.   This argument has been supported by Seligman (1982).

17.   Although there has been little formal economic analysis of bidding behavior in the movie business, game theory provides many economic bidding models that could be readily adapted; for example, see Davis (1973).

18.   More details on this can be found in section 4.3 where a sample calculation illustrating split percentages and minimum conditions can be found.

19.   In mid-1983, a U.S. District Court ruled that splits are a form of price fixing and an illegal market allocation in violation of the Sherman Antitrust Act. According to the court's ruling, split agreements entered into by Milwaukee exhibitors caused the amounts paid to distributors to be reduced by 92% from $1.8 million in 1977 to $140,000 in 1981. The ruling has been appealed by the defendant exhibitors (see *Hollywood Reporter,* June 22, 1983, *Variety,* March 23, 1988, and other legal transcriptions regarding the Kerasotes Theater cases).

20.   Real-estate value is the key determinant as to whether or not existing theater sites can be used more profitability for office buildings, parking lots, or other purposes. Standard-discounted-cash-flow and internal-rate-of-return modeling, as explained by Van Horne (1968), can be applied.

To illustrate, consider a theater generating an average annual net income of $100,000 over its expected 10-year life. The internal rate of return on an original $500,000 investment will be just over 15%. However, if the required rate of return is 18%, then, using the net-present-value (NPV) method, the net present value of this theater is about $450,000.

21.   If each household pays four dollars, if one-third of that is remitted as rental to the distributor (the remainder to cable operators and program wholesalers), and if there are 15 million households, then $20 million will be generated. There is an additional benefit to the distributor because of the much faster cash return than from theaters.

22. Details on this particular situation can be found in *Variety,* December 21, 1977. Also, to get around this problem, exhibitors occasionally "piggyback" one film with another in violation of their contracts.

23. The correlation between number of releases and rentals percentage is about -0.4.

24. Those technologies included the so-called Electronic Video Recording (EVR) system, developed by Dr. Peter Goldmark at CBS Laboratories in the late 1960s, and Cartrivision. See Lessing (1971) for a description of Cartrivision and Donnelly (1986) for a quick overview of the development of EVR.

25. The optical video disc was at the time promoted by MCA and Pioneer, while RCA spent hundreds of millions of dollars before scrapping the capacitance system in 1984. Although early optical videodiscs obviously did not gain wide acceptance, modern formats that are compatible with compact disc players for music (see also Chapter 5) are likely to coexist with magnetic tape technologies for the foreseeable future. Indeed, the importance of optical media will increase once low-cost recordable and erasable discs are made available to consumers over the next few years.

26. This despite the fact that the studios initially fought hard against the introduction of VCRs into the home. See the Chapter 5 discussion of the First Sale Doctrine.

27. Disney was able to exceed Paramount's *Top Gun* numbers with its Christmas 1987 release of *Lady and the Tramp* (3 million units) and Christmas 1988 release of *Cinderella* (7.2 million units). MCA did even better with its 1988 issue of *E.T.,* which sold 15 million units at a retail price (after a $5 rebate) of around $20. Warner's *Batman* in 1989 also generated unit sales of over 10 million at a $20 retail price point.

28. This is because of the First Sale Doctrine. However, if special arrangements known as pay-per-transaction were agreed upon in advance, there is no theoretical reason for the distributor not to participate in subsequent rental income. National Video and several other companies have, with varying degrees of success, actually established such pay-per-transaction operations.

29. Perhaps the best-known home video independent is Vestron, which went public in 1985 in the hopes of becoming an important video alternative to the releasing arms of the majors.

In return for making a commitment to finance (or partially finance) the picture, the independent home-video distributor will, however, insist that the picture receive a predetermined amount of support in initial theatrical release through spending on prints and advertising (or p & a as it is known). Such p & a commitments are very important because they in effect "legitimize" the picture by bringing name recognition to what is hoped will be a broad audience for the home videocassette. Home video distribution rights contracts with independent filmmakers will typically extend over seven years.

30. The video store's profit is derived from fast turnover of the tape in the first six months after release in videocassette format. In 1988, the typical cassette was rented an average of some 60 times. With overhead and other costs, the normal retailer would probably require at least 30 turns in order to break even – although this would obviously be a function of the wholesale cost of the tape and the type of film.

In recent years, large video superstores such as Blockbuster Entertainment have emerged. Such stores compete on service by carrying many thousands of titles, and by having great depth-of-copy (i.e., lots of copies) of the most popular films.

Because of this, they may very well be able to resist the inroads being made by PPV cable.

31. Most royalties would be in the area of 5% of the value of wholesale shipments, but the percentages can reach higher. The most recent example of how lucrative merchandising can be is provided by the 1989 release of *Batman,* in which the distributor, Warner Bros., received licensing fees ranging from $2,000 to $50,000 plus royalties of 8% to 10% on revenues estimated to be $250 million in the first year of release. See especially Lipman (1990).

32. On a cost-per-thousand (CPM) basis, the cost of an average 30-second network prime-time spot rose about 129% from 1970 to 1980; the price per minute rose by 180%.

33. Independent producers in particular also incur additional costs in attempting to market their pictures directly at various international marketing conventions, the most important of which are the American Film Market (AFM) based in Los Angeles in March, the Cannes Film Festival held in Cannes, France, in early May, and MIFED, a somewhat similar event held in Milan, Italy, each October.

Television producers and distributors also have several marketing conventions, including the midwinter National Association of Television Program Executives (NATPE) held in the United States and the March Internationale des Programmes de Television (MIP) held each spring in France.

34. Estimates of average negative and marketing costs for major (MPAA-member) studios provide a somewhat misleading impression of the whole industry, because every year there are many low-budget releases by smaller companies. Because of their lower costs, many such films can be profitable.

35. A simple ROI estimate for a purely hypothetical distributor-financed project that ignores the effects of typical cash-flow delays, compounding of interest, and taxes might be made as follows: The assumed distributors' gross from all sources is $30 million.

(*a*) Distributor profit from distribution fee, overhead charge, and other sources: $5 million
(*b*) Distributor share of net profit: $3 million
(*c*) Producer share of net profit: $3 million
(*d*) Cost of capital: $2 million
(*e*) Total investment including negative and marketing (prints and ads): $30 million

The return on investment (over two years) is

$$\text{ROI} = 100\,(a + b + c + d)/e = 100\,(5 + 3 + 3 + 2)/30 = 43.4\%$$

or 21.7% per annum.

To be placed in proper perspective, this rate should then be annualized and compared with the risk-free rate of return available on government securities during the period the film project went through its life cycle (from production start to ancillary-market release).

Chapter 4

1. Copyright 1951 and 1952 by Paramount–Roy Rogers Music Co., Inc. Copyright renewed 1979 and 1980 and assigned to Paramount–Roy Rogers Music Co., Inc.

2. Litigation concerning *Bad News Bears,* which was licensed to ABC by Paramount for $6.75 million as part of an $18.5-million package, helped set legal precedent in a 1979 lawsuit. More details can be found in *Variety,* January 21, 1981, and July 2, 1980.

3. There were also some 16mm screenings at educational and penal institutions.

4. Growth in television revenues is illustrated by the following: In 1956, MGM received about $250,000 for a network showing of *Gone with the Wind;* in 1979, based on a $35-million face-value 20-year contract with CBS, the average per run was over $1 million.

5. For example, when Lorimar-Telepictures was acquired by Warner Communications in early 1989, over $450 million of its equity was eliminated through adoption of Warner's more conservative accounting practices.

The sensitivity of reported earnings to relatively small changes in early period revenue estimates is also substantial. As a rule-of-thumb, a 10% increase in total estimated revenues could normally be expected to at least double profit margins in such early periods.

Also, companies with high inventory-to-sales ratios will generally correlate with optimistic projections of income ultimates and vice versa.

6. Leedy (1980, p. 9) expresses the view that accrual accounting would be to the detriment of outside participants.

7. As applied here, the "quasi" is a form of purchase accounting in which the film library is assessed on a picture-by-picture basis, with some written up and some written down. New amorization rates are then established for recent releases and in-process productions, and a fair market valuation of the company's distribution system is made. In the case of Filmways, an immediate cash infusion of $26 million (in exchange for issuance of debt and equity securities) combined with sale of assets and various accounting adjustments gave the company a new lease on life under the name of Orion Pictures. Although according to the rules, tax credits previously accumulated from the Filmways net operating losses had to be abandoned, the film library (composed of over 600 theatrical and television motion pictures) was written up by $18.2 million. In addition, the distribution system, which had not been on the balance sheet as such, was assigned an estimated fair-market value of $14 million (out of the eliminated $22.2 million in goodwill carried on the prior company's books).

Welles (1983) discusses Orion's quasi-reorganization and overhead-amortization accounting policies in a generally critical vein. Management, however, notes that a quasi is not all that uncommon and that the reorganization was done in consultation with various regulatory agencies and under the guidance of auditors from Arthur Young & Co. Filmways' auditor had been Arthur Anderson & Co.

MGM's acquisition in 1981 of United Artists Corporation from Transamerica Corporation provides another example of applied purchase-method accounting. The $380-million purchase price was allocated to the assets and liabilities of United Artists based on independent appraisals of such assets and liabilities. That portion of the acquisition cost not allocated to specific assets – in other words, goodwill – and the appraised value of the worldwide distribution organization acquired in the purchase of United Artists were to be amortized on a straight-line basis, over a 40-year period. The interesting contrast here, though, is that MGM's assigned distribution-system value of $190 million is being amortized over 40 years, whereas Orion's distribution system is being amortized on a straight-line basis over only 25 years. A faster amortization rate, of course, places a greater burden on current reported income.

8. A notable exception to the standard 30% theatrical rate existed in the 1970s when United Artists distributed MGM's products for 22.5% of gross.

9. Return on investment in this example is, simplistically, 54% (i.e., $8.1 million/ $15 million). However, many other factors, including length of time needed to make the movie, taxes, and so forth, would need to be known in order to make useful comparisons.

10. Curran (1986) discusses the financing alternatives for independent filmmakers and producers in considerable depth.

11. A study sponsored by the National Association of Concessionaires and Coca-Cola indicated that in dollar terms, about 40% of refreshment-stand sales come from popcorn, 40% from soft drinks, and 20% from candy.

12. For instance, in its 1988 annual report, Cineplex Odeon shows a significant operating income figure, yet if profits from real estate transactions are excluded, it can be seen that the company's basic theater business operated at a loss. Also, see Wechsler (1989).

13. The cost of establishing a major domestic-distribution organization was around $25 million as of the late 1980s. Annual direct operating expenses are estimated to be at least $20 million. See also Wechsler (1990).

14. This example follows Garey (1983, p. 104).

15. The old rule of thumb is that the box-office gross must be two or three times the negative cost to reach break-even. However, for major-event pictures, this can shrink to less than two times.

16. The following is a partial list of companies that since the early 1970s have attempted to enter production and either have failed totally or, at one time or another, have substantially withdrawn from the field: ABC Pictures (ABC's first venture distributed by Cinerama in the early 1970s), Associated Communications, Avco-Embassy, Cannon Group, Cinema Center Films (CBS's first venture distributed by National General in the early 1970s), De Laurentiis Entertainment Group, Filmways (now reconstituted as Orion), General Cinema Corp., and Time-Life Films. Some of these production entities had considerable financial backing and experience, and yet (the new-media revolution notwithstanding) were not effective in bucking the odds.

17. See *Daily Variety,* October 24, 1979.

18. Quoted from *Daily Variety,* October 24, 1979. Litman in Kindem (1982) discusses pricing of series and movies from the perspectives of the 1970s.

19. "War and Remembrance" was noted for its high-quality production values, but also for its huge cost and the over $20 million in losses that the ABC network sustained on its original broadcast of the 32-episode $110 million miniseries that was shown in the fall of 1988 and the spring of 1989. See Kneale (1988).

20. The high costs and generally unrepresentative nature of pilots, and the great probability that most will not be extended into full series, have led many in the television industry to question the wisdom of using this massive and wasteful spending system for program-development purposes. Unfortunately, satisfactory alternatives to this system have yet to be discovered.

21. Prior to the phasing out of investment tax credits in 1986, 6⅔% of production costs had qualified for tax credits – a factor that had considerably eased the production deficit problem

22. Indeed, because it is so difficult to generate positive cash flows in the start-up phase of production, many production companies have encountered financial difficulties and have been forced to co-venture or to merge with larger organizations or studios.

23. The issue of deficit financing is at the heart of the financial interest and syndication rule debate that has been raging since the early 1980s. In return for paying higher license fees for original programming, the networks feel entitled to participation in some of the so-called "back-end" syndication profits, which, at least through 1990, they are barred from sharing. Deficits had risen from an average of around $64,000 a half-hour show in 1982–3 to over $170,000 by 1986–7. For hour-long shows, the deficits are estimated to have risen from $198,000 to over $370,000 in the same period.

24. According to Lorimar Research, the longest running TV series through the 1988–9 season were "Gunsmoke" with 402 episodes, "Bonanza" with 318, "Dallas" with 307, "The Love Boat" with 255, and "Knots Landing" with 237.

25. In the late 1960s and early 1970s, the probability of making a syndicatable, highly profitable series was greater than in the late 1970s, and early 1980s. By the 1980s, viewers had become increasingly discriminating in their choices. Because of disruptions by strikes and other factors, the start of the TV season had become irregular, and cable, videocassette, and movie-of-the-week viewing alternatives had become more numerous.

26. The increasing competitive influence of pay-TV implies that in the future, producers may be less willing to tie up their best properties for long periods. The relative values of syndicated half-hour and hour series episodes, as well as typical contract terms, may therefore be in a state of flux. Also, networks may have a strategic interest in "warehousing" best-drawing feature films in order to prevent their rapid appearance on competing pay-cable networks.

27. For a show with the potential to last three years or more on a network, program-distribution companies may be willing to guarantee, in installments, say, at least $50,000 per episode against a percentage of anticipated syndication profits. Here producers may sacrifice some percentage of ownership in return for immediate cash, and distributors may obtain long-term project commitments on which they can rely to keep the pipelines filled. The risk to the distributor is that the program will be canceled or that the show will, over time, lose its audience appeal. Should the producer enter into such an agreement, an important issue for negotiation is which party will pay what percentage of talent residuals and royalties. As in features, however, residuals would normally be expected to come out of the producers' side.

28. An important recent exception has been the distributor King World, which has been able to sign stations to three-year contracts on the basis of the incredible ratings strength of its shows "Wheel of Fortune" and "Jeopardy!"

29. Barter prices naturally ride on the back of the network cost per thousand (CPM) prices, and are usually 80% of what a network might charge. Barter, however, clearly shifts the financial burden from the station to the syndicator, who must arrange to aggregate and sell the time to national advertisers.

30. The costs of network prime-time productions, as shown in Table 4.12 of the first edition of this book, are estimated to have risen at a 14.4% compound annual rate during the 1970s. Although comparable data are not available for the 1980s, it seems fair to assume that the cost of production has probably continued to rise by an average of 10% a year between 1980 and 1990.

31. Soon after the record price for "Magnum" was obtained, television industry demand for hour-long series plummeted, and through the second half of the 1980s, most off-network hour-long series could not command more than $300,000 to $400,000 per episode, which is scarcely enough to cover the costs of marketing and of residual payments. Licensing to cable networks has thus developed as an alternative to syndicating to local TV stations. Hour-long series sold to such networks for prices up to $250,000 an episode include "Murder She Wrote," "Cagney and Lacey," and "Miami Vice."

32. Constraints on self-production were the result of a 1980 consent decree that limited each network to in-house production of 2½ hours on average per week until the fall of 1985, when the cap began to gradually rise toward 5 hours per week in 1988. In actuality, however, networks have to date not proven to be particularly efficient in production. An episode of the one-hour ABC-network-produced series "Moonlighting" reportedly set a record at a cost of $3 million.

33. Both the Syndication and Financial Interest and the Prime Time Access rules were adopted by the FCC in 1970 in response to conditions that had existed in the 1960s, when the networks had been at the peak of their relative competitive strength. The disallowance of network financial interest went into effect on August 1, 1972, and of network syndication on June 1, 1973.

In 1980, the three national networks also entered into consent decrees in connection with antitrust suits brought against each of them by the Department of Justice in the early 1970s. These consent decrees contain provisions that parallel but are not identical to the original Syndication and Financial Interest Rules.

In 1983, movement toward deregulation encouraged networks to challenge some of the restrictions, and there ensued a bitter political battle between the networks on one side and independent producers, independent television stations, and movie studios on the other. The independents feared that the networks would stifle their creative and financial well-being, while the networks contrarily argued that they were no longer oligopolistic because of the inroads made by strongly competitive cable and home video industries. See section 6.1, and also Crandall (1972), Landro and Saddler (1983), Colvin (1983), and *Variety,* August 10, 1983.

34. It might be noted that the Fox network evolved in the late 1980s. Because Fox does not program a full week's schedule, and because it thus does not fall under the FCC's definition of a network, it is free to own syndication interests in its self-developed shows. Thus, News Corp., the parent company, owned a movie studio, a quasi-network, and a television syndication arm prior to any modifications of the rules.

35. Mr. Garner's "Rockford Files" (NBC, 1974–80) agreement with Universal had entitled him to 37.5% of the net profits of the show in return for taking a smaller upfront fee. By 1988, receipts from the show had reached $119.3 million according to Universal's own accounting. Nevertheless, Universal claimed that the show would have to earn another $1.6 million before it would realize net profits as described in Garner's contract.

According to the accounting statement, as described by Scholl (1989a), subtracted from the $119.3 was $32.6 million for distribution fees. Then another $14.6 million is deducted for distribution expenses including the cost of prints and storage. Then another $57.8 million is taken off for production costs, which leaves only $14.2 million. That $14.2 million, however, by Universal's accounting was insufficient to cover the $15.8 million in interest expenses that the company (and most other studios) charges on the theory that the money spent on production could have been invested at risk-free rates.

However, according to Garner's auditors, Universal overstated costs and/or underestimated receipts by at least $10.9 million. For example, the auditors claimed that Universal received quantity discounts (of $443,000) on development of extra print copies that it failed to pass along.

Another issue involved whether to count print and dubbing costs as gross receipts or as expense reimbursements. If counted as the former, Universal would take a 50% fee off the top, whereas in the latter case, it is a direct expense reduction that leads to faster profitability for the participant. An even larger amount ($7.9 million), and one that is at the crux of the interest payments charges issue, involved Universal's alleged practice of immediately recording expenses while deferring the recording of revenues and profits until cash was in hand.

However, as Scholl (1989b) describes, the Garner suit, initiated in 1983, was settled in 1989 for approximately $10 million.

36. This topic is also treated in Salemson and Zolotow (1978).

37. During periods of high interest rates and economic duress, playing the float is obviously not unique to entertainment businesses.

38. Piracy is estimated to cost the industry at least $500 million per year. A bill signed by President Reagan in 1982 makes piracy a felony punishable by five years in prison.

39. The practice of settlements appears to be on the ethical borderline and, interestingly, does not seem to apply in reverse. That is, if a picture performs better than expected, distributors do not ordinarily extract stiffer terms from exhibitors. Settlements are much less likely to be found in exhibitor contracts that are bid rather than negotiated.

40. Blocked currency funds have occasionally served as a source of new film production financing. Normally, such funds are accumulated by different companies or industries operating in a country, and as long as the funds are used within that country, it does not matter that the funds were generated in selling, say, automobiles or textiles.

41. There are several foreign sales organizations, but most are relatively small. The most famous of these, mentioned in Paris (1984) and Salamon (1984), was Producers Sales Organization, which eventually went out of business.

Chapter 5

1. According to the International Federation of Phonogram and Videogram Producers (IFPI), an international industry trade organization, direct world sales of records and cassettes totaled $17.0 billion in 1987. Unit sales were 590 million LPs, 1,150 million tapes, and 260 million CDs.

2. As noted by Eliot (1989, p. 15). For detailed history of recorded sound, also see Gelatt (1977), Read and Welch (1976), and White (1988).

3. It was not until 1941 that the originally formed ASCAP (American Society of Composers, Authors and Publishers) settled on the same royalty formula (based on 2¾% of radio stations' annual advertising revenues) as had been standardized by BMI (Broadcast Music Inc.) – the organization that had been formed in 1939 to compete with ASCAP.

4. The musicians' union (American Federation of Musicians) sought compensation from the record companies for income lost as demand for live performances had declined with the increasing use of recorded performances.

5. New majors of the latter half of the 1950s included Capitol, MGM, and Mercury, for a total of six dominant companies in all.

6. The role of managers is comprehensively covered in Frascogna and Hetherington (1978).

7. Disputes in this area have mostly concerned music rights in syndicated television programming and commercials. Stations generally do not receive music rights along with the other rights conveyed in consideration of their broadcast license fees. Instead, they normally operate under blanket music licenses – by definition nonspecific as to the music used in the show – for which they are charged by ASCAP and BMI about 2% of adjusted station gross receipts, and which entitle stations to use any of the approximately 4 million titles in the ASCAP and BMI catalogs.

A blanket license, however, is only one of four ways in which to license music for a show: (a) a blanket license that covers any music used in the composers' rights catalogs; (b) through each composer; (c) on a per-program basis; and (d) through the producer, who has already obtained a license. See Boucher (1986), *Broadcasting,* February 1, 1988, p. 44, and especially Flick (1988), who provides a cogent description of the situation, and Zollo (1989).

8. Between January 1, 1988, and January 1, 1996, this rate is adjusted every two years in proportion to changes in the Consumer Price Index. Whatever CPI changes occur, the rate cannot fall below 5 cents for each record of a composition or $0.95 per minute or fraction thereof, whichever is larger, nor exceed the previous rate by more than 25% for any two-year span.

9. This compulsory license system, in which the copyright owners have the opportunity to be the first to record and distribute their works, is intended to provide such owners with fair remuneration while preventing the owners from retaining a monopoly over all future uses of a particular musical composition.

10 Since 1978, the Copyright Royalty Tribunal has also been collecting and distributing license fees from cable-television operators. Of the total license pool of $20.6 million in 1979, movie producers and program syndicators received 70%, sports organizations 15%, noncommercial broadcasters 5.25%, commercial broadcasters 4.5%, performing-rights societies 4.25%, and National Public Radio 0.25%. See Carlson (1984).

11. However, several pay-per-transaction schemes have been developed that would allow producers and distributors to participate directly in the revenues from each and every rental transaction. See also section 3.4.

12. According to the new copyright law, which largely parallels those in other countries, an author retains a copyright for life plus 50 years.

13. The financial dynamics of a concert tour are discussed by Kronholz (1984) and in Newcomb (1989).

14. After the 1982 introduction of a so-called musical-instrument digital interface (MIDI) that converts musical control information into a uniform computer code, the productivity of recording studios, musicians, and composers increased substantially as several electronic instruments could then be recorded simultaneously.

15. It is estimated that there are 1,200 record companies and over 2,600 labels in the United States. However, most of the recording activity is concentrated with the largest dozen firms.

16. At CBS and Capital Records, the major domestic pressing companies of the late 1970s, short-run demand outstripped production capacity when release of the until then all-time best-selling (20-million-plus) *Saturday Night Fever* album (surpassed by Michael Jackson's 30-million *Thriller* in 1984) and the deaths of Elvis Presley and Bing Crosby occurred within an 18-month span. As of the late 1980s, Warner Communications also had a major CD pressing facility.

17. However, there may still be isolated instances in which stations (and also record stores) overstate a song's popularity to the chart services in return for record-company advertising. Because such overstatements are not based on actual sales, but just on inflated figures put down on paper, they are known in the industry as "paper adds" (Hull 1984). Also, as described by Goldberg (1988), it would appear that the extensive use of independent promotion men who are paid large fees for getting songs added to station play lists may have, in effect, recently again contributed to the spread of payola.

18. As with most other entertainment company assets, including film libraries, movie theaters, broadcast stations, and gaming casinos, music-related assets are generally evaluated on the basis of projected pretax, preinterest cash-flow multiples.

Although there have been several significant corporate asset transfers in recent years that include the sale of CBS Records to Sony, of RCA Records to Bertelsmann, and of Chappell Music Publishing to Warner Communications, financial information as to the precise cash-flow multiples used in these transactions has been difficult to obtain. A rough estimate of the Sony/CBS deal is that the transfer price was probably at around nine times projected cash flow.

The key financial figure in evaluating music publishers, however, is called the *net publisher's share* (NPS), and it is equal to all the royalties the company takes in minus everything it must pay out to writers and artists. As described by Flack (1989), the multiple of NPS rose from the area of 5 or 6 times to around 10 times in the 1989 SBK/EMI deal.

On the average, and using another rough rule-of-thumb, song publisher catalogs seem to have been transferred in the late 1980s at a going rate of around $1,000 per title. See also Gubernick (1989a).

19. Kronemyer and Sidak (1986) analyzed the industry for the years 1970–84 and provide the most comprehensive market share data available. Unfortunately, however, it is generally not possible to easily update the market share data.

As for Polygram, it was almost merged with Warner Communications in 1984, but the merger was blocked by the Federal Trade Commission because of antitrust considerations. At the time, Polygram had sales of around $700 million. Polygram, with 1989 sales of over $1.5 billion, sold 20% of its shares to the public in December 1989.

20. In the 1970s, Pickwick International was the largest rack jobber in the United States. It was acquired by American Can Co., which in 1984 sold most of the Pickwick assets to Handelman.

21. Although suggested retail list prices are used to compile industry sales figures, these numbers are misleading because record stores normally do not charge suggested list.

22. According to the American Music Conference (Chicago, Ill.) annual survey, musical instrument retail sales rose to $3.7 billion in 1988 up from a recent low of $2.2 billion in 1980. Aggregate figures, however, mask the variation in popularity of different instruments. For instance, in the 1960s and 1970s, unit shipments of guitars gained rapidly, while shipments of pianos plateaued.

Chapter 6

1. FM frequencies are between channels 6 and 7 on the VHF television spectrum; that is, channels 2 through 6 operate at 54 to 88 megahertz (MHz), and channels 7 through 13 operate at 174 to 216 MHz. Harmonic distortions prevent the use of channel 1 in VHF television transmissions.

2. Measurement techniques have become increasingly sophisticated and dependent on technological improvements. Nielsen had long relied on "audimeters" (audience meters) in the largest markets (and diaries in the smaller ones), but sampling has been enlarged, and now depends on People Meters that require viewers to log in their presence on a console attached to the television set. As Berry (1984) describes, Britain's AGB Research had accelerated a movement toward using more sophisticated audience sampling methods than had previously been used by Nielsen and Arbitron, and efforts continue toward development of "passive" people meters. Also see Couzens (1986).

   Both Arbitron and The Birch Scarborough Research companies are perhaps better known for radio audience measurements.

3. Barter syndication is discussed in section 4.4. The growth of the business is shown in Table 4.10.

4. In theory, allocation of scarce frequency space probably would be more efficient if free-market auction bidding were permitted.

5. Government regulation of all aspects of broadcasting is generally much more stringent in foreign countries.

6. In the old NTSC system, for example, the electron beam produces 30 different pictures, or frames, per second and each frame is made up of 525 scanning lines. By contrast, movies show 24 different frames a second interrupted by a shutter in the projector that reduces flicker by showing each frame twice.

   To reduce flicker in the TV picture, however, each frame is separated in half and each half-frame (field) is shown separately, which means that each field composed of either odd or even scan lines is on the screen for one-sixtieth of a second. The process is known as interlacing.

7. As of the early 1990s, an HDTV (1,250 line, 60 MHz) system known as MUSE (Multiple Sub-Nyquist Sampling and Encoding) was just beginning to be implemented in Japan, while it had not yet been determined which of several competing systems would prevail in the United States and Europe. In Europe, the plans for HDTV are to use 1,250-line 50-Hz signals based on a MAC (multiplexed analog component) signal standard for direct broadcast satellite distribution. In the United States, as of early 1990, an HDTV standard had not yet emerged.

8. Only half of UHF viewers are counted in determining such audience percentage figures.

9. As of 1989, Fox had operated a full schedule of prime-time programming on three nights of the week (Saturday, Sunday, and Monday), and owned and operated stations in the three major markets. However, according to FCC definitions, Fox is not a network because it provides less than 15 hours a week of programming. (A network, by FCC definition, must also provide interconnected program service to at least 25 affiliated licensees in 10 or more states.) This has significance with regard to the financial interest and syndication rules (discussed in Chapter 4) because, as a "non-network," Fox is permitted to have a financial interest in the programming that it develops and distributes.

10. In the late 1980s, long-standing affiliate compensation relationships began to shift as the networks sought to lower their expense ratios in recognition of their diminished share of audience. New affiliate compensation contracts appear to be evolving toward payments related to local market ratings performance. Also, there have been instances in which stations actually pay the networks for the privilege of affiliation. See *Broadcasting,* August 8, 1983, and September 3, 1988. Also see Cox (1989) for a complete review.

11. As it happens, ABC's ratings also began to improve, and by the late 1970s ABC finally ended the dominance CBS had held for over 20 years. There immediately ensued considerable switching of the affiliates of other networks to ABC, but by the early 1980s, such reshuffling had essentially come to an end.

12. In Canada, for example, the Canadian Radio-Television and Telecommunications Commission (CRTC) is charged with the authority to license, regulate, and supervise all aspects of the Canadian broadcasting industry, which includes five major television networks. Two of the five are operated by the Canadian Broadcasting Corporation (a federal crown corporation with a budget of over C$1 billion), and provide basic national services in both English and French. The CTV Television Network Limited (CTV) operates a national, privately owned English-language network, and Les Télé-Diffuseurs Associes (TVA) and Quatre Saisons do the same in French-speaking areas.

In many countries, one significant difference from the American system, however, is the use of programming quotas, which are not of regulatory concern in the United States. As of 1989, for example, the CRTC required that Canadian television stations devote 60% of their programming throughout the day and 50% of it in prime time to Canadian material. However, sports and news programming can be counted against these limits.

13. A good analogy is to an inverted yield curve in the bond market.

14. From Barwise and Ehrenberg (1988), p. 36.

15. Barwise and Ehrenberg (1988, p. 44) cite sociologist William McPhee as having recognized and named the "double jeopardy" effect. In the same discussion, they also note that the percentage of audience in one week that watches another episode of the following week is only about 40% in the United States and probably no more than 50% in Britain. Even among the most popular series, only a small percentage of the audience, perhaps under 2% or so, may see every episode of the season.

16. In 1982, a federal district court judge ruled that the NAB's code, which placed certain restrictions on the scheduling of and number of commercials, violated antitrust regulations. See "The Coming Avalanche of 15-second TV Ads." *Business Week,* February 11, 1985.

17. One of the best known of these is Turner Broadcasting's Atlanta-based WTBS, which transmits Atlanta Braves baseball games as far away as Alaska. Reimposition of syndication exclusivity rules in the late 1980s, however, has limited the growth potential for superstations. See *Broadcasting,* November 30, 1987, for a complete discussion and history.

18. PBS television stations have from time to time considered the possibility of carrying a limited amount of commercial advertising in order to supplement their income. This idea was discussed in "PBS May Get a Few More Words From Its Sponsors," *Business Week* No. 2811 [(October 10, 1983):70]. Tucker (1982) also discusses the costs of operating public television. And *Broadcasting,* May 11, 1987, p. 60, provides a thorough review of the 20 years of CPB history.

19.   The correlation between advertising expenditures and corporate profits for the post–World War II period is approximately 0.97.

20.   Movies and books have characteristics of both public and private goods: Content here is a public good, but delivery is in the manner of a private good, in which consumption by one person makes the product or service unavailable for someone else (Owen, Beebe, and Manning 1974, p. 15).

21.   For example, Peterman and Carney (1978) found evidence that "larger buyers of network TV advertising do not purchase time at prices significantly below those charged smaller buyers." Fisher, McGowan, and Evans (1980) studied the audience–revenue relationship for local television stations. Wyche and Wirth (1984) described a mathematical model that can be used to project future financial performance for a station. And Crandall (1972) analyzed the implications of FCC rules barring network investments in ancillary program rights.

A most important article on the economics of advertising is by Stigler and Becker (1977). A follow-up on this, which suggests a net positive relationship between a firm's advertising and product output, is by Hochman and Luski (1988).

22.   As suggested in Chapter 4, prime-time program producers may directly recover only 80% to 85% of the total production cost through the network license fees. Also, as noted, the proportion of self-produced versus licensed programming has been proportionately stable since the 1970s, when antitrust cases against the three networks were settled by consent-decree agreements that limited networks to producing no more than 2.5 hours per week of entertainment prime-time programming in the early years of the agreements.

23.   As a percentage of operating costs at independent stations, film amortization of syndicated television series has risen from 35% in the mid-1970s to over 45%-50% in the late 1980s. This compares with levels of about 25% for affiliates, who regularly receive about 65% of their programming from the networks.

24.   The FCC had a rule against "trafficking" that prevented turnover of a broadcast property more frequently than every three years. Under deregulation, this rule was abolished in November 1982, and the rate of station trading has increased. There were $3.5 billion of radio and television station transactions and $1 billion of cable-system transactions in 1988. In 1988, for example, the average price for a radio station was $928,368 (AM was $508,754, and FM $1,280,305), and the average price for a VHF television facility was $24.0 million (UHF was $11.4 million).

25.   Buyers often pay 30% down and receive a loan from sellers for up to 70% of the station's value. The loan is usually repaid in 10 annual installments. These terms appear to have evolved in response to capital-gains-tax treatments that were in effect during the 1960s and 1970s. Also, in the late 1970s, for example, with real interest rates low and credit readily available, the prices of television and FM-radio properties rose steeply. As inflationary psychology took hold, transfer prices for television stations began to be affected by the asumption that there would be high inflation of land and time prices well into the future.

26.   Depreciation and amortization policies may vary from one company to another, but treatments of these items tend toward uniformity. Also, an important aspect of station trading prior to the Tax Reform Act of 1986 was the ability of station owners to cash in on a station's increased market value at capital-gains tax rates. The tax code had allowed owners to trade up to more expensive properties without paying any capital-gains taxes at all through use of tax-deferral certificates. The certificates had been granted for like-type exchanges or upgrades that produced the effect of deconcentrating local-media ownership. Such exchanges were very appealing to owners, who, after depreciation had been exhausted, faced the prospect of paying taxes on a rising stream of earnings.

Another important tax-related issue for the broadcasting and cable industries involves amortization of intangible assets. Amortizable intangible assets may include leasehold interests, broadcast rights, and program licenses. Nonamortizable intangibles may include FCC licenses and network affiliation agreements. This whole area is significant in considerations of a station's asset value, but appears to be in a state of flux vis-à-vis the Internal Revenue Service. See *Broadcasting,* September 1, 1986, and August 7, 1989, for more details.

27. See "Limited Partnerships and Leveraged Buyouts: Growing Means to Broadcast Ownership," *Broadcasting,* November 14, 1983, p. 40.

28. Loss of television-message penetration is further accelerated by use of a VCR's fast-forward speed or by use of devices that automatically detect commercials and omit them from the tape.

Chapter 7

1. A detailed historical review of the cable industry's development is found in Whiteside (1985).

2. This is also discussed in the notes to section 2.4.

3. In 1983, The Movie Channel and Showtime were merged in order to compete with HBO, which in terms of subscribers (12 million) was substantially larger than the other two services combined. As of 1989, Showtime was half-owned by Viacom.

4. The jointly owned Mattel/General Instruments Playcable channel, for example, provided properly equipped households with cable-interactive games and was one of the first unconventional experimental channels. The experiment was discontinued in 1984.

5. In fact, competitive and cost pressures were so great that CBS, for example, discontinued its advertiser-supported cable venture in 1982 with a write-down of about $30 million, and a year later, RCA discontinued its Entertainment Channel at a cost of over $60 million.

6. See *Broadcasting,* June 25, 1984.

7. In an important 1985 decision involving a suit by Preferred Communications, Inc. against Los Angeles, it was decided that a city may not create an artificial monopoly (Kelley 1985).

8. In 1983 and 1984, bills were proposed in Congress to limit cities' power vis-à-vis operators. Passage of such legislation would have made it difficult for cities to refuse franchise renewals, would have allowed companies to modify onerous contracts under a significant change of circumstances, and would have limited municipal fees to 5% of gross annual revenues (Cohen 1983). In 1985, a compromise agreement included essentially all of these elements, but most significantly terminated (by 1987) a municipality's right to regulate the price of basic cable services. As of 1985, cable systems were also no longer required to carry local broadcast signals, although legal battles on this issue have dragged on for several years. See also note 23.

9. In the early 1980s the bidding procedure for a franchise was fraught with political considerations. In practice, that often meant that bidders would have to employ so-called "rent-a-citizen" schemes whereby local prominents would be offered shares of stock in the cable company at below market prices in return for supporting the company's bid. The issue, as seen from the perspective of the late 1980s, is discussed in *CableVision,* May 22, 1989.

10. One way to arrive at the 25% figure is to assume that the average major-film rental is 25 cents per subscriber and that there is an average of 10 such films per month, for a total of $2.50. This is around 25% of the total monthly retail charge.

11. Of course, should commercial advertising begin to appear more regularly, cable offerings are likely to more closely resemble those found on commercial television, where the theory of least objectionable programming – programs appealing to the largest mass audience – has held sway.

12. Presumably, the higher the price of the service, the less advertising will be tolerated. In the limiting case of "free" over-the-air broadcasts, people would be expected to tolerate the most advertising.

A 1983 Benton & Bowles (ad agency) survey indicated that 17% of all current or previous cable subscribers canceled at least one pay service for reasons other than changing residence: 51% said shows were repeated too often; 42% said it was not worth the money. Only 10% of subscribers bought three pay channels at once, and 7% bought four or more (Landro 1983). It has been estimated that on the average, pay tiers are discontinued (disconnected) by about 3.5% of system subscribers each month (sometimes rates are as high as 8%). This is at least double the rate for other utilities (telephone, gas, etc.) that are disconnected when households move.

13. In terms of total operating costs, a typical system might have payroll accounting for about one-third of the total expenses, and programming costs (for pay-cable programs) about 40% of the same. Franchise fees may amount to around 4% of basic-service revenues.

14. In practice, of course, it may cost $15,000 per mile to build a rural or suburban system, and $100,000 per mile or more to build an urban franchise.

15. In general, the early 12-channel systems might currently provide the highest margin of profit (up to 65% per subscriber) because they are not burdened by the costs of investment in modern equipment. However, the growth potential of such an old system is likely to be very limited. On newer systems, some with more than 55 channels, revenues per subscriber may be twice as high as on 12-channel systems. Yet because labor expenses for administration and maintenance rise sharply with an increase in the number of pay programming options, and because capital costs are higher, margins on the newer systems may average 40% or less. See *Broadcasting* of December 19, 1983.

16. See note 26 of chapter 6 for more detail.

17. As of the late 1980s, response rates to PPV offerings have generally fallen into the 2% to 5% range of addressable homes with access to PPV services. Reiss Media Enterprises, Inc., which owns and operates Request Television, and Viewer's Choice, partly owned by The Walt Disney Company, Viacom, and several MSOs are the leading PPV wholesaler/distributors. Reiss, for example, is in over 5 million cable homes, and began operations in November 1985 by effectively employing with each of its studio-suppliers a "time-shared condominium" concept. Each program year was divided into 10 units, each of which entitled holders to 10% of the program exhibition time on a channel. The separately contracted unit holders were originally 10 movie studios and/or suppliers for which Reiss provides transmission services, enters into affiliation agreements with cable systems, and bills and collects payments for a fixed fee plus a variable fee that is based on revenues generated. The first Request Channel provided between two and four new movies each week, augmented by special sporting and concert events. In these arrangements, the studios in effect each own an equal share of the PPV time that is available, and they have the flexibility to swap or to sell channel time among themselves while retaining approximately half of the PPV revenues generated at retail. An Automatic Number Identification (ANI) system technology makes it possible for one-way addressable cable households to order virtually on impulse, without the severe delays often encountered by ordinary phone dial-up systems.

The first notable PPV experiment, however, was in early 1983, when with about 2 million addressable converters in place, MCA offered its *Pirates of Penzance* first-run feature film to MSOs for a minimum of $6 per household. In charging viewers an average of $10 for the privilege of seeing the movie, MSOs are believed to have profited by about $4 million that night.

18. For a description of "wireless" cable see *Broadcasting,* December 4, 1989, p. 86.

19. DBS signals, transmitted via high-power satellites, are receivable from rooftop or window-mounted antenna dishes (or flat surfaces) that cost about $300 at retail. In Europe, Rupert Murdoch's Astra, and British Satellite Broadcasting were two of the early entrants. In the United States, however, DBS service applications to the FCC in the early 1980s were originally sponsored by several major communications companies including Comsat, RCA, and General Instruments. After several false starts and substantial losses, most of the early entrants decided to withdraw from participation in DBS. Yet, eventually, DBS may be used in the United States to reach about 10 million rural homes, for which provision of regular cable service would be uneconomical. See *Broadcasting,* "The Uncertain Future of DBS," March 13, 1989, for a full historical discussion.

20. In Los Angeles, for example, in the early 1980s, ON-TV and SelecTV services were quite popular. And nationwide, STV subscribers numbered 2 million at the peak. STV has, however, fared much better in France, where Canal Plus has, since 1984, signed up approximately 3 million subscribers, and has proven to be a great financial success.

21. Many other signal-distribution schemes have been either proposed or tested, but none of them flourished. American Broadcasting, for example, initially implemented and then withdrew (in 1984) an addressable system in which a scrambled VHF signal was sent during unused network overnight hours to homes equipped with a descrambler and a VCR. The system was intended to allow subscribers to play back relatively recent full-length feature films at their own convenience. Also, in late 1977, Warner Communications was the first company to attempt two-way cable service in Columbus, Ohio, under the trade name QUBE, but the financial performance of the system was disappointing.

22. See "Heard on the Street," *Wall Street Journal,* May 20, 1983.

23. See for example, Andrews (1989), in which the potential for a significant speed-up in fiber optic transmission capability using solitron waves is discussed.

24. The cable industry has historically fought legislative and regulatory battles with broadcasting interests. The most recent important conflicts have been over "must-carry" rules, and over syndicated program exclusivity. The must-carry rules had, according to the FCC, required cable systems to carry all local broadcast signals. The cable industry found this to be cumbersome because of the limited channel capacity of many older systems, and sought to have the rules changed (The Washington, D.C., Court of Appeals repealed must-carry rules in 1985). Syndication exclusivity is important to broadcasters who pay substantially for the rights to license programs and do not want to see their investment jeopardized by having the same program imported into their market by cable. Compromises on both issues were reached in the late 1980s.

Chapter 8

1. See, for example, Watkins (1986), and especially Stern and Schoenhaus (1990) for elaborate discussion of the toy development process.

2. For example, it is usually easy enough to make more prints so that a popular movie can be shown in more theaters; it is next to impossible to make and to deliver more copies of a popular toy the week before Christmas.

3. Software is the instruction set that controls a machine's functions.

4. By that time, the worldwide market had become fairly mature and predictable, with Gottlieb (eventually renamed Mylstar, and later discontinued by its owner, Coca-Cola) and Williams holding dominant market positions. In the late 1980s, Bally sold its pin and video business to a successor company of Williams, WMS Industries.

5. The Sanders patents were eventually licensed to all major home video-game manufacturers.

6. With sales of only 1,500 units, this model was not a commercial success, and the rights to it were sold to Nutting Associates, the small firm that had originally agreed to produce it.

7. Nolan Bushnell's early associates included Ted Dabney and Al Alcorn. Bushnell subsequently bought controlling interest in the company and then sold the renamed Syzygy (Atari) to Warner Communications. Among the companies he then helped found were the following: the Pizza Time Theater restaurant chain; Androbot, the personal-robot manufacturer; and Catalyst Technologies, the umbrella venture-capital company that has spawned at least a dozen other independent corporate start-ups. See Owen (1983) and Kubey (1982).

8. Losses at Fairchild and at Warner's new Atari division continued into 1977, when both companies introduced new cartridge-loaded programmable consoles that they hoped would turn the tide. But although these models were a distinct improvement over the previous generation of dedicated machines, they did little to excite the average consumer. Game-design capabilities were at a primitive stage, and the semiconductor chips used in consoles and cartridges had very small and relatively expensive memories: There was no software.

Around this time, Bally Manufacturing and RCA also made major efforts to enter the programmable market, but both companies soon found their participation unrewarding. Bally sold its loss-plagued division to Astrocade, a private company that eventually folded, and RCA discontinued its line. Long-suffering Fairchild also gave up on the business.

9. Intellivision's key selling point was pictorial resolution (graphics) superior to that of Atari's 1977-vintage Video Computer System® (VCS) and to the older Odyssey® line. In short order, Mattel garnered about a 16% share of market – second only to Atari's.

Nevertheless, Intellivision was vulnerable in two areas: Its price was relatively high compared with that of the VCS (at retail over $200, versus about $150 for

Atari), and it was largely dependent on a software library of generic sports-related games instead of arcade hits. This provided Coleco, a late (1982) entrant, with the opportunity to surpass Mattel's unit volume with Coleco Vision® – a lower-priced product that successfully combined high-resolution graphics with top licensed arcade titles.

Although Atari and Mattel initially had complete control of titles for their own cartridge formats, by late 1981 growth of console shipments had attracted several other plug-compatible software designers and manufacturers, including Activision, Parker Bros. (a division of General Mills), Coleco, CBS, and Imagic.

10. Unit sales in that year climaxed at an estimated 8.3 million consoles and 77 million cartridges.

11. The microcomputers included the Texas Instruments (TI) model 99/4A and the Commodore model VIC-20.

12. Computerized-entertainment industry, major-company profits and losses for the calendar year 1983 (excluding results for several smaller manufacturers for arcade and home video):

Company	Profit or loss ($ million)
Activision	−11.3
Atari	−538.6
Bally Mfg.	−34.6
Coleco	−22.3
Commodore[a]	141.2
Mattel	−361.0
Milton Bradley	−30.2
Texas Instruments	−660.0
Total	−1,516.8

[a]Atari and Commodore both lost another $400 million combined in 1984.
Source: Company financial reports.

13. Nintendo was jointed in this revival by a much shrunken Atari, and by another Japanese-based company, Sega Enterprises Ltd. However, Nintendo's software, particularly titles such as *Super Mario Bros. 2*® and *The Legend of Zelda*®, which each sold over 3 million copies, were especially important in maintaining the company's leading share of market. (*Super Mario Bros.*®, introduced in 1987, sold 9.1 million units.) In 1988, in fact, the company delivered 7 million hardware units and 32.5 million software units. From the fall of 1986 through year-end 1989, the company estimated that 19 million Nintendo hardware units and 101.5 million Nintendo and Nintendo-licensed software units had been sold. Industry totals for the same period were estimated at 24.5 million hardware units and 125 million software units. By 1990, though, a serious challenge to Nintendo's primacy was launched by NEC, also a large Japanese consumer electronics company. See also Pollack (1986).

14. At the peak in 1982, for example, it is estimated that video games absorbed about 25% of all 16K ROMs (read-only memories) and up to 50% of all 32K ROMs produced by the then economically depressed semiconductor manufacturers.

15. Operators and location owners exercise control over the pricing and frequency of play perhaps, and have obvious opportunities to divert cash if strict accounting is not enforced. All estimates as to the annual coin-drop are thus approximations based on number of units in use and average play per machine.

16. Servicing is the responsibility of the operator, who is often indirectly supported for parts, labor, and financing by local wholesaler/distributor branches.

17. In the early 1980s, the Atari VCS (Video Computer System) had an installed base of over 10 million, and hits such as *Asteroids, Space Invaders,* and *Pac-Man* were bought by at least 50%, and perhaps up to 75% of console owners.

18. The profit dynamics of games are obviously quite similar to those of other entertainment industry segments. In the heyday of the early 1980s, the similarities extended to the software designers, who were able to command business arrangements with their employers that resembled those that authors and composers have with their publishers. See Chace (1983).

19. According to a 1982 survey by *Play Meter,* a video machine required an average of $117 per week over a 10.5-month period in order to break even after considering operating costs for rent, taxes, and license fees.

Street operators will try to extend the useful life of a machine by "rotating" it to a different location. And arcade operators will use variable pricing on tokens in order to be able to collect more during times of peak demand, and to encourage greater use at slower times of the day. But the income per week and resale value for a typical machine usually declines rapidly during the first year. And once a machine's drawing power begins to noticeably decline, the owner has to make a financial decision based on projected cash-flows, taxes, and salvage values.

20. It is interesting to note that when a new game is introduced, players' skills specific to that game obviously are not well honed, and many coins per unit time are dropped. But as familiarity with the machine's features increases, players are able to endure longer on a single coin, thereby reducing the operator's return. In recognition of this, operators sometimes use "speed-up" kits that make the game more challenging to skilled players.

Chapter 9

1. The Flamingo Hotel was designed by Siegel to attract the rich and famous to the middle of the desert. The hotel started a building boom that was not to slow until the early 1980s, when more than 50,000 hotel rooms were available to host some of the largest business conventions in the world. Also see Puzo (1976).

2. Taxes are currently at a rate of 5¾% of gross winnings in Nevada, and 8% in New Jersey, where a surcharge of 1¼% of gross revenues to be invested in urban development over 25 years also exists.

3. However, the average length of stay of Atlantic City visitors is probably a little less than a day, and for many visitors, just a few hours. In Las Vegas, the average length of stay is about 3.8 days.

4. According to *Gaming Business,* in 1983 there were 92 thoroughbred racing associations that attracted 51.1 million patrons and handled about $7.2 billion, and 62 standardbred (harness) racing associations that reported a total annual handle of $2.81 billion and a total attendance of 23.3 million. In more recent years, these figures have not changed appreciably.

5. Net revenues retained by the states would normally be about half as much. The rest, after deduction of administrative and selling expenses, is returned to the public as prizes. So these figures suggest that average annual net per-capita spending on lotteries – i.e., the actual tax burden on citizens – is approaching $35.

6. From surveys, Scarne (1974) estimated a bingo handle of about $3 billion. However, Abt, Smith, and Christiansen (1985) estimated that same handle for 1982; also see Christiansen (1989) and Cook (1979).

7. Similar charity-designated games are also conducted in two Canadian provinces, Alberta and Manitoba. Also, legalized casino gaming is expected to be operational on Mississippi riverboats in Iowa and Illinois sometime in the early 1990s.

8. These numbers are also not to be confused with the gross amounts bet, or the handle, which is estimated to be around $250 billion. Scarne (1974) conducted surveys that indicated much larger numbers – numbers that most observers believe to be highly exaggerated. As of the early 1970s, Scarne estimated that the total U.S. gambling handle (defined as the money handled, the total amount wagered, or the annual gambling exchange) amounted to an astonishing $500 billion. Of this, he estimated that the actual cost to the betting public was about 10% of $500 billion, or $50 billion. Extrapolated into current dollars, a comparably estimated sum would now be larger still, especially because high inflation and tax rates of the late 1970s and early 1980s stimulated the growth of the so-called underground economy, a largely cash-transactions economy, that exists beyond the official statistics and tax-collection system. See Scarne (1978).

9. There is evidence to suggest that the majority of players consider gaming to be a form of entertainment. As the survey in U.S. Congress (1976) indicates, 81% of respondents said that one of the reasons they bet at a casino is to have a good time. See Table S9.1.

10. Judging by history, the industry has only experienced one important setback in the postwar period (in 1981), and that coincided with a recession. It is not clear, however, whether the difficulties the industry encountered were exacerbated by the new competition that came on-stream from Atlantic City at that time.

11. Acting on the wishes of the legislature, the commission specified the following:

minimum size of table bets
numbers of tables and slots of different denominations and type allowed in each
    casino
hours of operation
number of square feet of public space relative to number of rooms
numbers of security guards required
number of days per week that live entertainment had to be provided (in the first
    off-peak seasons there were days when there were more performers on stage than
    people in the audience)
various other aspects of hotel-casino operations, including limitations on marketing
    that are normally considered in the province of management

12. For example, as of 1989, public companies include Hilton, Holiday Corp., Aztar, Bally, Circus Circus Enterprises, Caesars, Sahara Resorts, and Showboat. Racing includes General Instruments, Hollywood Park, San Juan Racing, Santa Anita Consolidated, and United Tote. Bingo includes Bingo King. Lotteries include

Bally, GTECH, and General Instruments. And slot machines include International Game Technology, Jackpot Enterprises, and United Gaming.

13. For example, in May 1989 the Atlantis (originally Playboy) hotel-casino next to the convention center in Atlantic City closed. Long operating under bankruptcy laws, it failed for a number of reasons, but mostly because it was never able to overcome its initial design handicap of having a casino on three levels.

14. It is interesting to observe, for example, that on a total investment of $4.2 billion as of 1988, New Jersey's 12 casinos netted (see Tables S9.2 and S9.3) about $15 million. But total "casino" cash flow (EBITD) was a more impressive $684 million.

15. Multiples have generally ranged between five and nine in recent years.

16. However, Binion's Horseshoe in downtown Las Vegas has a unique policy whereby the player's limit is as high as his first bet. Also, a group of very high stakes players can "pool" their play.

17. *Gambling Times,* August 1983, p. 16.

18. Interestingly, the definitions of hold percentage are somewhat different in Nevada and in New Jersey. New Jersey's definition includes all cash and markers, but Nevada's definition does not include markers redeemed at the table. All other things being equal, New Jersey hold figures should normally be a bit lower than those of Nevada.

19. If, however, as is more likely, players initially buy many more chips than they bet on each decision (some lose, and some tend to walk away from a table without betting all the chips initially bought), then the ratio of handle to drop does not grow as rapidly as in this example.

20. Win rates, of course, also depend on game rules, which may vary (especially in Nevada) according to the discretion of management.

21. It is estimated that perhaps 20% of the high-rollers may account for 80% of the upper-end business.

22. Junkets, in which rooms and meals and travel costs may be picked up, i.e., "comped" by the casino, have diminished in popularity as the casinos have found that junkets are not as profitable as they had been thought to be. For instance, a casino wanting to earn at least $100 should know that if it costs $400 to bring a junket player in the door, it must – assuming a 20% hold (win/drop) – realize a minimum drop that averages $2,500.

23. The volume increase is a direct function of the credit extension itself, and may also be indirectly affected by the exciting atmosphere that surrounds high-stakes tables, where smaller noncredit bettors may feel that they should become less conservative with their funds.

24. Prior to June 1983, gaming debts were not legally enforceable in Nevada. See also Rose (1986).

25. For instance, in 1983, receivables in Atlantic City casinos rose at about twice the rate of win, and foreshadowed the potential for a noticeably slower growth of revenues (win) in 1984.

Chapter 10

1. Gate receipts are shared 65:35 between home and visiting teams. In 1980, the net profit margin for NFL teams was 5.2%, and net income was $694,000. This compares with total television payments of only $926,000 for the NFL title game in 1963 (Michener 1976, p. 360). Under the 1982 television contract, teams derived an average of $14.2 million per year from television. Also see the Kent-sponsored "Sports Business" advertisements in *The Wall Street Journal,* April 2, 1982, and April 16, 1982.

2. See, for example, the discussion by Frank (1984) of the United States Football League.

3. Relaxation of antitrust-law restraints enables leagues to bargain with networks as a unit. In this respect, the sports business has an advantage not available to other entertainment segments. Also see Rivkin (1974).

4. In the NBA and NHL, gate receipts are not shared with the visiting team; the home team takes 100%. In baseball, there is limited sharing of gate receipts, but not nearly to the extent of that in the NFL. See Waggoner (1982).

5. For example, in 1982 the New York Yankees and the Philadelphia Phillies each received $6.5 million from local television stations. This sum excludes cable, which can in addition easily provide well in excess of $1 million per year for those clubs. (Cable and pay-TV revenues are split 75% home club, 25% visitors.) License fees from sales of network television rights, however, are also of increasing significance. As of the mid-1980s, baseball franchises began splitting the income from network broadcasts, with each major-league team deriving about $7 million annually (before other possible deductions) from this source. In total, radio, television, and cable-rights fees paid to baseball's major-league teams rose from $44.5 million in 1975 to almost $268 million in 1984.

6. In 1989, for example, a sports bidding war erupted among the cable and broadcast networks. CBS paid $1.1 billion for 4 years of major league baseball, and NBC paid $600 million for 4 years of N.B.A. games. See La Pointe (1989).

But teams may not be directly profitable. In the 1980–1 season, only 5 of 23 basketball teams were profitable, and the entire NBA claimed losses totaling more than $13 million. In hockey, about half of NHL teams are unprofitable. In baseball, only 8 of 26 teams are estimated to have made money or broken even in 1982; in aggregate, the 26 teams lost $58 million. Weighing heavily on the future profitability and solvency of major sports organizations are deferred player salaries, which have become important liabilities for professional teams.

7. However, appreciation of broadcast rights can no longer be taken for granted by college and other amateur-sports organizations. Whereas a degree of immunity from application of antitrust laws exists for professional teams, a 1984 Supreme Court decision found that the National Collegiate Athletic Association's (NCAA) exclusive agreements with three television networks violated federal antitrust statutes. That decision left NCAA colleges free to negotiate individual contracts with commercial broadcast and cable networks, and nullified the NCAA's traditional role as sole exclusive negotiator for broadcast rights to college football games.

Although the Supreme Court decision increases opportunities for cable and regional sports networks and independent broadcasters to bid for licenses to show games of local interest, the amounts being paid by these new bidders have in the aggregate proved to be below the amounts that had regularly been obtained in contracts negotiated by the NCAA. The demand for such programming has remained fairly steady, but the supply has in effect been increased.

8. Another famous case of *Flood* v. *Kuhn* in 1972 served to advance some of the issues that ultimately led to free-agency. The original reserve system was secretly adopted in 1879 and first implemented by the National (baseball) League in 1880. It was designed to minimize players' bargaining power and to prevent a few wealthy

owners from destroying a league's competitive balance by buying all the best talent. But, in fact, as Demmert (1973) indicates, competitive balance has generally not been attainable: The richest teams in the most lucrative markets, regardless of new-talent draft policies, have over the long term tended to field clubs with the highest overall athletic quality.

Prior to free-agency, baseball's so-called waiver rules had restricted the sale of a player's contract to a team outside the league, and an owner wishing to make such a sale had to first secure agreement from each team owner in the league to relinquish the right to purchase the player's contract at a fixed price. Union contracts still generally require a player testing free-agency to give his old club an opportunity to match a new team's offer – in other words, to provide the old team the right of first refusal. Also, teams losing valuable players may be entitled to receive some compensation.

9. Several times during the 1960s and 1970s, the National Football League attempted to obtain immunity from the Sherman Anti-trust Act of 1890, which declared "every contract, combination . . . or conspiracy in restraint of trade or commerce to be illegal." One of the key cases was *John Mackey et al.* v. *National Football League,* which was filed in 1972 by the players' union to fight against the so-called Roselle Rule. As Harris (1986, p. 71) notes, this rule, named after the League's commissioner, suggested that "any franchise whose contract with a player expired had the right to compensation from the player's new employer should that player subsequently work for another franchise. The compensation was to be a player of equal caliber, selected by the commissioner." The effect of this, Mackey argued, was to suppress player salaries by reducing competition between franchises. Mackey won the original case, but an appeals court decision in October of 1976, in effect, said that the labor issues should be settled by collective bargaining. Both sides agreed on a 76-page contract in February of 1977.

Public-policy implications deriving from baseball's immunity to antitrust laws and the previously severe restrictions on the economic mobility of players enmeshed in the reserve system are extensively reviewed in the studies cited in section 10.3, and in Markham and Teplitz (1981).

10. The effectiveness of free-agency was, however, severely questioned in 1987, as team owners apparently stopped aggressively bidding against each other. See, for example, Spitz (1987).

11. In the 1980s, for example, there were numerous strikes or threats of strikes. Baseball players went on strike in 1981, 1985, and 1987, and football players in 1982.

The 1982 National Football League Players Association strike was based on an attempt to gear compensation to a fixed percentage of gross revenues and to create a salary scale based on seniority and performance. The players did not achieve their initial primary objective of sharing a percentage of gross revenues from network television and therefore did not significantly alter the balance of power of owners over athletes. But their collective salary pool totaling $1.6 billion over five years amounted to just under 50% of gross revenues, as compared with 35%–44% before the strike. In addition, a modest salary scale – and the right to bargain for income above minimums that started at $30,000 per year for rookies and went up to $200,000 per year for veterans – was established.

The outcome in football was not unlike the situation in the 1981 Major League Baseball Players Association strike, in which the primary issue was compensation to clubs losing players through free-agency transfers. The complicated settlement delineates rules for player rankings and performances under which such transfers are conducted.

The Basketball Players Association in the NBA and the National Hockey League Players Association negotiated with team owners on issues similar to those in football and baseball, but the financial positions of basketball and hockey teams have historically been much weaker than those in the other major sports.

A new revenue-sharing agreement was developed in the NBA in 1983, and it has thus far worked well. The agreement is designed to prevent richer franchises from dominating the game, to create more consistent competition between teams, and to stop cost escalation due to free agency. Beginning in the 1984–5 season, the NBA guaranteed players 53% of the league's gross revenue – which included money from rapidly growing sales of regional pay-cable rights. The 53% is to be distributed among 23 teams, with a "cap" for the richest teams and a "floating minimum" for the poorest. See "The NBA's Ingenious Move to Cap Players' Salaries," *Business Week,* October 31, 1983, p. 81.

12.   Two additional regulations concerning amortization of intangibles and the distinction between nonamortizable goodwill and amortizable intangibles in 1974 also helped set the stage for employing sports-franchise ownership as a tax shelter.

13.   *Laird* v. *United States; First Northwest Industries of America, Inc., Houston Chronicle Publishing Co.* v. *United States; KFOX Inc.* v. *United States.*

Chapter 11

1.   In looking at this, an interesting fact noted by Baumol and Baumol (1984) is that over the 50 years following the Great Depression, top Broadway prices rose about 14-fold, while movie-ticket prices rose 35-fold.

2.   According to Hirsch (1987), Ringling played in 1987 before 11 million people in 89 cities at ticket prices ranging from $6.00 to $11.50. Revenues in 1987 were $250 million. Labor costs are 50% of budget, ads and promotion consume another 25%, and the remainder of the budget is absorbed by train costs, arena rentals, props, and equipment and insurance expenses. Most circuses cover their costs at the gate and make profits with concessions. RB&BB's yearly advertising and promotion budget is between $10 million and $12 million, with half of this total going to TV and 25% to newspapers, according to *Advertising Age,* December 12, 1983. For a good review of the RB&BB history at age 100, see *Variety,* January 11, 1984.

3.   In practice, copyright considerations are often illegally ignored in small off-off-Broadway or regional productions. Copyrights would, of course, be enforced in any important commercial production.

4.   The New York State Attorney General's office had compiled statistics on offering prospectuses for Broadway and off-Broadway shows. Over the 11 seasons between 1972–3 and 1982–3, for example, some 948 shows in this sample (which included shows that never opened, but excluded some very prominently successful shows in which funding was privately raised) lost a grand total of $66.6 million on capitalizations of $267.5 million. There was not a single season in which these shows, in the aggregate, generated profits.

Nevertheless, the other side of the coin is that when shows are successful, they are incredibly so. "Cats," according to *Variety* of February 15, 1989, has become the most profitable (in absolute dollars) theatrical production to date, earning net profit in North America (United States and Canada) of approximately $44 million (and another $14.5 million from the London and other foreign editions). The base investment made by the Shubert Organization, ABC Entertainment, Metromedia Corp., and Geffen Records in 1982 was $3.9 million. In other words, the Andrew Lloyd Webber production returned over 11 times the investment in North America alone. Because Webber, as author, and the other royalty participants receive about 25% as a license fee plus royalties, the actual gross profit was $58 million. As of 1989, "Cats" on Broadway was still grossing almost $400,000 a week, and generating weekly net profit of around $45,000.

Other big winners have included "Hello, Dolly," which netted $9 million on a $420,000 investment (a 21-to-1 return with investors splitting the profit equally with the producer David Merrick) and "Fiddler on the Roof," which earned $12.4 million on a $375,000 investment.

Yet, as Rothstein (1988) has noted, in the 17 months after "Starlight Express" opened (in March 1987), this show took in $35 million and was seen by more than 925,000 people – and it had not yet recouped its investment. Reibstein (1986) suggests that in order to succeed, straight plays should generally have weekly production costs that are half or less of the theater's box-office capacity, although musicals will usually range higher.

Table S11.4 shows the income and expense characteristics for a sample of non-profit theaters between 1984 and 1988. Also, see Passell (1989).

5. If x = utilization percentage, then the formula is $x = \$100,000/(500$ seats $\times \$30$ ticket price $\times 8$ performances).

6. Although all Broadway productions follow contract-specified minimum-scale guidelines, the percentage of unemployed members of performing-arts unions is chronically high, and for smaller productions, union specifications are often ignored or waived. For instance, in order to encourage low-budget productions that will provide good experience for new performers, Equity waives many of its minimums in theaters with seating of under 100.

7. Additional topics of potential interest to economists, all in the volume edited by Hendon, Shanahan, and MacDonald (1980), include a mathematical model for support of the arts (Seaman 1980), an analysis of artistic innovation using information theory (Owen and Owen 1980), development of a composer supply function (Felton 1980), and estimation of a demand function for Broadway-theater tickets (Kelejian and Lawrence 1980). In a separate study, however, the economics of the theater are presented in great detail by Moore (1968), who developed a model of demand for theater as a function of income, the supply of shows, and the real price of tickets.

8. However, Grillo (1983) noted that, at least to date, theater productions have not found a wide audience or comfortable home on cable television.

Chapter 12

1. The 160-acre site for Disneyland was selected by the Stanford Research Institute.

2. In attempts to emulate Disney's concepts on a smaller scale, the Marriott Corporation, Taft Broadcasting, Six Flags, and others began a construction boom that lasted throughout most of the 1970s. A total of at least $500 million was spent in the construction of parks such as Busch Gardens Old Country, Great Adventure, Kings Dominion, Great America, and Canada's Wonderland. However, many of the companies that built these parks are no longer in the business. As of 1989, the two largest park operators after Disney in terms of total admissions were Anheuser Busch (Sea World parks) and Wesray (Six Flags).

3. That was, of course, followed by another initial investment of $1.1 billion to open the EPCOT Center in 1981, and $500 million for the Studio Tour that opened in 1989.

4. A subset of the themed-amusement business involves regularly scheduled state fairs and regional expositions. These fairs are, in essence, movable, impermanent theme parks that have operating characteristics similar to those of permanent facilities. According to compilations by *Amusement Business,* the industry trade journal, in 1989 the top 50 fairs attracted combined attendance of 48.7 million. But because only about 60% of all admissions are paid, the industry generates under $150 million at the gate. Several times this amount, however, is derived from activities conducted within the fairs.

Waterparks, another subset, have also become popular in recent years. In 1988, the top 10 waterparks in the United States, as measured by *Amusement Business* (December 24, 1988), generated an average of over 400,000 visits a year.

A substantial overview of the theme park business in the United States is presented in Lyon (1987).

5. A number of major European parks date to the early 1900s. As shown in Brown and Church (1987), Alton Towers in the United Kingdom was opened in 1924, and Kantoor (Duinrell) in the Netherlands, in 1935. Alton Towers and De Efteling in the Netherlands attract well over 2 million visitors a year. The new EuroDisney park to open in 1992 outside of Paris, however, will attract over 11 million visitors.

Asian parks are also becoming important, especially in Japan, Indonesia, and Korea. Tokyo Disneyland, for example, attracts over 12 million visitors a year.

6. Both traditional carnival-type games and electronic video games also generate high marginal profits.

7. Occasionally it may be analytically convenient to view theme parks as hotels – where guests happen to stay during the day rather than at night. Capital-expenditure and amortization patterns are quite similar in these two types of operations.

8. Also, the recent selling prices of similar properties. Significant transactions in the 1980s included:

The sale of Six Flags to Wesray Capital Corp., by Bally Mfg. in 1987 for approximately $350 million plus assumption of $250 million of debt, a price of about 15 times estimated operating cash flow.

Marriott's 195-acre Santa Clara property to the city of Santa Clara for $101 million, and the 325-acre Gurnee, Illinois, park to Bally Mfg. for about $114.5 million in 1984. Gurnee attracted some 2.6 million visitors and generated revenues of over $50 million.

The purchase by Gaylord Broadcasting, in 1983, of Opryland, which included a 120-acre park, a theater, the Opryland Hotel (1,068 rooms), two radio stations, and the Nashville Network (cable), for an estimated $270 million.

Kings Entertainment Company, which bought from Taft Broadcasting Kings Island, Kings Dominion, Carowinds, and Hanna Barbera Land for $167.5 million in 1983. Together these parks earned $10.7 million on revenues of $97.2 million.

The purchase, in 1982, of the Six Flags parks (six facilities with 1982 attendance of approximately 12.6 million) for $147 million plus assumption of about $100 million in debt by Bally Mfg. Operating income in 1982 was $36 million on revenues of $259 million.

Appendix A
Sources of information

The most convenient sources of macroeconomic data for use in entertainment-industry studies include the following regular U.S Department of Commerce publications:

Survey of Current Business, especially the July issue containing personal-consumption expenditure figures for the preceding four years.

Business Conditions Digest, especially for detailed industrial price data.

U.S. Labor Department *Monthly Review* and *Handbook of Labor Statistics* for articles and data on labor and employment issues.

U.S. Census of Manufactures and, especially, *Census of Selected Services,* which contains regional data on revenues, employment, and productivity.

U.S. Statistical Abstract for historical series.

U.S. Industrial Outlook, published every year with forecasts for the next five years.

Information on specific entertainment-business topics is also widely available in the following regularly published non-government-sponsored magazines and newspapers:

Sources of information

Advertising Age
American Film
Amusement Business
Billboard
Broadcasting
CableVision
Cash Box
Channels

Electronic Media
Gaming & Wagering Business
Hollywood Reporter
Play Meter
Public Gaming
Replay
Television Digest
Variety (daily and weekly)

Appendix B
Major games of chance

In studying the financial economics of gaming, it is essential to have at least a cursory knowledge of how the major games are conducted. This appendix is designed to provide such knowledge, but it is by no means intended as a complete guide. Many other widely available books contain far greater detail concerning the finer points of play strategy and money management (i.e., the number of units wagered at each betting decision).[1] Tax consequences may also have some relevance.[2]

Blackjack

In blackjack, alternatively known as twenty-one or vingt-et-un, the player's goal is to receive cards totaling more than those of the dealer, but not exceeding 21 – and to do this before the dealer has to show his hand. A 1 (ace) card can be counted as either 1 or 11, other numbers count as their actual values, and picture cards count as 10. Suits do not matter. The payoff to a winning player is equivalent to the amount bet, that is, even money – except in the case of "blackjack" (a "natural" 21 on the first two cards), when the payoff is three units to two.

The player is initially dealt two cards that must compare against the dealer's two cards – positioned in front of the dealer, one face down and one face up. Although casino rules vary, the dealer generally must "stand" (i.e., cannot draw another card) on the total of 17. Players have an option to request another card (called getting "hit") whenever they want, as long as the cards they already hold total less than 21.

Depending on casino rules, players may also "double down" on certain totals (usually, with a 9, 10, or 11), which means the initial bet can be doubled while drawing one, and only one, more card. Also, if the first two cards are of the same number, a split into two betting hands is permitted, but not always advisable.

The player or dealer exceeding 21 is said to go "bust," and tie hands, in which no money is exchanged, are a "push." (Technically, however, if both player and dealer bust, that kind of tie is won by the dealer, because sequencing requires that players show their hands and relinquish the bets first.)

After seeing that the dealer's face-up card is an ace, a player can also take "insurance," which allows protection against losing in case of a dealer's blackjack (an ace and a 10 card). Insurance is a side bet, at most equal to one-half the amount of the original bet. If the dealer indeed has a natural, the insurance is paid at 2 to 1; otherwise it is lost. The original bet is then settled in the usual way regardless of the decision on the side bet.

Strategies on whether to stand (not request an additional card) or to hit, on how to evaluate a "soft" total (composed with an ace), and on when to double down or to split have been devised by experts in probability theory and computer-simulation techniques. By assigning point values to cards already dealt and by playing proper strategy in response, a "card counter" can obtain information as to the shifting probabilities in the remaining deck. A remaining deck rich in 10-value cards would, for example, make it relatively easier than otherwise for the player to attain a two-card hand close to 21.

The game operator's advantage on blackjack is difficult to compute at any point of play. However, from the top of a deck, blackjack ordinarily provides the house with an edge of a little over 2%.[3] As the game progresses, however, the house edge (which depends importantly on the fact that the dealer turns over his cards *after* the player has gone bust) may disappear, and a skilled card counter can take advantage of such moments by increasing the size of the bet at that time. Blackjack is thus the only casino game that can be beaten by players, and it is this well-advertised fact that has made blackjack the most popular of casino table games.

To win consistently, however, skills in card counting, in play strategy, and in money management must be employed simultaneously in the typical high-speed, pressurized casino environment. But because attainment of such skills requires innate ability in mathematics and extensive study and practice (the patience for which is not apt to be found in most players), the threat to casino profits from self-proclaimed card counters is usually more imagined than real.

The presence of card counters has nonetheless tended to unnerve managements, and rather than simply foiling recognized counters by setting low betting limits, casinos have devised a multitude of card-cutting and multideck variations – the effect of which is to slow the rate of play and to probably reduce profitability.

Craps

Craps (Figure B.1) has long been a favorite in American casinos and, along with poker, is a quintessential American game. It evolved from the English game hazard, and was adopted and refined by American blacks in New Orleans in the early 1800s. Thereafter it spread to immigrant neighborhoods on the East Coast. In contrast to 21, in which probability calculations are especially complicated, the house edge in bank craps as regularly conducted in casinos can be readily computed.

Two cubes (dice) – each die's surfaces marked one through six with embedded dots – are thrown by the player ("shooter") against a backboard on the opposite side of the table. Betting decisions are dependent on the sum of dots on the top surfaces of the dice after they come to rest.

There are 36 possible outcomes (6 × 6), and the probabilities of a number being thrown are measured against those outcomes. With two cubes there are more ways (six) to make a seven (i.e., 1:6, 2:5, 3:4, 4:3, 5:2, 6:1) than to make any other number [Table B.1(a)], and craps uses this as a central theme for decision making.

The game focuses on what number the shooter makes on the first roll, the "comeout" throw. A 7 or 11, also known as a natural, provides an even-money win for players betting with the shooter on the "pass line" and a loss for those betting against the shooter on "don't pass." If the outcome is a 2, 3, or 12 (known as craps), the converse is true. However, either the 2 or the 12 is selected by local custom to be used as a "push" or standoff number. In other words, there are no winners or losers if the sum on the top faces of the dice agrees with the designated standoff number that is indicated by diagram on the table's felt-cloth layout. Probabilities and game strategies remain the same whichever number is designated for this purpose.

If the comeout throw was neither a natural (7, 11) nor a craps (2, 3, 12), then one of the other possible numbers (4, 5, 6, 8, 9, 10) was thrown. One of those numbers then becomes the "point." Players on the pass line are betting that the point number will appear again before a 7 appears. Don't-line bettors are hoping that 7 appears before the point. Winners are paid even money.

Although there are many additional bets that can be made at any stage

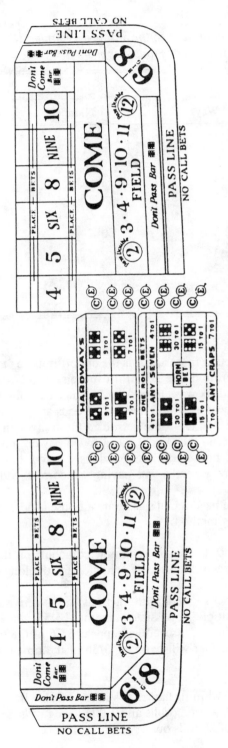

Figure B.1. Craps-table layout. *Source:* Reprinted by permission of the Putnam Publishing Group from *Playboy's Guide to Casino Gambling* by Edwin Silberstang. Copyright © 1981 by Edwin Silberstang.

329

Table B.1. *(a) Number of ways to throw a given number with two dice, and (b) point numbers and odds that 7 appears first*

(a)		(b)	
Roll	Ways	Number	Odds
2	1	4	2 to 1
3	2	5	3 to 2
4	3	6	6 to 5
5	4	8	6 to 5
6	5	9	3 to 2
7	6	10	2 to 1
8	5		
9	4		
10	3		
11	2		
12	1		
Total	36		

in the game, of particular importance is the opportunity to "take the odds" or "lay the odds." From Table B.1(a) it can be seen that there are three ways to make a 4 and six ways to make a 7. Thus, over the long run, 7 is twice as likely to appear as 4, and the correct odds are 2:1 in favor of the number 7 [Table B.1(b)]. On some bets (e.g., those involving "taking" or "laying" the odds behind the "line"), casinos will pay off the correct odds, thereby lowering the house edge. As previously noted, however, casinos make their profits by generally *not* paying off correct odds to winners (Table B.2).

So-called front-line bets in craps generate a house edge of 1.41%, calculated by the following method:

Assume a perfect dice shooter on each new comeout roll throws each of the 11 numbers exactly as often as predicted for the long run by probability theory.

To avoid complicated arithmetic with fractions and to derive a lowest common multiple, multiply 36 possible outcomes by 55, which is 1,980.

Then, out of 1,980 throws, a seven will appear 6/36 of the time (i.e., 330 times). Similarly, a four will be made 3/36 of the time (or 165 times), and so forth.

After adding all the winning figures as shown in Table B.3, it can be seen that there will be 976 winning rolls and 1,004 losing rolls, the house edge being the difference of 28 rolls out of 1,980, or 1.41%.

Table B.2. *Craps payout odds*

Bet	Payout odds
Pass line bet	1 to 1
Come bet	1 to 1
Pass line odds, come bet odds and buy bets	
Points of 4 or 10	2 to 1
Points of 5 or 9	3 to 2
Points of 6 or 8	6 to 5
Place bet to win:	
Points of 4 or 10	9 to 5
Points of 5 or 9	7 to 5
Points of 6 or 8	7 to 6
Field bets:	
3, 4, 9, 10, or 11	1 to 1
2 or 12	2 to 1
Proposition bets:	
Any 7	4 to 1
Any craps	7 to 1
Two craps or twelve craps	30 to 1
Three craps or eleven	15 to 1

Bet	Payout odds
Don't pass line bet	1 to 1
Don't come bet	1 to 1
Don't pass line lay odds: don't come lay odds and lay bets:	
Points of 4 or 10	1 to 2
Points of 5 or 9	2 to 3
Points of 6 or 8	5 to 6
Big six or eight:	
Bets of $6 or multiples thereof	7 to 6
Bets of less than $6 or odd multiples	1 to 1
Hard ways:	
Hard 6 or 8	9 to 1
Hard 4 or 10	7 to 1

Horn high bets: payout based on 2 craps, 3 craps, 12 craps, and 11 payout odds shown above

Table B.3. *Front-line bets*

Number	Times thrown	Winning rolls
Natural 7	330	330
Natural 11	110	110
Craps 2, 3, 12	220	—
Point 4	165	55
Point 10	165	55
Point 5	220	88
Point 9	220	88
Point 6	275	125
Point 8	275	125
Totals	1,980	976

Source: Scarne's Guide to Casino Gambling. Copyright © 1978 by John Scarne Games, Inc. Reprinted by permission of Simon and Schuster, Inc.

Roulette

Historians disagree on the origin of roulette. Some say it was invented by the French mathematician Blaise Pascal in 1655; others support more arcane theories. In any event, the game has evolved into European and American versions – the European wheel with a single zero, the American with zero and double zero (Figure B.2).

Mixed in standardized format around the roulette wheel are the numbers 1 through 36 and, in addition, depending on the version, either zero or both zero and double zero. The numbers on the wheel have adjacent background colors that alternate red and black and are arranged so that alternate low and high, odd and even, and red and black numbers are as mathematically balanced as possible. A perfect balance cannot be achieved, because the sum of the numbers 1 through 36 is 666, but the odd numbers sum to 324, and the even numbers sum to 342.

By placing one or more chips on a number, color, or odd or even, the player is betting that a ball spinning near the rim of the wheel will stop on that number, color, or number type. Payoffs on winning odd–even or black–red bets are 1:1, but for a specific number the payoff is 35:1. With an American double-zero wheel, there is a total of 38 positions, with the correct odds being 37:1. Thus, the casino keeps 2/38, or 5.26% in the American game, or 1/37 (2.70%) in the European game.

Other betting variations that are often offered by casinos normally do not significantly affect the casino's percentages. For instance, the *en prison* option reduces the house advantage by half on even-money bets (i.e., color, high–low number, or odd–even). On such bets, when zero or double zero is the outcome of the last spin of the wheel, players may settle for half the original wager or let the original amount ride (imprison the wager). If the

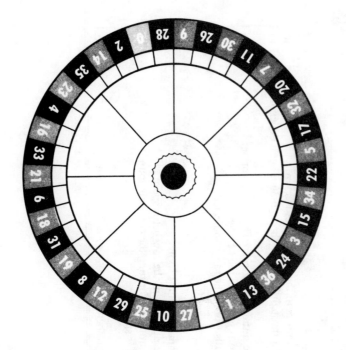

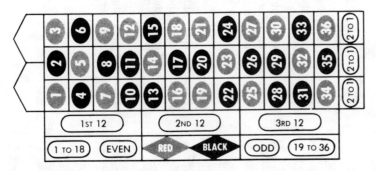

Figure B.2. Roulette wheel and table layout. *Source:* Reprinted by permission of the Putnam Publishing Group from *Playboy's Guide to Casino Gambling* by Edwin Silberstang. Copyright © 1981 by Edwin Silberstang.

choice is to let it ride and the following spin is a winner, the original bet is returned intact. Roulette bets and odds are given in Table B.4.

Baccarat

Baccarat (Figure B.3) and its close cousins, chemin de fer and Punto Banco, are popular high-stakes games in casinos all over the world. All cur-

Table B.4. *Roulette bets and odds*

Position	Description	Payout odds
Straight bets		
Straight up	All numbers, zero & double zero	35 to 1
Column bet	Pays off if any of the 12 numbers in the column bet is spun	2 to 1
Dozen	Pays off if 1 through 12, 13 through 24, or 25 through 36 is spun depending on the dozen bet	2 to 1
Red or black	Pays off if the color on the number spun corresponds to color bet	1 to 1
Odd or even	Pays off if number spun corresponds to the bet made	1 to 1
1 to 18 or 19 to 36	Pays off if number spun falls within the range indicated	1 to 1
Combination bets		
Split	Pays off if either of two numbers split is spun	17 to 1
Row	Pays off if any of the three numbers in the row bet is spun	11 to 1
Corner	Pays off if any of the four numbers forming the corner is spun	8 to 1
Five numbers	Pays off if 0, 00, 1, 2, or 3 is spun	6 to 1
Six numbers	Pays off if any of the six numbers in the two rows bet is spun	5 to 1

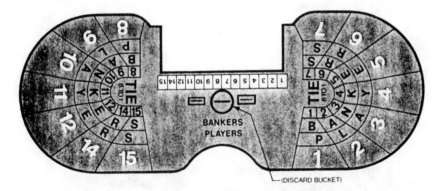

Figure B.3. Baccarat-table layout. *Source:* Reprinted by permission of the Putnam Publishing Group from *Playboy's Guide to Casino Gambling* by Edwin Silberstang. Copyright © by Edwin Silberstang.

rent versions are derived from the Italian *baccara,* first introduced into France circa 1490 and later adopted as a favorite game of the nobility. But it was not until the late 1950s that modern baccarat was taken seriously by Las Vegas casinos.

The earlier chemin de fer is played the same way as baccarat, except that in chemin, the casino takes no risk because players bet against each other – the house merely acts as a "cutter" for a standard 5% charge taken from the player-banker's winning bet (coup).

In American baccarat, eight standard 52-card decks are shuffled and placed in a "shoe." There may be as many as 12 people seated at the table, and each makes a bet by placing chips for the *Player,* for the *Banker,* or for a tie hand. Winning bets (subject to commissions, as discussed later) are paid even money, and ties usually are paid at 8:1.

A bettor and the dealer are each ritualistically dealt two cards, with picture cards and 10 counting as zero, and number cards counting their actual face values. Should the two-card sum be in double digits (i.e., 10 or more), then the right-hand digit is considered the card count. In other words, a two-card sum of 14 would be counted a 4.

Normally, the gamer's goal is for the side he is betting on – either Player or Banker – to have a two-card count of 9. However, if either side has less than 8 or 9, a "natural," there are fairly standardized rules (Table B.5) that specify when additional cards may be drawn. A count of zero is "baccarat."

Through complicated arithmetic it has been determined, according to Scarne (1978, p. 266), that the chance of the Player's side winning is about 49.33%, and for the Banker's side, 50.67%. The Player's disadvantage, or cost to participate, is thus about 1.34%. However, in order to even out the sides, the casino retains a 5% "commission" out of the Banker's winnings. [Because the Banker's side, on average, wins 50.67% of the hands dealt, the

Table B.5. *Baccarat rules*

Player having		
1–2–3–4–5–10	Draws a card	
6–7	Stands[a]	
8–9	Natural. Banker cannot draw.	

Banker having	Draws when giving	Does not draw when giving
3	1–2–3–4–5–6–7–9–10	8
4	2–3–4–5–6–7	1–8–9–10
5	4–5–6–7	1–2–3–8–9–10
6[a]	6–7	1–2–3–4–5–8–9–10
7	Stands	
8–9	Natural. Player cannot draw.	

Note: Pictures and tens do not count.
[a] If player takes no card, banker stands on 6.

actual charge is 2.53% (0.5067 times 5%).] In so reducing the aforementioned Banker's advantage of 1.34% by 2.53%, the Banker's cost of play after commission then nets to about 1.19%. Thus, the casino's edge is somewhere between 1.19% and 1.34%.[4] But on bets that Banker and Player have tie hands, casinos usually pay 9 for 1 (i.e., at 8:1 odds) and have an edge of 14.36%.

Because most of the play is concentrated on Player or Banker – where the margins are thin – over the short term the casino win results for baccarat are generally far more volatile than for any of the other games.

Slots

Slot machines have steadily evolved since Charles Fey first introduced them in San Francisco in 1887, and for most casinos they now draw over 40% of revenues and an even larger share of profits.

In recent years, slots and their video-game relatives discussed in Chapter 8 have all been greatly enhanced by development of sophisticated electronic microprocessors. Nonetheless, the basic concept of slot play remains the same as always: to line up certain randomly generated symbols on a window or video screen. In return for so doing, players are rewarded with various levels of monetary prizes determined proportionally by the probability of occurrence.

For example, in a mechanical three-reel model with 20 different symbols per reel, and with each reel spinning independently, the probability of three of the same figures lining up is $1/20 \times 1/20 \times 1/20$, or 0.000125, which is 1 in 8,000. Of course, as in other games, the casino will profit by setting the actual payout to be less than 7,999 to 1. In New Jersey, by law, slot machines cannot pay out less than 83% of the drop, but there is no such rule in Nevada.

Slot machines today come in many different versions, including "progressives" (which are linked to the coin-drop in other machines), color-action (non-reel) videos, and multi-line-payoff models. But whatever the type, the chief advantages to casinos are the low operating costs and relatively high hold percentages of slots as compared with table games. Indeed, because of the low operating costs, coin-operated machine adaptations of blackjack and poker have also been emphasized by casinos.

Other casino games

Poker

America's all-time favorite private card game, poker, is believed to have evolved from French and Persian card games in the early 1800s. It was refined by active use on the Mississippi riverboats of the last century.

The principal concept in the game's many variations is to arrange the dealt cards in sequence of value and in suits, and to determine the relative ranking of each player's final hand to establish a winner of the money pool (pot) generated during the course of play. Players bet according to the actual and perceived strengths of the various hands, with bluffing a normal part of strategy.

Despite poker's popularity in private settings, it has not been an important contributor to the earnings of publicly owned casino companies. Most licensed poker-club operators (in California and Nevada) charge an hourly fee for playing based on the minimum-size bet. Casino operators will more generally charge 5% of the pot.

In the future, however, low-denomination electronic video poker machines will represent an increasing proportion of casino coin-operated devices. Payout percentages on these machines usually are set by management.

Keno

Keno, which is normally a more important profit maker for Nevada casinos than is poker, will also benefit from conversion to electronic video units. Keno is played by marking several numbers (spots) out of a total of 80 with a crayon (in the manual version) or with a light pen (in the electronic version). Winning spots are then determined by a random-number generator, and payoffs are made to winners in proportion to how many spots match the preselected choices of the bettor. According to calculations by Scarne (1974, p. 499), the house percentage on a keno ticket varies between approximately 20% and 25%, and depends on the number of spots on the ticket.

Big Six wheel

The Big Six wheel is fairly popular in Atlantic City, and it has been a staple in Nevada for a long time. In older versions, the wheel's rim is divided into 54 spaces, in each of which are representations of faces of three dice bearing different combinations of the numbers 1 through 6. Bets are placed on a layout containing those numbers. After the wheel is spun and its ratchet peg comes to rest, for every bet that corresponds to a number in the section where the peg stops, there is a winner who is paid even money. In other words, if the player bets $1 on the number 2, and the section on the wheel where the peg stops shows dice with faces 1, 2, and 2, the bettor will receive $2 (a dollar for each 2) plus return of his original bet. Similarly, if the number is 5, and the stop is at 5-5-5, the payback will be $3 plus the original dollar. The Atlantic City version, however, merely has the numbers 1, 2, 5, 10, 20, and two jokers distributed over the 54 spaces. There are 24 ones, 15 twos, 7 fives, 4 tens, 2 twenties, and 2 jokers. A bet on 1 pays 1:1, on 2 pays 2:1, and so forth, except for jokers, which pay 45:1. The Big Six operator normally has a favorable advantage ranging to over 22%, which makes this game one of the most profitable for casinos. As can be seen from Atlantic City monthly statistics, casino hold percentages often approach 50% on the Big Six.

Bingo

Bingo, an offspring of the Italian lotto game, is not too important to gaming casinos. However, it is one of the most popular and widely legalized of wagering activites, and is normally very profitable for operators.

The traditional game is played to fill a card's row, column, or diagnoal containing numbers between 1 and 75 under the word "bingo." A random-number selector or caller picks the numbers that qualify to fill the card, and the first card so filled is declared prize winner. The house edge for bingo is calculated to be around 22%.

Pai Gow, Fan Tan, Sic Bo

Players from the Orient have a long history of interest in gambling, and this is reflected in marketing studies of Nevada and Atlantic City casinos indicating that such players are among the most avid. To accommodate these good customers, Nevada casinos have introduced three favorite Chi-

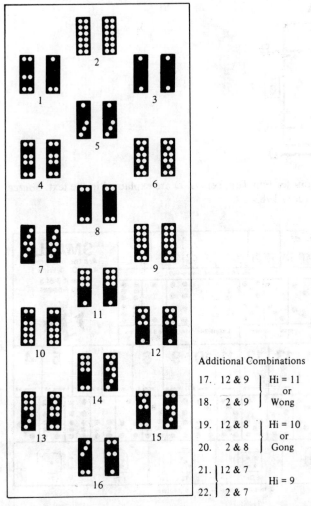

Additional Combinations

17.	12 & 9	Hi = 11
		or
18.	2 & 9	Wong
19.	12 & 8	Hi = 10
		or
20.	2 & 8	Gong
21.	12 & 7	
		Hi = 9
22.	2 & 7	

Figure B.4. Pai Gow: The chart lists 16 pairs and 4 combinations that compose the top-ranking 20 hands. Hand number 1 is called the king pair; each subsequent pair or hand is one value lower than the hand preceding it. The rank of each lesser hand is determined by the numerical value of the hand after discarding 10's from the total. Examples: Two dominoes 12 and 7 = 19, which becomes a 9 after the 10 is discarded; 8 and 7 = 15, which likewise becomes a 5. The higher number is the winning hand. *Source: Gambling Times,* November 1982.

nese games, Pai Gow, Fan Tan, and Sic Bo, of which the first is the most important.

Originated in ancient China, *Pai Gow* (Figure B.4) is played with 32 specially designed dominoes that are scrambled and then placed in eight stacks of four. The dealer and as many as seven players are each dealt one stack

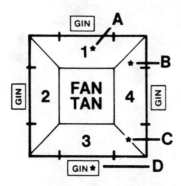

Figure B.5. Table layout for Fan Tan; bets A–D are explained in the text. *Source: Gambling Times,* February 1983.

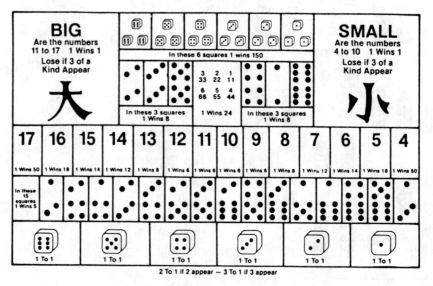

Figure B.6. Sic Bo. *Source: Gambling Times,* January 1983.

of four specially marked dominoes (or cards), with the player to receive the first stack determined by rolling three dice.

The objective is to make two hands of the highest possible value from four dominoes – with both of the player's hands of higher value than the banker's corresponding hands. The player loses if both hands are lower, but if one hand is higher and the other lower, no one wins or loses. The house retains a 5% commission on all winning bets.

Fan Tan (Figure B.5), in contrast, is basically a game of guessing the number of beans in a cup. (A card game has taken the same name, but it is not similar.) A pile of beans is "cut" with a long, thin wand, four at a time, until 4, 3, 2, or 1 is the winning number or section. Figure B.5 illustrates the possibilities: (a) straight up on a number pays 3 to 1; (b) the corner inside the hash mark of a side pays 2 to 1 if the side hits; (c) a split of any two sides pays even money; (d) a gin bet pays even money if the closest side hits, and is a standoff if adjacent sides hit. The house retains 5% of all winning bets as commission.

Sic Bo (Figure B.6) was first brought into the United States by migrant Chinese in the mid-1800s. Three dice are played in a sealed shaker, and bettors select individual numbers or combinations of numbers that will appear on the dice after shaking. Winning payoffs are made according to the game layout in Figure B.6.

Pan

Pan, short for *panguingue,* is sometimes found in Nevada casinos or is played in commercial clubs. It is a card game related to rummy. The standard 52-card deck is modified by eliminating all eights, nines, and tens. The sevens are in sequence with jacks, and aces rank low, below deuces. Eight decks are generally used, and to each hand, 10 cards are dealt, 5 at a time.

By discarding and drawing, a meld or grouping of three cards of the same rank, or a sequence of three in the same suit, is composed. Several rules govern the game, in which the object is to be the first to meld exactly 11 cards.

As in poker or the Chinese games, the house will normally take a percentage of the pot (5%) for conducting the game.

Trente-et-quarante (Rouge et Noir)

This card game is rarely found in U.S. casinos, but is quite popular in Europe. In *trente-et-quarante* (literally, thirty-and-forty) (Figure B.7), a dealer and croupier cut and shuffle a six-deck shoe in which cards are dealt face up in two rows: The first and farthest away is the black row, and the nearest is the red row. Dealing continues until the sum of points on the cards exceeds 30 but never 40.

The black row is dealt until the critical value of 40 or less is reached; then the red row is similarly presented. Suits have no value; face cards count ten, aces one, and others their pip value.

Players can bet on four even-money propositions: red versus black, and color versus inverse. The color row whose total is closer to 30 is the winner. When the color of the first card dealt in the black row is the same as the color of the winning row, then color wins; otherwise inverse wins. The bank makes its money when – on an average of once every 47 hands – the total for each row is 31 (called the *refait* or *un après*). The bank then collects half of each player's stake, which provides an advantage of 1.25%.[5] All

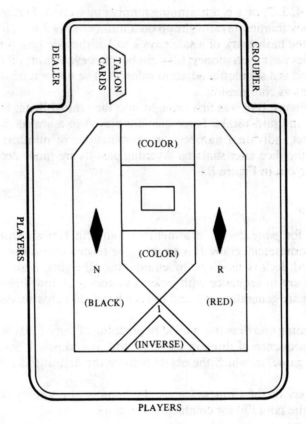

Figure B.7. Table layout for *trente-et-quarante. Source: Gambling Times,* December 1983.

other ties are disregarded, and as in roulette, an *en prison* option may be available.

Mathematical studies of this game have indicated that as in blackjack, there may be times during the course of play in which the house may have little or no edge. However, it is not clear that effective card-counting strategies exist.

Lotteries

Lotteries have been around a long time and have been used for many purposes. For instance, the concept appeared in classical Greek mythology, and Roman emperors entertained dinner guests with door-prize drawings. But the first recorded money lottery designed to raise funds for government appeared in Italy in the year 1530. A British defense lottery also was held in 1566. Yet it was the Virginia Company, which colonized Virginia, that provided the prototype for other early American colonial lottery financings. Indeed, founding fathers Benjamin Franklin and George Washington both sponsored lotteries, and many public-works programs and educational institutions, including Harvard, Yale, Columbia, and Princeton, were in part financed through this means.

Although lottery drawings were very popular in the early 1800s, several large swindles cooled the fervor, and by midcentury most states had banned sales of lottery tickets. Of course, illegal lottery sales then flourished, and these became especially common in the 1920s and 1930s.

It was not until 1964, when the state of New Hampshire introduced a sweepstakes game, that lotteries were legally renewed. But by the end of the 1980s, a majority of the states, the District of Columbia, and all Canadian provinces had legalized lotteries as a means of raising funds for welfare and public-works grants. In total, North American lottery-ticket sales as of 1989 have exceeded $16.0 billion.

As a percentage of sales, states typically net about 36%–38%: Administrative expenses absorb up to 6%, system operators and designers receive 2%–3%, retail vendors receive a commission of 5%, and winning players receive an average of about 50%. However, payouts of 50% to players appear to be relatively generous only until comparison is made against casino-game payouts, which exceed 85%. Moreover, states may pick up extra income from interest earned on funds escrowed in the time between prize drawings and payments to winners (out of annuities).

Modern lotteries have evolved in several distinct stages. The original New-Hampshire-style lotteries employed a sweepstakes concept that had limited appeal because of relatively small payoffs, and a long time between ticket purchase and event decision. However, that was remedied in a second stage of development in which many more "instant-winner" scratch-off-type tickets and on-line three-digit daily number games were introduced, with significant increases in sizes of cash prizes and in numbers of retail outlets handling sales.

By the late 1970s, a third phase of expansion was initiated as greater sophistication of on-line computer systems made it possible to introduce games of the so-called lotto variety. These games select winners on almost a daily basis and allow for buildup of substantial prize money over several drawings: If the major prize is not won, the money spills over into the pool used for subsequent drawings.

Lotto players must correctly select 6 numbers from a field of between 36 and 49 numbers. In the state of New York, for example, the player (prior to 1985) selected 6 out of 44 numbers on two "boards" – panels with boxes labeled 1 to 44. The cost to play two boards is $1, and there are 10 boards on a card. Prizes are paid on a pari-mutuel basis, wherein for each draw (twice a week), 40% of that draw's sales revenue (less 2% Prize Fund Reserve) is allocated as the winning pool for payment of the prizes under the conditions and odds indicated in Table B.6.

Table B.6. *New York State Lotto-game payout (pre-1985)*

First prize: 50% of the winning pool plus any first-prize money carried forward from previous draws. Six winning numbers in one game panel, with odds on a $1 bet (two panels) 1:3,529,526.

Second prize: 12.5% of the winning pool for that draw. Any five winning numbers in one game panel. Odds on a $1 bet, 1:15,480.

Third prize: 25% of the winning pool for that draw. Any four winning numbers in one game panel. Odds on a $1 bet, 1:335.

Fourth prize: 12.5% of the winning pool for that draw. Any three winning numbers plus the supplementary number in one game panel. Odds on a $1 bet, 1:265.

Overall odds of winning a prize are 1:146 for a $1 bet.

Source: New York State Lottery.

Another variation, seen in the Lottario (Ontario, Canada) version, is a combination ticket, where 5 selected numbers are placed in combination with the remaining 34 out of 39 numbers. The cost of this combination ticket is $34.00.

As of the mid-1980s, the industry entered a fourth phase featuring the placement of microprocessor-controlled lottery machines – video lottery terminals (VLTs) – that may use bingo, keno, or other similar random-number-generator-based concepts. Such machines are essentially hybrid slot and video-game units.

Tracks

Horse races were popular during the reign of England's Henry II (1154–89), and they were regularly scheduled by New York's first English governor in 1665. But to this day, horse and dog racing is where direct government participation in legalized betting is greatest.

There are many betting variations now allowed at tracks specializing in thoroughbred racing, harness racing, or greyhound racing. In addition to standard wagering on *win* (bettor collects if the selection bet to win finishes first), *place* (collects on first or second finish), and *show* (collects on first, second, or third finish), more exotic bets such as the quinella, exacta, and daily-double have been designed to heighten public interest.

The variations, however, have not changed the operational economics whereby the state may take up to 20% of pari-mutuel sales, and so-called breakage (actually a rounding of winners' payout to the last nickel or dime) further adds to the state's advantage. The following example paraphrasing Scarne (1974, p. 51) well illustrates how pari-mutuel betting pools are shared by the state.

Supposing that a race is conducted "where the combined mutuel take of state and track is 15%," and breakage is to a nickel. "Assume that $129,400 was bet on all horses in the win (straight) pool, and the red-hot favorite and eventual winner was backed to the amount of $100,000." The combined state and track deduction of 15% of $129,400 is $19,410, leaving $109,990 in the win pool. The $100,000 wagered on the winner is then deducted from the net $109,990, leaving $9,990 to be divided among holders of winning tickets. "The $100,000 bet on the winning animal is set aside so that it may be returned to the winners."

Dollar odds, meaning earnings on each $1 unit bet on the winner, are then calculated by dividing $9,990 by $100,000 to give "a dollar-odds figure of $9\frac{99}{100}$ cents." Breakage to the last nickel is then performed, which leaves an additional 4.99 cents on each dollar to the track and the state. That is, the winners give up an additional $4,990, the state and track total becomes $24,400, and the winning wagerers' earnings on each dollar are reduced from 9.99 cents to 5.0 cents per dollar. As reported in newspapers, the standard $2.00 win bet in this example would have returned $2.10.

To calculate the return on place bets, "the total amount of money (gross place pool) bet on all the horses to place (run first or second)" is used as the base on which to apply state and track percentages. After subtracting the appropriate percentages from the gross place pool, the amount bet on first and second finish is then deducted to arrive at the net place pool. This is then divided by 2 because half the pool goes to holders of place tickets on the horse that finished first, the other half to the holders of place tickets on the horse that finished second. The resulting "(half net place pool) is divided by the amount bet to place wagers on the horse whose place payoff is being calculated." Breakage is then deducted.

"The method . . . to compute show mutuels [is] the same as . . . for place mutuels except that three horses who finished first, second, and third share in the show pool."

Depending on the betting variations used and the aggressiveness with which winners reinvest their gains in other races, the player's disadvantage at the track generally ranges upward of 17%.

Sports book

Wagering on sports events is probably the most common type of gaming, and it is certainly among the most widespread of illegal activities in the United States. Legal sports betting based on the same principles used by neighborhood bookies is sanctioned and available only in Nevada gaming establishments, or at betting shops in England.

The underlying concept used in both the legal and illegal varieties is that of *point spread,* which in theory mathematically compensates for the different abilities of competing teams. As calculated by expert handicappers, the spread is how many points the winning team's score must exceed the losing team's score in order for wagers on the winning team to be paid. For example, if team *A* is favored to beat team *B* by 4 points, and it does so by only 3 points, wagers on the underdog win.

Sports-book operators generally attempt to equalize the amounts bet on both sides of the book and to avoid a "push" (making the exact point spread) by adjusting the spread, or *line,* that is offered to bettors. In football, for example, the odds are usually 11:10 – which means that whether betting favorite or underdog, in effect you wager $11 to win $10. The bookie thus retains a $1 commission known in the vernacular as vigorish or "vig." Electronic terminals and computers – able to automatically and instantaneously equalize the book by adjusting the spread – will eventually be legally playable in some jurisdictions.

Notes

1. Economists familiar with the efficient-market hypothesis will recognize many of the concepts (a martingale, for instance) that are involved in money management. A martingale is any system of trying to make up losses in previous bets by doubling or otherwise increasing the amount bet. The pyramid or D'Alembert system is also popular.

2. Players should also be aware that the IRS requires bingo and slot-machine winners of over $1,200, and keno winners of over $1,500, to file form W-2G. In the case of lotteries and racetrack winners, witholding of 20% for federal taxes may begin at $1,000.

3. Estimates are approximate and assume application of basic strategy.

4. Silberstang (1980, p. 388) has slightly different figures of −1.36% for Player and −1.17% for Banker. Also see Thorp (1984).

5. Numbers are from Barnhart (1983), and differ from those of Scarne (1978).

Appendix C
Supplementary data

Entertainment industry data of interest to economists and investors are voluminous, and the material most significant to the flow of discussion has been placed in the text. But so much more is available that it makes sense to include the best of it in a supplement organized according to chapter topics. The material is largely self-explanatory, and generally historical.

Table S1.1. *Aggregate economic statistics relating to spending on recreational goods and services, 1929–88 ($ billion)*

Year	Disposable income	Personal consumption expenditures	PCE on recreation	Recreation as % of disp. inc.	Recreation as % of total PCE
1929	81.70	77.30	4.331	5.30	5.60
1930	73.00	69.90	3.990	5.47	5.71
1931	62.90	60.50	3.302	5.25	5.46
1932	48.00	48.60	2.442	5.09	5.02
1933	44.90	45.80	2.202	4.90	4.81
1934	51.60	51.40	2.441	4.73	4.75
1935	57.90	55.80	2.630	4.54	4.71
1936	65.80	62.00	3.020	4.59	4.87
1937	70.50	66.70	3.381	4.80	5.07
1938	64.80	64.10	3.241	5.00	5.06
1939	69.70	67.00	3.452	4.95	5.15
1940	75.00	71.00	3.761	5.01	5.30
1941	91.90	80.80	4.239	4.61	5.25
1942	116.40	88.60	4.677	4.02	5.28
1943	132.90	99.50	4.961	3.73	4.99
1944	145.60	108.20	5.422	3.72	5.01
1945	149.20	119.60	6.139	4.11	5.13
1946	158.90	143.90	8.539	5.37	5.93
1947	168.80	161.90	9.249	5.48	5.71
1948	188.10	174.90	9.692	5.15	5.54
1949	187.90	178.30	10.010	5.33	5.61
1950	207.50	192.10	11.147	5.37	5.80
1951	227.60	208.10	11.659	5.12	5.60
1952	239.80	219.10	12.299	5.13	5.61
1953	255.10	232.60	13.027	5.11	5.60
1954	260.50	239.80	13.506	5.18	5.63

Year					
1955	278.80	257.90	14.528	5.21	5.63
1956	297.50	270.60	15.447	5.19	5.71
1957	313.90	285.30	15.783	5.03	5.53
1958	324.90	294.60	16.235	5.00	5.51
1959	344.60	316.25	17.549	5.09	5.55
1960	358.90	330.66	18.366	5.12	5.55
1961	373.80	341.14	19.119	5.11	5.60
1962	396.20	361.92	20.633	5.21	5.70
1963	415.80	381.74	22.289	5.36	5.84
1964	451.40	409.31	24.400	5.41	5.96
1965	486.80	440.69	26.666	5.48	6.05
1966	525.90	477.26	30.657	5.83	6.42
1967	562.10	503.55	32.895	5.85	6.53
1968	609.60	552.46	36.446	5.98	6.60
1969	656.70	597.85	39.629	6.03	6.63
1970	715.60	640.01	42.718	5.97	6.67
1971	776.80	691.55	45.587	5.87	6.59
1972	839.60	757.57	50.983	6.07	6.73
1973	949.80	837.22	57.160	6.02	6.83
1974	1038.40	916.55	62.994	6.07	6.87
1975	1142.80	1012.77	70.233	6.15	6.93
1976	1252.60	1129.35	77.992	6.23	6.91
1977	1379.30	1257.22	85.480	6.20	6.80
1978	1551.20	1403.50	95.656	6.17	6.82
1979	1729.30	1566.75	106.207	6.14	6.78
1980	1918.00	1732.56	114.972	5.99	6.64
1981	2127.60	1915.14	128.626	6.05	6.72
1982	2261.40	2050.66	138.321	6.12	6.75
1983	2428.10	2234.54	152.052	6.26	6.80
1984	2668.60	2430.46	168.322	6.31	6.93
1985	2838.70	2629.00	185.689	6.54	7.06
1986	3013.30	2797.44	201.205	6.68	7.19
1987	3205.90	3010.82	224.527	7.00	7.46
1988	3477.80	3235.10	246.845	7.10	7.63

Source: U.S. Department of Commerce

Table S1.1. *(cont.)*

Year	Commercial theater	Movies	Toys	Pari-mutuel betting	Spectator sports	Coml. partic. amusements	Total recreation services	Consumer price index (1983 = 1.00)[a]
1929	0.127	0.720	0.336	0.008	0.066	0.170	1.696	0.17
1930	0.095	0.732	0.281	0.007	0.065	0.167	1.650	0.17
1931	0.078	0.719	0.266	0.006	0.057	0.144	1.533	0.15
1932	0.057	0.527	0.207	0.004	0.047	0.108	1.187	0.14
1933	0.041	0.482	0.181	0.006	0.050	0.099	1.072	0.13
1934	0.042	0.518	0.200	0.019	0.065	0.111	1.172	0.14
1935	0.044	0.556	0.216	0.026	0.072	0.116	1.261	0.14
1936	0.050	0.626	0.242	0.029	0.083	0.135	1.417	0.14
1937	0.053	0.676	0.269	0.038	0.089	0.159	1.570	0.14
1938	0.058	0.663	0.268	0.044	0.095	0.135	1.513	0.14
1939	0.064	0.659	0.285	0.041	0.098	0.150	1.548	0.14
1940	0.071	0.735	0.306	0.055	0.098	0.162	1.683	0.14
1941	0.079	0.809	0.362	0.065	0.107	0.172	1.836	0.15
1942	0.092	1.022	0.404	0.069	0.090	0.175	2.098	0.16
1943	0.118	1.275	0.393	0.079	0.062	0.176	2.416	0.17
1944	0.142	1.341	0.459	0.131	0.080	0.198	2.672	0.18
1945	0.148	1.450	0.553	0.153	0.116	0.233	2.979	0.18
1946	0.174	1.692	0.840	0.241	0.200	0.311	3.686	0.20
1947	0.187	1.594	0.907	0.255	0.222	0.332	3.773	0.22
1948	0.180	1.506	1.076	0.257	0.232	0.349	3.803	0.24
1949	0.182	1.451	1.170	0.247	0.239	0.351	3.797	0.24
1950	0.183	1.376	1.394	0.239	0.222	0.368	3.837	0.24
1951	0.186	1.349	1.662	0.255	0.221	0.392	4.005	0.26
1952	0.190	1.319	1.708	0.327	0.222	0.412	4.215	0.27
1953	0.198	1.292	1.694	0.372	0.225	0.439	4.448	0.27
1954	0.222	1.373	1.624	0.368	0.229	0.457	4.735	0.27
1955	0.248	1.474	1.803	0.381	0.237	0.504	5.107	0.27

1956	0.272	1.541	1.952	0.414	0.245	0.564	5.513	0.27
1957	0.293	1.238	2.048	0.438	0.252	0.636	5.560	0.28
1958	0.304	1.085	2.116	0.454	0.261	0.729	5.748	0.29
1959	0.324	1.043	2.365	0.503	0.311	0.879	6.241	0.29
1960	0.349	1.045	2.478	0.539	0.364	1.068	6.812	0.30
1961	0.333	1.044	2.665	0.569	0.412	1.231	7.311	0.30
1962	0.356	1.033	2.891	0.650	0.469	1.362	7.852	0.30
1963	0.361	1.029	3.115	0.694	0.527	1.463	8.365	0.31
1964	0.390	1.038	3.379	0.769	0.587	1.561	8.945	0.31
1965	0.397	1.163	3.591	0.814	0.660	1.584	9.427	0.32
1966	0.444	1.219	4.047	0.848	0.744	1.688	10.211	0.33
1967	0.489	1.227	4.282	0.881	0.780	1.815	10.847	0.34
1968	0.491	1.400	4.781	0.947	0.959	1.926	12.186	0.35
1969	0.506	1.507	5.234	1.035	1.053	2.121	13.447	0.37
1970	0.531	1.629	5.498	1.096	1.136	2.367	14.672	0.39
1971	0.530	1.733	5.826	1.195	1.222	2.612	15.888	0.41
1972	0.571	1.744	6.572	1.263	1.198	3.046	17.111	0.42
1973	0.624	1.647	7.447	1.449	1.207	3.545	19.182	0.45
1974	0.702	2.022	8.168	1.559	1.249	4.187	21.901	0.50
1975	0.787	2.197	8.954	1.662	1.333	4.858	24.691	0.54
1976	0.943	2.074	9.953	1.802	1.423	5.605	27.559	0.57
1977	1.083	2.368	10.843	1.883	1.582	6.358	30.514	0.61
1978	1.327	2.784	12.062	1.928	1.735	7.322	34.120	0.66
1979	1.526	2.890	13.449	1.996	1.894	8.374	38.233	0.73
1980	1.786	2.671	14.633	2.095	2.033	9.666	43.186	0.83
1981	2.049	2.853	16.005	2.229	2.027	11.677	50.274	0.91
1982	2.141	3.326	16.826	2.240	2.332	12.471	55.153	0.97
1983	2.389	3.583	18.004	2.269	2.629	13.606	61.489	1.00
1984	2.678	3.936	19.747	2.566	2.921	14.145	66.633	1.03
1985	2.973	3.571	21.127	2.569	2.909	15.124	74.090	1.07
1986	3.342	3.909	23.106	2.631	2.918	15.956	81.253	1.09
1987	3.992	4.223	26.196	2.707	3.046	17.129	90.884	1.12
1988	4.424	4.225	28.118	2.800	3.236	18.936	100.838	1.17

^aActual index = 100 for December 1982. Rounding and averaging effect makes it equal 1.00 in 1983.

Table S1.2. *Average hours worked by wage and salary workers (except agricultural workers), May of 1968, 1973, 1978, and 1979*

Sex and occupation	All schedules					Full-time schedules				
	Number[a] of workers, 1979	Average weekly hours				Number[a] of workers, 1979	Average weekly hours			
		1968	1973	1978	1979		1968	1973	1978	1979
All workers										
White collar, total	42,980	39.6	39.3	39.1	39.3	34.112	43.1	43.1	42.9	42.9
Professional, technical, and kindred workers	13,527	40.8	40.6	40.5	40.5	11,253	44.0	43.4	43.6	43.3
Managers and administrators	8,340	46.0	46.0	45.2	45.5	7,702	46.9	47.0	46.2	46.6
Sales workers	4,851	36.5	38.8	36.2	36.9	3,331	44.5	44.4	43.8	43.9
Clerical workers	16,262	37.4	35.9	35.8	35.7	11,825	40.1	40.1	40.0	39.9
Blue collar, total	28,296	40.5	40.3	39.9	40.0	23,226	42.8	42.7	42.5	42.4
Craft and kindred workers	10,884	42.3	42.0	41.7	41.6	9,553	43.2	43.1	42.9	43.0
Operatives	13,087	40.8	40.5	40.3	40.2	10,819	42.8	42.8	42.7	42.4
Nonfarm laborers	4,326	35.0	35.5	34.6	34.9	2,854	41.4	41.4	40.9	40.8
Service workers	11,342	33.5	33.0	31.9	32.2	6,214	43.6	42.6	41.7	41.7
Men										
White collar, total	19,748	43.4	43.6	43.4	43.7	17,666	45.3	45.5	45.3	45.4
Professional, technical, and kindred workers	7,511	43.0	43.2	43.5	43.4	6,771	44.8	44.7	45.0	44.7

Managers and administrators	6,294	47.1	47.1	46.6	47.1	5,976	47.7	47.8	47.2	47.7
Sales workers	2,746	42.5	42.5	41.7	42.5	2,328	46.2	46.1	45.4	45.6
Clerical workers	3,197	39.8	39.6	39.2	38.8	2,591	42.3	42.3	42.3	41.9
Blue collar, total	23,000	41.2	41.0	40.6	40.7	19,274	43.4	43.3	43.0	43.0
Carft and kindred workers	10,248	42.4	42.1	41.9	41.8	9,045	43.3	43.2	42.9	43.1
Operatives	8,903	42.2	42.0	41.9	41.8	7,649	44.1	44.1	43.9	43.7
Nonfarm laborers	3,850	35.0	35.6	34.6	35.1	2,579	41.4	41.5	40.8	41.1
Service workers	4,417	39.2	37.5	36.3	36.7	3,030	45.7	44.2	43.4	43.8
Women										
White collar, total	23,232	35.5	35.0	35.3	35.5	16,446	40.3	40.2	40.2	40.3
Professional, technical, and kindred workers	6,017	37.4	37.0	36.8	36.9	4,482	42.4	41.5	41.5	41.3
Managers and administrators	2,045	39.7	41.1	40.3	40.6	1,727	42.2	43.3	42.4	42.9
Sales workers	2,105	29.8	28.4	29.2	29.7	1,003	40.0	39.8	40.0	40.0
Clerical workers	13,065	35.3	34.7	34.8	34.9	9,235	39.2	39.3	39.3	39.3
Blue collar, total	5,296	37.4	37.1	37.0	36.7	3,952	39.7	39.7	40.2	39.7
Craft and kindred workers	636	38.7	38.7	38.5	38.5	508	40.3	41.2	41.6	41.3
Operatives	4,184	37.3	37.3	37.1	37.0	3,171	39.6	39.6	39.9	39.5
Nonfarm laborers	476	35.4	33.1	34.1	32.6	274	40.5	40.2	41.2	39.0
Service workers	6,925	30.4	30.2	29.2	29.3	3,184	41.9	41.2	40.2	39.8

[a]In thousands; numbers have been rounded out.

Source: Hedges and Taylor (1980).

Table S1.3. *Household participation in leisure-time activities, by selected type, 1983*[a]

Type of activity	Number (million)	Percentage[b]
Watching television	68	81
Listening to music	54	64
Sewing/needlepoint	27	32
Going to the movies	36	42
Vegetable gardening	35	42
Pleasure trips in cars	37	44
General exercise/physical fitness	26	31
Watching professional sports (TV)	33	39
Fishing	26	31
Camping	17	20
Vacation trips in U.S.	29	34
Bicycling	19	22
Tennis	10	12
Workshop/home repair	25	29
Jogging	16	19
Bowling	17	20
Hunting	14	16
Photography	17	20
Hiking	12	14
Golf	10	12
Swimming in own pool	7	8
Horseback riding	8	9
Racquetball	6	7
Skiing (downhill)	5	6
Boating (power)	8	10
Vacation trips outside U.S.	5	6
Snowmobiling	3	4
Cross-country skiing	3	4
Archery	3	4

[a]As of mid-July 1983. Based on national sample survey of 1,500 households conducted by the Gallup Organization, Inc.
[b]Percentage of all households.
Source: Gardens for All; The National Association for Gardening, Burlington, Vt.; *National Gardening Survey;* unpublished data.

Table S1.4. *Census of selected service industry data[a] by major entertainment categories, 1963–87*

Year	No. establishments	Receipts ($ thousands)	Payroll ($ thousands)	Paid employees	Receipts per establish. ($)	Receipts per employee ($)	Payroll/ receipts (%)	Employees/ establish.
Selected service industries, total								
1987	1,624,622	752,474,203	283,224,996	15,688,243	463,169	47,964	37.6	9.7
1982	1,339,229	426,981,971	158,624,502	11,106,144	318,827	38,446	37.1	8.3
1977	725,096	164,219,449	56,054,955	6,337,275	226,480	25,913	34.1	8.7
1972	683,614	95,675,519	33,424,040	5,305,181	139,955	18,034	34.9	7.8
1967	521,410	55,527,000	17,524,045	3,841,174	106,494	14,456	31.6	7.4
1963	504,356	41,023,378	12,192,105	3,261,541	81,338	12,578	29.7	6.5
Motion-picture prod./dist. services								
1987	11,242	19,916,629	4,973,497	171,328	1,771,627	116,249	25.0	15.2
1982	8,347	10,117,034	2,451,083	127,209	1,212,056	79,531	24.2	15.2
1977	5,473	5,314,465	1,376,657	88,372	971,033	60,137	25.9	16.1
1972	4,704	2,856,799	795,490	64,660	607,313	44,182	27.8	13.7
1967	3,375	2,169,424	699,072	64,581	642,792	33,592	32.2	19.1
1963	2,829	1,510,315	479,207	48,806	533,869	30,945	31.7	17.3
Motion-picture theaters								
1987	7,776	3,977,078	584,337	94,086	511,455	42,271	14.7	12.1
1982	10,020	3,575,737	566,647	103,461	356,860	34,561	15.8	10.3
1977	10,696	2,570,309	461,950	112,210	240,306	22,906	18.0	10.5
1972	11,670	1,815,916	381,065	127,435	155,605	14,250	21.0	10.9
1967	11,478	1,283,003	281,126	112,109	11,779	11,444	21.9	9.8
1963	12,040	1,058,224	249,999	112,521	87,892	9,405	23.6	9.3
Dance groups and artists								
1987	104	32,981	11,477	717	317,125	45,999	34.8	6.9
1982	142	27,125	10,246	980	191,021	27,679	37.8	6.9
1977	425	20,660	8,249	1,776	48,612	11,633	39.9	4.2

Table S1.4. (*cont.*)

Year	No. establishments	Receipts ($ thousands)	Payroll ($ thousands)	Paid employees	Receipts per establish. ($)	Receipts per employee ($)	Payroll/ receipts (%)	Employees/ establish.
Symphony orchestras, opera companies, chamber-music groups								
1987	56	26,474	9,639	989	472,750	26,768	36.4	17.6
1982	61	17,911	5,958	730	293,623	24,536	33.3	12.0
1977	87	10,302	5,281	785	118,414	13,124	51.3	9.0
Producers of legitimate theater								
1987	940	809,222	201,536	11,199	860,874	72,258	24.9	11.9
1982	873	750,487	203,423	13,449	859,664	55,802	27.1	15.4
1977	750	304,100	98,626	9,113	405,467	33,370	32.4	12.2
1972	934	277,209	99,842	10,622	296,798	26,098	36.0	11.4
1967	586	223,133	73,948	9,814	380,773	22,736	33.1	16.7
Professional sports clubs, managers, and promoters								
1987	807	1,904,388	1,354,231	26,566	2,359,836	71,685	71.7	32.9
1982	498	1,128,428	684,139	19,430	2,265,920	58,077	60.6	39.0
1977	526	937,148	366,131	14,693	1,781,650	63,782	39.1	27.9
1972	537	512,904	207,019	14,515	955,128	35,336	40.4	27.0
1967	455	226,067	116,648	10,321	496,851	21,904	51.6	22.7
1963	445	158,804	70,862	8,663	356,863	18,331	44.6	19.5
Racing, including track operation								
1987	2,377	3,118,806	692,922	48,957	1,312,077	63,705	22.2	20.6
1982	1,862	2,290,039	485,879	43,017	1,229,881	53,236	21.2	23.1
1977	2,133	1,551,660	351,511	38,804	727,454	39,987	22.7	18.2
1972	2,196	1,007,375	226,431	33,793	458,732	29,810	22.5	15.4
1967	1,946	700,534	158,928	29,010	359,987	24,148	22.7	14.9
1963	1,647	537,444	177,662	21,374	326,317	25,145	33.1	13.0

Coin-operated amusement devices

1987	4,450	1,396,312	296,688	24,924	313,778	56,023	21.2	5.6
1982	5,434	1,422,726	285,438	26,886	261,819	52,917	20.1	4.9
1977	2,665	486,892	115,955	14,525	182,699	33,521	23.8	5.5
1972	2,061	297,406	72,027	10,165	144,302	29,258	24.2	4.9
1967	2,400	257,514	57,252	10,641	107,298	24,200	22.2	4.4
1963	3,074	260,640	50,175	11,142	84,789	23,393	19.3	3.6

Amusement parks

1987	744	3,469,836	819,552	60,414	4,663,758	57,434	23.6	81.2
1982	491	1,823,728	603,104	46,464	3,714,313	39,250	33.1	99.7
1977	663	1,172,419	352,645	37,014	1,768,354	31,675	30.1	55.8
1972	682	467,718	159,043	20,399	685,804	22,928	34.0	29.9
1967	786	174,105	56,000	8,339	221,508	20,878	32.2	10.6
1963	997	115,939	41,846	4,733	116,288	24,496	36.1	4.7

Carnivals and circuses

1987	351	266,952	39,648	3,572	760,547	74,735	14.9	10.2
1982	298	196,271	32,992	3,851	658,628	50,966	16.8	12.9
1977	368	155,404	28,522	3,175	422,293	48,946	18.4	8.6
1972	337	97,565	19,726	3,205	289,510	30,441	20.2	9.5
1967	548	62,857	13,844	2,229	114,703	28,200	22.0	4.1
1963	363	46,536	11,250	1,730	128,198	26,899	24.2	4.8

[a]Because of changes in classifications and in scope of data collected, data from one year often are only roughly comparable to those of another.

Table S2.1. *Frequency of motion-picture attendance, 1981–3*

Admissions by age groups

Age (years)	Percentage of total yearly admissions			Percentage of resident civilian population (as of 1/83)
	1983[a]	1982	1981	
12–15	13	12	16	7
16–20	25	25	24	11
21–24	16	14	15	9
25–29	14	13	13	11
30–39[b]	18	16	17	18
40–49	6	8	6	12
50–59	3	5	5	12
60+	4	6	4	20
Total	100	100	100	100
12–17	27	22	26	11
18+	73	78	74	89

Frequency of attendance (%)

Frequency	Total public (ages 12+)			Adult public (ages 18+)			Teenagers (ages 12–17)		
	1983	1982	1981	1983	1982	1981	1983	1982	1981
Frequent[c]	23	26	25	20	24	22	54	49	50
Occasional[d]	32	29	29	32	29	30	30	30	32
Infrequent[e]	9	9	10	10	10	10	4	9	5
Never	36	35	36	38	36	38	12	11	12
Unreported	<0.5	1	<0.5	<0.5	1	<0.5	0	1	1

[a]The total number of moviegoers ages 12 and over slipped moderately from 123.6 million in 1982 to 121.6 million in 1983.
[b]The bulk of motion-picture admissions continues to be generated by those moviegoers under age 40, accounting for 86% of total yearly admissions.
[c]Frequent moviegoers (those who attend movies at least once a month) constitute only 23% of the public ages 12 and over, but account for 84% of admissions.
[d]Attend movies once in 2–6 months.
[e]Attend movies less than once in 6 months.
Source: MPAA study conducted by Opinion Research Corp.

Table S2.2. *Average weekly movie attendance in America, 1926–80*

Year	Average weekly attendance	Year	Average weekly attendance
1926	50,000,000	1955	46,000,000
1927	57,000,000	1956	47,000,000
1928	65,000,000	1957	45,000,000
1929	95,000,000	1958	40,000,000
1930	90,000,000	1959	42,000,000
1931	75,000,000	1960	40,000,000
1932	60,000,000	1961	42,000,000
1933	60,000,000	1962	43,000,000
1934	70,000,000	1963	44,000,000
1935	75,000,000	1964	— [a]
1936	88,000,000	1965	44,000,000
1937	85,000,000	1966	38,000,000
1938	85,000,000	1967	17,800,000
1939	85,000,000	1968	18,800,000
1940	80,000,000	1969	17,500,000
1941	85,000,000	1970	17,700,000
1942	85,000,000	1971	15,800,000
1943	85,000,000	1972	18,000,000
1944	85,000,000	1973	16,600,000
1945	90,000,000	1974	19,400,000
1946	90,000,000	1975	19,900,000
1947	90,000,000	1976	18,400,000
1948	90,000,000	1977	20,400,000
1949	87,500,000	1978	21,800,000
1950	60,000,000	1979	21,600,000
1951	54,000,000	1980	19,600,000
1952	51,000,000		
1953	46,000,000		
1954	49,000,000		

[a]Not reliably reported.
Source: Reel Facts. © Random House, Inc.

Table S2.3. *Average price of a movie ticket in America, 1933–80*[a]

Year	Admission price	Year	Admission price
1933	23¢	1957	50.5¢
1934	23¢	1958	50.5¢
1935	24¢	1959	51¢
1936	25¢	1960	69¢
1937	23¢	1961	69¢
1938	23¢	1962	70¢
1939	23¢	1963	84.6¢
1940	24.1¢	1964	92.5¢
1941	25.2¢	1965	$1.010
1942	27.3¢	1966	$1.094
1943	29.4¢	1967	$1.198
1944	31.7¢	1968	$1.310
1945	35.2¢	1969	$1.419
1946	40.3¢	1970	$1.552
1947	40.4¢	1971	$1.645
1948	40.1¢	1972	$1.695
1949	46¢	1973	$1.768
1950	52.8¢	1974	$1.874
1951	52.8¢	1975	$2,048
1952	60¢	1976	$2.128
1953	60¢	1977	$2.230
1954	44.7¢	1978	$2.340
1955	49.8¢	1979	$2.510
1956	49.7¢	1980	$2.690

[a]Between 1942 and 1953, there was an amusement tax on movie tickets. In 1942 the tax was 2.7 cents; in 1953, 10 cents. The figures given for those years include the tax.
Source: Reel Facts, © Random House, Inc. Through 1962 these statistics were compiled by *Film Daily Yearbook.* The Research Department of the Motion Picture Association of America is the source of the figures beginning in 1963.

Table S2.4. *Domestic rentals of films doing over $10 million summed by year and major distributor ($ thousand)*

Year	Buena Vista	Columbia	MGM/UA	Paramount	T.C.–Fox	Universal	Warner Bros.	Orion
1988	170,246	54,200	134,931	195,300	128,600	117,833	79,000	55,100
1987	229,106	107,038	71,778	250,374	132,900	104,116	149,900	136,638
1986	95,155	154,100	37,612	330,727	84,200	77,312	103,400	91,089
1985	0	213,804	101,339	48,500	134,200	240,154	217,900	10,937
1984	34,103	300,855	75,704	326,500	121,420	59,219	282,200	64,753
1983	14,674	57,960	92,231	204,008	247,027	103,603	215,700	35,118
1982	16,704	201,732	129,220	164,392	129,450	359,871	94,950	
1981	29,812	119,396	88,113	146,598	110,153	173,736	117,200	
1980	0	123,678	10,102	179,435	230,700	157,414	143,800	
1979	42,595	140,954	172,293	158,899	111,130	129,607	107,200	
1978	10,452	62,654	99,307	213,689	58,633	198,018	181,600	
1977	53,735	127,634	86,683	120,255	271,831	112,803	233,939	
1976	32,836	61,958	105,538	78,378	79,804	21,610	116,200	
1975	16,580	60,928	96,643	30,404	129,520	162,078	34,300	
1974	27,200	10,662	11,618	114,014	26,634	61,156	92,400	
1973	29,249	22,457	32,636	16,559	0	146,443	120,600	
1972	11,426	13,110	0	86,275	42,000	0	90,500	
1971	0	0	57,968	0	26,315	0	88,000	
1970	26,462	11,645	14,661	62,250	94,550	45,220	31,400	
Total	840,335	1,844,765	1,418,377	2,726,557	2,159,067	2,270,193	2,500,189	393,635

Source: Data compiled from *Variety* anniversary issues.

Table S2.5. *Major-distributor North American theatrical rental market shares in percent, 1970–88*[a]

Year	Columbia[b]	Disney	Fox	MGM/UA[c]	Orion[d]	Paramount	Tri-Star[b]	Warner[e]	Universal	Total
1988	3	20	11	10	7	16	6	11	10	94
1987	4	14	9	4	10	20	5	13	8	87
1986	9	10	8	4	7	22	7	12	9	88
1985[f]	10	3	11	9	5	10	10	18	16	92
1984	16	4	10	7	5	21	5	19	8	95
1983	14	3	21	10	4	14	—	17	13	96
1982	10	4	14	11	3	14	—	10	30	96
1981	13	3	13	9	1	15	—	18	14	86
1980	14	4	16	7	2	16	—	14	20	93
1979	11	4	9	15	5	15	—	20	15	94
1978	11	5	13	11	4	24	—	13	17	98
1977	12	6	20	18	4	10	—	14	12	96
1976	8	7	13	16	5	10	—	18	13	90
1975	13	6	14	11	5	11	—	9	25	94
1974[g]	7	7	11	9	4	10	—	23	19	90
1973[h,i]	7	7	19	11	3	9	—	16	10	82
1972	9	5	9	15	3	22	—	18	5	86
1971	10	8	12	7	3	17	—	9	5	71
1970	14	9	19	9	3	12	—	5	13	84
Mean	10.3	6.8	13.3	10.2	4.4	15.2	1.7	14.6	13.8	90.1
Variance	11.4	17.1	15.2	13.5	3.9	21.5	9.4	19.7	39.4	40.2

a Feature film rentals from U.S. and Canadian theaters, expressed in percentages of total industry rentals (including those of minor distributors). Percentages do not add to 100% in any year; the residual amount is accounted for by smaller and/or defunct distributors.

b Tri-Star Pictures began operations in April 1984, absorbed Columbia Pictures late 1987; corporate name changed to Columbia Pictures Entertainment. Columbia and Tri-Star retain separate marketing controls, but certain administrative functions are performed by Triumph Releasing, an entity which has no operational significance.

c MGM/UA means the present distribution company as well as the "old" UA, which took over domestic distribution of MGM product late in 1973.

d Includes old American International Pictures (1970–9), and Filmways Pictures (1980–1). Name changed to Orion in 1981.

e Allied Artists Pictures had a 4% market share in 1974. Insignificant in other years. Lorimar acquired assets in 1981. Lorimar began domestic distribution operations in August 1987. Warner Bros. acquired Lorimar in late 1988.

f Embassy Pictures market shares as follows: 3% in 1980, 5% in 1981, 1% in 1983 and 1985, nil in 1984, insignificant in other years. Company bought by Columbia Pictures in 1985. Dino De Laurentiis acquired Embassy's theatrical production-distribution operations from Columbia later in 1985. Name changed to De Laurentiis Entertainment Group, distribution operations resumed June 1986. Market share for 1986 just over 2%; for 1987, just over 1%.

g Pre-'74, the "old" MGM market shares as follows: 4% in 1970, 9% in 1971, 6% in 1972, and 5% in 1973. Company exited distribution late in 1973.

h National General Pictures (most of its release schedule being CBS-Cinema Center Films) market shares as follows: 7% in 1970, 8% in 1971, 3% in 1972, and 8% in 1973. NGP also released First Artists product under a commitment transferred to Warner Bros. in 1974 when NGP folded.

i Cinerama Releasing Corp. (most of its releases being ABC Pictures product) market shares as follows: 3% over 1970–3 period. CRC folded thereafter.

Source: Variety, January 18, 1989. © A. D. Murphy.

Table S2.6. *Approximate movie theater admissions[a] in seven major developed countries, 1970–88*

Year	Total	England	France	Germany	Italy	Japan	Netherlands	Sweden
1988	583.6	83.5	122.4	108.9	92.5	144.1	14.84	17.4
1987	604.6	78.4	132.5	108.1	108.8	143.8	15.47	17.5
1986	659.2	74.0	163.4	105.2	124.9	160.5	14.86	16.4
1985	660.8	70.2	175.0	104.2	123.1	155.1	15.32	17.9
1984	672.4	53.8	190.8	112.1	131.6	150.5	16.53	17.1
1983	761.4	65.7	198.8	125.3	162.0	170.4	20.23	19.0
1982	782.7	64.0	201.9	124.5	195.4	155.2	22.01	19.7
1981	829.9	86.0	189.2	141.3	215.2	149.5	26.68	22.1
1980	877.8	101.0	174.8	143.8	241.9	164.4	27.93	24.0
1979	927.7	111.9	178.1	142.0	276.3	165.1	28.40	25.9
1978	979.8	126.1	178.5	135.5	318.6	166.0	30.52	24.5
1977	984.3	103.5	168.7	124.2	373.9	165.2	26.29	22.5
1976	1,072.1	103.9	177.3	115.1	454.5	171.0	26.52	23.7
1975	1,167.6	116.3	181.7	128.1	513.7	174.0	28.33	25.4
1974	1,234.4	138.5	179.4	136.2	544.4	185.7	28.10	22.1
1973	1,234.0	134.2	176.0	144.3	544.8	185.3	26.54	22.9
1972	1,283.5	156.6	184.4	149.8	553.7	187.4	24.98	26.7
1971	1,321.6	176.0	177.0	161.4	535.7	216.8	28.70	26.0
1970	1,376.9	193.0	184.4	167.4	525.0	254.8	24.14	28.2

[a]In millions.
Source: Annual country statistical abstracts and trade publications.

364

Table S2.7. *United Artists' revenues and operating income by division,*
1972–9

Year	Revenues ($ thousand)		Operating income ($ million)		Margin (%)	
	Theatrical	Television	Theatrical	Television	Theatrical	Television
1979	380,997	57,000	23.2	18.9	6.1	33.2
1978	294,490	76,010	31.8	19.1	10.8	25.1
1977	318,483	59,691	38.7	16.8	12.1	28.1
1976	229,482	55,543	16.6	10.9	7.2	19.6
1975	187,399	29,626	14.2	4.8	7.6	16.2
1974	142,667	40,606	8.0	8.7	5.6	21.4
1973	163,843	51,725	14.8	14.1	9.0	23.3
1972	152,749	50,620	9.1	11.0	6.0	21.7

Source: UA-Transamerica corporate reports.

Table S4.1. *Average rental-flow table: an example (as average percentage*
of estimated ultimate rentals realized)

Source	Number of quarters after initial release								Subsequent	Total estimated theatrical rentals
	1	2	3	4	5	6	7	8		
Domestic	71	19	5	2	1	1	—[a]	—	1	100
Foreign	4	33	24	14	7	5	3	2	8	100
Total	47	24	12	6	3	2	1	1	4	100

Note: Data are based on films released during fiscal years 1976–8. TV, pay-TV, and
other nontheatrical revenues are excluded from these statistics.
[a]Less than 1%.
Source: Columbia Pictures Industries (1982), p. 39.

Table S 4.2. *All-time rental champions adjusted by GNP deflator (base: 1972 = 100)*

Rank	Title	Release year	*Variety* rank	Historical dollars ($ million)	1982 constant dollars ($ million)
1	Gone With the Wind	1939	13	76,700	321,603
2	Star Wars	1977	1	193,500	272,085
3	Jaws	1975	4	133,435	213,455
4	The Sound Of Music	1965	10	79,748	208,833
5	E.T. The Extra-Terrestrial	1982	2	187,000	187,000
6	The Godfather	1972	8	86,275	177,841
7	The Empire Strikes Back	1980	3	140,000	160,062
8	The Exorcist	1973	7	88,600	152,723
9	The Sting	1973	11	79,419	139,741
10	Grease	1978	6	96,300	130,892
11	The Ten Commandments	1956	42	43,000	129,950
12	Dr. Zhivago	1965	36	46,550	118,658
13	Raiders of the Lost Ark	1981	5	112,000	117,415
14	Ben-Hur	1959	60	36,650	113,525
15	Mary Poppins	1964	39	45,000	110,143
16	Close Encounters of the Third Kind	1977	12	77,600	109,004
17	Love Story	1970	31	50,000	107,921
18	The Graduate	1968	33	49,078	105,758
19	Superman	1978	9	82,700	104,654
20	Airport	1970	38	45,609	102,107
21	Saturday Night Fever	1977	14	74,100	101,729
22	Nat'l Lampoon's Animal House	1978	15	74,000	98,436
23	Butch Cassidy and the Sundance Kid	1969	37	46,039	97,543
24	American Graffiti	1973	24	56,662	96,634
25	One Flew Over the Cuckoo's Nest	1975	22	59,188	92,313

26	Snow White	1937	92	26,900	87,890
27	Smokey and the Bandit	1977	21	61,055	87,714
28	The Poseidon Adventure	1972	43	42,000	82,100
29	Rocky	1976	26	55,905	81,876
30	Mash	1970	59	36,720	81,667
31	Fiddler on the Roof	1971	50	40,499	76,703
32	Thunderball	1965	84	28,530	75,703
33	Jaws II	1978	27	55,608	75,370
34	Blazing Saddles	1974	35	47,800	74,880
35	Cleopatra	1963	98	26,000	73,981
36	Around the World in 80 Days	1956	124	23,120	72,304
37	Kramer vs. Kramer	1979	20	61,734	71,496
38	Nine To Five	1980	16	65,350	68,814
39	Star Trek	1979	25	56,000	68,744
40	Superman II	1981	17	64,500	68,333
41	Heaven Can Wait	1978	32	49,400	67,100
42	Every Which Way But Loose	1978	30	51,900	65,375
43	Guess Who's Coming to Dinner	1968	101	25,500	63,989
44	Rocky III	1982	18	63,450	63,450
45	Goldfinger	1964	127	22,860	63,035
46	On Golden Pond	1981	19	63,000	63,000
47	Patton	1970	87	28,100	62,838
48	Billy Jack	1971	69	32,500	62,583
49	West Side Story	1961	166	19,450	62,520
50	Stir Crazy	1980	23	58,408	61,906
51	The Robe	1953	192	17,500	61,828
52	Young Frankenstein	1975	54	38,823	61,495
53	Funny Girl	1968	95	26,325	61,243
54	Earthquake	1974	61	36,250	60,559
55	It's a Mad, Mad, Mad, Mad World	1963	147	20,800	57,806

Table S4.2. (*cont.*)

Rank	Title	Release year	*Variety* rank	Historical dollars ($ million)	1982 constant dollars ($ million)
56	The Goodbye Girl	1977	45	41,800	57,394
57	2001: A Space Odyssey	1968	111	24,100	56,574
58	Bonnie and Clyde	1967	129	22,800	56,094
59	The French Connection	1971	96	26,315	55,757
60	A Star Is Born	1976	56	37,100	54,865
61	What's Up Doc?	1972	88	28,000	54,584
62	My Fair Lady	1964	330	12,000	54,580
63	King Kong	1976	58	36,915	54,484
64	Lady and the Tramp	1955	105	25,218	54,446
65	Bridge on the River Kwai	1957	196	17,195	53,739
66	Porky's	1982	28	53,500	53,500
67	Rocky II	1979	44	41,836	53,376
68	South Pacific	1958	193	17,500	53,364
69	The Dirty Dozen	1967	154	20,300	52,684
70	This Is Cinerama	1952	234	15,400	52,055
71	An Officer and a Gentleman	1982	29	52,000	52,000
72	The Jerk	1979	41	43,551	51,947
73	The Jungle Book	1967	91	27,317	51,713
74	Alien	1979	40	45,000	51,404
75	Valley of the Dolls	1967	160	20,000	50,226
76	The Love Bug	1969	121	23,150	50,215
77	You Only Live Twice	1967	167	19,400	50,166
78	The Longest Day	1962	191	17,600	50,141
79	The Godfather, Part II	1974	76	30,673	50,109

80	The Odd Couple	1968	161	20,000	50,040
81	Cinderella	1949	100	25,539	49,919
82	Bambi	1942	89	27,850	49,884
83	Swiss Family Robinson	1960	156	20,155	49,618
84	This Is the Army	1943	486	8,500	48,739
85	To Sir With Love	1967	172	19,100	48,730
86	Tom Jones	1963	206	16,950	48,160
87	Best Little Whorehouse in Texas	1982	34	48,000	48,000
88	Hooper	1978	66	34,900	47,705
89	How the West Was Won	1962	321	12,150	47,067
90	Lawrence of Arabia	1962	213	16,700	47,022
91	101 Dalmations	1961	130	22,792	46,964
92	All the President's Men	1976	79	30,000	46,898
93	Airplane	1980	48	40,610	46,850
94	The Best Years of Our Lives	1946	356	11,300	46,796
95	Duel In the Sun	1946	357	11,300	46,431
96	The Way We Were	1973	106	25,000	46,388
97	The Deep	1977	73	31,300	46,288
98	Coal Miner's Daughter	1980	51	40,302	46,215
99	Smokey and the Bandit II	1980	52	40,002	46,021
100	Greatest Show on Earth	1952	270	12,800	45,768

Note: How the table was formulated: This presentation uses as its base the table of annual "All-Time Film Rental Champs" (U.S. and Canadian market) for the year 1982, as published in *Variety's* 77th anniversary edition of January 12, 1983. Laventhol & Horwath has prepared its table from the best financial and economic information available, but is not responsible for the accuracy of its source material.

Notes to Table S.4.2. (*cont.*)

It is important to underscore that the annual *Variety* table is made up solely of U.S. and Canadian motion-picture rentals and does not reflect rentals from overseas markets. Neither does it reflect what a film has produced at the box office, domestically or overseas. However, the table, a valid barometer of a given motion picture's revenues, is the only published record of its kind that gives the motion-picture industry a basis for comparison and assessment.

Analysis of indexes. There are two indicators that can be used to interpret inflation. One is the consumer price index (CPI), as published by the U.S. Bureau of Labor Statistics (BLS): the other is the "gross national product implicit price deflator," as devised by the U.S. Department of Commerce. Both of these statistical indexes are widely used by financial economists. The CPI uses 1967 as a base (1967, 100); the GNP deflator uses 1972 as a base (1972, 100). Most recognized economists prefer the GNP deflator to make adjustments for inflation, as the CPI index tends to give even greater purchasing power to pre-1962 dollars. Therefore, in this presentation, the GNP deflator was used as the common denominator, as being a somewhat more conservative approach.

Using the GNP deflator, there are two further options for interpreting for inflation: (1) The 1982 dollar is worth 48.2¢ in relation to the 1972 dollar, or (2) the 1972 dollar is worth $2.07 in terms of 1982's $1 purchasing value. (In this context, the 1950 dollar was worth $3.87 in terms of the 1982 dollar, or had roughly almost four times as much purchasing power.) The table is in 1982 dollars because we felt it would be less confusing. Consideration was also given to correlating the rental figures with average box-office ticket prices, but we felt using the GNP deflator was more relevant.

To arrive at the all-time rental value of each motion picture, it was first necessary to establish (according to annual *Variety* tables since 1946) the actual historical dollars the film has produced in U.S. and Canadian rentals *each* year since its release date. The dollar figure for each applicable year was then translated into constant dollars (a term invented by economists to set forth the purchasing power of today's dollar in terms of what it might have bought in 1967 or 1972) by the given factor for that year. These constant figures were then totaled.

Source: Variety, May 4, 1983.

Table S5.1. *Market profile of spending on records, 1983 (percentages of dollars spent)*

	Total	Rock	Country	Pop/easy listening	Black/dance	Classical	Gospel	Children's	Jazz	Soundtracks/ shows
Age										
10–14	4	7	1	2	5	1	1	2	0	3
15–19	15	26	7	9	18	3	8	1	6	13
20–24	24	32	19	21	26	15	14	12	22	18
25–34	25	22	25	24	30	23	32	53	35	27
35 +	32	13	48	44	21	58	45	32	37	39
Race										
White	89	95	97	91	50	94	87	93	77	96
Nonwhite	11	5	3	9	50	6	13	7	23	4
Sex										
Male	55	63	47	47	48	63	44	22	82	54
Female	45	37	53	53	52	37	56	78	18	46

Source: Recording Industry Association of America (RIAA).

Table S5.2. *Sales of blank audiocassettes and videocassettes in the United States, 1981–8*

	Audio		Video	
Year	Value ($)[b]	Units[b]	Value ($)[b]	Units[b]
1988	354	366,355	936	296,947
1987	364	392,892	1,006	273,830
1986	292	296,681	1,235	296,253
1985	263	245,682	1,050	233,021
1984	256	228,119	770	133,088
1983	250	235,000	540	65,000
1982	219	186,447	357	33,529
1981	242	201,439	—[c]	—[c]

[a]Statistics reflect all U.S. shipments in retail, industrial, and bulk sales.
[b]Value in millions; units in thousands.
[c]Not available in a consistent series.
Source: Electronics Industry Association.

Table S6.1. *Spot television, time sales, historic and projected*

Year	Total time sales (independent + affiliates)		Total independent		
	Sales ($ million)	Percent increase	Sales ($ million)	Percent increase	Percent share
1975	2,521.2	9	403.4	17	16
1976	3,302.5	31	561.4	39	17
1977	3,546.7	7	602.9	7	17
1978	4,313.6	22	776.4	29	18
1979	4,805.7	11	865.0	11	18
1980	5,404.0	12	1,080.8	25	20
1981	6,190.0	15	1,361.8	26	22
1982	7,101.0	15	1,633.2	20	23
1983	8,009.0	13	1,922.2	18	24
1984	9,240.0	15	2,217.6	15	24
1985	10,199.0	10	2,549.8	15	25
1986	11,356.0	11	2,725.4	7	24
1987	11,871.0	5	2,967.8	9	25
1988	12,464.6	5	3,145.8	6	25
1989	13,337.1	7	3,366.0	7	25
1990	14,404.0	8	3,635.3	8	25

Note: Total time sales do not include network compensation.
Source: FCC 1975–80, INTV/TvB Estimates 1981–90.

Table S6.2. *Television stations on air, 1950–89 (as of January 1 for each year)*

Year	VHF coml.	VHF ETV	Total VHF	UHF coml.	UHF ETV	Total UHF	Total coml.	Total ETV	Grand Total
1950			98			—			98
1951			107			—			107
1952			108			—			108
1953			120			6			126
1954	233	1	234	121	1	122	354	2	356
1955	297	8	305	114	3	117	411	11	422
1956	344	13	357	97	5	102	441	18	459
1957	381	17	398	90	6	96	471	23	494
1958	411	22	433	84	6	90	495	28	523
1959	433	28	461	77	7	84	510	35	545
1960	440	34	474	75	10	85	515	44	559
1961	451	37	488	76	15	91	527	52	579
1962	458	43	501	83	19	102	541	62	603
1963	466	46	512	91	22	113	557	68	625
1964	476	53	529	88	32	120	564	85	649
1965	481	58	539	88	41	129	569	99	668
1966	486	65	551	99	49	148	585	114	699
1967	492	71	563	118	56	174	610	127	737
1968	499	75	574	136	75	211	635	150	785
1969	499	78	577	163	97	260	662	175	837
1970	501	80	581	176	105	281	677	185	862
1971	503	86	589	179	113	292	682	199	881
1972	508	90	598	185	123	308	693	213	906
1973	510	93	603	187	137	324	697	230	927
1974	513	92	605	184	149	333	697	241	938
1975	514	95	609	192	152	344	706	247	953
1976	511	97	608	190	162	352	701	259	960
1977	515	101	616	196	160	356	711	261	972
1978	515	102	617	201	164	365	716	266	982
1979	515	107	622	209	167	376	724	274	998
1980	516	109	625	218	168	386	734	277	1011
1981	519	111	630	237	171	408	756	282	1038
1982	517	112	629	260	176	436	777	288	1065
1983	519	114	633	294	179	473	813	293	1106
1984	523	117	640	318	180	498	841	297	1138
1985	520	121	641	363	193	556	883	314	1197
1986	522	121	643	397	195	592	919	316	1235
1987	524	121	645	444	201	645	968	322	1290
1988	539	122	661	489	212	701	1028	334	1362
1989	545	124	669	516	218	734	1061	342	1403

Source: Television & Cable Factbook, No. 57. Washington, D.C.: Warren Publishing Inc., 1989.

Table S6.3. *AM and FM radio stations 1950–89 (as of January 1 for each year)*

Year	AM stations		FM stations	
	Licenses and CPs	On air	Licenses and CPs	On air
1950	2246	2045	791	728
1951	2351	2199	706	672
1952	2410	2306	654	640
1953	2516	2377	648	612
1954	2644	2451	602	550
1955	2782	2662	583	549
1956	2941	2814	557	536
1957	3140	3024	559	528
1958	3289	3180	588	537
1959	3423	3318	686	571
1960	3527	3456	839	677
1961	3667	3547	1018	821
1962	3826	3618	1136	894
1963	3941	3760	1312	1050
1964	4050	3854	1358	1126
1965	4181	4044	1597	1205
1966	4126	4065	1951	1730
1967	4185	4121	2200	1904
1968	4266	4190	2418	2124
1969	4308	4265	2558	2330
1970	4343	4292	2695	2468
1971	4379	4343	2885	2624
1972	4462	4374	3053	2775
1973	4471	4395	3241	2936
1974	4495	4407	3457	3094
1975	4520	4445	3722	3299
1976	4540	4471	3920	3511
1977	4559	4497	4117	3676
1978	4585	4510	4289	3870
1979	4610	4526	4435	4016
1980	4679	4523	4599	4043
1981	4724	—	4637	—
1982	4760	—	4701	—
1983	4815	—	4863	—
1984	4880	—	5141	—
1985	4973	—	5386	—
1986[a]	4718	—	5106	—
1987[b]	4866	—	5208	—
1988	4902	—	5342	—
1989[c]	4948	—	5576	—

Note: CPs = construction permits; dash indicates data not available.
[a]Totals for 1986 from official FCC figures as of February 25, 1987.
[b]Totals for 1987 from official FCC figures as of March 11, 1988.
[c]Totals for 1989 from official FCC figures as of March 31, 1989.
Source: TV & Cable Factbook, No. 57. Washington, D.C.: Warren Publishing Inc., 1989.

Table S6.4. *TV sets, major developed free countries, 1989 estimates*

Country	No. sets (thousand)	Sets per thousand pop.	Country	No. sets (thousand)	Sets per thousand pop.
United States	195,600	797	Asia		
Canada	15,701	600	China (Taiwan)	6,009	296
Europe			Hong Kong	1,350	242
Austria	2,700	379	India	13,000	16
Belgium	3,000	303	Indonesia	7,000	38
Denmark	1,930	379	Japan	30,400	247
France	21,450	385	S. Korea	8,001	178
Greece	1,751	174	Philippines	6,000	99
W. Germany	23,001	375	Singapore	530	200
Italy	14,600	255	Thailand	8,900	163
Netherlands	4,601	314	Total	81,190	
Spain	14,771	372	Oceana		
Sweden	3,290	393	Australia	6,000	368
Switzerland	2,300	355	New Zealand	970	287
United Kingdom	19,601	347	Total	6,970	
Total	137,295		Central & South America		
			Argentina	7,150	217
Africa			Brazil	35,000	232
Algeria	1,500	61	Chile	2,300	181
Egypt	2,510	47	Colombia	5,000	159
S. Africa	2,600	74	Mexico	9,100	106
Total	6,610		Venezuela	2,750	145
			Total	59,000	
Middle East			Approximate number of free-world sets outside of U.S. and Canada	305,301	
Israel	655	150			
Jordan	249	83			
Kuwait	800	414			
Lebanon	830	297			
Saudi Arabia	3,701	297			
Turkey	8,001	147			
Total	14,236				

Source: Television Age International, April 1989.

Table S6.5. *The top Arbitron TV markets, 1985*

'85–86	Market	Households	'85–86	Market	Households
1	New York	6,696,000	34	New Orleans	638,500
2	Los Angeles	4,401,300	35	Buffalo, N.Y.	613,500
3	Chicago	3,006,300	36	Oklahoma City	611,100
4	Philadelphia	2,640,400	37	Greenville-Spartanburg, S.C.-Asheville, N.C.	604,200
5	San Francisco	2,043,800	38	Raleigh-Durham, N.C.	602,600
6	Boston	2,005,800	39	Salt Lake City	582,600
7	Detroit	1,661,700	40	Memphis	576,900
8	Dallas-Fort Worth	1,541,500	41	Grand Rapids-Kalamazoo-Battle Creek, Mich.	576,200
9	Washington	1,522,100	42	Providence, R.I.-New Bedford, Mass.	561,200
10	Houston	1,417,500	43	Charleston-Huntington, W. Va.	525,100
11	Cleveland	1,392,300	44	Harrisburg-York-Lancaster-Lebanon, Pa.	521,600
12	Pittsburgh	1,238,900	45	San Antonio, Tex.	521,200
13	Seattle-Tacoma	1,178,400	46	Norfolk-Portsmouth-Newport News-Hampton, Va	511,300
14	Miami	1,173,100	47	Birmingham, Ala.	508,300
15	Atlanta	1,167,400	48	Dayton, Ohio	502,900
16	Minneapolis-St. Paul	1,164,200	49	Louisville, Ky.	500,900
17	Tampa-St. Petersburg, Fla.	1,056,900	50	Greensboro-Winston Salem-High Point, N.C.	493,400
18	St. Louis	1,034,400	51	Albany-Schenectady-Troy, N.Y.	481,200
19	Denver	1,011,600	52	Tulsa, Okla.	459,100
20	Sacramento-Stockton	914,700	53	Shreveport, La.-Texarkana, Tex.	442,800
21	Baltimore	878,800	54	Flint-Saginaw-Bay City, Mich.	442,700
22	Phoenix	829,500	55	Little Rock, Ark.	438,900
23	Indianapolis	820,500	56	West Palm Beach, Fla.	431,800
24	Hartford-New Haven	810,700	57	Mobile, Ala.-Pensacola, Fla.	425,700
25	Portland, Ore.	777,700	58	Wilkes Barre-Scranton, Pa.	421,000
26	San Diego	765,300	59	Wichita-Hutchinson, Kan.	419,300
27	Orlando-Daytona Beach	718,900	60	Knoxville, Tenn.	418,200
28	Milwaukee	693,500	61	Jacksonville, Fla.	406,100
29	Cincinnati	692,900	62	Albuquerque, N.M.	404,400
30	Kansas City	688,400	63	Richmond, Va.	403,300
31	Nashville	665,100	64	Fresno-Visalia, Calif.	396,100
32	Charlotte, N.C.	655,300	65	Toledo, Ohio	382,500
33	Columbus, Ohio	643,700	66	Des Moines, Iowa	375,300

Source: Arbitron

Table S7.1. *Estimated growth of the cable industry (as of January 1 of each year)*

Year	Operating systems	Total subscribers
1952	70	14,000
1953	150	30,000
1954	300	65,000
1955	400	150,000
1956	450	300,000
1957	500	350,000
1958	525	450,000
1959	560	550,000
1960	640	650,000
1961	700	725,000
1962	800	850,000
1963	1,000	950,000
1964	1,200	1,085,000
1965	1,325	1,275,000
1966	1,570	1,575,000
1967	1,770	2,100,000
1968	2,000	2,800,000
1969	2,260	3,600,000
1970	2,490	4,500,000
1971	2,639	5,300,000
1972	2,841	6,000,000
1973	2,991	7,300,000
1974	3,158	8,700,000
1975	3,506	9,800,000
1976	3,681	10,800,000
1977	3,832	11,900,000
1978	3,875	13,000,000
1979	4,150	14,100,000
1980	4,225	16,000,000
1981	4,375	18,300,000
1982	4,825	21,000,000
1983	5,600	25,000,000
1984	6,200	29,000,000
1985	6,600	32,000,000
1986	7,500	37,500,000
1987	7,900	41,000,000
1988*	8,500	44,000,000
1989	9,050	47,500,000

Note: The change in the number of systems operating each year is determined by three factors: (1) New systems which began operation during the year. (2) Older systems coming to the attention of *Television & Cable Factbook* for the first time and therefore included in the total for the first time. (3) The splitting or combining of systems by operators.
*Revised.
Source: Television & Cable Factbook, No. 57. Washington, D.C: Warren Publishing Inc., 1989.

Table S8.1. *Estimated unit sales of best-selling coin-op video games*

Game	Company	Year introduced	Estimated unit sales
Ms. Pac-Man	Bally Midway	1982	114,000
Pac-Man	Bally Midway	1980-1	96,500
Donkey Kong	Nintendo	1981	80,000
Asteroids	Atari	1980	75,000
Space Invaders	Bally Midway	1979	58,000
Defender	Williams	1980-1	55,000
Centipede	Atari	1981	50,000
Tempest	Atari	1981	45,000
Galaxian	Bally Midway	1980	41,500
Missile Command	Atari	1980	40,000
Gorf	Bally Midway	1981	21,000

Table S9.1. *Reasons for gambling*

Reasons for betting[a]	%	Reasons for not betting[a]	%
To have a good time	81	Not available	48
For excitement	47	Don't know about it	27
Challenge	35	Not interested	26
To make money	35	Other things to do	23
To pass the time	23	Don't think about it	22
Something to look forward to	21	Odds against you	22
Chance to get rich	11	Don't want to lose money	16
Net activity reasons	94	Don't have the money	16
Net money reasons	43	Waste of money	14
		Illegal	10
		Not lucky	8
		Net money reasons	53
		Net activity reasons	55
		Net moral reasons	8
		Net legal reasons	12

[a]Respondents chose one, two, or three reasons from a list of 11 reasons provided for betting and 18 reasons provided for not betting.
Source: U.S. Congress (1976).

Table S9.2. The New Jersey casino industry, 1978–88: operating profits before taxes, interest, and depreciation ($ million)

Casino	1988	1987	1986	1985	1984	1983	1982	1981	1980	1979	1978	Grand totals
Atlantis	-3.4	-1.7	8.1	2.9	22.8	29.4	2.8	0.2				61.0
Bally Park Place	97.3	88.6	77.2	81.8	85.8	83.1	15.8	9.8	61.1	0.7		601.0
Bally's Grand[a]	63.7	75.9	87.9	83.6	70.8		61.4	50.7				493.9
Caesars	89.0	85.2	68.8	64.1	50.8	40.3	48.5	52.7	52.3	21.6		573.3
Claridge	26.7	26.5	23.7	26.6	27.0	2.2	4.1	-0.1				136.6
Harrah's Marina	91.4	80.6	77.8	67.2	83.6	82.1	65.7	34.9				583.4
Resorts	60.2	69.6	73.9	73.3	87.7	91.2	55.5	51.5	70.9	128.4	89.2	851.2
Sands	44.5	46.4	51.3	42.9	22.2	37.9	32.7	11.7	-11.0			278.5
Showboat	29.1	32.2										61.3
TropWorld	42.6	42.1	51.8	48.7	55.3	47.8	17.3	-1.1				304.5
Trump Plaza	86.6	66.0	56.7	43.4	28.5							281.2
Trump's Castle	56.7	65.2	65.9	33.5								221.2
Total	684.3	676.5	642.9	567.9	534.4	413.9	303.8	210.1	173.3	150.6	89.2	4,447.1

[a]Formerly Golden Nugget (prior to 1987).
Source: New Jersey Casino Control Commission.

Table S9.3. *The New Jersey Casino Industry: net income (loss) by casino, 1978–88 ($ million)*

Casino	1988	1987	1986	1985	1984	1983	1982	1981	1980	1979	1978	Grand totals
Atlantis	−76.6	−28.3	−31.77	−33.62	−8.92	0.50	−10.77	−25.55				−215.0
Bally Park Place	38.4	26.6	22.34	23.50	23.25	20.57	10.17	4.51	2.55	8.50		180.5
Bally's Grand[a]	−1.0	2.2	−12.21	1.57	4.34	35.93	20.64	18.64	−8.20			61.9
Caesars	29.7	17.3	14.07	9.65	12.68	10.04	12.80	10.34	13.21	5.36		135.2
Claridge	−20.4	−15.3	−20.09	−14.75	−14.74	−21.57	−30.39	−16.22	−6.86			−153.5
Harrah's Marina	72.8	59.0	48.80	48.77	60.30	68.73	38.57	1.34				391.5
Resorts	−47.1	5.1	2.80	3.17	21.68	29.67	16.79	19.73	31.22	76.26	41.31	200.6
Sands	6.4	0.6	5.35	4.33	1.75	17.02	14.02	−5.91	−15.45			28.2
Showboat	−15.5	−13.7										−29.2
TropWorld	−2.1	0.9	6.53	6.23	18.12	7.84	−14.94	−26.57				−4.0
Trump Plaza	33.2	17.9	15.45	0.87	−0.24							67.1
Trump's Castle	−3.1	1.7	3.74	1.85								4.2
Total	14.7	74.0	55.0	51.5	118.2	168.7	56.9	−19.7	16.5	90.1	41.3	667.3

[a]Formerly Golden Nugget (prior to 1987).
Source: New Jersey Casino Control Commission.

Table S9.4. *Nevada percent of total win by source,*[a] *1975–89*

	Major table games					Slots				Keno	Other games
Year	Blackjack	Craps	Roulette	Baccarat	Total	$1.00	$0.25	$0.05	Total	Keno	games
1975	27.2	21.4	3.0	5.9	57.4	2.6	7.7	15.8	26.2	6.9	9.5
1976	27.6	19.9	2.7	4.8	55.0	4.0	8.6	15.8	28.3	7.0	9.7
1977	27.7	18.3	2.7	3.9	52.5	10.6	8.2	13.3	32.1	6.4	9.1
1978	27.1	16.8	2.7	4.0	50.6	16.3	8.5	11.1	35.9	5.9	7.6
1979	26.8	15.6	3.3	4.2	49.9	18.7	9.4	9.4	37.6	5.5	7.1
1980	26.3	14.5	2.7	5.1	48.6	19.2	10.8	8.9	38.8	5.4	7.2
1981	24.5	12.8	2.7	6.2	46.1	19.9	13.1	8.1	41.1	5.4	7.4
1982	22.8	12.2	2.3	6.3	43.6	20.7	15.8	8.0	44.5	5.1	6.8
1983	22.0	11.1	2.2	4.3	39.6	22.0	18.4	8.1	48.5	4.8	7.1
1984	22.3	10.7	2.1	3.9	39.1	22.6	19.7	8.0	50.3	4.7	6.0
1985	22.7	10.6	2.4	3.7	39.5	22.2	21.6	7.6	51.5	6.0	3.1
1986	21.2	10.1	2.1	3.0	36.4	21.7	23.0	7.5	52.3	3.9	7.4
1987	20.2	9.5	2.4	3.9	35.9	21.5	24.1	7.3	52.9	3.6	7.6
1988	19.7	9.0	2.4	5.2	36.2	22.3	25.4	7.2	54.9	3.4	5.5
1989	19.0	8.6	2.5	6.5	36.5	21.9	26.2	7.1	55.2	3.1	5.1
Mean	23.8	13.4	2.5	4.7	44.5	17.8	16.0	9.5	43.3	5.1	7.1

[a] Fiscal years ended June 30 beginning in 1984.

Table S9.5. *Comparison of individual bets at craps*

Bet	House advantage (%)	Average no. of rolls for decision	Cost per roll[a]
Pass line or come odds	0.00		0
Pass line or come	1.41	3.38	0.0042
Place 6 or 8	1.51	3.27	0.0046
Place 5 or 9	4.00	3.60	0.0111
Place 4 or 10	6.67	4.00	0.0167
Buy of 10 (5% vigorish)	4.76	4.00	0.0119
Hard-way 4 or 10	11.11	4.00	0.0278
Hard-way 6 or 8	9.09	3.27	0.0278
Any craps (7-to-1 odds)	11.11	1	0.1111
2 or 12 (30-to-1)	13.90	1	0.1390
2 or 12 (30 for 1)	16.67	1	0.1667
3 or 11 (15-to-1)	11.11	1	0.1111
3 or 11 (15 for 1)	16.67	1	0.1667
Big 6 or 8 (even money)	9.09	1	0.0909
Any 7	16.67	1	0.1667
Field bets			
2–3–4–9–10–11–12 (2 & 12 pay double)	5.26	1	0.0523
2–3–4–9–10–11–12	11.11	1	0.1111

[a] As a percentage of money bet.
Source: Rouge et Noir Newsletter, March 1984, p. 16.

The minimum average pass bet (x) that generates an average casino win of \$2,000 in 15 hours of play at an assumed 75 rolls per hour is calculated as follows:

$$\$2,000 = (15 \text{ hours}) \left(\frac{75 \text{ rolls}}{\text{hour}} \right) (x) \left(\frac{0.0042}{\text{roll}} \right)$$

$$x = \frac{(\$2,000)}{(15)(75)(0.0042)} = \$423.28$$

Table S9.6. *Financial data for major Nevada hotel-casinos, fiscal 1988 (amounts represent 40 locations)*

Aggregate balance sheet			Dollars	Percent
Assets				
Current assets				
Cash			398,795,482	9.0
Receivables:	Total	Allowance		
Casino	186,177,065	77,407,585	108,769,480	2.4
Trade	53,622,614	3,641,055	49,981,559	1.1
Sundry	18,168,883	265,831	17,903,052	0.4
Notes	34,769,653	139,177	34,630,476	0.8
Prepaid expenses			62,549,942	1.4
Other current assets			83,366,538	1.9
Total current assets			755,996,529	17.0
Fixed assets	Cost	Depreciation		
Land	534,953,579		534,953,579	12.0
Land imprv.	67,554,001	10,672,052	56,881,949	1.3
Bldg. & imprv.	2,436,327,363	401,807,894	2,034,519,469	45.7
Furn. & equip.	1,072,046,823	519,539,326	552,507,497	12.4
Lease imprv.	149,589,126	51,068,828	98,420,298	2.2
Constr. in prog.	112,749,805		112,749,805	2.5
Total fixed assets			3,390,132,597	76.2
Other assets			304,490,952	6.8
Total assets			4,450,620,078	100.0
Liabilities and capital				
Current liabilities				
Accounts payable – trade			103,753,345	2.3
Accounts payable – other			36,361,863	0.8
Current portion of long-term debt			89,619,499	2.0
Accrued expenses			242,825,541	5.5
Other current liabilities			165,913,534	3.7
Total current liabilities			638,473,782	14.3
	Total owing	Current portion		
Long-term debt				
Mortgages	473,076,177	25,389,941	447,687,076	10.1
Debent. & bonds	247,922,424	1,700,000	246,222,424	5.5
Notes	496,423,430	52,402,462	444,020,968	10.0
Contracts	48,936,996	9,353,257	39,583,739	0.9
Other	222,140,062	774,745	221,365,317	5.0
Total l-t debt	1,488,499,029	89,619,505	1,398,879,524	31.4
Other liabilities			426,770,001	9.6
Total liabilities			2,464,123,307	55.4
Capital				
Owners capital accounts			115,736,407	2.6
Capital stock and other capital			634,797,966	14.3
Retained earnings			1,235,962,397	27.8
Total capital			1,986,496,770	44.6
Total liabilities and capital			4,450,620,077	100.0

Table S9.6. (*cont.*)

Aggregate income statement	Dollars	Percent
Revenue		
Gaming	2,742,519,301	59.3
Rooms	726,767,760	15.7
Food	539,709,011	11.7
Beverage	309,086,703	6.7
Other	308,117,614	6.7
Total revenue	4,627,100,389	100.0
Cost of sales	350,922,568	7.6
Gross margin	4,276,177,821	92.4
Departmental expenses	2,251,279,611	48.7
Departmental income (− loss)	2,024,898,210	43.8
General and administrative expenses		
Advertising and promotion	114,688,843	2.5
Bad debt expense	3,798,294	0.1
Complimentary expense (not reported in operation departments)	53,495,812	1.2
Depreciation – buildings	110,233,767	2.4
Depreciation and amortization – other	138,556,791	3.0
Energy expense (electricity, gas, etc.)	74,109,760	1.6
Equipment rental or lease	9,719,470	0.2
Interest expense	175,469,026	3.8
Music and entertainment	116,368,349	2.5
Payroll taxes	30,322,037	0.7
Payroll – employee benefits	65,128,157	1.4
Payroll – officers	16,049,102	0.3
Payroll – other employees	282,820,153	6.1
Rent of premises	61,549,229	1.3
Taxes – real estate	29,201,677	0.6
Taxes and licenses – other	3,876,626	0.1
Utilities (other than energy expense)	9,119,077	0.2
Other general and administrative expenses	226,105,229	4.9
Total general and administrative expenses	1,520,611,399	32.9
Net income (− loss) before federal income taxes and extraordinary items	504,286,811	10.9

Table S9.6. (*cont.*)

Aggregate casino department statement	Dollars	Percent
Revenue		
Pit revenue (includes keno and bingo)	1,229,517,962	44.8
Coin-operated devices	1,383,813,628	50.5
Poker and pan	58,146,522	2.1
Racebook	48,997,316	1.8
Sports pool	22,043,873	0.8
Total revenue	2,724,519,301	100.0
Departmental expenses		
Bad debt expense	49,703,366	1.8
Commissions	12,356,384	0.5
Complimentary expense	324,272,574	11.8
Gaming taxes and licenses	201,765,651	7.4
Junket expenses (no complimentaries)	21,282,139	0.8
Payroll taxes	44,265,871	1.6
Payroll – employee benefits	104,442,326	3.8
Payroll – officers	2,986,918	0.1
Payroll–other employees	425,258,795	15.5
Race wire fees	6,866,380	0.3
Other departmental expenses	153,911,214	5.6
Total departmental expenses	1,347,111,618	49.1
Departmental income ($-$ loss)	1,395,407,683	50.9

Statistical averages

Average pit revenue per room per day	88.88
Average slot revenue per room per day	100.03
Average food sales per room per day	39.01
Average beverage sales per room per day	22.41
Average rooms department payroll per room per day	15.93
Average room rate per day	52.53

Table S9.6. (*cont.*)

Ratios	Percent
Total current assets to total current liabilities	118.4
Total capital to total liabilities	80.6
Total capital to total current liabilities	311.1
Total current liabilities to total liabilities	25.9
Total complimentary expense to gaming revenue	14.1
Music and entertainment expenses to gaming revenue	4.2
Total revenue to average total assets	102.0
Total revenue less comp sales to average total assets	94.2
Return on invested capital[a]	17.4
Return on average assets[b]	15.0

[a] Return on invested capital is equal to the total of net income (before federal income taxes and extraordinary items) and interest expense divided by the total of average total assets less average current liabilities.

[b] Return on average assets is equal to the total of net income (before federal income taxes and extraordinary items) and interest expense divided by the average total assets.

Table S9.7. *Total illegal gambling in the U.S., 1982–8*

Year	Total	Sports books	Horse books	Sports cards (or other)	Numbers
Gross wager (handle), $ billion					
1988	42.02	26.31	8.13	2.04	5.55
1987	32.31	19.20	6.07	1.49	5.55
1986	32.31	19.20	6.07	1.49	5.55
1985	31.65	18.64	6.07	1.44	5.50
1984	30.08	17.56	6.07	1.36	5.09
1983	28.79	16.80	5.80	1.30	4.89
1982	25.50	14.50	5.50	1.13	4.37
CAGR[a]	8.7	10.4	6.7	10.3	4.1
Gross revenues (win), $ billions					
1988	6.63	1.20	1.38	1.22	2.83
1987	5.63	0.87	1.03	0.89	2.83
1986	5.63	0.87	1.03	0.89	2.83
1985	5.55	0.85	1.03	0.87	2.80
1984	5.24	0.80	1.03	0.82	2.60
1983	5.01	0.76	0.99	0.78	2.49
1982	4.52	0.65	0.92	0.68	2.27
CAGR[a]	6.6	10.6	7.1	10.3	3.7

[a] Compound annual growth rate (%). *Source: Gaming amd Wagering Business* (Christiansen, 1989).

State	Bingo	Card rooms	Casinos	Charitable gaming	Slot machines	Sports betting	Lottery: General	Instant	Lotto	Numbers	Passives	VLT's	Parimutuels: Greyhound	Jai-alai	Harness	Quarter horse	Thoroughbred	Off-track: Interstate intertrack	Intrastate intertrack	OTB, race/sports books	Telephone betting	Teletheaters
Alabama	•												•		▶	▶	•					
Alaska	•	•		•									•		□	•	•	•	•			•
Arizona	•							•	•				•		□	•	•	•	•			•
Arkansas													•			•						
California	•	•		•				•	•	▶					•	•	•	•	•			•
Colorado	•			•	•			•	▶		□		•		□	•	□	•	•			
Connecticut	•			•				•	•	•	□		•	•	▶		▶			•	•	•
Delaware	•					□		•	•	•	□				•	•	•	•			•	▶
Florida	•							★	★				•	•	•	•	•	•			•	▶
Georgia	•																					
Hawaii																						
Idaho	•												▶			•	•	•				
Illinois	•			★				•	•	•	□	□			•	□	•	•	•	★		▶
Indiana																						
Iowa	•	•		★				•	•			▶	•		▶	▶	▶					
Kansas	•							★	★				▶		▶	▶	▶					
Kentucky	•			•											•	•	•	•	▶		•	
Louisiana	•			•											□	•	•			★	★	★
Maine	•			•				•	•	•	□				•	□						
Maryland	•	•		•	★			•	•	•	□				•	•	•			★		▶
Massachusetts	•			•				•	•	•	□			•	□	•	•					
Michigan	•			•				•	•	•	□				•	•	•	•				
Minnesota	•			•											□	•	•	•		▶		
Mississippi	★																					
Missouri	•							•	•	•						•	★	▶				
Montana	•	•			•	•		•							▶	•	•					
Nebraska	•			•								□				•	•					

Figure S9.1. Legalized gambling in the United States by state, 1988.
Source: Gaming and Wagering Business, 1988.

State	Bingo	Card rooms	Casinos	Charitable gaming	Slot machines	Sports betting	Lottery: General	Lottery: Instant	Lottery: Lotto	Lottery: Numbers	Lottery: Passives	Lottery: VLT's	Parimutuels: Greyhound	Parimutuels: Jai-alai	Parimutuels: Harness	Parimutuels: Quarter horse	Parimutuels: Thoroughbred	Off-track: Interstate intertrack	Off-track: Intrastate intertrack	Off-track: OTB, race/sports books	Off-track: Telephone betting	Off-track: Teletheaters
Nevada	•	•	•		•	•							□	□	□	•	□			•	•	•
New Hampshire	•			•				•	•	•	□		•		□			•	•			
New Jersey	•		•	•				•	•	•	□				•			•	•	•		
New Mexico	•			•												•	•	•				
New York	•			►				•	•	•	□				•	□		•	•	•	•	•
North Carolina	•																					
North Dakota	•	•		•												►	►	►				
Ohio	•			•				•	•	•	•					•	•	•	•			
Oklahoma	•															►	•	•	•			
Oregon	•	•		★				•	•	•	•					•	•	★	►	►		►
Pennsylvania	•							•	•	•	□					•		•	•		•	
Rhode Island	•			•				•	•	•	•		•	•	□		□					
South Carolina	•																					
South Dakota	•			•			►	★					•		►	•	•		►			►
Tennessee	•															►	►	►				
Texas	•			•									►			►	►	►				
Utah																						
Vermont	•	-						•	•	•	□		•			□			□			
Virginia	•			•			►	►														
Washington	•	•		•				•	•	•						□		•	•	•	►	►
Wash., D.C.	•							•	•	•												
West Virginia	•							•	•	•	★		•			□		•	•	►		
Wisconsin	•						►	►					►			►	►	►				
Wyoming	•															►	•	•	•			►
Puerto Rico	•		•	•							•						•					
Virgin Islands								►			•											

Explanation of symbols
• legal and operative
★ implemented since July 1987
► authorized but not yet implemented
□ permitted by law and previously operative

Figure S9.1. (*cont.*)

Table S10.1. *Network-television-rights fees for Olympic Games, 1960–94*

Year	Winter location	Network	Amount paid ($ million)	Summer location	Network	Amount paid ($ million)
1960	Squaw Valley	CBS	0.05	Rome	CBS	0.4
1964	Innsbruck	ABC	0.6	Tokyo	NBC	1.5
1968	Grenoble	ABC	2.5	Mexico City	ABC	4.5
1972	Sapporo	NBC	6.4	Munich	ABC	7.5
1976	Innsbruck	ABC	10.0	Montreal	ABC	25.0
1980	Lake Placid	ABC	15.5	Moscow	NBC	87.0
1984	Sarajevo	ABC	91.5	Los Angeles	ABC	225.0
1988	Calgary	ABC	309.0	Seoul	NBC	300.0
1992	Albertville	CBS	243.0	Barcelona	NBC	411.0
1994	Lillehammer	CBS	300.0			

Table S11.1. *Broadway theater statistics*

Season beginning:[a]	Season attendance (millions)	Average price per ticket ($)
1970	7.4	7.43
1971	6.5	8.00
1972	5.4	8.33
1973	5.7	8.07
1974	6.6	8.64
1975	7.2	9.86
1976	8.8	10.60
1977	8.6	12.05
1978	9.1	14.05
1979	9.4	15.29
1980	10.8	17.97
1981	10.7	22.07
1982	8.1	25.07
1983	7.9	28.68
1984	7.2	29.06
1985	6.5	29.20
1986	7.0	29.74
1987	8.1	31.65
1988	8.0	32.88

[a]Note 1970–4 figures from League of American Theatres and Producers.
Source: Variety, May 31, 1989 and League of American Theatres and Producers.

Table S11.2. *Broadway productions by category, 1972–88*

Years	Plays		Musicals		Return shows	Pre-opening flops	Total
	New	Revival	New	Revival			
1972–73	22	14	18	3	1	0	58
1973–74	21	12	12	3	0	2	50
1974–75	25	17	11	3	2	1	59
1975–76	18	21	16	5	0	2	62
1976–77	27	11	13	11	0	1	63
1977–78	20	7	7	5	0	14	54
1978–79	22	5	17	3	0	0	47
1979–80	29	7	20	5	2	4	67
1980–81	25	7	19	7	2	7	67
1981–82	24	4	12	4	4	5	53
1982–83	24	9	13	4	0	0	50
1983–84	14	7	11	4	0	0	36
1984–85	14	9	5	2	1	0	31
1985–86	12	9	11	1	0	0	33
1986–87	16	11	11	2	0	0	40
1987–88	11	3	14	3	0	0	31
1988–89	13	7	7	1	1	0	29

Source: Variety, May 31, 1989.

Supplementary data   391

Table S11.3. *Broadway long runs*[a]

Show[b]	No. of performances
Oh, Calcutta (M–R)* (1976–77)	5,852
A Chorus Line (M)* (1975–76)	5,752
42nd Street (M) (1980–81)	3,486
Grease (M) (1972–73)	3,388
Fiddler On The Roof (M) (1964–65)	3,242
Life With Father (P) (1939–40)	3,224
Tobacco Road (P) (1933–34)	3,182
Hello Dolly (M) (1963–64)	2,844
Cats (M)* (1982–83)	2,773
My Fair Lady (M) (1955–56)	2,717
Annie (M) (1976–77)	2,377
Man of LaMancha (M) (1965–66)	2,328
Abie's Irish Rose (P) (1921–22)	2,327
Oklahoma (M) (1942–43)	2,212
Pippin (M) (1972–73)	1,944
South Pacific (M) (1948–49)	1,925
Magic Show (M) (1973–74)	1,920
Deathtrap (P) (1977–78)	1,792
Gemini (M) (1976–77)	1,788
Harvey (P) (1944–45)	1,775
Dancin' (M) (1977–78)	1,774
La Cage aux Folles (M) (1983–84)	1,761
Hair (M) (1967–68)	1,750
Wiz (M) (1974–75)	1,672
Born Yesterday (P) (1945–46)	1,642
Ain't Misbehavin' (M) (1977–78)	1,604
Best Little Whorehouse in Texas (M) (1977–78)	1,584
Mary, Mary (P) (1960–61)	1,572
Evita (M) (1978–79)	1,567
Voice Of The Turtle (P) (1943–44)	1,557
Barefoot In The Park (P) (1963–64)	1,530
Dreamgirls (M) (1981–82)	1,521
Mame (M) (1965–66)	1,508

[a]Broadway shows that have played at least 1,500 performances, not including previews. Excluded are multiple productions: In most instances, those listed are the original productions, but an exception is "Oh, Calcutta," in which both original and revival played more than 1,000, so both are listed.
[b]Designations are as follows: (P), play; (M), musical; (R), revival; an asterisk means the show is continuing. Figures are as of May 28, 1989.
Source: Variety, May 31, 1989.

	1984	1985	1986	1987	1988
Contributed income					
Individuals	7,038	8,026	9,200	10,049	10,200
Corporations	5,757	6,588	7,468	8,356	8,959
Foundations	4,357	4,708	5,800	6,542	8,127
United arts funds	4,565	5,916	6,378	6,191	6,812
Federal	4,591	5,038	5,974	5,520	5,735
State	4,814	4,841	6,008	5,461	5,614
City and county	560	628	1,066	1,602	1,849
Fund-raising events/guilds	2,382	2,703	3,427	3,812	3,921
All other	4,215	4,695	4,421	5,627	6,262
Total	38,279	43,143	49,742	53,160	57,479
Earned income					
Box office	54,182	59,109	61,724	67,510	73,191
Touring	2,266	2,383	3,348	2,436	2,207
Booked-in events	1,808	1,949	1,793	3,197	2,689
Educational programs	2,044	1,993	2,064	2,368	2,260
Interest and dividends	1,902	1,749	1,322	1,197	1,506
Endowment income	726	947	1,210	1,560	1,784
Royalty income	562	332	538	487	533
Concession/advertising and rental	3,385	3,918	4,105	4,133	4,187
All other	2,730	1,565	2,841	1,661	2,031
Total	69,605	73,945	78,945	84,549	90,388
Total income and expenses					
Earned income	69,605	73,945	78,945	84,549	90,388
Total expenses	109,255	119,845	128,531	137,057	147,792
Earnings gap	−39,650	−45,900	−49,586	−52,508	−57,404
Contributed income	38,279	43,143	49,742	53,160	57,479
Total income	107,884	117,088	128,687	137,709	147,867
Surplus/deficit	−1,371	−2,757	156	652	75

Source: American Theatre, April 1989.

Glossary

This abbreviated glossary has been compiled with help (and permission) from two sources: *Dictionary of Marketing and Related Terms in the Motion Picture Industry,* by Donn Delson, Bradson Press, Thousand Oaks, California, 1979 (recommended as an in-depth lexicon of motion picture terminology); *The McGraw-Hill Dictionary of Economics,* McGraw-Hill, New York, 1974. The *Dictionary of Economic and Statistical Terms,* U.S. Department of Commerce was supplementary. Additional references include Oakey (1983) and Konigsberg (1987).

Above-the-line costs: Those production-period costs related to acquiring the story rights and screenplay and signing the producer, director, and major members of the cast.

ADI (area of dominant influence): An Arbitron (ARB) audience-market classification designating a certain market area in which local stations have partial or complete signal dominance over stations from other market areas. Commonly referred to as a television broadcast area. Similar to Nielsen DMA (designated market area).

Advance: Monies paid by an exhibitor to a distributor prior to the opening of a film in a market as an "advance" against film rentals due. Advances, unlike guarantees, are refundable if the film does not generate enough box-office revenue at the exhibitor's theater to justify the advance film-rental monies paid out. The portion not earned by the distributor in film rental will be returned to the exhibitor.

Affiliate: Generally, an independently owned broadcast station that contracts with a network to show that network's programming in certain time periods. Each of the three major U.S. networks (ABC, NBC, and CBS) has approximately 200 affiliated stations, which compose the bulk of television broadcasting facilities.

Aggregate: The familiar type of summary series shown in most statistical reports. Generally, it is a total, such as the gross national product or retail sales, but sometimes it is an average, such as the index of industrial production or the index of wholesale prices.

AM (amplitude modulation): Technically, the variation of the amplitude of a radio wave in accordance with the sound being broadcast. AM-radio broadcasting is from 535 to 1,605 kilohertz. Signal reception occurs in two ways: either via ground waves that follow the curvature of the earth or via bounced sky waves that are reflected off the ionosphere back to earth. AM signals are subject to atmospheric or local interference, but generally are unimpeded by topographic or physical obstructions.

Amortization of debt: A gradual reduction of a debt through periodic payments covering the interest and part of the principal. Generally, amortization is used when the credit period is longer than a year. Common examples of amortization of debt are mortgage payments on homes, which extend over a period of 20 years or more.

Amortization of negative costs: Accounting procedure by which negative cost is charged against film revenue.

Answer print: A positive print made from the original negative that is color- and sound-balanced. "Answers" the question affirmatively that a viable working negative exists from which prints can be made for commercial presentation.

ARB (American Research Bureau): One of the major companies involved in national research for television and radio. ARB publishes numerous audience-market surveys throughout the year, rating the comparative audience viewing and listening habits for each medium, both locally and nationally.

Aspect ratio: A ratio of the horizontal to the vertical dimensions of a movie or television screen.

Asset: A physical property or intangible right, owned by a business or an individual, that has a value. An asset is useful to its owner either because it is a source of future services or because it can be used to secure future benefits. Business assets are usually divided into two categories: current and fixed.

Asset values: The implied price buyers might be willing to pay in order to obtain control of an asset's profit- and/or cash-generating potential. Asset values fluctuate according to changes in general economic conditions, in interest rates, and in expected returns.

Audience, primary or target: A particular audience composition or demographic to which a message is believed to have the most appeal and is therefore primarily directed.

Availability: 1. The date when a motion picture is able to be shown commercially in a market as offered by the distributor to the exhibitor. 2. Commercial-broadcast time periods available for purchase, including radio time periods (such as Drive Time, Housewife Time, etc.) and television programming (such as "Charlie's Angels," "M*A*S*H," etc.).

Basic service: Initial cable-television service that usually consists of 12 to 20 channels available off-the-air, and satellite channels supported by advertising.

Below-the-line costs: All costs, charges, and expenses incurred in the production of a motion picture other than the above-the-line costs, including such items as extras, art and set costs, camera, electrical, wardrobe, transportation, raw-film stock, etc.

Bicycling (print): The use of one print in two theaters for staggered showings. Originated with the transporting by bicycle of consecutive reels of film from one theater to another and back again.

Bid: A written notification from a theater-exhibition company in response to a bid solicitation from a distribution company, competing for the right to license a motion picture for showing in a given market beginning on or about a specific date. This notification usually includes commitments, if applicable, for minimum playing time, clearances, guarantees, advance, film-rental terms, advertising terms, etc.

Bid request: A written notification from a distributor to all motion-picture exhibitors who own or operate theaters in a market area, notifying them that a specific motion picture is available for showing in that area on or about a certain date, and inviting them to submit a bid to license that picture. This request may contain suggestions such as length of playing time, guarantees, advances, film-rental terms, advertising terms, deadlines for submission, etc. Such a bid request usually specifies that bid offers must be received by a certain time and date, usually no later than 10 days subsequent to its issuance.

Blind bidding: The practice by which film-distribution companies, through a bid-request letter and without having previously screened the film, request that interested exhibition companies submit bids to license a motion picture for showing in a market.

Block booking: Governed by the Paramount consent decree of 1948, major distributors were forbidden to employ the practice of the tying together of one or more motion pictures for licensing within a market. The basic premise of this decree is that motion pictures must be licensed picture by picture, theater by theater, so as to give all exhibitors equal opportunities to show a given film.

Bond: 1. A written promise to pay a specified sum of money (principal) at a certain date in the future or periodically over the course of a loan, during which time interest is paid at a fixed rate on specified dates. Bonds are issued by corporations, states, localities (municipal bonds), foreign governments, and the U.S. government, usually for long terms (more than 10 years), although any security issued by the U.S. government for more than five years is defined as a bond. 2. In movies, *completion bonds* are insurance policies that assure distributors and/or financiers that their investments in the movie will not be lost due to incompletion.

Book value: The value of a corporation according to its accounting records. It is computed by subtracting all debts from assets; the remainder represents total book value. Total book value is also referred to as net assets. If a corporation has assets of $300,000 and debts of $100,000, its total book value is $200,000. In reports of corporations, the book value is usually represented on a per-share basis. This is done by dividing the total book value by the number of shares. In the example given above, if the corporation had 10,000 shares outstanding, its book value would be $20 per share. The book value differs from the par value of the shares and also from the market value.

Booker: Responsible for all aspects of monitoring and trafficking the actual motion-picture prints throughout the markets over which the branch office has jurisdiction.

Box-office receipts: The money that has been paid by the public for admission (tickets) to see a specific motion picture.

Branch: The office located in a given city, staffed by employees of a film-distribution company, responsible for bidding out (licensing) the film company's products, servicing prints to legitimate customers, and collecting on film rentals due. Business is generally conducted with exhibitors within certain geographic regional boundaries of relative proximity to the branch.

The major distribution companies will have individual branches in 25 to 30 major U.S. cities. Branch staffs consist of the branch manager, salesmen, bookers, cashiers, clerical personnel, etc.

Break: 1. Each stage of the release of a motion picture within a market (first-run break, second-run break, etc.) consisting of a distinct array of theaters playing a motion picture in a given "availability." 2. The commercial time available for sale either within a particular show or between two shows on television or radio. 3. A short hiatus in production activity for meals, personal needs, etc.

Break-even point: The specific volume of sales at which a firm neither makes nor loses money. Above this point, a firm begins to show a profit; below it, a loss. Break-even-point analysis is used to compute the approximate profit or loss that will be experienced at various levels of production. In carrying out this analysis, each expense item is classified as either fixed (constant at any reasonable level of output) or variable (increasing as output increases and decreasing as output declines).

Business cycles: Alternate expansion and contraction in overall business activity, evidenced by fluctuations in measures of aggregate economic activity, such as the gross national product, the index of industrial production, and employment and income. A business cycle may be divided into four phases: expansion, during which business activity is successively reaching new high points; leveling out, during which business activity reaches a high point and remains at that level for a short period of time; contraction, during which business volume recedes from the peak level for a sustained period until the bottom is reached; recovery, during which business activity resumes after the low point has been reached and continues to rise to the previous high mark.

Cable-TV: Transmission of a television signal for home viewing by wire (cable), as opposed to airwave broadcast. A fee or monthly subscription charge is assessed. Often used in remote or isolated viewing areas, many cable systems offer subscribers an opportunity to see movies, sporting events, and other special programming not available on free TV.

Capitalized value: The terms applied to a technique used to determine the present value of an asset that promises to produce income in the future. To calculate the present value, the total future income expected must be discounted, that is, offset against the cost (as measured by the current interest rate) of carrying the asset until the income has actually been realized. If the asset promises a stream of income, its capitalized value is calculated by adding together the present discounted value of the income in each year. The general formula for this calculation is $I/(1 + r)^t$, where I is the annual income, r is the current rate of interest, and t is the number of years involved. In this manner, an investor confronted with a choice of properties can determine which alternative is the most remunerative, though the formula tells nothing about the relative risks involved.

Cash flow: The sum of profits and depreciation allowances. (Instead of profits, many economists use retained earnings, which are profits after taxes and after deductions for dividend payments.) Gross cash flow is composed of total profits plus depreciation; net cash flow, of retained earnings plus depreciation. Thus, cash flow represents the total funds that corporations generate internally for investment in modernization and expansion of plants and equipment and for working capital. The growth of depreciation allowances over the years has made them a much more important part of cash flow than retained earnings. To facilitate comparisons of property values, however, entertainment businesses often take cash flow to be prior to deductions of interest, depreciation, and taxes.

Clearance: The relative exclusivity a theater specifies as a condition to licensing a motion picture within a market. A theater may request an exclusive run within an entire market or may request exclusivity for exhibition of a motion picture only over those theaters that are in geographic proximity and may be considered competitive.

Commercial: An advertisement broadcast on a television or radio station for which the station receives some form of compensation (also called spot announcement).

Common stock: The capital stock of a corporation that gives the holder an unlimited interest in the corporation's earnings and assets after prior claims have been met. Common stock represents the holder's equity or ownership in the corporation. Holders of common stock have certain fundamental legal rights, including the following: preemptive rights; the right, in most cases, to vote for the board of directors, who actually manage the company; the right to transfer any or all shares of stock owned; the right to receive dividends when they are declared by the board of directors.

Competition: The condition prevailing in a market in which rival sellers try to increase their profits at one another's expense. In economic theory, the varieties of competition range from perfect competition, in which numerous firms produce or sell identical goods or services, to oligopoly, in which a few large sellers with substantial influence in the market vie with one another for the available business. Early economists envisioned perfect competition as the most effective assurance that consumers would be provided with goods and services at the lowest possible prices.

Consent decree of 1948: A decree issued by the U.S. Supreme Court ordering all motion-picture companies to divest themselves of all motion-picture-theater holdings. This put an end to vertical integration, through which the motion-picture companies produced, distributed, and showed their products to the public. The intention was to afford competitive theaters an equal opportunity to license a motion picture for commercial presentation. This began the era of the independent motion-picture exhibitor.

Contract: The mutually binding licensing agreement between a distribution company and an exhibition company for the showing of a motion picture at a particular theater on or about a given date. Included are the terms for computing payment for film rental, playing time, clearance, advertising sharing, etc.

Convertible debenture: A certificate issued by a corporation as evidence of debt that can be converted at the option of the holder into other securities (usually common stock, but sometimes preferred stock) of the same corporation. Each debenture can be converted into a specified number of shares of stock at a stipulated price for a certain period. There are two advantages to convertible debentures for the issuing corporation: (a) The conversion privilege makes the debentures more attractive to investors and tends to reduce interest costs. (b) The debentures facilitate the extinction of debt, because debt declines and equity (stock) increases as holders convert their debentures. The major disadvantage is discrimination against the company's stockholders, whose equity is diluted as the holders of debentures convert them. At all times during the conversion period, there is a price relationship between the debenture and the stock. It is based on the conversion price, the number of shares into which each debenture can be converted, and the value that the market puts on the conversion privilege. For example, a $1,000 debenture that can be converted into 50 shares of common stock at $20 per share will normally trade in the market at a price higher than $1,000 because of the conversion privilege.

Copyright Royalty Tribunal: A special review board that was established by Congress in the 1976 Copyright Act. It has powers to set and distribute royalties.

Correlation: The statistical technique that relates a dependent economic variable to one or more independent variables over a period of time in order to determine how close the relationship between the variables is. This technique can be used for business forecasting. When more than one independent variable is used, the relationship is called a multiple correlation.

Cost per thousand: Determined by dividing the cost of a print or broadcast advertisement or of a total advertising campaign by the total estimated audience, computing the total audience on a base of thousands.

Cost recovery: Accounting method of amortization in which all costs are charged against earned revenue and no profit is recognized until cumulative revenue equals cumulative costs. This method is not acceptable for financial-statement reporting under generally accepted accounting principles.

Current assets: Cash or other items that will normally be turned into cash within one year, and assets that will be used up in the operation of a firm within one year. Current assets include cash on hand and in the bank, accounts receivable, materials, supplies, inventories, marketable securities, and prepaid expenses.

Current liabilities: Amounts owed that will ordinarily be paid by a firm within one year. The most common types of current liabilities are accounts payable, wages payable, taxes payable, and interest and dividends payable.

Day and date release: Simultaneous (same day, same date) release of a motion picture in two or more theaters in a given market. Also used to indicate simultaneous opening in two or more markets (i.e., "L.A. and New York, day and date openings," or "opening 50 markets in the United States day and date").

Debenture: A bond that is not protected by a specific lien or mortgage on property. Debentures (debts), which are issued by corporations, are promises to pay a specific amount of money (principal) at a specified date or periodically over the course of the loan, during which time interest is paid at a fixed rate on specified dates. The distinction between a debenture and a note of a corporation is that the debenture, like a bond, is issued under an indenture or deed of trust.

Demand: The desire, ability, and willingness of an individual to purchase a good or service. Desire by itself is not equivalent to demand: The consumer must also have the funds or the ability to obtain funds in order to convert the desire into demand. The demand of a buyer for a certain good is a schedule of the quantities of that good that the individual would buy at possible alternative prices at a given moment in time. The demand schedule, or the listing of quantities that would be bought at different prices, can be shown graphically by means of the demand curve. The term *demand* refers to the entire schedule of possibilities, not only to one point on the schedule. It is an instantaneous concept, expressing the relationship of price and the quantity that is desired to be bought, all other factors being constant.

Depreciation: A reduction in the value of fixed assets. The most important causes of depreciation are wear and tear (loss of value caused by the use of an asset), the effects of the elements (i.e., decay or corrosion), and gradual obsolescence, which makes it unprofitable to continue using some assets until they have been fully exhausted. The annual amount of depreciation of an asset depends on its original purchase price, its estimated useful life, and its estimated salvage value. A number of different methods of figuring the amount of depreciation have been developed. Using the simple straight-line method, which considers depreciation a function of time, the annual depreciation cost is calculated by dividing the cost of the asset (original minus salvage cost) equally over its entire life.

Designated market area: Nielsen audience-market classification that designates a certain market area in which local stations have partial or complete dominance over stations from other market areas. Similar to Arbitron ADI.

Direct-distribution expense: Expense incurred in relation to the distribution of a specific picture: The largest two items relating to the release of any picture are prints and advertising and publicity costs. Other direct expenses include such things as checking costs, freight, guild payments, trade-association fees and assessments, market research, certain taxes, etc.

Discounted-cash-flow method: A method of measuring the return on capital invested. The value of a project is expressed as an interest rate at which the project's total future earnings, discounted from the time that they accrue to the present, equal the original investment. It is more precise than most of the other methods used to measure return on capital invested, because it recognizes the effect of the time value of money. It can be used to determine whether a given project is acceptable or unacceptable by comparing each project's rate of return with the company's standard.

Discretionary spending: A measure, developed by the National Industrial Conference Board, that reflects the extent of consumer spending as the result of a decision relatively free of prior commitment, pressure of necessity, or force of habit. It includes all personal expenditures not accounted for specifically or in equivalent form in imputed income, fixed commitments, or essential outlays. The series measures the growth and the ability of American consumers to exercise some degree of discretion over the direction and manner of their spending and saving.

Distribution fee: Contractual rate assessed by a distributor on the gross film revenue. Used in computation of contingent compensation (i.e., profit participation).

Drop: A term used in the gaming industry to indicate the total monetary-equivalent value of cash, IOUs ("markers"), and other items that are physically deposited or dropped into a cash box of a gaming table or slot machine.

Econometrics: The branch of economics that expresses economic theories in mathematical terms in order to verify them by statistical methods. It is concerned with empirical measurements of economic relations that are expressible in mathematical form. Econometrics seeks to measure the impact of one economic variable on another in order to be able to predict future events or advise economic-policy choices to produce desired results. Economic theory can supply qualitative information concerning an economic problem, but it is the task of econometrics to provide the quantitative content for these qualitative statements.

Economic growth: An increase in a nation's capacity or an area's capacity to produce goods and services coupled with an increase in production of these goods and services. Usually, economic growth is measured by the annual rate of increase in a nation's gross national product, as adjusted for price changes.

Economic model: A mathematical statement of economic theory. Use of an economic model is a method of analysis that presents an oversimplified picture of the real world.

Economics: The social study of production, distribution, and consumption of wealth. With improvements in the tools used by modern economists in their analyses and the discarding of out-of-date theories, economics is becoming more a science and less an art.

Elastic demand: The percentage change induced in one factor of demand divided by a given percentage change in the factor that caused the change. For example, if the price of a commodity is raised, purchasers tend to reduce their buying rate. The relationship between price and purchasing rate, which is known as the elasticity of demand, expresses the percentage change in the buying rate divided by the percentage change in price.

Elasticity: The relative response of one variable to a small percentage change in another variable.

Equilibrium: The state of an economic system in which all forces for change are balanced, so that the net tendency to change is zero. An economic system is considered to be in equilibrium when all the significant variables show no change over a period of time.

Equity: 1. Amount of capital invested in an enterprise. It represents a participative share of ownership, and in an accounting sense is calculated by subtracting the liabilities (obligations) of an enterprise from its assets. 2. The shorthand name for the Actors Equity labor union.

Excess reserves: The surplus of cash and deposits owned by commercial member banks of the Federal Reserve System over what they are legally required to hold at Reserve Banks or in their own vaults. The excess-reserve position of a bank is an indication of its ability to invest in government bonds or to make loans to customers. Therefore, if the Federal Reserve System is trying to stimulate business in periods of economic sluggishness, it buys government bonds from private sellers, thus increasing bank reserves; and vice versa.

Film rental: The monies paid by the exhibitor to the distributor as rental fees for the right to license a film for public showing. Generally computed weekly on a consecutive seven-day basis (Wednesday through Tuesday or Friday through Thursday, depending on the day on which the film first opens in the market). Film rental may be determined by several different methods, including a 90:10 basis, sliding scale, fixed percentage, minimums (floors) that relate specifically to the gross box-office receipts, or a flat-fee basis that is a predetermined, unchanging amount. The film rental earned usually changes from week to week, with the distributor's relative share generally decreasing and the exhibitor's share increasing from the first through subsequent weeks.

FM (frequency modulation): Technically, the variation of the frequency of a radio wave in accordance with the sound being broadcast. Radio (audio) transmission from 88 to 108 megahertz. Signal is unaffected by atmosphere interference, but it is a high-fidelity, line-of-sight beam impeded by topographic or physical obstructions.

Foreign exchange: All monetary instruments that give residents of one country a financial claim on another country. The use of foreign exchange is a country's principal means of settling its transactions with other countries.

Fourier analysis: A technique for analyzing periodic movement in composite time series – hence, a form of harmonic analysis. It treats the variable under study as the sum of a series of sine and cosine terms in which the unknown periods of component series are not necessarily identical. Variances of deviations from a fitted Fourier series provide estimates of the variance of the error term.

Four-wall: A technique used by some distribution companies in which theaters are offered a flat weekly rental fee that is guaranteed to the exhibitor regardless of the film's revenue intake at the box office. The distributor pays all advertising expenses and usually hires personnel to be at each theater for supervision and nightly collection of all monies taken in at the box office. The exhibitor has virtually no risk in that rental income is guaranteed. The distributor incurs a greater risk, but is also in the position, should the film be successful, of reaping the benefits of 100% of the monies taken in at the box office, less advertising, administrative, and rental costs.

Franchise: 1. Between a cable operator and a government body, a contractual agreement that defines the rights and responsibilities of each party in the construction and operation of a cable system within a specified geographic area. 2. A territorial agreement between a league and team owners.

Free reserves: The margin by which excess reserves exceed borrowings at Federal Reserve Banks. They are a better indicator of the banking system's ability to expand loans and investments than excess reserves. Manipulation of the net free-reserve position of member banks is an indication of the monetary policy that the Federal Reserve wishes to pursue.

Gross national product (GNP): The most comprehensive measure of a nation's total output of goods and services. In the United States, the GNP represents the dollar value at current prices of all goods and services produced for sale plus the estimated value of certain imputed outputs, that is, goods and services that are neither bought nor sold. The rental value of owner-occupied dwellings and the value of farm products consumed on the farm are the most important imputed outputs included; the services of housewives are among the most important nonmarket values included. The GNP includes only final goods and services; for example, a pair of shoes that costs the manufacturer $2.50, the retailer $4.50, and the consumer $6.00 adds to the GNP only $6.00, the amount of the final sale, not $13.00, the sum of all the transactions. The GNP can be calculated by adding either all expenditures on currently produced goods and services or all incomes earned in producing these goods and services.

Gross rentals: The total of the distributor's share of the money taken in at the box office computed on the basis of negotiated agreements between the distributor and the exhibitor (also called gross proceeds).

Gross win: For a casino, gross win is equivalent to revenues or sales in other businesses. It is from the win that operating expenses must be deducted.

GRP (gross rating point): A rating basis for determining the estimated percentage of households or target audience exposed to a broadcast commercial or magazine advertisement (newspaper GRP data generally are not readily available). GRPs are the sums of all rating points and an indication of potential exposure. One rating point is equal to 1% of the population of the total universe in which the advertising campaign is being run. However, this does not mean that 100 GRPs provide advertising exposure to 100% of the population, because it does not eliminate audience duplication from its number totals. GRPs can be computed on the basis of reach multiplied by average frequency.

Handle: In the gaming industry, the handle is the total dollar amount bet on the outcome of an event.

Head end: The electronic-origination center of a cable system, and the site of signal-processing equipment.

Hold: A term used in the gaming industry to indicate how much of the drop is retained (won) by the game operator through the course of play. Hold can be expressed as a percentage of the drop, in which case it is known as the hold percentage, often in a shorthand way called "win."

Holdover figure: A minimum weekly dollar figure for monies taken in at the theater box office that a film must reach in order to be held over for another week. This figure is mutually agreed on by the exhibitor and distributor when the terms under which the film will be played are originally established. It is an objective means by which either the exhibitor or the distributor may insist that the picture continue if the figure was achieved or, if not, cease to be shown in a specific theater.

Home passed: The number of households in a market that a cable system has the ability to serve. This does not mean that these homes have elected to utilize the cable system.

Homes using television: The estimated percentage of the homes in which people are viewing television at any given time. The result of extrapolations made on the basis of audience-measurement techniques.

Income effect: A term used in demand analysis to indicate the increase or decrease in the amount of a good that is purchased because of a price-induced change in the purchasing power of a fixed income. When the price of a commodity declines, the income effect enables a person to buy more of this or other commodities with a given income. The opposite occurs when the price rises. By using indifference curves, it is possible to separate the income effect from the so-called substitution effect, in which the demand for a price-reduced good rises as it is substituted for other goods whose prices have remained constant.

Indifference curve: A graphic curve that represents the various combinations of two goods that will yield the consumer the same total satisfaction. For example, a household may receive the same satisfaction from consuming four pounds of steak or one pound of chicken. By assuming that the two commodities can be substituted for each other, it is possible to draw an indifference schedule that contains all of the possible combinations of the commodities that will yield the same satisfaction. When the schedule is plotted on a graph, with one commodity along the vertical axis and another along the horizontal axis, the curve that connects the points is called an indifference curve.

Inelastic demand (inelasticity): A term used to describe a proportionately smaller change in the purchase rate of a good than the proportional change in price that caused the change in amount bought. When the demand for a product is inelastic, a relatively large price change is necessary to cause a relatively small increase in purchase. To calculate the elasticity of demand, the percentage change in buying rate (the quantity bought per period of time) is divided by the percentage change in price.

Inflation: A persistent upward movement in the general price level. It results in a decline in purchasing power. According to most economists, inflation does not occur until price increases average more than 2.5% per year for a sustained period.

Interest: The price paid for the use of money over a period of time. Individuals, businesses, and governments buy the use of money. Businesses pay interest for the use of money to purchase capital goods because they can increase production and productivity through the introduction of new plants and new machines.

Inventory: The supply of various goods kept on hand by a firm in order to meet needs promptly as they arise and thus assure uninterrupted operation of the business. In manufacturing, for example, inventories include not only finished products awaiting shipment to selling outlets but also raw materials, nuts and bolts, paper and pencils, and countless other major and minor items required for the production and distribution of the product.

Labor force: According to the concept of the U.S. Department of Labor and the U.S. Bureau of the Census, the noninstitutionalized population, 16 years of age or older, who either are employed or are looking for work.

Lead–lag relationship: A term that describes the timing of changes in one statistical series in relation to changes in another series. It is frequently used in sales forecasting, which makes use of the timing pattern between a company's sales and a particular economic indicator.

Legs: A term used in the movie business to indicate that a film attracts strong audience interest and that it will therefore run (play) in theaters for a relatively long time.

Liabilities: The debts or amounts of money owed by an individual, partnership, or corporation to others. Considered from another point of view, liabilities are the claims or rights, expressed in monetary terms, of an individual's or a corporation's creditors. In accounting, liabilities are classified as either short-term or long-term liabilities or as secured or unsecured liabilities. Short-term liabilities are those that will be satisfied, or paid, within one year.

Macroeconomics: Modern economic analysis that is concerned with data in aggregate as opposed to individual form. It concerns itself with an overall view of economic life, considering the total size, shape, and functioning of economic experience rather than the workings of individual parts. More specifically, macroeconomics involves the analysis of the general price level rather than the prices of individual commodities, national output or income rather than the income of the individual firm, and total employment rather than employment in an individual firm.

Make-good: An offer by a medium to rerun, at no additional charge, an advertisement or commercial that appeared incorrectly because of some error on the part of the medium. Generally of equal or greater value than the original placement.

Marginal cost: The additional cost that a producer incurs by making one additional unit of output. If, for example, total costs were $13,000 when a firm was producing two machine tools per day and $18,000 when it was producing three machine tools per day, the marginal cost of producing one machine tool was $5,000. The marginal cost may be the same or higher or lower in moving from three to four machine tools. The concept of marginal cost plays a key role in determining the quantity of goods that a firm chooses to produce. The purely competitive firm, which faces a given price set in the market, increases its output until marginal cost equals price. That point is the firm's best-profit output point. The imperfectly competitive firm equates marginal cost to marginal revenue (additional revenue) to obtain the highest profits. For most firms, marginal costs decline for a while and then begin to rise. The pattern of the marginal-cost graph depends on the nature of the firm's production function and the prices of the goods that it buys.

Marginal revenue: The additional revenue that a seller receives from putting one more unit of output on the market.

Margins: See Profit margins.

Market share: The ratio of a company's sales, in units or dollars, to total industry sales, in units or dollars, on either an actual basis or a potential basis for a specific time period.

Mechanical rights (royalties): The rights to reproduce and to distribute to the public copyrighted materials. So-called mechanical royalties, usually on a per-copy basis, are paid to obtain such rights.

Microeconomics: Modern economic analysis concerned with data in individual form, as opposed to aggregate form. It is concerned with the study of the individual firm rather than aggregates of firms, the individual consuming unit rather than the total population, and the individual commodity rather than total output. Microeconomics deals with the division of total output among industries, products, and firms and the allocation of resources among competing uses. It is concerned with the relative prices of particular goods and the problem of income distribution.

Model: In econometrics, an equation or set of equations depicting the causal relationships that are believed to generate observed data. Also, the expression of a theory by means of mathematical symbols or diagrams.

Modern portfolio theory: A theory that enables investment managers to classify, estimate, and then control the sources of investment risk and return.

Monopoly: A market structure with only one seller of a commodity. In pure monopoly, the single seller exercises absolute control over the market price at which he sells, because there is no competitive supply of goods on the market. He can choose the most profitable price and does so by raising his price and restricting his ouput below what would be achieved if there were competition.

Monopsony: A market structure with a single buyer of a commodity. Pure monopsony, or buyer's monopoly, is characterized by the ability of the single buyer to set the buying price. In the case of a monopsonist who maximizes profits, both his buying price and the quantity bought are lower than they would be in a competitive situation.

MSO (multiple-system operator): A company that owns and operates more than one cable-television system.

National income: The total compensation of the elements used in production (land, labor, capital, and entrepreneurship) that comes from the current production of goods and services by the national economy. It is the income earned (but not necessarily received) by all persons in the country in a specified period.

Negative cost: All of the various costs, charges, and expenses incurred in the acquisition and production of a motion picture. These include such items as facilities (sound stage, film lab, editing room, etc.) and raw material (set construction, raw-film stock, etc.). Typically segregated as above-the-line production-period costs and post-production-period costs.

Negotiated deal: If the film-distribution company rejects all bid offers submitted by exhibitors for the right to license a film for exhibition within a market, the branch office will in turn either rebid the picture suggesting different terms or send out a notice to all exhibitors by which it offers to negotiate openly in an effort to award the film to the theater that offers the most attractive deal.

Net profits (contractual): Generally, the amount of gross receipts remaining after deducting distribution fees, distribution expenses, negative cost (including interest), and certain deferments, and gross participations.

Nielsen station index (NSI): A service provided by the A. C. Nielsen Company for rating television viewing habits, audience profiles, etc., on a local basis or within a given broadcast area.

Nonborrowed reserves: A reserve aggregate consisting of total bank reserves (deposits of the Federal Reserve and vault cash) minus borrowings by member banks from the Federal Reserve.

Oligopoly: A type of market structure in which a small number of firms supplies the major portion of an industry's output. The best-known example in the U.S. economy is the automobile industry, in which three firms account for 92% of the output of passenger cars. Although oligopolies are most likely to develop in industries whose production methods require large capital investments, they also cover such diverse items as cigarettes, light bulbs, chewing gum, detergents, and razor blades. In economic theory, the term *oligopoly* means a mixture of competition and monopoly, and the benefit or harm done to the economy at large by oligopolies remains in dispute.

Operating cash flow: In the cable and broadcasting industries, earnings before depreciation and amortization, interest, other income, and taxes.

Operating income: Earnings before interest, other income, and taxes.

Opportunity costs: The value of the productive resources used in producing one good, such as an automobile, instead of another good, such as a machine tool. With relatively fixed supplies of labor and capital at any given time, the economy cannot produce all it wants of everything.

Paretian optimum: A situation that exists when no one (say person *A*) in a society can move into a position that *A* prefers without causing someone else (person *B*) to move into a position that *B* prefers less. In other words, a situation is not a paretian or social optimum if it is possible, by changing the way in which commodities are produced or exchanged, to make one person better off without making another person (or persons) worse off. (See Second-best theory.)

Partnership: A type of business organization in which two or more persons agree on the amounts of their contribution (capital and effort) and on the distribution of profits, if any. Partnerships are common in retail trade, accounting, and law.

Pay-per-view: A cable service that makes available to a subscriber an individual movie, sporting event, or concert on payment of a fee for that single event.

Pay-TV: A generic term used to indicate subscriber-paid-for television, presented in an uncut and uncensored format.

Periodic-table computation method: An accounting method of amortization in which cost is related to gross revenue recorded during a period; may be based on an average table established from experience with previously released films.

Personal-consumption expenditures: Personal-consumption expenditures reflect the market value of goods and services purchased by individuals and nonprofit institutions or acquired by them as income in kind. The rental value of owner-occupied dwellings is included, but not the purchases of dwellings. Purchases are recorded at cost to consumers, including excise or sales taxes, and in full at the time of purchase whether made with cash or on credit.

Personal income: According to the concept of the U.S. Department of Commerce, the amount of current income received by persons from all sources, including transfer payments from government and business, but excluding transfer payments from other sources. Personal income also includes the net incomes of unincorporated businesses and nonprofit institutions and nonmonetary income, such as the estimated value of food consumed on farms and the estimated rental value of homes occupied by their owners.

Price/earnings ratio: The current market price of a company's stock expressed as a multiple of the company's per-share earnings.

Print: 1. A copy made from the master for the purpose of motion-picture presentation. For all intents and purposes, the print is the specific motion-picture release, because the master is preserved for additional duplication. A distribution company may make only a few copies or more than 1,500 prints depending on the expected or experienced success with a particular motion picture. 2. Advertising placed in newspapers as part of an advertising campaign.

Production function: The various combinations of land, labor, materials, and equipment that are needed to produce a given quantity of output. The production function expresses the maximum possible output that can be produced with any specified quantities of the various necessary inputs. Every production function assumes a given level of technology; once technological innovations have been introduced, the production function changes.

Production overhead: Those costs and expenses incurred for the production of motion pictures in general that cannot be directly charged to specific pictures. They include such things as salaries of production-department executives and their related expenses, story-abandonment costs, certain studio-facility costs, and general and administrative costs relating to the production area.

Productivity: The goods and services produced per unit of labor or capital or both; for example, the output of automobiles per person-hour. The ratio of output to all labor and capital is a total productivity measure; the ratio of output to either labor or capital is a partial measure. Anything that raises output in relation to labor and capital leads to an increase in productivity.

Profit margin: The percentage that net profit from operations is of net sales. This percentage measures the efficiency of a company or an industry. Nevertheless, profit margins vary widely among industries and among companies within a given industry. (See Returns.)

Profits: The amount left over after a business enterprise has paid all its bills.

Prospectus: Any communication, either written or broadcast by radio or television, that offers a security for sale. The prospectus contains the most important parts of the registration statement, which must give all information relevant to the issue.

Reach: The number of households or the target audience exposed to an advertising message at least one time over a predetermined period of time (also called *cume*).

Reach and frequency: Criteria for evaluating the level of cumulative audience exposure for an advertising campaign on the basis of a percentage of all persons or households who are exposed to the advertising (reach) and the average number of exposures (frequency) over a given period of time: reach $\times$ frequency = gross rating points.

Regression line: A statistical term that indicates a relationship between two or more variables. The regression line was first used by Sir Francis Galton to indicate certain relationships in his theory of heredity, but it is now employed to describe many functional relationships. A regression, or least-squares, line is derived from a mathematical equation relating one economic variable or another. The use of regression lines is important in determining the effect of one variable on another.

Required reserves: The percentages of their deposits that U.S. commercial banks are required to set aside as reserves at their regional Federal Reserve Bank or as cash in their vaults. Reserves requirements vary according to the category of the bank.

Returns: 1. The earnings or profit compensations received for owning assets or equity positions. Also, returns on sales are equivalent to profit margins. 2. The term used in the record business in regard to goods sent back to the manufacturer or distributor for credit.

Risk: The exposure of an investor to the possibility of gain or loss of money. Profit is the investor's reward for assuming the risk of economic uncertainty, such as changes in consumer tastes or changes in technology. The financial risk is based on natural, human, and economic uncertainties.

Scatter market: In network television, the remnants of unsold commercial time that remain after preseason up-front buying has been completed.

Second-best theory: A theory that analyzes alternative suboptimal positions to determine the second best, when some constraint prevents an economy from reaching a paretian optimum. (See Paretian optimum.)

Secular trend: A statistical term denoting the regular, long-term movement of a series of economic data. The secular trend of most economic series is positive, or upward, indicating growth, the angle of the trend depending on how fast or how slow the growth rate is.

Share of audience: The percentage of total households or population (either local or national depending on survey criteria) that are using television or radio during a specific time and that are also tuned into a particular program.

Sherman Antitrust Act: A U.S. federal statute, enacted in 1890, that forbids all contracts in restraint of trade and all attempts at monopolization. The main purposes of the act were to prevent the exercise and growth of monopoly and to restore free enterprise and price competition.

Spectral analysis: In statistics and econometrics, a technique for isolating and estimating the duration and amplitudes of the cyclical components of time series. It results in separating the random from the systematic components of time series.

Spot TV: Local-TV commercial time purchased on a given TV station within a specific market, through a local salesperson within that market or through a national representative of the station.

Stripping: Generally applied to the use of off-network syndicated series episodes several times a week, as in a continuous strip.

Supply: The ability and willingness of a firm to sell a good or service. The firm's supply of a good or service is a schedule of the quantities of that good or service that the firm would offer for sale at alternative prices at a given moment in time. The supply schedule, or the listing of quantities that would be sold at different prices, can be shown graphically by means of a supply curve. The term *supply* refers to the entire schedule of possibilities, not to one point on the schedule. It is an instantaneous concept expressing the relationship of price and the quantity that would be willingly sold, all other factors being constant.

Syndication: Usually a term applied to the process whereby previously exhibited or recorded material is reused by (licensed to) a collection of buyers such as independent television and radio stations.

Tax credit: A legal provision permitting U.S. taxpayers to deduct specified sums from their tax liabilities.

Tax deduction: A legal provision permitting U.S. taxpayers to deduct specified expenditures from their taxable income.

Terms: The conditions under which the distributor agrees to allow the exhibitor to show its product in a given theater, and whereby the exhibitor agrees to show the product. Relates to such items as the basis on which film rental will be paid (as a percentage of weekly gross box-office receipts or flat fee), the playing time (number of weeks), choice of theater, dollar participation in cooperative advertising expenditure, clearance over other theaters, etc.

Time series: A set of ordered observations of a particular economic variable, such as prices, production, investment, and consumption, taken at different points in time. Most economic series consist of monthly, quarterly, or annual observations. Monthly and quarterly economic series are used in short-term business forecasting.

Trade union: An association of workers who do the same kind of work. It bargains collectively on behalf of its members with single employers, business firms, or associations of employers. Trade unions are generally limited to skilled or semiskilled workers who have learned crafts.

UHF (ultrahigh frequency): Television signals in the range 300 to 3,000 megahertz. Television channels 14 through 83.

Underwriter: Any person, group, or firm that assumes a risk in return for a fee, usually called a premium or commission.

Unemployment rate: The number of jobless persons expressed as a percentage of the total labor force. The U.S. counts as unemployed anyone 16 years of age or over who is out of work and would like a job (even if that person is doing little about finding one).

Up-front buying: In network television, the preseason purchasing of commercial time in selected program blocks.

Utility: The ability of a good or a service to satisfy human wants. It is the property possessed by a particular good or service that affords an individual pleasure or prevents pain during the time of its consumption or the period of anticipation of its consumption. The degree of utility of a good varies constantly. Thus, utility is not proportional to the quantity or type of the good or service consumed.

VHF (very high frequency): Television signals in the range of 30 to 300 megahertz. Television channels 2 through 13.

Warrant: An option that gives the holder the privilege of purchasing a certain amount of stock at a specified price for a stipulated period. There are two types of warrants: *stock-purchase warrants* and *subscription warrants*. Stock-purchase warrants (also called option warrants) are sometimes issued with or attached to bonds, preferred stock, and, infrequently, common stock. They entitle the holder to buy common stock in the same corporation at a certain price. Some of these warrants limit the right to buy to a specified period; others are perpetual. Stock-purchase warrants are sometimes attached to the underlying issue and cannot be detached; their value is a part of the bond or preferred stock. Others are detachable, sometimes after a waiting period, and frequently have inherent value that depends on the current price of the common stock.

Win: See Gross win.

Working capital, net: The excess of current assets over current liabilities. These excess current assets are available to carry on business operations. As demand increases in prosperous times, a large volume of working capital is needed to expand production.

Workweek, average: The number of weekly hours per factory worker for which pay has been received, including paid holidays, vacations, and sick leaves. In the United States, workweek figures cover full-time and part-time production and related workers who receive payment for any part of the pay period ending nearest the 15th of the month. Because of increasing amounts of paid holidays, vacations, and sick leave, the paid workweek exceeds the number of hours actually worked per week. The average-work-week series compiled from payroll data by the U.S. Bureau of Labor Statistics differs from the series of weekly hours actually worked that is compiled from household surveys by the U.S. Bureau of the Census. It also differ from the standard or scheduled workweek, because such factors as absenteeism, part-time work, and stoppages make the average workweek lower than the standard workweek.

Write-off: The act of removing an asset from the books of a company. The term *write-off* is related to *write-down,* but the latter is more closely associated with partial reduction of the book value of the asset rather than with removing the asset from the books entirely.

Yield: The percentage that is derived from dividing the annual return from any investment by the amount of the investment.

References

Abt, V., Smith, J. F., and Christiansen, E. M. (1985). *The Business of Risk: Commercial Gambling in Mainstream America.* Lawrence: University of Kansas.

AICPA (1984). *Audits of Casinos,* New York: American Institute of Certified Public Accountants.

Akst, D., and Landro, L. (1988). "In Hollywood's Jungle the Predators Are Out and Feasting on Stars," *Wall Street Journal,* June 20.

Ambrose, J. F. (1981). "Recent Tax Developments Regarding Purchases of Sports Franchises – The Game Isn't Over Yet," *Taxes* (Chicago: Commerce Clearing House) 59(11)(November):739–61.

Andrews, E. L. (1989). "Mysterious Waves May Speed Fiber Optics," *New York Times,* July 5.

Asch, P., Malkiel, B. G., and Quandt, R. E. (1984). "Market Efficiency in Racetrack Betting," *Journal of Business* 57(2)(April):165–75.

Bagamery, A. (1984). "We Sell Space, Not Fantasy," *Forbes* 133(3)(January 30): 60–4.

Balio, T., ed. (1976). *The American Film Industry.* Madison: University of Wisconsin Press, rev. ed. 1985.

Barnhart, R. T. (1983), "Can Trente-et-Quarante Be Beaten?" *Gambling Times,* 3(8)(December):74–7.

Barrett, N. S. (1974). *The Theory of Microeconomics Policy.* Lexington, Mass.: Heath.

Barwise, P., and Ehrenberg, A. (1988). *Television and Its Audience,* London: Sage.

Baskerville, D. (1982). *Music Business Handbook,* 3d ed. Denver, Colo.: Sherwood Company.

Baumol, W., and Baumol, H. (1984). "In Culture, the Cost Disease Is Contagious," *New York Times,* June 3, Section 2, p. 1.

Baumol, W. J., and Bowen, W. G. (1968). *Performing Arts – The Economic Dilemma.* New York: Twentieth Century Fund; Cambridge, Mass.: M.I.T. Press.

Becker, G. S. (1965). "A Theory of the Allocation of Time," *Economic Journal* LXXV(299)(September):493–517.

Berger, A. J., and Bruning, N. (1979). *Lady Luck's Companion.* New York: Harper & Row.

Berry, E. J. (1984). "Nielsen May Face U.K. Rival in Researching TV Audiences," *Wall Street Journal,* February 2.

Biederman, D., and Phillips, L. (1980). "Negotiating the Recording Agreement," in *Counseling Clients in the Entertainment Industry,* edited by M. Silfen. New York: Practising Law Institute.

Blaug, M., ed. (1976). *The Economics of the Arts.* Boulder, Colo.: Westview Press; London: Martin Robertson.

Bloomfield, P. (1977). *Fourier Analysis of Time Series: An Introduction.* New York: Wiley.

Bluem, A. W., and Squire, J. E., eds. (1972). *The Movie Business: American Film Industry Practice.* New York: Hastings House.

Boucher, F. C. (1986). "Performing Music Licensing Procedures," *Billboard,* November 24.

Boyer, P. J. (1988). "Sony and CBS Records: What a Romance," *The New York Times Magazine,* September 18.

Breglio, J. F., and Schwartz, S. (1980). "Introduction to Motion Picture Production and Distribution and Motion Picture Financing," in *Counseling Clients in the Entertainment Industry,* edited by M. Silfen. New York: Practising Law Institute.

Brown, A. C. (1984). "Europe Braces for Free-Market TV," *Fortune* 109(4)(February 20):74–82.

Brown, J., and Church, A. (1987). "Theme Parks in Europe," *Travel & Tourism Analyst,* London: The Economist, February.

Browne, Bortz & Coddington (1983). *An Analysis of the Television Programming Market.* Denver, Colo.: Browne, Bortz & Coddington (prepared for ABC).

Burck, C. G. (1977). "Why the Sports Business Ain't What it Used to Be," *Fortune* XCV(5)(May):295.

Burton, J. S., and Toth, J. R. (1974). "Forecasting Long-Term Interest Rates," *Financial Analysis Journal* 30(5)(September/October):73–87.

Carlson, M. B. (1984). "Where MGM, the NCAA, and Jerry Falwell Fight for Cash," *Fortune* 109(2)(January 23):169–71.

Chace, S. (1983). "Computer Game: Key Software Writers Double as Media Stars in a Promotional Push," *Wall Street Journal,* December 12.

Christiansen, E. M. (1989). "1988 U.S. Gross Annual Wager," *Gaming and Wagering Business* 10(7)(July):7, and 10(8)(August):1.

Cohen, L. (1983). "Cable-Television Firms and Cities Haggle Over Franchises That Trail Expectations," *Wall Street Journal,* December 28.

Columbia Pictures Industries (1982). *Columbia Pictures Industries Financial Factbook, 1981.* New York: Columbia Pictures Industries.

Colvin, G. (1983). "The Battle for TV's Rerun Dollars," *Fortune* 107(7)(May 2):116–20.

Cook, J. (1979). "Bingo!" *Forbes* 124(3)(August 6):37–45.

Couzens, M. (1986). "Invasion of the People Meters," *Channels* (June):40.

Cox, M. (1989). "Networks Overhaul Payouts for Affiliates," *Wall Street Journal,* May 31.

 (1989). "The 'Toxic Avenger' May Not Win Any Prizes, But Fans Don't Care," Wall Street Journal, August 18.

Crandall, R. W. (1972). "FCC Regulation, Monopsony, and Network Television Program Costs," *Bell Journal of Economics* 3(2)(autumn):483–508.

Curran, J. J. (1984). "How High the Bull?" *Fortune* 109(3)(February 6):44–9.

Curran, T. (1986). *Financing Your Film: A Guide for Independent Filmmakers and Producers.* New York: Praeger.

Davis, L. J. (1989). "Hollywood's Most Secret Agent," *New York Times Magazine,* July 9.

Davis, M. D. (1973). *Game Theory: A Nontechnical Approach.* New York: Basic Books.

De Grazia, S. (1962). *Of Time, Work and Leisure.* New York: Twentieth Century Fund.

Dekom, P. J. (1984). "Transition in the Motion Picture Industry – Financing and Distribution, 1984," in *Counseling Clients in the Entertainment Industry,* edited by M. Silfen, pp. 189–203. New York: Practising Law Institute.

Demmert, H. G. (1973). *The Economics of Professional Team Sports.* Lexington, Mass.: Heath.

DeSerpa, A. C. (1971). "A Theory of the Economics of Time," *Economic Journal* (December):828–46.

Donnelly, W. J. (1986). *The Confetti Generation.* New York: Henry Holt.

Durso, J. (1986). "Mets a Baseball 'Jewel' In Attendance, Revenue," *New York Times,* August 22.

Eadington, W. R., ed. (1976). *Gambling and Society.* Springfield, Ill.: Thomas.

Eliot, M. (1989). *Rockonomics: The Money Behind the Music.* New York: Franklin Watts.

Felton, M. (1980). "Policy Implications of a Composer Labor Supply," in *Economic Policy for the Arts,* edited by W. S. Hendon, J. L. Shanahan, and A. J. MacDonald, pp. 186–98. Cambridge, Mass.: Abt Books.

Fielding, R., ed. (1967). *A Technological History of Motion Pictures and Television: An Anthology from the Journal of the Society of Motion Picture and Television Engineers.* Los Angeles: University of California Press.

Financial Accounting Standards Board (1983). *Accounting Standards: Original Pronouncements.* Stamford, Conn.: FASB.

Findlay, J. M. (1986). *People of Chance: Gambling in American Society from Jamestown to Las Vegas.* New York and Oxford: Oxford University Press.

Fisher, F. M., McGowan, J. J., and Evans, D. S. (1980). "The Audience–Revenue Relationship for Local Television Stations," *Bell Journal of Economics* 11(2)(autumn):694–708.

Flack, S. (1989). "The Real Music in Music Publishing," *Corporate Finance*, March.

Flax, S. (1982). "Why Cable TV is a High-Risk Investment," *Forbes* 130(6)(September 13):36–7.

(1983). "Squeeze on the Networks," *Fortune* 108(5)(September 5):84.

Flick, R. (1988). "Ascaps's Out of Tune with Composers." *Wall Street Journal*, May 27.

Frank, A. D., (1984). "The USFL Meets the Sophomore Jinx," *Forbes* 133(4)(February 13):41–2.

Frascogna, X. M., and Hetherington, H. L. (1978). *Successful Artist Management.* New York: Watson-Guptill/Billboard.

Friedman, B. (1974). *Casino Management.* Secaucus, N.J.: Lyle Stuart.

Friedman, M., and Savage, L. J. (1948). "The Utility Analysis of Choices Involving Risk," *Journal of Political Economy* 56(4)(August):279–304.

Frude, N. (1983). *The Intimate Machine: Close Encounters with Computers and Robots.* New York: New American Library.

Garey, N. H. (1983). "Elements of Feature Financing," in *The Movie Business Book,* edited by J. E. Squire, pp. 96–106. New York: Simon & Schuster/ Fireside.

Gelatt, R. (1977). *The Fabulous Phonograph, 1877–1977,* Second Revised Ed. New York: Macmillan.

Ghez, G. R., and Becker, G. S. (1975). *The Allocation of Time and Goods Over the Life Cycle.* New York: National Bureau of Economic Research.

Gibbs, N. (1989). "How America Has Run Out of Time," *Time,* 133(17)(April 24):58.

Goldberg, M. (1988). "Inside the Payola Scandal," *Rolling Stone,* January 14.

Gottman, J. M. (1981). *Time Series Analysis: A Comprehensive Introduction for Social Scientists.* New York: Cambridge University Press.

Grillo, J. B. (1983). "The Final Act?" *CableVision,* July 11.

Gubernick, L. (1989a). "Last Laugh," *Forbes,* 143(4)(May 15):56.

(1989b). "Living Off the Past," *Forbes,* 143(12)(June 12):48.

Hagin, R. (1979). *Modern Portfolio Theory.* Homewood, Ill.: Dow Jones–Irwin.

Halliday, J., and Fuller, P., eds. (1974). *The Psychology of Gambling.* New York: Harper & Row.

Hansmann, H. (1981). "Nonprofit Enterprise in the Performing Arts," *Bell Journal of Economics* 12(2)(autumn):341–61.

Harmelink, P. J., and Vignes, D. W. (1981). "Tax Aspects of Baseball Player Con- tracts and Planning Opportunities," *Taxes* (Chicago: Commerce Clearing House) 59(8)(August):535–46.

Harris, D. (1986). *The League: The Rise and Decline of the NFL.* New York: Bantam.

Harris, W. (1981). "Someday They'll Build a Town Here, Kate," *Forbes* 128 (Octo- ber 26):135–9.

Hedges, J. N., and Taylor, D. E. (1980). "Recent Trends in Worktime: Hours Edge Downward," *Monthly Labor Review* (U.S. Department of Labor) 103(3)(March):3–11.

Henderson, J. M., and Quandt, R. E. (1971). *Microeconomic Theory: A Mathe- matical Approach,* 2d ed. New York: McGraw-Hill.

Hendon, W. S., Shanahan, J. L., and MacDonald, A. J., eds. (1980). *Economic Policy for the Arts.* Cambridge Mass.: Abt Books.

Hirsch, J. (1987). "Big Business Under the Big Top," *New York Times,* October 4.

Hochman, O., and Luski, I. (1988). "Advertising and Economic Welfare: Comment," *American Economic Review,* 78(1)(March).

Horvitz, J. S., and Hoffman, T. E. (1976). "New Tax Developments in the Syndication of Sports Franchises," *Taxes* (Chicago: Commerce Clearing House) 54(3)(March):175–84.

Hotelling, H. (1929). "Stability in Competition," *Economic Journal* (March).

Hull, J. B. (1984). "Music Charts Move Against False 'Hits'," *Wall Street Journal,* February 16.

Ignatin, G., and Smith, R. (1976). "The Economics of Gambling," in *Gambling and Society,* edited by W. R. Eadington, pp. 69–91. Springfield, Ill.: Thomas.

Johnson, R. (1984)."Applying the Utilization Theory to Slot Decisions," *Gaming Business,* April.

Johnson, W. (1985). "The Economics of Copying," *Journal of Political Economy,* Vol. 93, No. 11.

Kelejian, H., and Lawrence, W. (1980). "Estimating the Demand for Broadway Theater: A Preliminary Inquiry," in *Economic Policy for the Arts,* edited by W. S. Hendon, J. L. Shanahan, and A. J. MacDonald, pp. 333–46. Cambridge, Mass.: Abt Books.

Kelley, D. (1985). "Cable Television Unshackled? The Courts Have Just Struck a Blow for Freedom of Speech," *Barron's,* Aprill 22.

Kilbey, J. (1985). "Estimating Revenue Through Bet Criteria," *Gaming and Wagering Business* 6(3)(March):57.

Kindem, G., ed. (1982). *The American Movie Industry: The Business of Motion Pictures.* Carbondale: Southern Illinois University Press.

Klein, H. J. (1982). "Gaming's Growing Slice of the American Leisure Pie," *Gaming Business* 3(9).

Kneale, D. (1988). "How Wouk Epic Became a Sure Loser," *Wall Street Journal,* November 11.

Knight, A. (1978). *The Liveliest Art: A Panoramic History of the Movies.* New York: Macmillan.

Konigsberg, I. (1987). *The Complete Film Dictionary.* New York: New American Library.

Koopmans, L. H. (1974). *The Spectral Analysis of Time Series.* New York: Academic Press.

Kraus, R. (1978). *Recreation and Leisure in Modern Society,* 2d ed. Santa Monica, Calif.: Goodyear Publishing Co.

Kronemyer, D. E., and Sidak, J. G. (1986). "The Structure and Performance of the U.S. Record Industry," *1986 Entertainment and the Arts Handbook.* New York: Clark Boardman.

Kronholz, J. (1984). "Pop and Rock Tours Like Michael Jackson's Grow More Complex," *Wall Street Journal,* July 9.

Kubey, C. (1982). *The Winners' Book of Video Games.* New York: Warner Books.

Kyriazi, G. (1976). *The Great American Amusement Parks: A Pictorial History.* Secaucus, N.J.: Citadel Press.

Landro, L. (1983). "Pay-TV Industry Facing Problems After Misjudging Market Demand," *Wall Street Journal,* June 29.

  (1984). "Merger of Warner Unit, Polygram Angers Troubled Record Industry."*Wall Street Journal,* April 12.

Landro, L., and Saddler, J. (1983). "Network, Film Moguls Blitz Capital in Battle for TV Rerun Profits," *Wall Street Journal,* November 8.

La Pointe, J. (1989). "Television Lavishes Money on Sports, But Does it Pay?" *New York Times,* December 3.

Lardner, J. (1987). *Fast Forward: Hollywood, The Japanese, and the VCR Wars.* New York: W. W. Norton.

Lawson, C. (1983). "Broadway Is in Its Worst Slump in a Decade," *New York Times,* January 3.

Leedy, D. J. (1980). *Motion Picture Distribution: An Accountant's Perspective.* Los Angeles: David Leedy, C.P.A., P.O. Box 27845.

Lessing, L. (1971). "Stand By for the Cartridge TV Explosion," *Fortune,* April, LXXXIII(4).

Levy, H., and Sarnat, M. (1972). *Investment and Portfolio Analysis.* New York: Wiley.

Linder, S. B. (1970). *The Harried Leisure Class.* New York: Columbia University Press.

Linfield, S. (1987). "The Color of Money," *American Film,* Vol. 12, No. 4.

Lipman, J. (1990). "Movie Merchandising Takes Off, Bat-Style." *Wall Street Journal,* January 5.

Lowe, P. M. (1983). "Refreshment Sales and Theater Profits," in *The Movie Business Book,* edited by J. E. Squire, pp. 344–9. New York: Simon & Schuster/ Fireside.

Lyon, R. (1987). "Theme Parks in the USA," *Travel & Tourism Analyst,* London: The Economist Publications, January.

Mahon, G. (1980). *The Company That Bought the Boardwalk.* New York: Random House.

Mair, G. (1988). *Inside HBO: The Billion Dollar War Between HBO, Hollywood and the Home Video Revolution.* New York: Dodd, Mead.

Mangels, W. F. (1952). *The Outdoor Amusement Industry: From Earliest Times to the Present.* New York: Vantage Press.

Markham, J. W., and Teplitz, P. V. (1981). *Baseball Economics and Public Policy.* Lexington, Mass.: Heath.

Marx, S. (1975). *Mayer and Thalberg: The Make-Believe Saints.* New York: Random House.

Michener, J. A. (1976). *Sports in America.* New York: Random House (paperback, Fawcett Crest/Ballantine Books, 1983).

Moore, T. G. (1968). *The Economics of the American Theater.* Durham, N.C.: Duke University Press.

Murphy, A. D. (1982). "21 Fundamental Aspects of U.S. Theatrical Film Biz," *Daily Variety,* October 26.

  (1983). "Distribution and Exhibition: An Overview," in *The Movie Business Book,* edited by J. E. Squire, pp. 244–62. New York: Simon & Schuster/ Fireside

Murphy, J. M. (1976). "Why You Can't Win," *Journal of Portfolio Management* (fall):45–9.

Nardone, J. M. (1982). "Is the Movie Industry Contracyclical," *Cycles* 33(3)(April):77.

Nash, C., and Oakey, V. (1974). *The Screenwriter's Handbook.* New York: Barnes & Noble (Harper & Row).

Netzer, D. (1978). *The Subsidized Muse: Public Support for the Arts in the United States.* New York: Cambridge University Press.

Neulinger, J. (1981). *To Leisure: An Introduction.* Boston: Allyn and Bacon.

Newcomb, P. (1989). "Negative Ratings," *Forbes* 143(3)(February 6):138.

Noll, R., ed. (1974). *Government and the Sports Business.* Washington D.C.: Brookings Institution.

Noll, R. G., Peck, M. J., and McGowan, J. J. (1973). *Economic Aspects of Television Regulation.* Washington, D.C.: Brookings Institution.

Oakey, V. (1983). *Dictionary of Film and Television Terms.* New York: Barnes & Noble.

Owen, B. M., Beebe, J. H., and Manning, W. G., Jr. (1974). *Television Economics.* Lexington, Mass.: Heath.

Owen, D. (1983). "The Second Coming of Nolan Bushnell," *Playboy* 30(6)(June):128.

(1986). "Where Toys Come From," *The Atlantic Monthly,* October.

Owen, J. D. (1970). *The Price of Leisure.* Montreal: McGill-Queen's University Press.

(1976). "Workweeks and Leisure: An Analysis of Trends, 1948–75," *Monthly Labor Review* (U.S. Department of Labor) 99(8)(August):3–8.

Owen, V., and Owen, P. (1980). "An Economic Approach to Art Innovations," in *Economic Policy for the Arts,* edited by W. S. Hendon, J. L. Shanahan, and A. J. MacDonald, pp. 102–11. Cambridge, Mass.: Abt Books.

Paris, E. (1984). "Ronald Reagan Is not the Only Actor Who Made Good," *Forbes* 133(5)(February 27):154–6.

Passell, P. (1989) "Broadway and the Bottom Line," *New York Times,* December 10.

Peterman, J. L., and Carney, M. (1978). "A Comment on Television Network Price Discrimination," *Journal of Business* 51(2)(April):343–52.

Poggi, J. (1968). *Theater in America: The Impact of Economic Forces, 1870–1967.* Ithaca, N.Y.: Cornell University Press.

Pollack, A. (1986). "Video Games, Once Zapped, In Comeback," *New York Times,* September 27.

Puzo, M. (1976). *Inside Las Vegas.* New York: Grosset & Dunlap.

Quirk, J., and Hodiri, M. (1974). "The Economic Theory of a Professional Sports League," in *Government and the Sports Business,* edited by R. Noll, pp. 33–80. Washington, D.C.: Brookings Institution.

Raabe, W. (1977). "Professional Sports Franchises and the Treatment of League Expansion Proceeds," *Taxes,* Chicago: Commerce Clearing House, July.

Read, O., and Welch, W. L. (1976). *From Tin Foil to Stereo: Evolution of the Phonograph.* Indianapolis: Bobbs-Merrill and Howard W. Sams.

Reibstein, L. (1986). "Broadway 'Angels' Often Settle for Glitz, but the Prospects for Profit Are Improving," *Wall Street Journal,* January 28.

Rivkin, S. (1974). "Sports Leagues and the Federal Antitrust Laws," in *Government and the Sports Business,* edited by R. Noll, pp. 387–410. Washington, D.C.: Brookings Institution.

Robinson, J. P. (1989). "Time's Up," *American Demographics,* 11(7)(July):33.

Root, W. (1979). *Writing the Script: A Practical Guide for Films and Television.* New York: Holt, Rinehart & Winston.

Rose, I. N. (1986). *Gambling and the Law.* Los Angeles: Gambling Times.

Rosen, D., and Hamilton, P. (1987). *Off-Hollywood: The Making and Marketing of American Specialty Films.* New York and Colorado: The Independent Feature Project and The Sundance Institute.

Rothstein, M. (1988). "'Starlight Express' Out of the Tunnel?" *New York Times,* August 20.

Royal Commission on Gambling (1978). *Final Report.* London (July), Vol. 2.

Salamon, J. (1984). "Blue Dots: Selling U.S. Films Abroad," *Wall Street Journal,* May 22.

Salemson, H. J., and Zolotow, M. (1978). "It Didn't Begin With Begelman: A Concise History of Film Business Finagling," *Action* (Los Angeles: Directors Guild of America) 11(7)(July/August):40–9.

Sansweet, S. (1983). "As New Studio Starts Work, It Seeks Credibility," *Wall Street Journal,* May 23.

Scarne, J. (1974). *Scarne's New Complete Guide to Gambling.* New York: Simon & Schuster.

     (1978). *Scarne's Guide to Casino Gambling.* New York: Simon & Schuster.

Scholl, J. (1989a). "The Rockford File," *Barron's,* February 6; 51.

     (1989b). "No Rockford Trials," *Barron's* April 3, 33.

Schumer, F. R. (1982). "More Than Merely Colossal," *Barron's,* June 21.

Seaman, B. (1980). "Economic Models and Support for the Arts," in *Economic Policy for the Arts,* edited by W. S. Hendon, J. L. Shanahan, and A. J. MacDonald, pp. 80–95, Cambridge, Mass.: Abt Books.

Seligman, D. (1982). "Who Needs Unions," *Fortune* 106(1)(July 12):54–66.

Sharp, C. H. (1981). *The Ecomonics of Time.* Oxford: Martin Robertson.

Shemel, S., and Krasilovsky, M. W. (1985). *This Business of Music,* Fifth Revised Ed. 1988. New York: Billboard.

Silberstang, E. (1980). *Playboy's Guide to Casino Gambling.* New York, Playboy Press.

Skolnick, J. H. (1978). *House of Cards.* Boston: Little, Brown.

     (1979). "The Social Risks of Casino Gambling," *Psychology Today* 13(2)(July):52–64.

Smith, S. J. (1986). "The Growing Diversity of Work Schedules," *Monthly Labor Review,* U.S. Department of Commerce, BLS, November, Vol. 109, No. 11.

Spitz, B. (1987). "Is Collusion the Name of the Game?" *New York Times Magazine,* July 12.

Squire, J. E., ed. (1983). *The Movie Business Book,* New York: Simon & Schuster/ Fireside.

Stanley, R. (1978). *The Celluloid Empire: A History of the American Motion Picture Industry.* New York: Hastings House.

Stern, S., and Schoenhaus, T. (1990). *Toyland: The High-Stakes Game of the Toy Industry.* Chicago: Contemporary Books.

Sternlieb, G., and Hughes, J. W. (1983). *The Atlantic City Gamble.* New York: Twentieth Century Fund; Cambridge, Mass.: Harvard University Press.

Stigler, G. J., and Becker, G. S. (1977). "De Gustibus Non Est Disputandum," *American Economic Review,* 67(March):76–90.

Swertlow, F. (1982). "How Hollywood Studios Flimflam Their Stars," *TV Guide* 30(18)(May 1):6–14.

Thomas, B. (1976). *Walt Disney: An American Original.* New York: Simon & Schuster (Pocket Books, 1980).

Thorp, E. O. (1984). *The Mathematics of Gambling.* Secaucus (N.J.): Lyle Stuart.

Throsby, C. D., and Withers, G. A. (1979). *The Economics of the Performing Arts.* New York: St. Martin's Press.

Trachtenberg, J. A. (1984). "Low Budget," *Forbes* 133(7)(March 26):116–17.

Trost, C. (1986). "All Work and No Play? New Study Shows How Americans View Jobs," *Wall Street Journal,* December 30.

Tucker, W. (1982). "Public Radio Comes to Market," *Fortune* 106(8)(October 18):205–10.

U.S. Congress (1976). *Gambling in America.* Washington, D.C.: Commission on the Review of the National Policy Toward Gambling.

(1989). *Survey of Home Taping and Copying.* Washington, D.C.: Office of Technology Assessment.

U.S. Congress (1989). *Copyright and Home Copying: Technology Challenges the Law.* Washington D.C.: Office of Technology Assessment, OTA-CIT-422, U.S. Government Printing Office.

U.S. National Endowment for the Arts (1985). *Survey of Public Participation in the Arts. U.S. Statistical Abstract* (Department of Commerce).

Van Horne, J. C. (1968). *Financial Management and Policy.* Englewood Cliffs, N.J.: Prentice-Hall.

Veblen, T. (1899). *The Theory of the Leisure Class.* New York: Macmillan (paperback, New American Library, 1953).

Vecsey, G. (1981). "In Sports, Money Is the Main Issue," *New York Times,* March 16.

von Neumann, J., and Morgenstern, O. (1944). *Theory of Games and Economic Behavior.* New York: Wiley.

Waggoner, G. (1982). "Money Games," *Esquire* 97(6)(June):49–60.

Watkins, L. M. (1986). "A Look at Hasbro's 'Moondreamer' Dolls Shows Creating a Toy Isn't Child's Play," *Wall Street Journal,* December 29.

Wechsler, D. (1989). "Every Trick in the Books," *Forbes,* 143(11)(May 29):46–48.

(1990). "Profits? What Profits?" *Forbes* 145(4)(February 19):38.

Welles, C. (1983). "How Accountants Helped Orion Pictures Launch Its Financial Comeback," *Los Angeles Times,* May 15.

White, A., ed. (1988). *Inside the Recording Industry: An Introduction to America's Music Business.* Washington, D.C.: Recording Industry Association of America.

Whiteside, T. (1985). "Onward and Upward with the Arts, Cable Television," *New Yorker* 61(13)(May 20):45–87; 61(14)(May 27):43–73; 61(15)(June 3):82–105.

Wyche, M. C., and Wirth, M. O. (1984). "How Economic and Competitive Factors Affect Station Results," *Television/Radio Age,* January 9.

Zeisel, J. S. (1958). "The Workweek in American Industry 1850–1956," in *Mass Leisure,* edited by E. Larrabee and R. Meyerson. Glencoe, Ill.: The Free Press.

Zollo, P. (1989). "The Per-Program License: Broadcaster's New Cost-Cutting Initiative," *Hollywood Reported,* August 29.

Index

425